Public Policy and
Social Institutions

**PUBLIC POLICY STUDIES: A MULTI-VOLUME
TREATISE, VOLUME 1**
Editor: Stuart Nagel, *Department of Political Science, University of Illinois*

PUBLIC POLICY STUDIES
A Multi-Volume Treatise

General Editor: Stuart Nagel, Department of Political Science, University of Illinois

Public Policy and Social Institutions

Edited by HARRELL R. RODGERS, JR.
Department of Political Science
University of Houston

JAI PRESS INC.

Greenwich, Connecticut   *London, England*

Library of Congress Cataloging in Publication Data
Main entry under title:

Public policy and social institutions.

  (Public policy studies ; v. 1)
  Includes bibliographies and index.
  1. United States—Social policy—Addresses, essays,
lecture. 2. Policy sciences—Addresses, essays, lec-
tures. I. Rodgers, Harrell R. II. Series: Public
policy studies (Greenwich, Conn.)
HN59.2.P83 1984   361.6′1′0973   84-9680
ISBN 0-89232-377-9

CONTENTS

ACKNOWLEDGMENTS

A project of this type requires a great deal of group cooperation and professionalism. I am pleased to thank the individual authors of this volume for meetings and exceeding these standards. Through numerous revisions and seemingly endless correspondence the authors maintained good humor, flexibility and a commitment to sound scholarship that enabled the project to be carried to its completion. I extend my sincerest thanks.

I would also like to thank Stuart Nagel, the series editor, for his assistance, support and guidance. There are few people in this profession who would attempt to direct such a complex series, and even fewer who could do the job so well.

Norman Furniss and Neil Mitchell would like to express their thanks to Alfred Diamant and Elizabeth Trousdell for their comments on their chapter. Laura L. Vertz would like to express her thanks to John P. Frendreis for his helpful comments in the preparation of her chapter.

Harrell Rodgers

PART I

THE ART AND SCIENCE OF POLICY ANALYSIS

INTRODUCTION

Harrell R. Rodgers, Jr

This volume is concerned with the art and science of policy analysis. At a broad theoretical level the volume attempts to help us understand the policy-making processes and abilities of government, and the immediate and broader implications of policy decisions for citizens and political entities. The individual chapters provide insights into such topics as why governments select some policies rather than others, how the selected policies impact upon individuals and society (i.e., both their intended and unintended impacts), what the policy decisions reveal about a society, and the implications and limits of comparative policy analysis for informing national policymaking. The individual chapters also provide insights into the methodological techniques and issues that must be mastered and dealt with in order to carry out viable policy analysis. Some of the chapters have been designed to show how policy analysis and prescription can be melded with a theoretical understanding of the policy environment to produce viable policy alternatives and rational policy debate.

In the first essay Norman Furniss and Neil Mitchell provide an excellent theoretical focus for an analysis of the role of the government in the formulation and implementation of social policy. Furniss and Mitchell analyze how social welfare provisions differ among western industrial nations, and relate these differences to the public philosophies that guide the economic and political systems of each nation. Furniss and Mitchell show, in other words, that each of the major western nations has a complex public philosophy which sets limits on, and defines the role of, the state in the economic and political systems. To isolate the similarities and differences between the nations, Furniss and Mitchell elaborate a framework for analyzing social welfare systems based on three major criteria: (1) the design and goals of the programs; (2) the political, economic and social priorities reflected by them; and (3) the impact of the programs on recipients and on the political and economic systems. This analytical framework produces four state types:

The Positive State

Social welfare programs are designed primarily to protect holders of property from the difficulties of unregulated markets and from demands for redistribution of income. Welfare policy, in other words, is a means of social control. The United States and Australia approximate this type.

Social Security State

Here social welfare programs establish a guaranteed national minimum as a right of citizenship and thus aims to ensure economic security, educational opportunities, and access to acceptable health care. Great Britain and the Federal Republic of Germany approximate this type.

Social Welfare State

This type of social welfare system is designed primarily to promote equality and solidarity. It seeks not only to produce a guaranteed minimum but to achieve a general equivalence of living conditions. The Netherlands and Sweden approximate this type of system.

Democratic Corporatist State

The adequacy of welfare provisions tends to correspond to whether one works within the state sector. Welfare provisions are targeted to groups, rather than to individuals; they are justified in terms of state or national interests. Examples of this type include France and Italy.

After developing their models, Furniss and Mitchell discuss a number of issues that are currently shaping the nature of the debate over the welfare system in each of the state types. The major issues are whether welfare provisions are a method of social control, whether welfare provision is aligned to "free market" principles, and whether welfare provision is associated with changes in the distribution of power.

Last, Furniss and Mitchell examine some of the problems common to all Western countries that have produced a consensus that the welfare state is "in trouble," and some of the political initiatives and philosophical debates about the role and obligations of the government that these problems have stimulated. As Furniss and Mitchell show, in the long run these tensions could alter the public philosophy in many of the western nations, which would result in alterations in the political and economic systems and the welfare provisions produced by them.

The second essay provides an excellent complement to the work of Furniss and Mitchell. Malcolm Goggin conducts an indepth analysis of the public philosophy of the United States. Goggin centers attention on the impact of the American public philosophy on the formulation and implementation of social policy. Goggin begins with a widely accepted point: the response of the Roosevelt administration to the Great Depression not only established the foundation of the American welfare state, but in so doing it created a philosophy about the role that the government should play in regulating and assisting the economy, and in helping to alleviate social problems. Scholars generally agree that this public philosophy has been the primary force in shaping public expectations and government economic and social policies since the New Deal.

The philosophy that grew out of the New Deal has been variously defined, but central to it was the acceptance by the federal government of the responsibility to use its powers to promote full employment, prosperity, and price stability. The public philosophy of the New Deal, in keeping with capitalist principles, assumed that private corporations would make the fundamental decisions about the allocation of resources. Washington was to use fiscal policy (determining whether the federal budget would be in surplus or deficit) and monetary policy (controlling the supply of money) to ensure that there would be adequate buying power to absorb the output of the corporations and thereby keep Americans at work, mainly in the private sector. Social welfare programs would be created to alleviate the suffering of the "legitimate" poor but to avoid creating a dependent class, benefits would be kept at a modest level.

Building on the New Deal social programs, and motivated and guided by the new public philosophy, the American welfare state grew slowly in the 1940s and 1950s but, in response to great social tensions, grew quite rapidly during the 1960s and early 1970s. As Goggin points out, the growth of the welfare state stimulated many concerns. An obvious one was that the new social welfare programs substantially increased the role and size of government. Another concern was that while the individual social welfare programs alleviated much pain and suffering and advanced many worthy public goals, the best evidence indicated that they were often poorly designed, badly administered, uncoordinated and generally less than optimally cost effective.

These findings stimulated a variety of reactions. Some scholars and policymakers called for actions designed to improve government policy making and administration. Along this line were calls for more policy research, the development of better tools of analysis, and special programs to teach policymakers and advisors about the design of public policies. Conservative scholars and public officials have often argued from a different perspective. They have generally argued that public policies are inherently inefficient and a drag on the economy. Their solution is fewer government policies and more reliance on the market. Goggin's primary focus is on President Reagan's efforts to gain acceptance of a new public philosophy which would reflect these conservative goals.

Goggin's analysis is in three parts. He first defines the major elements of Reagan's philosophy, and then evaluates the extent to which Reagan has been successful in convincing Congress to reshape public policies to reflect his philosophy. Last, Goggin assesses the long-term impact of the Reagan administration on specific social programs, and more broadly on the nation's public philosophy. Neither question can be answered definitively, but the analysis highlights the critical importance of the public philosophy in shaping the role of government in society.

Each of the next five chapters provides an analysis of policy issues in the major western nations. Four of the chapters employ a comparative analysis. Each chapter deals with a different policy topic, and each provides unique insights into the art of policy analysis, especially into the impact of political structures and political and economic values and priorities ("public philosophies") on public policies. The various analyses also provide important insights into the potentials and limits of comparative analysis.

In the third chapter Leichter examines the issue of health care cost containment. He begins with a discussion of the merits of a cross-national perspective. Leichter notes that the major western nations clearly borrow policy ideas from one another, and that regardless of public philosophy, some social programs can be remarkably similar across nations. All the major western nations, for example, with the exceptions of the United States and Great Britain (which has a public health system), have adopted some version of national health insurance. Similarly, all the major nations, with the exception of Great Britain, have struggled with spiraling health care inflation.

The specific topics considered by Leichter's essay include an analysis of the factors that have stimulated inflation in each of the nations, an examination by nation of the potential efficacy of various policy strategies to deal with the problem, a comparison of conservative and liberal perspectives within each nation about the specific policy options, and an evaluation of the policy options that nations might seriously consider.

Leichter's analysis takes place within a framework that provides insights into the impact of the public philosophy of each nation in filtering policy alternatives. The likely impact of a particular policy option is less important than whether that policy meshes with the political and economic values which prevail within the nation. The public philosophy, in other words, excludes certain types of policy responses regardless of their potential to deal with a public problem.

In chapter four Boneparth argues that to be successful, a major policy initiative must be framed so that it either meshes with or alters the public philosophy of the nation. The issue that Boneparth is concerned with is public assistance to single mothers. Boneparth notes that over the last couple of decades the status of many women in the United States has remained unchanged or even declined. The reason, she argues, is not simply because of unsympathetic male policymakers, but because women have failed to recognize the need to frame issues so that they will be widely enough accepted to alter the public philosophy.

The need for child care, for example, has been discussed in terms of children's needs, or as a method of making better use of women's labor. Boneparth believes that to be successful, policy issues of this type must be more broadly cast so that they can challenge the accepted approach. Thus child care should be promoted as a right of working mothers or, better, working parents. Casting "women's" issues in this manner, Boneparth believes, would require a feminist perspective.

A feminist perspective would have three parts: 1) a policy focus that considered the needs of all women, not just select groups of women; 2) policy analyses that made clear to men that women's issues do not "cost" them; and 3) an assessment of the long-term impact of policies in changing sex roles.

To illustrate the need for a feminist perspective, Boneparth provides a comparative case study of the impact of employment policies on single-parent female families. This analysis shows the limitations of traditional women's policy perspectives, and seeks to show how a different, broader perspective has worked more effectively in other western nations. Boneparth emphasizes that a feminist perspective is particularly compatable in those nations that function within the Social Welfare model.

Last, Boneparth discusses some of the specific policies that a feminist perspective would produce and the likely consequences of these policies.

In Chapter five, Rodgers centers attention on American housing problems, the housing policies that have been developed to deal with these problems, and major criticisms of these policies by both conservatives and liberals. In analyzing American housing programs, Rodgers shows how the values of the Positive state have influenced, and placed limits on, the housing programs adopted in America. Two overriding values that result from the American public philosophy are reliance on the private market to meet most housing needs (although this market is publically subsidized), and assistance primarily oriented toward those individuals who can afford to purchase housing in the private market.

A comparison of American housing policies with Western European policies illuminates the impact of national philosophies on this important public policy. Still, while there are substantial philosophical differences by state, housing policies in all the European nations are much more extensive than American policies, and much more equalitarian. Regardless of state type, in other words, all the European nations provide decent housing at reasonable costs for almost all of their citizens. Thus while the public philosophies of the Western nations vary, all the nations have reasons for helping their citizens obtain good housing, even though they often approach this objective in different ways.

The difference between European and American housing policies serves both to emphasize the impact of the public philosophy on a major policy, and also suggests the limitations of comparative analysis as a method of informing American policies. Some of the policies that have been quite popular in Europe, in other words, are not likely to be acceptable in the United States because of the differences in public philosophies.

The last section of this chapter compares conservative and liberal proposals to deal with American housing problems and then contrasts these proposals to those policies currently in effect in Western Europe. This analysis reveals two points: even the housing proposals suggested by American liberals are modest by European standards, and in the immediate future only a few of the European policies are likely to be acceptable within the American philosophical framework.

In the sixth chapter, Button and Scher examine a number of topics, a primary one being the limits imposed upon policy change by the AMRI/ can public philosophy. Button and Scher center attention on the impact that modern civil rights laws have had on the election of black elected officials in the American south, and the policy changes brought about by their election. They begin by examining the theoretical and methodological issues that must be considered in conducting this type of policy research. Next, by way of documenting how extensive recent changes have been, they review the history of black elected officials in the South. As late as 1968 there were only 248 black elected officials in the South. By 1980 there were some 2,600 black elected officials in this region, most of whom were serving on city councils and school boards.

Button and Scher's analysis reveals that the civil rights laws opened the door for black voting, but that certain macro- and micro-level factors play an important role in determining how many black officials will be elected in any given jurisdiction. Some of these factors, such as high concentrations of black voters, place upper limits on the potential number of black officials.

The analysis also examines the policy changes brought about by newly elected black officials. The evidence here is sparse, but there is evidence that black officials have been able to make some contributions toward improving the material conditions of their constituents. The evidence is also clear, however, that the impact has in many ways been modest and that it is not likely to greatly increase in the future. The authors also consider the symbolic impact that the election of black officials has brought about. The symbolic changes may be as important, or even more important, than the material changes.

Perhaps the most important conclusion of this essay is that the economy, and the American public philosophy about the economy, imposes serious restraints on the changes that the black vote or a limited number of elected officials can produce. In other words, the problems that afflict the economy (such as high unemployment and subemployment) greatly retard the ability of millions of black (and white) Americans to join the middle class, and the new black vote is too anemic to deal with such problems. The black vote has not been able to alter the public values about the role that the government should play in the economy, or correct the economic problems that plague millions of black Americans. The result is that the economy places serious limits on the amount of change in the condition of most low-income Americans that can be produced, and this includes the majority of all black Americans.

In chapter seven Kraft addresses an issue that provides some unique insights into governmental response to social issues. The issue, population policy, is unique because it is not addressed as an emergency in any of the western nations, and thus governmental response reflects substantially the extent to which the state is inclined to study long-term changes in society and to plan policies to deal with these changes.

The issue that Kraft addresses is birth rates. His data show that birth rates are at or below replacement levels in all the major Western industrialized nations. Kraft examines three major questions. First, how are nations responding to declining birth rates? Second, which public policies have been seriously considered and/or adopted and what type of policies might command attention in the future? Third, how can the differences among nations in the type and manner of their responses to population change be explained?

As might be expected, the nations that rely most heavily on the market to solve social and economic problems (the Positive state) are the least inclined to address such an issue. In the United States, for example, population dynamics have been carefully studied, but politically it is a nonissue. Equally interesting, even nations that have a stronger commitment to playing a role in social policy have difficulty planning for this type of future problem or social dynamic. Not all the nations, however, consider population declines to be a serious problem. In Sweden, for example, policymakers are aware of the issue, but do not see it as a problem. The factors that influence whether a nation will be concerned about the trend include a number of variables, but two of the most important are the political culture and ideology of the nation and the structure and influence of the interest group system. As Furniss and Mitchell pointed out, these variables are critical elements of a nation's public philosophy.

The eighth chapter, written by Loveman and Hofstetter, extends the analysis introduced by Kraft. In examining Mexican immigration into the United States, Loveman and Hofstetter consider an issue with direct implications for American population policy. But, as the authors point out, American public policy toward Mexican immigrants is hardly a result of national policy analysis, either long or short-term. In fact, the authors demonstrate that public beliefs about Mexican immigrants are generally quite at variance with the facts. Public beliefs on this topic primarily tend to reflect misinformation and bias. For a variety of reasons, public officials are often guilty of contributing to public ignorance and prejudice. A major problem, the authors conclude, is that the current debate ignores or rejects the domestic and foreign policy benefits that result from undocumented immigration.

A second focus of the Loveman and Hofstetter chapter is the implication of public ignorance for public policy. The authors note that public beliefs about Mexican immigrants are often so detached from reality that public policies that accurately reflected public opinion probably could not be enforced and would be detrimental if they were. For example, Loveman and Hofstetter attempt to demonstrate that the "modern reforms" in immigration laws that the public supports have no chance of controlling illegal entry into the United States. The authors argue that serious efforts to control or end immigration would be extremely costly, would require repressive enforcement measures that would seriously conflict with American civil liberties, would violate the liberties of many Americans who would be caught up in the enforcement net, would seriously damage many American businesses, and would have perilous implications for foreign policy.

Loveman and Hofstetter's conclusion is that the best policy solution for illegal immigration is probably not to be found in domestic policy. Rather the best solution, they argue, would be a foreign policy that helps Mexico deal with its extensive social and economic problems. A healthy Mexico would take better care of its own citizens.

Chapter nine by Cook and Skogan deals with the same policy problem addressed by Loveman and Hofstetter: the role that misinformation often plays in agenda setting. Agenda setting is the process by which an issue is defined as a social problem and thus becomes a political issue. The issue that Cook and Skogan examine is crime against the aged. The authors conduct a newspaper content analysis to demonstrate that the media has played a role in miseducating the public, and often public officials, about the impact of crime on the elderly population. The message of the media is that the elderly suffer more at the hands of criminals than do other groups in society.

Cook and Skogan analyze a number of different types of data to show that as a group the elderly do not suffer a high rate of actual crime, that when they are the victims of crime the consequences are not more severe, and that they do not manifest greater psychological harm as a result of fear of crime than other groups.

Cook and Skogan do not deny that elderly citizens are often the victims of crime, that the problems they suffer are serious and worthy of public response, or that some groups among the elderly have especially serious crime problems. Cook and Skogan's intent is simply to show that during the 1970s, misinformation about the crime problems of the elderly often misdirected anti-crime policy debates and even resources.

Cook and Skogan's essay provides excellent insights into how issues are placed on the public agenda (i.e., they capture some degree of public attention), and how public agenda issues are translated into formal agenda items (i.e., issues discussed by government bodies). They discuss three issue emergence models articulated by Cobb and Ross, and conclude that Cook's "convergence voice" model best explains how the crime against the elderly issue ended up on both the public and formal agendas in the 1970s.

In the last chapter Vertz also considers one dimension of agenda setting. Vertz is concerned with how a new issue displaces or seriously alters an established policy. Vertz examines a policy that has long been accepted, carries out an empirical analysis to determine the impact of that policy, and then argues that the policy conflicts with the rights of a newly emerging group and thus should be revised.

The issue Vertz examines is veterans' preference in government hiring. Veterans' preference consists of nonmerit advantages given to veterans by virtue of their status as veterans. As Vertz points out, women tend to view veterans' preference as a policy that discriminates against them, and thus as an impediment to the implementation of equal employment opportunity.

Vertz's sophisticated empirical analysis reveals that the primary impact of veterans' preference is that it influences the initial decision to hire: more veterans obtain federal employment than their qualifications would predict they are qualified for. The bias toward veterans reduces the number of women hired. Once the hiring decision is made, however, merit is the best predictor of job rank (i.e., G.S. level). Gender also has an independent impact on current G.S. level, with women having less representation in higher ranks than their qualifications would predict. This might be explained in part by seniority.

Since veterans' preference seems to have its primary impact on hiring decisions, Vertz recommends that hiring policies be revised. She suggests that federal policy be shifted from a benefits justification (i.e., a reward for past service) to a readjustment justification (i.e., rehabilitation and relocation of those suffering economic and social dislocation as a result of wartime service). A readjustment orientation would accommodate a compromise with equal employment opportunity goals, and would have a better chance of being adopted than a complete rejection of veterans' preference. Vertz articulates a six-part policy revision designed to reform the veterans' policy, and discusses some of the implications that would result from adoption of these reforms. Vertz's essay provides an excellent example of policy analysis and empirically-grounded policy formulation and prescription.

CONCLUSIONS

The insights provided by these essays are many, but clearly the most important is the illumination of the impact of a nation's public philosophy on public policy. Any attempt to analyze or account for the policy decisions of a given nation are greatly enhanced by an understanding of the theoretical environment in which the decision making process takes place.

The essays also provide valuable insights into the benefits and limits of comparative policy analysis. Most of the western nations clearly borrow policy ideas from one another, but the exportability of policy options is limited by many variables, not the least of which is the public philosophy of each nation.

Last, the essays make clear that public policy formulation and implementation is not an altogether rational process. Nations do not deal with social problems by objectively studying a problem and then formulating the best policy response possible. Instead, policies reflect the end product of a struggle that involves compromises that are compelled in part by vested interests, myths and ignorance, and circumscribed by the structure of the political process and the public philosophy upon which that system is based.

PART II

THE PUBLIC PHILOSOPHY AND PUBLIC POLICY

SOCIAL WELFARE PROVISIONS IN WESTERN EUROPE:

CURRENT STATUS AND FUTURE

POSSIBILITIES

Norman Furniss and Neil Mitchell

I. INTRODUCTION

This chapter aims first to present and then to order differences in social welfare provisions among West European countries. Both aims present challenges. On the first, there is no agreement on what "social welfare provision" entails.[1] Our strategy will be to approach the question from a number of different directions. We will offer comparisons among countries in the hope that a notion of what properly should be termed social welfare provision will "emerge" from the data. We will give brief descriptions of the national experiences in France, the Federal Republic of Germany, Italy, the Netherlands, Sweden, and the United Kingdom. We will then attempt to link these descriptions to general patterns of state policy.

This effort leads directly to the need to order differences in welfare provision in a systematic way, which leads in turn to a need to confront the terminological specter of the "welfare state." Although this term is widely used, there is no common agreement as to its reference. By some it is reduced to a level of spending, by others it is elevated to a moral principle. On the left it often refers to a functional response of late capitalism designed to promote false consciousness; on the right the welfare state often epitomizes the collectivist threat to individualism.[2] Even when the term is given a concrete measure such as ten percent of G.N.P. allocated to public expenditure on health and social security programs, analytical precision is not greatly enhanced because then almost every country in Europe, East and West, becomes a welfare state (Hage and Hanneman, 1980). As with that other twentieth century contribution to the labeling of political forms, totalitarianism, the ability to understand differences in the systems to which it commonly refers becomes lost. Faced with these normative and empirical confusions we have abandoned (or subdivided) the term "welfare state" and have attempted to construct a framework for aggregating social welfare provision in terms of analytically distinct policy patterns. These we associate with four state types: the positive state; the social security state; the social welfare state; the democratic corporatist state.

Our effort to show that these state types increase our understanding of social welfare provision is made in Part III. Here we make some preliminary distinctions between these "state types" in terms of underlying policy principles and principal beneficiaries. Public welfare provision under the positive state is conceived as a business-government partnership whose aim is to secure, with the least possible public intervention, property holders and the operation of a market economy from social and political conflict. The broader aim of public welfare provision under the social security state is to guarantee for all citizens a national minimum standard of living (health, housing, education, income) above which they are encouraged to rise. Under the social welfare state the aim becomes greater equality of result to be carried out by policies of redistribution. The aims of these state types can be arrayed along a continuum from active discouragement to active promotion of equality. The aim of the democratic corporatist state cannot be described in this way. As we will presently elaborate, the key concern is to promote state interests through group-state direction of economic and social affairs. The pattern of welfare provision flows from this concern and is targeted toward occupational groups that are able, from positions of economic and political importance to the state, to arrange special provisions.

These policy aims have consequences for policy content. From the positive state to the social security state to the social welfare state there is an expansion in coverage, in range of programs, and an increase in the generosity of benefits. With the democratic corporatist state, coverage, range of programs and benefits vary between groups and in accordance with their functional importance. All state types rely on a mix of financing mechanisms, both insurance based and general revenue financing. Only under the social welfare state does general revenue financing begin to replace insurance based financing. One final note: We do not expect to find any of these types represented in a pure form in the countries studied—such an expectation would require an entirely different epistemological orientation. We do intend to identify approximations. This exercise as well as promoting understanding of differing welfare provisions also leads to the conclusion that there are viable alternatives open to policy makers in advanced capitalist states. Policies are at least partially controllable within a market system and within a generally capitalist international economic order.

II. WEST EUROPEAN SOCIAL WELFARE PROVISION

We are primarily, though not exclusively, concerned with social welfare provision in six West European countries: France, the Federal Republic of Germany, Italy, the Netherlands, Sweden, and the United Kingdom. Social welfare provision in these countries traverses a range of welfare strategies. For analytic purposes, reference will also be made to developments in the United States and Australia as examples of positive states. At the end of this chapter we take advantage of the relatively recent general elections in America, Britain, France and Sweden to comment on the prospects for major policy change.

As Table I illustrates, similarly rich and developed countries allocate very different amounts to social welfare provision. Australia and the U.S.A. spend half of what Sweden and the Netherlands do, and their relative tax burdens are much lighter. These variations in receipts and expenditures cannot be attributed to variations in need between these rich countries. A large proportion of expenditures are devoted to old age benefits; yet as Table 1 shows, the Netherlands and the United States, for example have similar proportions of aged but very different expenditure patterns. Another indication of relative needs is provided by the "standardized" percentage of people below the poverty line in these countries. The United States has a relatively large number of poor but spends the least on social welfare provision. Interestingly more expenditure does not always coincide with less poverty, as is the case with France.

The ILO figures on social security include medical care, sickness benefits, old age benefits, unemployment benefits, employment injury bene-

Table 1.   Comparative Welfare Measures

	Social Security Receipts (% of GDP 1977)[1]	Taxes & Social Security Charges (% of GNP 1977)[2]	Over 65's (% of Pop. 1979)[3]	Poverty (% of Pop. Early 1970s)[4]
AUS	15.0	33	No Data	8
FR	26.0	44	14	16
FRG	23.0	45	15.4	3
IT	20.8	38	13.1	No Data
ND	31.4	52	11.3	No Data
SW	33.9	62	16.2	3.5
UK	18.8	40	14.6	7.5
USA	14.8	33	11.1	13

Sources: [1]ILO. The Cost of Social Security, (Geneva: ILO, 1981).

[2]Central Statistical Office Economic Trends, (London: HMSO, December, 1979).

[3]European Communities Statistical Office Basic Statistics of the Community, (1981).

[4]OECD, Public Expenditures on Income Maintenance Programs, (OECD, 1976).

fits, family benefits, invalidity benefits, and survivors' benefits. Costs provide one dimension of policy differences. They say nothing, however, of the content and purpose of particular social policies. When policy is treated in these terms additional cross-national differences are discovered. A brief country-by-country description of welfare provision with a focus on old age pensions, unemployment compensation, health care, and family allowances follows.

France

Welfare provision in France attained its present general character at the end of World War II. French welfare development is not associated with a dominant historical figure or single political party, which in part accounts for its complexity. There was no French counterpart to Bismarck in Germany or Beveridge in Britain. The latter's report (1942) achieved some prestige in France in the immediate post-war years, but its practical impact was limited. To Beveridge were attributed the principles of "generality" and "unity" in social welfare provision, yet it was not until 1978 that all Frenchmen received welfare protection. And it is still the case that French welfare provision operates under a general scheme as well as numerous special schemes (Rustant, 1980). A decree of 1946 enumerated occupations which are permitted special schemes. Among those included are central and local government offices, the mines, the railways, the gas and electricity industry, the Bank of France, la Comedie Francaise, and l'Opera-Comique (Dupeyroux, 1965, p. 193). There are also autonomous schemes for agricultural workers as well as for various non-agricultural self-employed and professions. Despite efforts at harmonization, one can still distinguish eighteen separate social security systems with the general system accounting for fewer than 70% of active members and fewer than 41% of benficiaries. As a rule, social welfare provision under the special schemes is more generous than under the general scheme. Just how much more generous varies according to occupation. It is no wonder that Rustant (1980, p. 36) concludes that "the system is so complex that it is practically impossible for the uninitiatied to understand anything about it."

The general scheme of old age pension provision is supervised by the Ministry of Health and Social Security. It is an insurance scheme with contributions required from insured persons and from employers, but not from the government. Minimum retirement age is 60 for men and women who receive full benefits with 37.5 years of coverage. Benefits are earnings related. Health insurance under the general scheme also covers about 70 percent of employees. The special schemes cover most of the remainder and means-tested public assistance for health care provides for those not insured, about 2 percent of the population (Abel-Smith and Maynard, 1979, p. 44). A specified length of employment is necessary to qualify under the general scheme. Contributions to the scheme are paid by employees, employers, and the government through a surcharge on automobile insurance premiums. Benefits take the form of partial cash refunds for the cost of medical care. The insured person normally pays about 25 percent of medical expenses. For certain expensive services the insured person may be fully reimbursed.

An unemployment insurance scheme was set up in 1959 through a collective agreement between employers' associations and labor covering about two-thirds of wage earners, which has since been extended into a compulsory insurance scheme (Laroque 1969). Unemployment insurance benefits require contributions from the insured person and the employer but not from the government. Benefits consist of a flat-rate and an earnings related component, and continue for a year, though they can be extended if the individual is over 50 years of age. Unemployment assistance, the full cost of which is borne by the government, is provided for the first three months of unemployment after which it is subject to means-test. While under the general supervision of the Ministry of Health and Social Security, employment organizations with bipartite bodies made up of management and labor administer unemployment benefits.

A basic concern underlying French welfare provision has been the birth rate and the family. According to Laroque "the system's stress on childbearing and the family has retained the greater part of its strength" (Laroque. 1969, p. 173). Women with three children, for example, receive certain pension advantages. The French equation of large families with national strength manifested itself in the enactment of the "Family Code" in July 1939 which aimed to extend the coverage of family allowances. This code has been described as "the defensive reaction of a Nation whose frontiers were threatened. . . ." (Laroque. 1963, p. 439). Current provision of family allowances began in 1946. An employers' payroll tax finances the universal scheme which covers all French families with more than one child; as we describe at the end of this chapter, this method of financing is due to change. There is also a prenatal allowance and a birth grant under the French scheme. Table 2 indicates the comparative importance of family allowances in the French welfare effort.

The lack of a unified system of welfare provision in France has been ascribed to the effective resistance of certain occupational groups anxious to maintain privileged positions and to governments anxious, for electoral reasons, to accede to their demands. With the Fifth Republic this "pluralist" explanation seems increasingly less plausible. A more fundamental reason for the maintenance of special schemes of social welfare provision has also been offered: these sehemes have assisted "the recruitment of those professional groups that are indispensable to the national effort" (Direction de la Securite Sociale en France, 1975, p. 63). According to Dupeyroux (1965, p. 67), "the care taken to maintain extensive socio-professional differentials gives the French system a very different look from the concepts outlined by Beveridge." The central thrust of French social welfare provision, Stephen Cohen and Charles Goldfinger (1975) argue, is not with providing assistance to the poor (France, as we saw in Table 1, combines high social welfare expenditure with high levels of poverty) or with redistribution, but with contributing to national strength and grandeur through improving the "nation's human capital." The "ultimate beneficiaries," they say, are "the Nation

Table 2.   Family Allowances
(% of Total Benefit Expenditure)

FR	11.1
FRG	5.1
IT	No Data
ND	6.5
SW	5.1
UK	2.8
US	0

Source: ILO The Cost of Social Security.

and the state" (p. 6). These characteristics we will associate in Part III with the policy pattern typical of a "democratic corporatist state."

Germany

Expenditure as a percentage of G.D.P. on social welfare provision in the Federal Republic of Germany is somewhat lower than in France. Before it is concluded that state effort therefore is somehow "less," it must be noted that contributions from general revenues are higher. And so, to further complicate comparisons, are contributions from individuals. The most straight-forward statement on financing that can be made is that French (and Italian) firms contribute far more toward welfare provisions than do firms in most of the rest of Europe. In terms of beneficiaries, comparison is easier: there are fewer special schemes in Germany than in France, though there is a generous social insurance scheme for civil servants.

Since the 19th century German governments have been involved in social welfare provisions. Public provision of pensions goes back to an 1889 scheme for manual workers. Pensions assumed their current earnings related form in 1957 and now include 98 percent of all employees (President's Commission on Pension Policy, 1980, Appendix A). The individual, the employer, and the government (about 16% of the cost) contribute to the scheme. There is an earnings ceiling for contribution purposes. Retirement is at age 63 with 35 years contributions or 65 with 15 years contributions for men and women. Benefits are earnings related. According to one of its administrators, the German statutory pension scheme "is designed to protect economically and socially weak classes of the population" (Lohman, 1973, p. 219). Since 1973 a floor of minimum pension benefits has been incorporated into the earnings related scheme in order to prevent payment of inadequate pensions. The Federal Ministry of Labor and Social Affairs supervises pensions as well as other social insurance schemes.

All workers below an earnings ceiling are compulsory members of the health insurance scheme. Coverage extends to approximately 93 percent of the population. Those earning over the ceiling can join on a voluntary basis or take out private insurance. Employers and employees contribute to the scheme with the government paying contributions for the unemployed. Comprehensive medical care is provided under the scheme with no share, barring a prescription charge, borne by the insured person.

Unemployment insurance is compulsory for employees. Employer and employee contributions plus government subsidies finance the scheme and benefits are earnings related. Unemployment assistance, subject to a means test, is paid to workers who have exhausted their regular benefits. Family allowances, financed by the government out of general tax revenue, cover all residents with children. The monthly allowance increases for each child up to and including the third. Begun in the 1950s the current system of family allowances had, according to its advocates, the goal of reducing the economic burden of raising a family (Kaim-Caudle, 1973, p. 175).

The aim of social insurance in the Federal Republic of Germany, correspondent with the social security state, "is substantially based on the principle that the workers who are producing the national produce . . . enable those not able to work, through no fault of their own, to live from the national product" (Schewe et al., 1972, p. 98). Social insurance is concerned with providing a living for those no longer able to earn one. Detlev Zollner (1972, pp. 324–5) says that "people want a guarantee not only of minimal physical subsistence, but of their entire social life." The earnings related nature of cash benefits lifts the floor provided for some claimants above subsistence levels, while retaining the established inequalities and cushioning the transition from work to nonwork. They represent an attempt to provide a guaranteed minimum for a life-style, not just life.

Italy

Social welfare in Italy functions through a variety of administratively separate schemes which are under the general supervision of the Ministry of Labor and Social Welfare. There is a compulsory general scheme of pension insurance for workers in industry which covers about 60 percent of the civilian labor force and many special schemes for different occupational categories: railway employees, air transport workers, industrial managers, seamen, liberal professions, public utilities, civil servants, merchants, self-employed artisans, journalists, and self-employed farmers. Approximately 95 percent of the population now has some form of social insurance (McArdle, 1978, p. 28). Old age pensions under the present general scheme were introduced in 1952. In 1968 an earnings related component was adopted. As a result of three months of recurring strikes in 1969 the government and the four largest unions agreed to a pension increase and to the introduction of a new social pension to persons over age 65 who had not been insured and had no other income. The agreement also increased union representation on the governing boards of the National Social Security Institute which administers the general scheme. As we shall relate later, this is the policy style typical of the "democratic corporatist state": at least one of the affected "corporate" parties—in this case employers—was told by the state what the new policy was to be. Separate institutes administer the special schemes. Pensions are financed by employees, employers, and government with lump-sum subsidies for each person. Retirement is at 60 for men and 55 for women with 15 year contributions. Benefits are earnings related above a minimum pension.

In 1978 Italy set up a National Health Service. Presently employees, employers, and the government finance health care. Patients pay a small charge for non-essential prescribed medicines. A compulsory unemployment insurance scheme is financed by employers and the government with no contribution from the insured person. Benefits are at a flat rate lasting for six months. Workers in industry are eligible for a special supplementary benefit of two-thirds of lost wages for six months. Employees with one or more children are eligible for family allowances. There are special schemes for employees in agriculture, insurance, tax collection, journalism, public utilities, maritime and air transport. Allowances are financed by employers with the government providing a subsidy toward the self-employed and agricultural employees allowances. A flat monthly benefit is paid for each child or adult dependent (a spouse or a grandparent). While administered by the National Social Insurance Institute, individual employers pay allowances directly to their own employees.

Employers carry a heavy share of the cost of Italian social welfare as do those in France. Also as in France, a limited coverage general scheme is combined with numerous occupation specific schemes, a combination identified with the democratic corporatist state in providing social welfare. The most universal program promises to be the National Health Service. Yet currently according to Abel-Smith (1979, p. 69), "provision of facilities is very unequal and so coverage in different parts of the country can mean radically different things with regard to access to quality and quantity of health care." Among the West European states we describe, Italy has by far the greatest gap between legal entitlement and actual provision. One's ability to approach (and through patronage arrangements attempt to exceed) entitlement depends to a large extent on one's place in the power structure and—the two are hardly exclusive—one's relationship to a regionally dominant party.[3]

The Netherlands

Old age pension insurance covers all residents. Pensions are financed from earnings-related employee contributions. Low income persons have their contributions paid for them by the government. Employers make no contribution to pension insurance. Retirement is at age 65. The Dutch pension scheme is unusual in that benefits are paid at a flat rate.

The combination of earnings-related contributions and flat rate benefits has a vertically redistributive effect. The Social Insurance Council administers the scheme with assistance at the regional level by employer-employee Labor Councils. As in most other countries, public servants receive more generous pensions.

There is a compulsory health insurance scheme for employees earning below an income ceiling. This scheme covers 73 percent of the population. There is also a heavy risk scheme covering the whole population. There are special schemes for miners, railway workers, seamen, and civil servants. Employees, employers, and the government finance health insurance. Medical care is paid for directly by the insurance scheme. Patients share the cost of maternity and long-term hospitalization (more than one year). Low income earners are exempted from cost sharing.

Employees, employers, and the government finance unemployment insurance. Unemployment benefits are earnings-related, unlike pensions. Dutch unemployment benefits have one of the highest earnings replacement ratios in Europe. (The Danish is higher.) After exhausting regular benefits the unemployed still receive 75 percent of earnings payable for two years.

All residents with three children or more are covered by the family allowances scheme. It is financed by an employers' payroll tax. Social insurance beneficiaries with one or more children also receive allowances, the cost of which is borne by the Government. The allowance rises incrementally up to the eighth child. Supervised by the Social Insurance Council, industrial associations administer allowances within each industry with larger enterprises paying allowances directly to their own employees.

Only Sweden spends more than the Netherlands on social welfare provision. In his ten country study of social welfare provision, P. R. Kaim-Caudle (1973, p. 301) ranks the Netherlands highest in terms of benefit standards across a range of programs. The Netherlands came

Table 3. Unemployment
Benefits % of Previous Gross
Earnings 1979–80

FR	70
FRG	68
IT	No Data
ND	80
SW	No Data
UK	66*

*Earnings related for a couple with two children.
Source: Economist (June 6, 1981), p. 62.

first with respect to employment injury, temporary disability, invalidity, unemployment, and family allowance programs. The other countries were Austria, Germany, Ireland, the U.K., Canada, the U.S.A., New Zealand, Australia, and Denmark. With its high spending above minimum standards and redistributive elements, Dutch social welfare provision approximates the social welfare state. With respect to health care and the heavy dependency on individual contributions the Netherlands falls short of this state type.

Sweden

All residents are covered by the universal pension scheme. In addition to the universal pension there is an earnings-related supplementary pension financed from employer contributions. The government does not contribute to the earnings-related pension. Combined, the two pensions aim to replace two-thirds of a recipient's previous average real earnings (President's Commission on Pension Policy, 1980, Appendix A). Combining the two pensions in terms of cost, the primary funding source is employer contributions (68%) followed by Central Government (15%) and local authorities (14%). Insured persons contribute only 3% of total funding. The entire administrative costs are borne by the Central Government. This mix represents a major shift toward greater reliance on employers to fund social security schemes. Taking social security financing as a whole, between 1962 and 1978 the funding share for insured persons has fallen from 19% to 1%. The share for employers has risen from 16% to 43% (Yearbook of Nordic Statistics, 1980, p. 277). All residents are covered by the health insurance scheme. As with pensions, individuals do not contribute. Employers pay a payroll tax and the government bears 15 percent of the cost. Hospital care is free to the patient. Patients pay a standard charge for visits to the doctor and prescription charges on some medicines.

Trade Unions run unemployment insurance schemes in Sweden. Coverage extends to about two-thirds of all employees. The employee and the employer pay contributions with the government covering about 46 percent of the cost. Benefits vary according to the particular scheme. The state's concern with unemployment has focused on prevention rather than compensation.

Sweden has pursued an active labor market policy comprised of regional development programs, relief work projects training programs, and information for the employer and the employee (Swedish Institute, 1979). All residents with children are paid family allowances, which are financed by the government. A flat benefit is paid quarterly for each child.

Table 4.   Unemployment % Rate
October 1982

AUS	7.4
FR	8.9
FRG	8.4
ND	13.1
IT	10.5
SW	3.0
US	10.4
UK	12.8

Source: Economist (November 13, 1981), p. 72.

Sweden allocates the highest percentage of GDP to social welfare provision. While public welfare provision goes back to the turn of the century, the period since 1932, which has seen the election and re-election of the Social Democrats up until 1976, has been most important for the development of public policy in this area. Swedish social welfare coverage is more a factor of citizenship and residency than of having made a personal contribution to a scheme. The liberal principle of individual social welfare insurance is weak in the Swedish system. The individual contributes directly only to the non-state unemployment compensation scheme. With redistributive effects the government, through general tax revenue, and employers bear most of the cost of Swedish social welfare provision. With these features, coupled with high employment, and excepting both the inegalitarian supplementary pension to which the state does not contribute and the limited coverage unemployment scheme, Sweden approaches the social welfare state. For this reason Sweden also is seen as the case of the "welfare state" going beyond its limits, encouraging dependency, eroding social control. A mark of this "dependency" could be seen in the ever increasing percentage of adults receiving their primary income from government. This percentage has risen from 23% in 1960 to 44% in 1979 (Schwerin and Heisler, 1982, p. 42). We will discuss the political implications, if any, as the chapter proceeds.

The United Kingdom

Of the six West European countries discussed, the United Kingdom spends the least on social welfare provision. The aim of state welfare provision has been to cover all residents with a subsistence minimum, above which individuals should make their own provision.

All resident's are covered by the universal flat rate pension. Over this basic pension there is an optional earnings-related component from which it is possible to "contract out" in favor of a private pension scheme. Employees, employers, and the government (about 18 percent of the cost) contribute to pensions. Even when contracted out, contributions from employers and employees to the state earnings related pension are still required, though at a reduced rate. Retirement is at age 65 for men and 60 for women. The present pension scheme began in 1978 and it will not be fully operative until 1998, with 20 years of contributions. As with other social insurance schemes, pensions are administered by the Department of Health and Social Security. Civil servants, teachers, white-collar National Health Service Workers, among others (about 20 percent of all employees), receive generous public service pensions (Inquiry into the Value of Pensions, 1981, p. 2).

The National Health Service provides free and comprehensive medical care to all residents. About 85 percent of the cost is paid by the government out of general tax revenue. The patient pays a prescription charge, from which low income people are exempt. Unemployment benefits cover employees earning more than a minimum and are financed by employees, employers, and the government. Up until January 1982 there was a flat rate benefit plus an earnings related supplement. Since then the earnings related supplement has been removed. Family allowances are paid to all residents with children under 16 years of age. There is a flat rate weekly benefit. The government pays the cost of family allowances.

Social welfare provision in the U.K. took its general form under the Attlee government, 1945–51 and was modeled in large part on the famous report by William Beveridge on Social Insurance and Allied Services which appeared during World War II. Since then and up to Mrs. Thatcher there has been considerable inter-party agreement over the methods and purposes of social welfare provision. Social welfare provision in the U.K. then, was primarily identified not with a particular political party but with a civil servant's report. William Beveridge's report contained the central principle of a guaranteed national minimum standard of living to be achieved through social insurance, family allowances, and a comprehensive National Health Service. This principle characterizes social welfare provision under what we call the social security state.

III. TOWARD AN UNDERSTANDING OF DIVERGENT WELFARE PROVISIONS

Social welfare provision is subject to at least two distinct analytical approaches. The first is transnational and transhistorical. The emphasis is on generalization. Inquiry is based at least implicitly on what are thought to be natural science research methods: the major aim, which is declared "value free," is to estimate relationships when all other things are held constant. In our area of concern this approach has led to an emphasis on the importance of economic development and its effects on social and political processes. The dependent variable "policy" is defined principally in terms of expenditures. Within this tradition fall the major works of Robert Jackman (1975 and 1980), Frederic Pryor (1968) and most centrally, Harold Wilensky (1975 and 1981). The basic findings yielded by this perspective are that cross-nationally two variables, the proportion of the population over sixty-five and the age of welfare programs, account for most of the variance in "welfare effort" (defined by Wilensky as welfare expenditures/GNP). Political processes, types of political parties, ideology, even (see Pryor) the nature of the economic system, are basically irrelevant. As one of us has commented, "what we end up with is policy without policy-makers" (Mitchell, 1983, p. 178).

The second orientation attempts to link public policies to historically grounded patterns of state development. Interest shifts to an engagement with the experience of a small number of states (not necessarily one). Moreover, albeit this implication too often is not considered explicitly, these states or cases need not be chosen because they are "representative" of some posited uniformity, they can typify distinct or "extreme" positions either analytically or from the perspective of desired outcomes. Rather than seeing significant patterns as consistent over time and space, outcomes are felt to be diverse, often unique, and at least partially controllable (Miller, 1981). "The interesting questions of policy analysis become those of problem-solving and public choice of how those in positions of authority, as well as those who advocate alternatives and otherwise engage in political argument, go about defining an appropriate response to a given set of circumstances and how appropriate their response turns out to be" (Anderson, 1975, p. 227). This approach, then, mandates that value questions be an integral part of any analysis. In the field of social welfare policy, the work of R. H. Titmuss provides a classic example. More recent efforts include the work of Francis Castles, Norman Furniss, Bruce Headey, and Timothy Tilton.[4]

Now, especially since we have made no effort to hide our preference (or prejudice), it is important to emphasize that the key issue between these two approaches is not which is "better" or "more accurate." Both, let us grant, yield findings of significance. The issue is which set of questions, which pattern of inferential reasoning, is more appropriate to the task at hand. If our concern with the contents of policy, policy choices, and future constraints leads us to choose the second, it is with the realization that the decision is not without costs. Specifically, we must forego cross-national budgetary comparison and with it the luxury of easy numeracy. More broadly, we must shift our aim from "explanation" as it is understood in natural sciences; our more modest goal becomes description and the identification of possible futures. A grander term for this is "understanding" (Verstehen).

A Description of State Types

We believe that the second perspective sketched above is particularly suited to our concern with social welfare policy because it helps us distinguish types of interventionist policies. With the advent of the Great Depression, even laggard "western" industrial states began to address the difficulties in welfare provision arising from the operation of unrestrained markets and the relative sanctity of existing property rights. This overthrow of what Harold Laski called the "negative state" was confirmed during World War II. As we outlined in Part II, however, to turn away from the ideal of some type of "market utopia" is not to adopt similar interventionist goals and practices. Not to see distinctions among sustained departures from the model of the "negative" laissez faire state is to invite overgenerality and an inability to describe insightfully how the goals of state intervention might be altered. In this part of the chapter our effort will be to show that these different forms of intervention can be described in terms of four types or models—the positive state, the social security state, the social welfare state, and the democratic corporatist state.[5] Since the first and last of these terms have been used much more broadly, they will need to be defined with particular care. After setting forth these types in rather abstract ways, we will attempt to compare and contrast their specific welfare efforts along a number of different dimensions.

The term "positive state" has been used by legal commentators (e.g. Miller, 1972) and by radical theorists (e.g., Greenberg, 1974) to categorize at least those capitalist states in which Lindblom's "privileged position of business" can be seen obviously to hold. Even more generally, the "positive state" has been made synonymous with "interventionist state" as in Clinton Rossiter's *Constitutional Dictatorship* (1948, p. 314): "You can't go home again; the positive state is here to stay, and from now on the accent will be on power, not limitations. Our problem is to make that power effective and responsible." We use the term in a narrower sense to mean a state with the primary aim of protecting existing property holders from the perils of unregulated markets and from redistributive demands. The latter involves extending public assistance when necessary to the most severe casualties of the industrial order. (The phrase, "when necessary", incorporates an unstable balance between political pressure and electoral cycles, with problems of legitimacy and patterns of incremental policy making superimposed.)

The general policy orientation of the positive state is thus government support of business initiatives aimed to promote economic growth and social stability. Full employment, for example, is a subordinate objective, and unemployment among unorganized groups can be viewed with a certain equanimity. In the field of welfare policy (not, we emphasize, elsewhere) the positive state hesitates to do anything inconsistent with market conceptions of economic efficiency. Public programs conform, in sum, to Titmuss's "residual welfare model" (1977). Within this model one can make the additional distinction between those "entitlements" resting on the principle of social insurance, which both deflects potential redistribution to noneconomic categories and extends benefits widely, and those in which the disabled, the poor, the "truly needy," are singled out for special treatment. The latter are particularly susceptible to cuts in times of financial stringency and political quiescence. Examples or approximations of the positive state include Australia and the United States.[6]

The social security state differs from the positive state on precisely this point of universality of welfare effort. Its primary aim can be described as the fulfillment of the vision of equal opportunity for all through the provision of a guaranteed national minimum. No one is to be prevented from achieving his or her potential because of inadequate health care, housing, or education. Further, it is recognized that the inherently nonproductive (the old, the severely disabled, the mentally ill) have a right to state assistance.

In the words of the Beveridge Report, the ideological foundation for welfare provision in Britain after World War II, every citizen is to be accorded as of right a level of benefits "adequate in amount, that is to say enough for subsistence without other resources, and adequate in time, that is to say as long as the need lasts." The writ of social policy, however, does not extend beyond this provision of decent security "from the cradle to the grave." As the Beveridge Report (1942, pp. 6–7) admonished, "the state in organizing security should not stifle incentive, opportunity, responsibility; in establishing a national minimum it should leave room and encouragement for voluntary action by each individual to provide more for himself and his family." Or as T. H. Marshall (1981, p. 52) has stated, "our society today is of such a complexion that it is bound to aim at the elimination of poverty while preserving an inegalitarian income structure, and the question of what range of inequality is acceptable above the 'poverty line' can only marginally, if at all, be affected by or affect the decision of where that line should be drawn." Examples or approximations of this state include Great Britain and the Federal Republic of Germany.

Particularly in light of the subsequent difficulties that beset the British "welfare state," some implications of this form of "guaranteed national minimum" might be set out. First, the establishment and maintenance of a national minimum is seen as a task quite apart from general economic organization. As Beveridge declared in a 1943 address (p. 13), "the Plan is neither a step towards Socialism nor a step away from it. . . . It is wanted under any economic system, because, under any economic system, men will be liable to interruption of work by sickness and accident, and will lose earning power in old age." In his elaboration of what he terms the "democratic-welfare-capitalist society," T. H. Marshall (1981) provides a more subtle account of the relationship. For Marshall all parts of this "hyphenated society" are necessary—the democratic component underpins citizenship, the capitalist liberty, the welfare security and solidarity. But while confirming social stability, the components display at least latent mutual tensions. To take only one instance, the "ethos of the normal processes of political and industrial democracy is out of harmony with the spirit required . . . in the field of welfare" because the duty of the welfare principle "is to provide not what the majority wants but what minorities need" (pp. 109,126). It is fairly easy to see how this "duty" could strike a responsive cord with social reformers in positive states. There is no need to discuss "socialism" or to tamper with the economic system; indeed such tampering would be most unwise. The task is to insert the welfare principle into the "democratic-capitalist society."

Second, the national minimum is to be "guaranteed" not by the affected individuals, either directly or through group representation, but by the administrative processes of the state itself. This stipulation, which once again is pleasing to most political reformers in positive states who are keen to restrict the action of "poor people" to voting for appropriate political parties, leads among other things to an ambivalent attitude toward trade unions. While necessary in the economic sphere, unions are always prone to cross the boundaries of the hyphenated society, to become greedy, to try to establish what in Germany has been called the "trade union state." Finally, we should note explicitly the stress placed on the altruism of those members of society unlikely to derive great benefits from the establishment of a national minimum. In his previously cited address, Beveridge presented the key psychological condition: "In the war all of us with incomes above the average have lowered our standards of comfort. . . Is peace so different from war? For my part, I would gladly go on with a lowered standard in peace—if that were necessary—to ensure that no sick or injured or old person, and no child in Britain need be in want or avoidable sickness. . . The appeal is to our sense of national unity and our feeling of Christian brotherhood." We will return to this condition later in assessing the future prospects of the social security state and possibilities for reform in the positive state.

These implications—deliberate inattention to the economic system, an emphasis on state provision, a reliance on the value of altrusim—help distinguish the social security state from the *social welfare state*. As Ernst Wigforss (see Furniss and Tilton, 1977, pp. 18, 19), one of the leading Swedish Social Democratic theoreticians argues, the wage earner

> cannot readily agree to that view of the welfare state . . . that it should secure a minimum livelihood for all, but allow whatever goes beyond this to be won through each individual's or each group's asserting itself in an unlimited competition for standards, wealth and power. That spirit clearly conflicts with the ideas that both the trade union movement and social democracy seek to follow in their public labors . . . that it still shall be the labor movement's ideas of equality, cooperation and solidarity, that shall set their stamp upon society's continuing transformation.

To actualize this vision requires a policy mix designed to lessen the importance of market relationships in daily life—to avoid economic segregation of housing, to promote public provision of education, health care, recreation and social activities. Concomitantly the social welfare state aims to redistribute resources in a more egalitarian fashion. "Solidaristic wage policy," as developed and practiced by the Swedish trade union movement, attempts to equalize pretax incomes by capturing relatively larger wage increases for low-wage workers. Industrial democracy and greater public direction of investment erode capitalist domination within the firm. Environmental planning injects social and collective values into domains previously ceded to private business. These policies mandate the collaboration of producer groups (in particular organized labor) and the state in wage, investment and employment decisions. Examples or approximations include the Netherlands and Sweden.

We see in this formulation a number of new things. First, the outlook toward capitalism is decidedly ambiguous. Capitalism can be a useful support for social welfare endeavors, a "milk-cow" in Adler-Karlsson's phrase, which after suitable motivation is best left undisturbed. Or it can be deemed no longer an adequate source of investment and thus liable to be displaced by, for example, the "wage earner funds" which were the subject of much political dispute during the two most recent Swedish elections. Or capitalism could be declared an intrinsic impediment to true solidarity defined as some type of "socialism."[7] The differences among these perspectives point to major tensions within the social welfare state. What they have in common is a rejection of Marshall's idea that capitalism contains the value of liberty and thus must be succored through hard times.

Second, in thinking about how the policy pattern of the social welfare state arose and operates it is necessary to merge Marshall's "democratic" and "welfare" components. How they come to be merged is subject to debate. Typically, the policy pattern associated with the social welfare state is linked to cases of political hegemony of the left (see Martin, 1975) or the associated proposition that the strategic balance between capital and labor has shifted in the direction of the latter (see Stephens, 1979). Sweden is offered as the prime example of both. The Netherlands, however, fits these propositions less well, combining social welfare policies and aims without the levening of a dominant left party aligned to a strong labor movement. (For a brief review of the Dutch experience see Hoogerwerf, 1977.) Third, and following from the above, there is a consistent effort to broaden the locus of power. As the Swedish Social Democratic Party Program states (quoted in Palme, 1980, p. 4f) to the party, "the demand for economic democracy is as self-evident as the demand for political democracy. . . . The aim is to make all members of society equal partners in the task of administering and increasing productive resources." The major tension inherent in this aim is between shifting decision-making power from employers to employees and increasing individual participation within all decision-making organizations.

Our final state type we call the *"democratic corporatist state."* As with the "positive state," but with more difficulty since "corporate" is so commonly used, we must start by indicating what we do not mean. It is quite clear that corporatist patterns (functional representation of interests) have developed not always harmoniously in all nations in Western Europe and North America. But to then label all these states "corporatist" invites the same problem as the universilization of "positive state" or "welfare state"—by being so broadly drawn, these generic terms fail to illuminate important differences. Again, it is possible to array our previous state types—positive, social security, social welfare—along a very rough continuum from "less" to "more" corporatist. Such an exercise is useful but only when one can hold the *type* of corporatism constant, for otherwise the continuum from "less" to "more" corporatist would not run along a single dimension. As we shall argue below, it is precisely a difference in the type of corporatism that distinguishes the "democratic corporatist state."

Fortunately, in recent years there has been an outpouring of work on the concept of corporatism, the most relevant being that of Gerhardt Lehmbruch (1979) and Philippe Schmitter (1974 and 1977); for their contributions we rely at the outset on the review by Alfred Diamant (1981). We begin with Schmitter's distinction (1974) between "state corporatism" and "societal corporatism." Under the former, groups "are created by and kept as auxiliary and dependent organs of the state"; in the second case, the groups are autonomous and it is they that penetrate the state. Lehmbruch has refined the latter concept as "liberal corporatism . . . a mixed system of governance in which corporatist features coexist with liberal democracy" (cited in Diamant, p. 108). This system is more than just rejuvinated "pluralism." As Lehmbruch explains, "the distinguishing trait of liberal corporatism is a high degree of collaboration among these groups themselves in the shaping of economic policy. For analytic reasons we may distinguish two levels of bargaining in liberal corporate systems; first, bargaining among the 'autonomous groups'; second, bargaining between government and the 'cartel' of organized groups" (cited in *ibid*). What remains to be articulated is the extent to which this bargaining is voluntary or prescribed. This distinction has been developed by Ruth and David Collier in terms of "inducement" and "constraint." (One need not think of these as dichotomous with appropriate scoring procedures.) Taking this distinction with Schmitter's state and societal corporatism, one has four abstract, hypothetical relationships: low inducement/low constraint (pluralism); low inducement/high constraint (tyranny); high inducement/high constraint (state corporatism); high inducement/low constraint (societal corporatism).

As presented and integrated here, this conceptual contribution is suggestive in pointing to the significance and general form of corporatist relationships. More development, however, seems necessary before the concept can illuminate key issues in the national experience of much of Europe. To argue with Schmitter, for example, that in general Southern Europe could be placed under the rubric of "state corporatism" has attractions in highlighting vital institutional legacies and in pointing to the often decisive role of the state. Organizations, however, are far from being "kept as auxiliary and dependent organs." But neither does the alternative model of "societal corporatism" seem appropriate. One hardly derives an insight into the policy pattern of France or Italy or Spain or Greece by proposing that autonomous groups collaborate first among themselves and then bargain with the state. On the other hand, in referring to a system in which corporatist features "coexist with liberal democracy" Lebmbruch presents a dimension that might be further developed. "Liberal democracy" injects a system of territorial representation that can be used to change radically patterns of "corporatist intermediation."

The most recent examples have been the electoral victories of the Socialist Parties in France, Greece and Spain. Even more important perhaps, the "democratic" component refers to civil rights which are individualistic in an active sense. That is, they include freedom of speech, religion, assembly, freedom to change association, to hold property, to enforce individual agreements. In short, civil rights "spell power" (Marshall 1981, p. 142), power that not only limits corporatist competence but which places a premium on "inducements" as opposed to "constraints." (The presence of this check differentiates Southern Europe from most Latin American experience and helps account in our view for how in most Latin American countries the mix of inducements and constraints over time can be so unstable.)

Our term "democratic state corporatism" then, refers to states in which constraints are much lower than our preliminary corporatist model would lead one to anticipate. Constraints are lower because of more or less institutionalized systems of territorial representation and because of guarantees of individual civil rights imbedded in some idea of civil society.[8] For these reasons also, general state policy patterns can be changed by others besides "dominant" state and corporate managers. What distinguishes these states from others in Western Europe are the following features. The first, as we mentioned, is the inapplicability of the model of "societal corporatism" or "liberal corporatism" as found for example in the Federal Republic of Germany. In the democratic corporatist state, groups do not "penetrate" the state nor do they engage in preliminary bargaining. Rather, bargaining takes place between the state and selected groups with decisions then imposed on other relevant actors. Examples include the establishment of the Italian *scala mobile* and the early French Plans. Second, historically the state must have assumed primary responsibility for economic growth and therefore *inter alia* for economic "welfare."

This responsibility must also be seen as a current charge, as it has been in France from the articulation of the First Plan to the nationalization of credit and as it is in a less coherent way in Italy through the activities of the great public holding groups (given the legal title "enti pubblici economici") IRI, ENI and EFIM. These groups are responsible for over 40 percent of all official Italian investment in a myriad of fields. In 1976 they accounted for over 60% of Italy's steel production, 75% of aerospace production, 97% of natural gas, 30% of petroleum, 15% of automobiles, 15% of textile production, 68% of synthetic rubber production, etc. (see Massera, 1981).

The final condition is that the state must be relatively differentiated from a dominant economic class; to use a current expression of some popularity, the state must have significant "relative autonomy." On this dimension Pierre Birnbaum (1980) offers an interesting contrast between Germany and France. In Germany "the state however highly developed or institutionalized, none the less emerged as the instrument of a dominant class. Thus social domination was clearly visible through political domination. It is thus understandable that the trade-union was subordinate to the (social democratic) party." In France, however, "the institutionalization of the state was accompanied by marked differentiation from the dominant class. . . Domination was thus experienced first in its political dimension, which perhaps explains the initial upsurge of anarchist theories and the subsequent spread of anarchosyndicalism" (p. 676). These remarks suggest another important feature of "democratic corporatist states": the weakness of traditional social democracy, and for reasons quite different from those in a "positive state." Typically in a positive state social democracy is deemed "too radical"; in a democratic corporatist state it is considered either too radical or not radical enough. There is also, as there is not in a "positive state," a strong impetus among opposition groups themselves toward corporatist action. This impetus restricts the scope of territorial representation and provides another support to the legitimacy of corporatist power.

In sum, the "democratic corporatist state" entails group-state direction of economic and social affairs with the state assuming a vital and independent role. This pattern, however, is modified both by the presence of individually based civil rights and by the potential impact of decisions from the institutions of territorial representation. The content as opposed to the form of policy direction is thus subject to radical change. Approximations or examples of this type include France and Italy. In the field of welfare policy there is certainly no obeisance paid to the strictures of "laissez faire"; one can anticipate expansive and expensive initiatives oriented at least in part toward perceived state needs or toward the needs of sectors under state tutelage. Even with this qualification characterization of welfare policy is likely to be difficult. The idea of a "national minimum" is too individually grounded, too "liberal," and the notion of income equality reflects too heavily the aspirations of social democracy.

State Types Applied and Contrasted

So far we have described the positive state, social security state, social welfare state, and democratic corporatist state with a focus on policy aims. We will now contrast the state type in terms of internal political orientation and patterns of income equality. Our first contrast is in political orientation. We begin by reproducing a figure from Castles and McKinlay (1979, p. 167) that indicates, roughly that *on their measures* public welfare decreases with the size of the vote for the major party of the right.[9] From this figure we see a sharp contrast between positive states [the United States (US) and Australia (AUL)] and social welfare states [Sweden (SWD) and the Netherlands (NE)]. We see no contrast between positive states and social security states [Britain (UK) and Germany (GE)] which suggests that welfare policy based on a national minimum can be established on "conservative" principles, the classic examples, of course, are the welfare reforms initiated under Bismarck. The position of the democratic corporatist states [France (FR) and Italy (IT)]

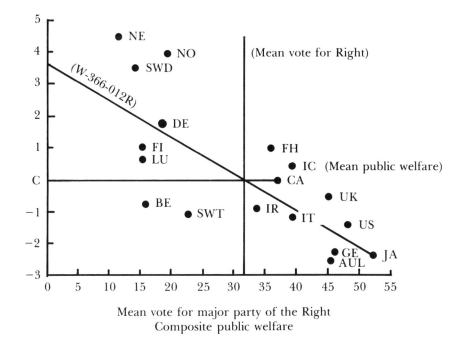

Mean vote for major party of the Right
Composite public welfare

is also enlightening. The "composite public welfare" is quite high (and would have been higher in Italy had a health measure other than infant mortality been used); politically the countries have been dominated by parties of the "right"—Italy continuously since World War II, France from 1958–1981. In more "qualitative" terms we can note major differences in the nature of the "left" party. In neither positive states nor democratic corporatist states is there a strong social democratic party. In positive states the "left" party is mildly reformist. (This statement fits the United States better than Australia. As we outline in footnote six, Australia remains a "positive state" more from the electoral weakness of the Labour Party than from its adherence to the gospel of free markets.) Democratic corporatist states have a "radical" and historically splintered left. Social security states are the home of "conservative social democrats" epitomized by Helmut Schmidt and James Callaghan. Social welfare states have social democratic parties willing to pursue the goal of equality.

Finally, we offer some correlations between the data presented in Part II and our state types. Aligning the effort on social security schemes with our examples, we see a nice progression from the positive state through the social welfare state. Within this progression the democratic corporatist state does not fit; it is distinguished not by the level, but by the

Table 5.   State Types and Social Security
Receipts

State Type	Country	Receipts
Positive State	AUS	15.0
	US	14.8
Social Security State	FRG	23.0
	UK	18.8
Social Welfare State	ND	31.4
	SW	33.9
Democratic Corporate State	FR	26.0
	IT	20.8

purposes of social security spending. Thus in France, for example, one can note the comparatively large expenditure on family allowances (see Table 2).

The correlation between state types and Malcolm Sawyer's findings (1976, p. 19) on the size distribution of post-tax income "standardized" by household size is even more instructive. Note that we do not propose that this distribution is "caused" by the level of welfare spending. Our claim is that our state types help structure the pattern of both welfare provision and income distribution (Table 6). Here we see that the commitment to a national minimum is associated in our social security states with higher shares of post-tax income for the bottom two deciles than are present in our positive states. When we look at the upper deciles, however, we see no patterned difference in income shares. This result we might anticipate from the emphasis placed (to cite the *Beveridge Re-*

Table 6.   State Types and Income Inequalities

State Type	Country	Decile Shares of Post-tax Income (early 1970s)	
		Bottom Two Deciles	Top Two Deciles
Positive State	AUS	4.8	40.9
	US	4.9	42.1
Social Security State	FRG	6.1	39.3
	UK	6.5	46.3
Social Welfare State	ND	9.1	35.3
	SW	7.3	35.0
Democratic Corporate State	FR	4.2	47.1
	IT	Data not available (But see footnote 10)	

port again) on individual "incentive, opportunity and responsibility" be-yond the national minimum. In contrast, our social welfare states reveal both the largest income share for the bottom two deciles and though still substantial, the smallest income share for the upper two deciles, again the situation we would expect. Finally we come to France, the most "unequal" case of all, despite having a "composite public welfare" index and social security expenditures significantly above those of Australia, the United States, Britain, and Germany.[10] The reason we suggest is not inefficiency or the Gallic temperament. Welfare provisions are targeted to groups (including families) not so much to individuals per se. There is little concern about a "poverty line" (see Table I). There was, under conservative French governments, even less concern about equality. It is this matter which the present socialist government proposes to change; prospects will be discussed below.

IV. THE FUNCTIONS AND FUTURES OF WELFARE PROVISION

We link functions and futures as a result of our basic orientation toward political inquiry outlined at the beginning of Part III: policy outcomes are at least partially controllable; the present therefore is the time to begin to forge the future. Put another way, basic, "qualitative" policy changes need not arise only from exogenous factors beyond the realistic ability of policy makers to foresee or affect. Note also that we do not mean to depict "incremental" changes that over time produce outcomes unanticipated in original debate. This outlook governs much of the liter-ature on the "welfare state" from both the political left and the political right—eventually, they say (unless a major reversal is undertaken now, etc.), we will all be living in Sweden. For us on the other hand, no state type has an automatic claim on the future. Not only does each state type considered abstractly exhibit strong "conservative," "system maintain-ing" tendencies, within each nation we have discussed there are signifi-cant political forces committed to implementing policy patterns more akin to those in an alternative state type. Thus we must outline "futur-es," not "the future."

The Functions of Welfare Provision

Our aim in this section is both to illuminate how welfare provisions currently work and to indicate tensions that could lead to change. Our questions are whether we can depict welfare provision as a means of social control; whether welfare provision is aligned to "free market" principles; and whether welfare provision is associated with changes in the distribution of power.

1. Does Welfare Provision Function as a Means of Social Control? The answer in positive states seems basically yes. The argument of Piven and Cloward that relief-giving tends to rise in periods when the poor and underprivileged are mobilized and to fall in periods of social passivity seems persuasive, and for the United States it has found support in recent time-series analyses of welfare spending.[11] The stability of the positive state, then, rests in part on "the poor" remaining unmobilized. When mobilization is tentatively undertaken (as during the "Great Society") welfare provisions based more on the principles of the "social security state" are likely. As an inducement to various occupational groups in democratic corporatist states the answer also seems affirmative. Gaullists, according to Cohen and Goldfinger (1975, p. 30), not only thought of welfare provision as a way of ensuring social peace but also "as an example of the association between Capital and Labor . . . the ideal form of social organization in Gaullist ideology." This position has obvious resonances with the Catholic ideas of "corporatism." It suffers from the same weakness—that in practice, "capital" and "labor" have differing views over what constitutes "the ideal form of social organization." For the social security state and the social welfare state, on the other hand, the answer is "no." By this we do not mean that ideas of "social control" may not have played a part in the *establishment* of welfare programs; one can easily depict both Bismarck's reforms as efforts to preempt the Social Democratic Party and the further "welfare state" measures in both Britain and Germany after World War II as (successful)) attempts to accommodate increased working class power in a way most acceptable to the capitalist order. What differentiates these state types is that in the *functioning* of welfare provision there is a deliberate decision not "to let the State use its power over those in distress for any purpose except to relieve distress" (Gilbert, 1966, p. 856). We return to this point in our discussion of the Thatcher government's proposals for welfare reform.

2. What are the Links Between Welfare Provision and the "Market Economy"? This question must be approached in a number of different ways. We move roughly from the more to the less specific. First, in the matter of whether welfare provision is never to undercut the "rigors" of the market, we can make a sharp distinction between the positive state and all other state types. In the positive state, Bentham's notion of "least eligibility" continues to animate welfare policy. Welfare is to be made as unpleasant as possible; those receiving welfare are instructed to find work. Elsewhere, it is recognized that in Marshall's words (1981, p. 107) "the central function of welfare is to supersede the market by taking goods and services out of it." In the social security state, welfare provision limits the severity of the consequences of market failure. At the same time, the emphasis on a national minimum is designed to give incentive to individuals to rise above it as best they can. The safety net is a good analogy for welfare provision in this state type—economic structures, roles, and performances are similar to the positive state, but a slip is less heavily penalized. Advocates of the social welfare state go further and maintain that taking goods and services out of the market is desirable. "The welfare state indeed undercuts the market. If it didn't it wouldn't be worth defending" (Esping-Andersen, 1982, p. 39). Within the democratic corporatist state, of course, the idea that the market is a force for good has never been a dogma. It is not hard to see that all these positions post difficulties. In the positive state one is instructed to find work; yet the fear of undercutting the rigors of the market also makes programs of "sheltered employment" less appealing. Elsewhere, the tension between market and nonmarket sectors remains unresolved and it is not proven how far the market can be "undercut" without incurring massive financial costs. Indeed in the Netherlands and in Scandinavian countries (except Sweden) we are witnessing attempts to reduce costs by instituting more market discipline.

Next we consider the form of welfare provision—to what extent is it designed to simulate market *mechanisms*. Once again, it is in the positive state that the attraction of "vouchers" and "negative income taxes" is strongest. Likewise, among "populist" critics there is a yen to substitute straight cash payments for what certainly are in many instances demeaning and second class services. The position in the social security state is more ambivalent. On the one hand, the market is considered an extremely efficient distributional system. On the other hand, it is recognized that welfare provision should further the establishment of different value standards. To promote this "welfare culture" (to use Gunnar Myrdal's term, 1960) becomes the goal of the social welfare state; the aim is to sever the link between welfare and exchange. In democratic corporatist states this link never has been strong.

Finally, we can note briefly the role welfare provision is seen to play in national economic strategy. In the positive state, where welfare is still seen as public "charity," no relationship is posited. Felix Rohatyn, New York investment banker, former Chairman of the Municipal Assistance Corporation for the City of New York, and a prominent figure in the search for "new ideas" to reanimate the Democratic Party, sees a gloomy future: "Will the middle class sacrifice to keep black mothers on welfare? I don't think so. We are coming toward a time of mutual terror" (quoted

by Reeves, 1982, p. 77). This revealing statement highlights the costs of
benign neglect in the field of welfare provision and suggests "latent
dysfunctions" in the positive state model. For the social security state,
while it is maintained that in the long run a minimum standard will
further equality of opportunity, welfare provision is essentially parasitic
on the existing economic order. It is assumed that the "mixed economy"
will deliver the goods. When it does not, as in Britain, or threatens not
to, as in Germany, the political temptation to cut welfare provision on
the grounds that the country can no longer afford such luxuries is great.

In the democratic corporatist state and in the social welfare state faith
in the mixed economy is less pervasive. The concern is to integrate
welfare provision into a coherent economic strategy. It is fair to say,
however, that no such strategy has been found effective in hard times.
No one would accuse the Italian government of economic "coherence."
As for France, the early plans do appear to have helped "modernize" the
economy toward the level of its neighbors to the east and north. And
today state direction still seems effective in certain industries requiring
large capital investment and subject to political marketing pressures;
aerospace is a prime example. This example, as the French government
discovered, cannot be repeated in all industrial sectors; the effort of the
Mitterand government to establish a "socialism of production" will be
discussed below. In our social welfare states, economic progress has
rested primarily on an effective labor market strategy which has encouraged productivity and discourged industrial disputes. We would not
deny that an effective labor market policy is furthered by appropriate
types of welfare provision, but it rests even more on an expanding international economy which is just what is in question.

3. Is Welfare Provision Linked to Changes in Power Relations? We look
at power in the Weberian sense of carrying out one's will even against
resistance. Does welfare provision increase power in this sense? In positive states, far from increasing power, the recipient of welfare provisions
loses power. For example, it has been judged by the courts in the United
States that certain property rights claims must be given up with the
acceptance of welfare. Welfare recipients may have their tax records
scrutinized, their homes searched, their sexual habits monitored. The
rationale is the same that pertained to laws in most of 19th century
Europe limiting the franchise to men of property. In the social security
state ideally power relations are to remain untouched. The right to
welfare "is not designed for the exercise of power at all" (Marshall, 1981,
p. 94). Welfare is not about power but about altruism, which leaves
welfare recipients in a tough position should benevolence be withdrawn.
In the democratic corporatist state, power is increased—often directly
through voting for social security oversight boards—but it tends to apply

to groups not to individuals. LaPalombara (1964) observes that one of the main constraints on group power in their relationship to the Italian state is that they must frame demands in terms of the "public interest." Discussing French social welfare provision Cohen and Goldfinger (1975) describe an "ideology of solidarity . . . grounded in an organic vision of the state, in theories of general interest and an ideology of nationalism" (p.5). The problem is that visions differ among relevant groups; there is no consensus on "what solidarity really means." We can say that the idea of "power" becomes divided between benefits bestowed by the state on those able to make requisite claims and rights seized from the state by a reinvigorated civil society. The latter often is the vision; the former usually is the rather uninspiring reality. In the social welfare state, as we noted earlier, there is a tension between the aim of making the individual more of an "actor" in the Weberian sense given above and of transferring "power" from employers to employees which in practice means employee *organizations.*

Common Problems and Political Prospects

The tensions we have identified briefly in the previous section we believe will structure the nature of political debate in each of the state types. This debate is likely to be intense. The conjunction of a number of problems common to all Western countries has produced rather general agreement that the "welfare state", wherever it may be, is "in trouble."[12] After reviewing these problems, we will consider a few current political initiatives that could be of more than fleeting interest.

Any discussion of problems in welfare provision common to Western industrialized countries must begin with adverse demographic trends. Populations are aging, creating more beneficiaries and leaving fewer workers to pay into social security schemes. There is a Multhusian flavor to this problem. The number of old people is increasing faster than the ability to support them. The Germans have come up with a specific term: the "Rentenberg" or pension mountain. The peak of this mountain is reached at different times in different countries, but the problem will become most severe after the year 2000, and generally sooner in Western Europe than in the United States (Horlick, 1979). This demographic trend, of course, affects far more than the financing of pensions. Among other things, the aging of populations also affects health costs. Technological advances in health provision add to the financial burden: To reattach a limb through micro-surgery is much more expensive than to amputate it. (See the discussion in the London *Sunday Times,* 2/14/1982, "Breaking Point: Why the Welfare State is Starting to Crack.")

Poor economic performance for the last decade has combined with these rising costs to make the financial problems of social welfare provision more serious. In the 1950s and 1960s, with steady economic growth, it was easier to increase expenditures on social welfare provision than in the economically depressed 1970s and 1980s. Further, a situation of mass unemployment, which is now characteristic of most Western industrialized countries, directly affects the number of people requiring support from state income maintenance programs. There are now (in 1982) approximately thirty-two million people unemployed in OECD countries. In most, the level of unemployment is higher than at any time since World War II (see table 4).

Apart from depressed economic conditions one cause of the unusually high unemployment rate is the entry of massive numbers of individuals into the world of looking for work. Instead of contributing to the leveling of the Rentenberg this (probably final) cohort of the post war "baby boom" too often finds itself on the dole. In sum, the long run pursuit of welfare (however defined in terms of minimal securities or maximal quality of life) depends first and foremost on re-establishing "a full employment economy with non-inflationary growth" (*The Welfare State in Crisis*, p. 24). It is fair to say that no country under review has succeeded in approaching both goals; most have failed to achieve either.

Recent efforts can be understood in terms of our state types. In the United States the Reagan administration has attempted with varying degrees of success to eliminate the accretion of "social security state" programs launched or given impetus in the mid 1960s. Food stamps and AFDC funds have been cut substantially. The percentage of unemployed receiving unemployment benefits is the lowest since World War II. Occupational safety regulations are enforced laxly, and so on. Some effects have been immediate. According to Census Bureau measures the proportion of the population below the "poverty line" rose in 1982 to 15.0%. (The figure was 11.4% in 1970, 11.7% in 1979, 13.2% in 1980.) The current percentage again reaches the level it was before the impact of "Great Society" programs (The New York *Times*, 2/24/1983, p. 8).

For now Rohatyn's question, "Will the middle class sacrifice to keep black mothers on welfare?", has been answered and while the "time of mutual terror," has not arrived, one of the sides at least is making preparations. In marked contrast to policies of the recent past, and despite financial stringencies, a massive program of prison construction is underway, and the long awaited deluge of public executions could be at hand. Ironically, none of this has led to reduced federal deficits or even to major reductions in the overall level of taxation. One reason is that the United States is a *positive* not a laissez faire state; the line of claimants for public largesse remains large. Of particular relevance is the status of pensioners whose benefits have not been cut significantly and whose "poverty rate" accordingly has not risen. The results of the 1982 congressional elections further show the limits of benefit cuts. There also seems to be a consensus among the Congressional Republican leadership that even the "truly needy" have sacrificed enough.

This result had been foreshadowed in Britain where the Prime Minister, Mrs. Thatcher, has aimed to move away from the provision of a national minimum. Supplementary benefits for strikers' families have been cut. The earnings related supplement on unemployment compensation has been abolished. Unemployment benefit levels are now dropping below the supplementary benefit line. The Thatcher government's solution to the problem of financing health care is to encourage the expansion of private medicine (see *Social Welfare in Britain,* 1980) . The article in the *Sunday Times* cited earlier mentions the prospect of the emergence of two nations in health care, concluding that "anything further from the welfare state envisaged by Beveridge and Bevan is hard to imagine." A key to her views on future policy initiatives has been recorded in a recent paper from the Central Policy Review Staff, Mrs. Thatcher's "think-tank." It suggests replacing the national health service with private health insurance, removing index-linking from benefits, and even ending state funding for higher education. (The fate of this document is discussed in *The Economist,* 9/18/82.)

Capturing the essence of the changed priorities of social welfare provision in Britain is the present preoccupation with fraud as a major problem. The worry is no longer the presence of unclaimed benefits, or individuals slipping through the safety-net. In June 1981 the government said that its campaign against fraud had saved 40 million pounds. The government have set up special teams to expose and investigate fraudulent claims. Claimants now become suspects. Abel-Smith concludes (1980, p. 17) that "if the government continues along this road it will be the end of the post-war Butskellite consensus on the welfare state." At the same time, and as with the positive state in America, forces to retain the status quo remain strong. Within the Conservative party, even within Mrs. Thatcher's cabinet, the position of what are called "the wets" has not been undermined. The "think tank" report was repudiated. Government spending as a percentage of gross national product has not declined. As in America, one is unable to show a link between reduced taxation for the highly paid and welfare cuts on the one hand and economic growth on the other hand. Without this coincidence, the appeal of additional taxation benefits and welfare cuts is sharply attenuated.

The aims of the French Socialist and Swedish Social Democratic governments stand in sharp contrast to these efforts in Britain and the United States. It is proposed in the French case at least to alter the balance of economic and political power within the "democratic corpora-tist" state in favor of the less privileged and in the Swedish case at least to consolidate the "social welfare state." In times of widespread talk of "limits", "bankruptcy" and "ungovernability", a discussion of these cases seems appropriate. In assessing policies we will concentrate on the French experience in part because the Swedish government has been in power only a short while and in part because French policies were pre-sented not only as a new hope for France but as a new hope for the world. As President Mitterrand declared in his Inaugural Statement in May, 1981, "It is in the nature of a great nation to conceive great plans. In the world of today, what higher calling can there be for our country than to achieve a new alliance of socialism and freedom? What finer ambition than to offer it to the world of tomorrow?" After almost two years the state of this "new alliance" can be legitimately reviewed.

We can divide the French governmental program in three parts: moves toward a more "liberal" society; moves toward a more "equal" society; moves toward modernizing the French economy and expanding its world position. On the first the government took a number of steps to bring France in line with northern European practice. Many of these steps also could be viewed as fulfilling the promise of Giscard's 1974 Presidential election campaign developed in his book, *French Democracy*. Capital punishment was abolished, as was the emergency "Court of State Security." The police were told to behave with respect. The law on "security and freedom," which opponents argued always sacrificed the latter to the needs of the former as perceived by state officials, is sched-uled to be repealed this spring. Immigrants were told they would not be expelled summarily. In the area of "decentralization" a whole range of initiatives have been launched including the abolition of "tutelle" (ad-ministrative supervision by prefects and other central government de-partments) and the devolution of more discretion to non central elec-toral bodies. These reforms have continued despite the ability of the opposition to win a number of symbolically important electoral contests. In brief, in regards to individual rights there so far has been a move away from the administrative structure typical of a "democratic corpo-ratist state."

The second thrust has been the effort, stated by Mitterrand at the conclusion of the Presidential "debate," to begin to establish in France "a little more equality," to begin to create a France "juste *et* solidaire." And, as we have seen in the area of income equality, there is much room for development; France in the mid 1970s could claim to be the OECD country with the greatest income inequalities. Upon taking office the government immediately increased the minimum wage and social se-curity benefits, reduced working hours, added a week to holidays, levied a much watered down "wealth tax", and launched a program to hire more government workers. These specific steps were instituted in the context of a renewed "Keynesian" macro-economic policy aimed primarily at reducing unemployment. A necessary feature was the early negotiation of a devaluation of the franc within the European Monetary System. (The Swedish crown was also devalued on the first day of the Social Democratic government.) There was also an effort to create more equality in the workplace. As a result of a series of bills proposed by the Minister of Labor, business and labor organizations are *obliged* to engage in "collective bargaining"; disciplinary powers are reduced; and yet another attempt is being made to institute a mild version of the German system of "co-determination."

In industrial policy the goal as stated by the Minister of Industry (Documents from France, 182/35) "is to generate the conditions that will allow us to build innovative industry which is capable of taking the offensive in two directions: technological progress, which is a factor in social progress, and improved competitiveness with multi-national companies. This is an ambitious goal, and it is clear that it can be achieved only at the national level." This goal is pursued from three directions. The first and most apparent has been a series of nationalizations of industrial groups, armament manufacturers or divisions and banks. The public banking sector now holds 90% of total deposits (up from 55%), and public companies are responsible for 29% of industrial sales (up from 16%). The "commanding heights" have been secured. Second, all industry is directed toward productivity. "Absolute priority," according to the 9th Plan, "must be given to industrial investment." As an aid, employers are to make decreasing contributions to social security; contributions to family allowances are to be phased out altogether. Finally, with the nationalization in place the government is moving toward the creation of trans-European rivals to American and Japanese corporations.

The major effort to date is by the newly nationalized electronics firm Thomson-Brandt (in 1981 ninth among electronics corporations in world sales) to take over the smaller but strategically placed German Grundig corporation and then to align with the Dutch Philips corporation. This grouping, if total sales—not net income—could be added, would be the largest in the world. The spirit behind this sort of initiative was articulated in one of Mitterrand's notations (1978, p. 309), "Only a Socialist Europe, daring to rely on itself, will construct its independence." This aim, the government claims, sets it apart from Scandinavian Social-Democracy. There the emphasis is on consumption. In France interest is said to turn toward establishing a "socialism of production" founded on the premise that industries owned or controlled by the state are the growth polls for France. (For a clear argument of the differences between French Socialism and Swedish Social Democracy see Duverger, 1981.)

In assessing this record the most obvious conclusion is that the easiest part of the Socialist program has been accomplished. The moves toward a more "liberal" society while (as with the abolition of the death penalty) not necessarily favored in the opinion polls, did have broad approval within the French "establishment." And, as we mentioned earlier, most were at least implicitly part of what was supposed to set the previous Giscardian government apart from its "gaullist" predecessors. The moves toward a "more" equal society were firmly supported by the Socialist Party electorate and parliamentarians. After some preliminary political skirmishing, including the rejection of a number of articles by the Constitutional Court, the nationalization bill was passed and the law implemented relatively smoothly.

In short, the measures taken thus far, while sometimes controversial, did not themselves use up too much political capital. In addition, their passage as discrete laws or decrees obscured ambiguities, as for example when in the interest of increased profits for investment, employer social security charges were lessened while the work week also was being reduced. During this period the opposition was in disarray, and Mitterand's political "honeymoon" continued with the public. But in late 1982 the SOFRES poll for the first time showed a minority of respondents expressing complete or a good deal of confidence in his leadership; this was also the time the opposition began mobilizing for the 1983 municipal elections. It is reasonable to project a more critical reception for further policy initiatives.

These measures were also effected with relative ease because they generally took the traditional French form of directives from on high which others were to carry out. This is, as we argued earlier, the policy style typical of "democratic corporatism." So, for example, instead of management and organized labor reading some accord and then negotiating with the state, the state *ordered* the sides to bargain, as it *ordered* the police to act nicely and so on. The limitations of this decision style are clear. More generally, when it comes to efforts to alter corporatist features and associated state privilege, to reform social relations, to bring the working class into decision-making, to liberate the "forces vives", directives are likely to be ineffective. (See the excellent discussion by Hoffmann, 1982.) The fate of "decentralization" is a key test.

The final element in any assessment must be a review of the economic record. Here, as with Reagan and Thatcher, there has been no correlation between economic policy and economic revival. The growth rate in the gross national product has risen slightly, in contrast to the first years of the Reagan and Thatcher administrations. But inflation has remained high, the franc has fallen dramatically on foreign exchange markets, the public deficit has grown, and the balance of trade had deteriorated. (A useful summary is given by Paul Lewis, "France's New Industrial Policy," The New York *Times,* November 28, 1982.) Nor have all these "trade-offs" enabled the government to achieve its declared priority of bringing down the unemployment level; spokesmen have been reduced to stating that the rate of increase has been less than in some neighboring countries. (See, for example, the interview with the Prime Minister in *Le Nouvel Observateur,* November 13, 1982.)

These economic troubles have necessitated a change in course, as they did in Britain with renewed public expenditures and in the United States with federal tax increases. Unlike Britain or America, however, the change has been overt: The government has delighted in proclaiming a new "politique de rigeur." Wages and prices were frozen, plans to expand public employment curtailed, jobless benefits have been reduced. Accompanying this change has been a renewed campaign to "reconquer the domestic market." Similar sentiments have been voiced in Sweden where the campaign is called the "defense of the Swedish economy."

What direction economic policy will now take is unclear, and what impact it will have is even less certain. The possibility that the "politique de rigeur" will mark the end of the Socialist economic experiment is there. The potential that the reconquest of the French economy, and the defense of the Swedish economy, will degenerate into pure protectionism is greater. The economic moves can also be seen as a sign of greater realism, which is not entirely the same thing. This realism is of two related kinds. First, on the individual level, as the Swedish Prime Minister Olof Palme remarked (1980, p. 22), "Prospects for increases in real wages in the years to come are bleak." Second, on the national level governments, especially governments of the left, to retain freedom of action must not permit consumption to exceed production. Andre Fontaine (*Le Monde,* June 17, 1981) presented the lesson directly: "If the left was ousted from power in Chile in 1973 and in Portugal two years later, it is because it already had lost [this] economic battle."

Certainly, the change in "rigeur" did not split the Socialist Party. The challenge is to institute a "socialism of production" in a nonfacilitating international economy and in time to have tangible results before the parliamentary elections scheduled in 1986. That this challenge must be met within the policy pattern of "democratic corporatism" adds yet another difficulty. As in Britain and the United States, to forecast failure for any policy initiative remains the most prudent course. Unlike Britain and the United States, the policy initiatives of the Mitterrand government carry the promise of both greater personal liberty and of greater social solidarity.

NOTES

1. Much of the argument over determinants rests on differing ideas on what the term includes. A prime example is found in the work of Harold Wilensky (1975) and—one is tempted to say "versus"—Francis Castles (1978). Differences are further elaborated in Francis Castles and R. D. McKinlay (1979). We will refer to the work of Castles and Wilensky throughout this chapter.

2. This confounding of the normative with the empirical lead Richard Titmuss (1968) to label the "welfare state" an "indefinable abstraction" (which, nevertheless, he continued to use in his own work).

3. This statement should not be confused with a "vulgar marxist" explanation. Thanks to the events of 1968–69 organized workers have established a relatively privileged position in the corporate structure. The keystone was the establishment of the *scala mobile* (wage indexation) which, despite numerous efforts to weaken it, remains relatively intact. French organized workers also achieved gains during this period. These gains brought more attention but less institutionalization.

4. On Titmuss see particularly (1976 and 1977). Other relevant citations would include Castles (1978), Furniss (1975), Furniss and Timothy Tilton, (1977), Bruce Headey (1978), Tilton (1979).

5. This effort began with Furniss and Tilton, especially chapters 1, 5, 6, 7. In that book only the first three types of interventionist states were elaborated; the "democratic corporate state" is new to this chapter. In addition, with the exception of the "positive state", we have made a number of modifications in the description of the other state types.

6. Australia is included for different political reasons than the United States. In the United States both of the major parties are oriented around the policy pattern of the "positive state" with the "left wing" of the Democratic Party aspiring toward the social security state and the "right wing" of the Republican Party casting nostalgic glances in the direction of the "negative" laissez faire state. Later in this chapter we will evaluate Reagan's efforts to move welfare policies in this direction. In Australia the policy pattern typical of the positive state arises more from the political hegemony of the right. Since 1949 conservative governments have been in office for all but three years. (The experience of the Whitlam government, which lies beyond the scope of this paper, shows at a minimum the tenacity with which the right believes in its claim to office.) The consequence, to quote Hugh Stretton (1979, p. 370) is that Australia is "by almost any standard the meanest country in the world to its unemployed, its blacks, and many of its other poor." Nevertheless, we should note that this policy pattern, by not resting on party consensus, is more subject to change than is the case in the United States. The welfare policy goals of the Australian Labour Party are similar to those of social democratic parties in social security states. A period of time in office would presumably enable the party to move policies in this direction.

7. Adler-Karlsson, (1969 pp. 65, 66). "Wage earner funds" would transfer a percentage of firms' profits to funds controlled by trade union organizations. (In the latest version control is to be decentralized.) For a general discussion linking social welfare theory to ideas of socialism see Tilton (1979).

8. It remains significant that the system of territorial representation and the guarantee

of individual civil rights is less firmly grounded than in the other states under review. One reason, surely, is the greater pull of "corporatist" tendencies as defined.

9.   The values of public welfare and the vote for the right they give as follows (p. 167):

Australia	−2.64	44.85
Austria	−2.40	44.14
Belgium	−0.84	16.02
Canada	−0.07	37.08
Denmark	1.67	18.76
Finland	0.81	15.96
France	0.96	35.15
Germany	−2.55	45.97
Iceland	0.37	39.46
Ireland	−0.99	33.40
Italy	−0.10	39.62
Japan	−2.38	52.10
Luxembourg	0.56	15.23
Netherlands	4.35	11.58
Norway	3.85	19.46
Sweden	3.42	14.84
Switzerland	−1.13	22.30
United Kingdom	0.60	45.25
United States	−1.42	48.02

Their index of public welfare standardizes the variables of education (expenses as a % of GNP), transfer payments (% of GDP), and infant mortality, and adds them. See their table 1, p. 158.

10.   Lest the French case be dismissed as an anomaly, we should note that Sawyer was able to compute for Italy size distribution of post-tax income *not standardized* by household size. The findings correspond to the French case: The bottom two deciles received 5.1% of post- ax income, the top two deciles received 46.5%.

11.   Piven and Cloward set out their arguments in *Regulating the Poor* (1971) and more generally in *Poor People's Movements* (1977). On support for many of the hypothesized relationships between capital accumulation and social security outlays see Larry Griffin *et al.* (1981). On support for the argument that the inner city riots were responsible for significant expansions in welfare payments see Larry Issac and William Kelly (1981). See also Albritton (1979).

12.   For an overview see Albert O. Hirschman (1981). That the diagnosis is correct is a view held on both the political left and right. See for example James O'Connor (1973) and Richard Rose and Guy Peters (1978).

REFERENCES

Abel-Smith, Brian, and Maynard, Alan. *The Organization, Financing, and Cost of Health Care in the European Community.* Brussels: European Communities Commission, 1979.

Abel-Smith, Brian. "The Welfare State: Breaking the Post-War Consensus." *Political Quarterly,* January, 1980.

Adler-Karlsson, Gunnar. *Functional Socialism: A Swedish Theory for Democratic Socialism.* Stockholm: Pisma, 1969.

Albritton, Robert. "Social Amelioration Through Mass Insurgency? A Reexamination of the Piven and Cloward Thesis." *The American Political Science Review* 73 (December 1979).

Anderson, Charles. "System and Strategy in Comparative Analysis." In *Perspectives on Public Policy Making*. Edited by W. B. Gwyn and G. C. Edwards. New Orleans: Tulane University Press, 1975.

Beveridge, William. *Social Insurance and Allied Services*. New York: Macmillan, 1942.

———. *Beveridge on Beveridge*. London: Social Security League, 1943.

Birnbaum, Pierre. "States, Ideologies and Collective Action in Western Europe." *International Social Science Journal* XXXII, No. 4 (1980): pp. 672–686.

Castles, Francis. *The Social Democratic Image of Society*. London: Routledge and Kegan Paul, 1978.

———, and McKinlay, R. D. "Public Welfare Provision, Scandinavia and the Sheer Futility of the Sociological Approach to Politics." *British Journal of Political Science* 9 (April 1979): pp. 151–171.

Central Statistical Office. *Economic Trends*. London: HMSO, December 1979.

Cohen, Stephen, and Goldfinger, Charles. *From Permacrisis to Real Crisis in French Social Security*. Berkeley: Institute of Urban & Regional Development, 1975.

Collier, Ruth Berins, and Collier, David. "Inducements versus Constraints: Disaggregating Corporatism." *The American Political Science Review* 73 (December 1979): pp. 967–986.

Diamant, Alfred. "Bureaucracy and Public Policy in Neocorporatist Settings: Some European Lessons." *Comparative Politics* 14 (October 1981): pp. 101–124.

Direction de la Securite Sociale en France. Paris: La Documentation Francaise, 1975.

Documents from France. Paris: French Embassy Press and Information Service.

Dupeyroux, Jean Jacques. *Securité Sociale*. Paris: Dalloz, 1965.

Duverger, Maurice. "Les Trois Visages." *Le Monde*, December 1981.

The Economist. London.

Esping-Andersen, Gosta. "After the Welfare State." *Working Papers IX* 3 (May/June 1982).

European Communities Statistical Office. *Basic Statistics of the Community*. International Publications Service, 1981.

Flora, Peter, and Heidenheimer, Arnold, eds. *The Development of Welfare States in Europe and North America*. New York: Transaction Books, 1981.

Furniss, Norman. "The Welfare Debate in Great Britain: Implications for the United States." *Public Administrative Review*, May/June 1975: pp. 300–309.

Furniss, Norman, and Tilton, Timothy. *The Case for the Welfare State*. Bloomington, Indiana: Indiana University Press, 1977.

Gilbert, Bentley. "Winston Churchill versus the Webbs: The Origins of British Unemployment Insurance." *American Historical Review*. 71 (April 1966): pp. 846–862.

Greenberg, Edward. *Serving the Few: Corporate Capitalism and The Basis of Government Policy*. New York: John Wiley, 1974.

Griffin, Larry, et. al. "Accumulation, Legitimation and Politics." Paper presented at the Annual Meeting of the American Sociological Association, Chicago, 1981.

Hage, Jerald, and Hanneman, Robert A. "The Growth of the Welfare State in Britain, France, Germany, and Italy: A Comparison of Three Paradigms." In *Comparative Social Research* III. Edited by Richard Tomasson. Greenwich, Conn.: JAI Press, 1980.

Headey, Bruce. *Housing Policy in the Developed Economy*. New York: St. Martin's Press, 1978.

Hirschman, Albert O. "The Welfare State in Trouble." *Dissent*, Winter 1981: pp. 87–90.

Hoffmann, Stanley. "Year One." *New York Review of Books* XXIX. No. 13 (1982).

Hoogerwerf, A. "De Groei van de Overheid in Nederland Sinds 1900." *Bestwurswetenschappen* 4 (July/August 1977): pp. 46–82.

Horlick, Max. "The Impact of an Aging Population on Social Security: The Foreign

Experience." INU.S. Department of Health, Education and Welfare, *Social Security in a Changing World*. Washington, D.C.: U.S. Department of Health, Education and Welfare, September 1979.

Inquiry into the Value of Pensions, Cmnd. 8147. London: HMSO, 1981.

International Labour Office. *The Cost of Social Security*. Geneva: ILO, 1981.

Isaac, Larry, and Kelly, William. "Racial Insurgency, the Welfare Expansion." *American Journal of Sociology* 86 (May 1981): pp. 1348–1386.

Jackman, Robert. *Politics and Equality*. New York: John Wiley, 1975.

————. "Socialist Parties and Income Inequalities in Western Industrial Democracies." *Journal of Politics*, February 1980, pp. 135–142.

Kaim-Caudle, P. R. *Comparative Social Policy and Social Security*. London: Martin Robertson and Company, 1973.

La Palombara, Joseph. *Interest Groups in Italian Politics*. Princeton: Princeton University Press, 1964.

Laroque, Pierre. *Social Welfare in France*. Paris: La Documentation Francaise, 1963.

————. "Social Security in France." In *Social Security in International Perspective*. Edited by Shirley Jenkins. New York: Columbia University Press, 1969.

Lehmbruch, Gerhard. "Liberal Corporation and Party Government." In *Trends Towards Corporated Intermediation*. Edited by Phillippe Schmitter and Gerhard Lehmbruch. Beverly Hills: Sage, 1979.

Lohmann, C. H. "The New Structure of Statutory Pension Insurance in the Federal Republic of Germany." *International Social Security Review* 263 (1979): pp. 214–224.

Marshall, T. H. *The Right to Welfare and Other Essays*. New York: Free Press, 1981.

Martin, Andrew. "Is Democratic Control of Capitalist Economies Possible:" In *Stress and Contradiction in Modern Capitalism*. Edited by Leon Lindberg, et al. Lexington, Mass: Lexington Books, 1975.

Massera, Alberto. "L'Efficacite des Entreprises Publiques en Italie." *Revue Français d'Administration Publique* 20 (October–December 1981): pp. 147–161.

McArdle, Frank B. "Italy's Indexing, Minimum Benefits, and Pension Reform." *Social Security Bulletin* 41 (August 1978): pp. 27–31.

Miller, Arthur. "The Legal Foundations of the Corporate State." *Journal of Economic Issues* 6 (March 1972): pp. 59–79.

Miller, Trudi, "Useful Knowledge about the Public Sector." In *Proceedings of a Conference on Knowledge Use*. Pittsburgh: University of Pittsburgh Press, 1981.

Mitterrand, Françoise. *L'Abeille et l'Architecte*. Paris: Flammarion, 1978.

————. *The Wheat and the Chaff*. London: Weidenfeld and Nicholson, 1981.

Mitchell, Neil. "Ideology or the Iron Laws of Industrialism: The Case of Pension Policy in Britain and the Soviet Union." *Comparative Politics* 15 (January 1983): pp. 177–201.

Le Monde.

Myrdal, Gunnar. *Beyond the Welfare State*. New Haven: Yale University Press, 1960.

The New York Times.

Le Nouvel Observateur.

O'Connor, James. *The Fiscal Crisis of the State*. New York: St. Martin's Press, 1973.

Palme, Olaf. "Democratizing the Economy." Address given in Washington D.C., 1980.

Piven, Francis, and Cloward, Richard. *Regulating the Poor*. New York: Vintage, 1971.

————. *Poor People's Movements*. New York: Pantheon, 1977.

The President's Commission on Pension Policy. *An International Comparison of Pension Systems*. Washington, D.C.: U.S. Government Printing Office, 1980.

Pryor, Frederic L. *Public Expenditures in Communist and Capitalist Nations*. Homewood, Ill.: R.D. Irwin, Inc., 1968.

Public Expenditures on Income Maintenance Programs, (OECD, 1976).

Reeves, Richard. "An American Journey." *The New Yorker,* April 12, 1982, pp. 48 et seq.

Rose, Richard, and Peters, Guy. *Can Governments Go Bankrupt?* New York: Basic Books, 1978.

Rossiter, Clinton. *Constitutional Dictatorship.* Princeton: Princeton University Press, 1948.

Rustant, Maurice. *La Securité Sociale en Crise.* Paris: Chronique Sociale, 1980.

Sawyer, Malcolm. "Income Distribution in OECD Countries." *OECD Occasional Studies,* July 1976.

Schewe, Dieter; Nordhorn, Karlhugo, and Schenke, Klaus. *Survey of Social Security in the Federal Republic of Germany.* Bonn: Federal Ministry of Labour and Social Affairs, 1972.

Schmitter, Philippe. "Still the Century of Corporation?" *Review of Politics,* (1974): pp. 85–131.

———. "Modes of Interest Intermediation and Models of Social Change in Western Europe." *Comparative Political Studies* 10 (1977): pp. 7–38.

Schwerin, Don S., and Heisler, Marin O. "Government as Paymaster: Public Employment and Dependence of Transfer Payments for Primary Income in the Nordic Countries." Institute of Political Science: University of Aarthus, 1982.

Stephens, John. *The Transition from Capitalism to Socialism.* London: Macmillan, 1979.

Stretton, Hugh. "The Australian War on the Poor." *New Society* November 15, 1979). *The Sunday Times,* (London).

Tilton, Timothy. "A Swedish Road to Socialism." *The American Political Science Review* 73 (June 1979): pp. 505–520.

Titmuss, Richard. *Commitment to Welfare.* London: George Allen & Unwin, 1968.

———. *Essays on the Welfare State.* London: George Allen & Unwin, 1976.

———. *Social Policy.* London: George Allen & Unwin, 1977.

U.S. Department of Health, Education and Welfare, *Social Security Programs Throughout the World.* Washington D.C.: Government Printing Office, 1980.

Weise, Robert. "Social Changes in Italy," *Social Security Bulletin,* 32, (June 1969).

The Welfare State in Crisis. Paris: OECD, 1981.

Wigforss, Ernst. "Forstomajtal 1962." In *Frihet och Gemenskap.* Stockholm: Tidens Forlag, 1962.

Wilensky, Harold. *The Welfare State and Equality.* Berkeley: University of California Press, 1975.

———. "Leftism, Catholicism, and Democratic Corporatism: The Role of Political Parties in Recent Welfare State Development." In *The Development of Welfare States in Europe and America,* (see above) Edited by Peter Flora and Arnold Heidenheimer. New Brunswick, N.J.: Transaction Books, 1981.

Yearbook of Nordic Statistics. Stockholm: Nordic Council.

Zollner, Detlev. "Social Security in the Federal Republic of Germany." *Journal of Social Policy,* October 1972, pp. 317–330.

SOCIAL POLICY AS THEORY:
REAGAN'S PUBLIC PHILOSOPHY

Malcolm L. Goggin

A philosophical realignment occurred in the United States in the after-math of the Great Depression. An outmoded set of capitalist principles which guided and justified public policy was replaced with a reconstruct-ed "public philosophy,"[1] one which Theodore Lowi calls "interest group liberalism" (Lowi, 1967; 1979). Prior to 1938, political leaders disagreed over how to use the power and resources of the Federal government for solving the nation's problems and for promoting the general welfare. Liberals, usually Democrats, favored an enlarged role for government. Conservatives, mostly Republicans, argued for less government.

Following the shared catacylismic experience of the Great Depression, liberals and conservatives, and Democrats and Republicans reached a consensus: the Federal government was to play a major "positive" role in creating jobs for the unemployed and in protecting American workers from the vagaries of a market economy by doing everything in its power to hold down rates of inflation and unemployment while stimulating economic growth.[2] Concomitantly, the legislative and executive branches of government were to parcel out to private interest groups the power to make public policy.[3] Politics was a means for interests who were involved in inter-group struggle to get what they wanted, while the unorganized received what they were told they needed (Edelman, 1974, p. 25). According to Lowi's formulation, interest group liberalism expects to use government in a positive and expansive role, it is motivated by the highest sentiments, and it possesses strong faith that what is good for government is good for the society . . . it sees as both necessary and good that the policy agenda and the public interest be defined in terms of the organized interests in society. In brief sketch, the working model of the interest group liberal is a vulgarized version of the pluralist model of modern political science (Lowi, 1967, p. 19).

Interest group liberalism embodied the set of principles which justified and guided the expansionary public policy initiatives which formed the basis of an incomes and services strategy from the late New Deal through the Great Society. Moreover, support for liberal policies was widespread among the public. For example, at approximately the midpoint in the period between the New Deal and the 1980 elections, about two-thirds of the American people supported the idea that the Federal government should use its power in order to achieve socially desirable objectives.[4] (Free and Cantril, 1968, pp. 21-22). Paradoxically, a large majority of those who favored liberal *policies* held conservative *beliefs* (Free and Cantril, 1968, p. 178).

I. POLICY AS THEORY

Ronald Reagan has compared himself to Franklin D. Roosevelt, and his program of economic recovery to FDR's New Deal. Ronald Reagan's 1980 election as president and his performance in office have raised a number of puzzling questions: Has Reagan's election ushered in another 20th century philosophical realignment? Is there an end to pluralism? Are we experiencing a deconstruction of the welfare state? Is there a new public philosophy under Ronald Reagan's direction? What is the underlying theory of this emerging public philosophy? Is it a return to pre-1938 conservatism or is "Reaganism" a new brand of conservative thinking?

This essay examines several of the Reagan administration's social policy proposals, treating them as hypotheses from which an underlying theory or public policy can be inferred.[5] In the first section, the construction of the welfare state is described. By the late 1960's, the *perception* of scholars and practitioners was that the social policies of the welfare state had failed to deliver on their promises. Following this analysis, several proposed 1970s solutions to the "failure" of these policies, one of which was to deconstruct the Great Society, are identified. In the concluding section, the Reagan administration's proposed health, welfare, job training, food stamp and school lunch proposals for fiscal year 1982, and the subsequent provisions of the Omnibus Budget Reconciliation Act of 1981,[6] are analyzed. These policies are interpreted in terms of the conservatives' efforts to deconstruct the welfare state.

The method of analysis is evaluation research, broadly defined to mean the measurement of the process by which political elites make decisions about the worth of a particular course of action (Anderson, 1979, p. 711). It is in its focus on principles that it differs from the evaluative research that has become a sub-speciality of policy analysis.

Using primary sources, budget decisions that the Reagan administration made during its first 100 days in office are reconstructed, and examined in the context of fifty years of national social welfare policy. The analysis treats public choice as argument—in the words of Charles Anderson, "a reasoned case for a preferred course of action" (Anderson, 1979, p. 712).

The research method aims at specifying the policy rationality that underlies these public choices. Ronald Reagan has a structured set of beliefs about what the nation's problems are, and how these problems can be solved. This essay articulates the policy rationality—the public philosophy—which has guided the Reagan administration's public choices in its first two and one half years in office. The critical question which is analyzed is whether this public philosophy is transitory or whether it will become, in the sense used by Walter Lippmann (1955), "the" public philosophy.[7]

II. CONSTRUCTING THE WELFARE STATE

The construction of the welfare state was neither facile nor mercurial. It took nearly seventy-five years and passed through three phases: a period of *protecting* those who had jobs from the trusts and the bosses, to an era of *economic growth,* and at its pinnacle, a period of planned *growth and equality of opportunity.*

The foundation was laid by the reforms of Progressives like Teddy Roosevelt and Woodrow Wilson. The frame was planned and erected in the aftermath of the traumas of two World Wars and a world-wide economic collapse by liberal architects like Franklin D. Roosevelt and John F. Kennedy; and an entire new wing was added while Lyndon B. Johnson was in office, between November of 1963 and the end of 1968.

The construction materials were social policies[8]—the authoritative decisions to intervene in the market place for the purpose of improving the social, material, and psychological well-being of those least able to provide for themselves. According to Harold Wilensky (1975, p. 1), the welfare state consists of "government protected minimum standards of income, nutrition, health, housing, and education, assured to every citizen as a political right, not as charity." Thus, the construction of the welfare state replaced nineteenth century Elizabethan Poor Laws[9] with twentieth century entitlements.

The Era of Protection

The period between 1896 and the Great Depression has been called the "Age of Reform" (Hofstadter, 1955). The major targets of reform were the trusts and the bosses. The primary goal of reform-minded politicians was to resurrect the type of economic individualism that many people believed existed earlier in America. Between 1896 and 1930, laws were enacted by Congress and signed by the President in order to reform working conditions, to reduce the work week, and to protect women and children in the work force. Because most of the social policies were aimed at helping those who already had jobs, improved working conditions took precedent over increased employment or productivity. Consequently, economic growth during the period was relatively slow.

According to a Brookings Institution study (Leven et. al, 1938), national income, after adjustments for rising prices and a growing population, increased at a modest 1.3% per year. Whereas there were substantial gains in economic equality during the first decade of the twentieth century, this progress was offset by accentuated inequality in the distribution of income in the 1920s (Gordon, 1974). The principal losers during the 1920s were members of the middle class. Although lower income workers improved their lot, both in terms of better pay and better working conditions, *relative* to those in the upper income brackets they did rather poorly (King, 1915, p. 231).

In spite of liberal reforms, some historians have argued that the era was neither progressive nor a movement. Challenging Richard Hofstadter's rosy assessment of the period, James Weinstein (1968), for example, writes that the reformers failed badly. The era was essentially conservative, largely because the reforms preserved and nurtured the existing system of private property and protected business interests. By 1930, much of the labor force, especially unskilled laborers and farmers, were still unorganized, poverty was widespread, and income inequalities were essentially the same as they were at the turn of the century.

The Era of Growth

By the time the 1932 elections were held, a majority of the American electorate, almost one of four who were out of work at the time, were discouraged and lacked faith in American business and government. They wanted a change in administrations and a more active government—one that would intervene in the economy to find jobs for the unemployed and insulate workers from the economic hardships of disability, unemployment, and retirement (Conkin, 1975).

The operative theme of the new Roosevelt administration was to guarantee every American a minimum subsistence as a right. Not charity, but earned entitlement was to be the clarion call of the New Deal. The Roosevelt administration, recognizing the dire needs of the American people, created a new mood of hope by designing policies to provide short-term aid to the temporarily deprived. Policy goals were full employment and insurance against temporary fluctuations in the economy.

Roosevelt's success with Congress during the famous fundred-day legislative session of 1933 provided a tremendous psychological boost to the nation, thus setting the stage for the incomes and social services policies which followed. The National Recovery Act of 1933, for example, was a case of business cooperation in the interest of national planning, and stressed the centralized control of federal public works programs. By employing one million Americans in 1933, the Civil Works Administration pumped one billion dollars of purchasing power into the lagging economy. In this "early" New Deal, a variety of interests and groups found a sympathetic listener in FDR, "a unifier of interests" (Conkin, 1975, p. 8).

Roosevelt also succeeded in getting social legislation through Congress during the "second" New Deal (Conkin, 1975, p. 21). The new regulatory bodies—the Securities and Exchange Commission, the Federal Reserve Board, the Federal Power Commission, and the Interstate Commerce Commission—symbolized a new partnership between big business and big government. Vigorous enforcement of the Wagner Act strengthened labor by granting unions the ability to bargain collectively with management. The 1935 Social Security Act and related laws addressed, if not solved, the problems of job insecurity and unemployment, inadequate housing, below-subsistence wages, and retirement and old age. Their enactment affirmed the federal government's role as a tool of beneficient action. However, while the federal insurance aspects of the Social Security Act had a pronounced welfare bias, it had limited applicability to the working poor.

By 1938, the dominant utilitarian theme of economic growth for the benefit of all was firmly in place. The goals were economic security and a higher standard of living for everyone. Roosevelt promised a better life for the poor:

> The test of our progress is not whether we add more to the abundance of those who have much; it is whether we provide enough for those who have too little (Roosevelt in Chambers, 1965, p. 73).

In his administration's policy behavior, however, the New Deal had the net effect of conserving and protecting capitalism while stifling meaningful participation by potentially revolutionary groups of industrial and agricultural workers (Leuchtenburg, 1963, p. 240). These policies did not have the "trickle down" effects that were promised. Reflecting on the legacy of the New Deal, Michael Harrington wrote in 1962:

> Out of the thirties came the welfare state. Its creation had been stimulated by mass impoverishment and misery, yet it helped the poor least of all . . . . If a man works in an extremely low-paying job, he may not even be covered by social security or other welfare programs. If he receives unemployment compensation, the payment is scaled down according to his low earnings . . . .
>
> Indeed, the paradox that the welfare state benefits those least who need help most is but a single instance of a persistent irony in the other America . . . .
>
> Today's poor, in short, missed the political and social gains of the thirties. They are, as Galbraith rightly points out, the first minority poor in history, the first poor not to be seen, the first poor whom the politicians could leave alone (Harrington, 1962, p. 16).

The most radical change between 1896 and 1938 was the universal acceptance of the idea of an enlarged role for the Federal government in the economy. While the political rhetoric included promises to make income distribution more equal, the operative theme of the Progressive era was *protection* of workers *and* managers, and the principal strategy of the New Dealers was economic *growth*. Thus, the major thrust between 1932 and 1938 was to expand the size of the pie, not to divvy it up in slices more equal in size.

Although Theodore Roosevelt's New Nationalism and Woodrow Wilson's New Freedom contained elements of Federal government intervention in the economy on behalf of the underpriviledged,[10] it took the cataclysmic events of wars and the Great Depression and the failure of private markets to convince American politicians and voters that many of the nation's social problems could not be solved by private charity or local or State governments alone.[11]

Besides the Employment Act of 1946, very few new programs were passed during the prosperity of the immediate post-World War II era. The 1946 Act reiterated the Federal government's responsibility for the performance of the economy. Economic growth became a bipartisan venture: Eisenhower's Great Crusade affirmed and legitimized the social policies of previous Democratic administrations, but few innovations were adopted during the Republican's tenure.

Even John F. Kennedy's New Frontier faltered, and failed to live up to the campaign rhetoric of helping the poor. In 1962, President John Kennedy changed to the familiar theme of growth: "Our primary challenge is not how to divide the economic pie, but how to enlarge it." It was not until shortly before his assassination in November of 1963 that Kennedy gave instructions to the Chairman of his Economic Advisors, Walter Heller, to formulate a set of anti-poverty programs upon which he might base his 1964 campaign for reelection.[12] However, actual legislative victories, for example, The Area Redevelopment Act, the Manpower Development and Training Act, and a program for the poor in Appalachia, represented only a symbolic, piecemeal approach to such a mammoth problem as poverty in America. In sum, the period between World War II and 1964 was a time when social welfare legislation was a low priority for Presidents and Congresses.

The Era of Growth and Equality of Opportunity

For a variety of reasons,[13] an explosion of liberal social policies followed the 1964 elections. What is significant about the social programs of the Johnson administration is that they attempted to combine "the Prometheon ambition and the egalitarian ideal" (Aron, 1968, p. 3). Not only was the size of the economic pie to be expanded dramatically, it was also to be divided up more equally. The most important means to a more equal distribution of America's benefits and burdens was equality of opportunity—equal access to timely and adequate health and medical care, adequate housing, a quality education, nutritional diets and a job. Throughout the course of Johnson's term as President, social policies were expanded not only in number, but also in expenditures, providers, clients, services, and new centers of power.

Expenditures for social welfare increased rapidly during the Johnson administration, going from 77.2 billion in FY 1964 to 113.8 billion in FY 1967, or after controlling for inflation, at an average annual rate of approximately 10 percent during the period (Table 1).

Social welfare expenditures not only increased in absolute dollars, but also in terms of per capita spending, as a percentage of Gross National Product, and in relation to outlays for defense (Table 2).

Table 1. Social Welfare Expenditures, FY 1964–FY 1967

Program	(in $ millions)			
	FY 1964	FY 1965	FY 1966	FY 1967
Social Insurance	$28,122.8	$31,934.4	$37,338.8	$42,739.3
Public Aid	6,283.4	7,301.1	8,811.0	11,091.7
Health Medical	6,246.4	6,938.0	7,628.0	8,458.6
Veterans' Program	6,031.0	6,358.2	6,898.5	7,246.8
Education	28,107.9	32,824.9	35,807.8	40,589.7
Housing	318.1	334.8	377.8	427.7
Other Social Welfare	2,065.7	2,309.0	2,848.4	3,285.4
Total	77,175.3	88,000.4	99,710.4	113,839.2

Source: *Statistical Abstracts of the United States*, 1964, and *Social Security Bulletin*, 34 (December 1971), p. 5.

Table 2.   Social Welfare Expenditures, Per Capita and as a Percentage
of GNP, FY 1964–FY 1967

Program	Year (% GNP)							
	FY 1964		*FY 1965*		*FY 1966*		*FY 1967*	
Social Insurance	$142.33	(4.3)	$159.66	(4.4)	$184.77	(4.7)	$209.33	(5.2)
Public Aid	31.96	(1.0)	36.69	(1.0)	43.80	(1.1)	54.56	(1.3)
Health Medical	31.77	(1.0)	34.87	(1.0)	37.92	(1.0)	41.61	(1.0)
Veterans' Programs	30.31	(.9)	31.60	(.9)	33.89	(.9)	35.20	(.9)
Education	142.77	(4.3)	164.71	(4.6)	177.79	(4.6)	199.47	(4.9)
Other Social Welfare	10.51	(.3)	11.60	(.3)	14.16	(.4)	16.16	(.4)
Total*	391.28	(11.8)	440.82	(12.2)	494.21	(12.9)	558.43	(13.8)

*Includes housing.
Source: *Statistical Abstracts of the United States–1964; Social Security Bulletin,* 34 (December 1971), p. 88.

In Fiscal Year 1964, outlays for national defense represented 8.8% of
GNP and social welfare expenditures accounted for 11.8%. By FY 1967,
the percentages changed to 9.1% and 13.8%, respectively.

Table 3 compares defense and social welfare expenditures in the U.S.
with spending in twenty-one other countries. In 1966, the United States
ranked third (with 9.1%) behind the Soviet Union (with 12.2%) and
Israel (with 11.9%) in military spending as a percentage of GNP. With
respect to social security spending as a percent of GNP in 1966, the U.S.
ranked twenty-first (with 7.9%) of twenty-two countries, with only Japan
trailing.

Authority structures also changed along with the growth in the size of
the budget. For example, community action programs mandated "maximum feasible participation" by the beneficiaries of the programs and
the laws established new power centers which bypassed traditional authority structures. In some cases, the loci of decision-making were devolved, e.g., in the case of community action, but in others, it was centralized. For example, in the Medicare program, a national rate board
set federal rates, fees, and standards and enforced them, and, in education, the Justice Department sought uniform implementation of school
desegregation guidelines.[14]

The public philosophy of interest group liberalism as the means to
expand both the size of the economic pie and the opportunities for
America's least advantaged was transformed into the social policy of the
mid-1960s. Social plans which had been on the liberal back burner for
decades were put into practice during the Johnson administration's
Great Society. The public aid and income maintenance strategies of the
New Deal were expanded greatly and a services strategy in health care,

Table 3. Social Security and Defense Spending as a Percent of GNP at Factor Cost for 22 Countries, 1966

Country	Social Security Amount/Rank	Defense Amount/Rank
Austria	21.0 (1)	1.5 (20)
Germany (Fr)	19.6 (2)	4.7 (7)
Belgium	18.5 (3)	3.3 (15)
Netherlands	18.3 (4)	4.1 (10)
France	18.3 (4)	5.9 (6)
Sweden	17.5 (6)	4.4 (9)
Italy	17.5 (6)	3.8 (12)
Czechoslovakia	17.2 (8)	6.3 (5)
East Germany	16.4 (9)	4.5 (8)
United Kingdom	14.4 (10)	6.5 (4)
Denmark	13.9 (11)	3.1 (16)
Finland	13.1 (12)	1.8 (19)
Norway	12.6 (13)	4.0 (11)
New Zealand	11.8 (14)	2.2 (18)
Ireland	11.1 (15)	1.5 (20)
USSR	10.1 (16)	12.2 (1)
Canada	10.1 (16)	3.6 (14)
Switzerland	9.5 (18)	2.8 (17)
Australia	9.0 (19)	3.8 (12)
Israel	8.3 (20)	11.9 (2)
United States	7.9 (21)	9.1 (3)
Japan	6.2 (22)	1.0 (22)

Source: Adapted from Harold L. Wilensky. *The Welfare State and Equality: Structural and Ideological Roots of Public Expenditure*, Table 2 and Appendix Table 4.

education, housing, community services, and job training firmly established the legitimacy of entitlements to these services. But what of the effectiveness of these policies? How great *was* the Great Society?

III. IN THE AFTERMATH OF THE GREAT SOCIETY

By the late 1960s and early 1970s, many people perceived the Great Society as a "failure".[15] Critics on the left emphasized the failure of the social policies to redistribute either income or power. Several blamed the escalation of the Vietnam War for sapping social programs of much needed federal dollars. Others stressed the co-optive functions of government, giving the poor just enough to "defang the revolutionary tiger" (Wilensky, 1975, p. 109). Critics launched a frontal attack on the politics of growth (e.g., Wolfe, 1981), and the ideology which holds to the illusion that "more" means "better" (Milner, 1972, p. 36). Some (e.g. Greenberg, 1974; Stockman, 1975) pointed to programs which bene-fited the rich, stressing examples of social welfare for the wealthy.

In education, Lee Hansen and Burton Weisbrod's analysis (1969) of grants policies of financing higher education in California concluded that the system of public higher education was regressive; and John Owen's findings (1970) demonstrated that intra-state spending patterns suggested that the gap between levels of support for public schools in rich and in poor states was widening, not narrowing.

In welfare, programs were deemed pro-poor and redistributive; how-ever, the levels of spending and the philosophy of subsistence precluded the possibility of *significant* redistribution, and some scholars claimed that welfare programs tended to be an instrument of social control to regulate the poor (Edwards, 1972; Piven and Cloward, 1971). Welfare programs helped a lot of poor people, but they also benefited the wel-fare service providers who resisted reforming the program. The radical Family Assistance Plan proposed by the Nixon Administration, accord-ing to Daniel P. Moynihan (1973, p. 306), "threatened interests associ-ated with a services strategy, and this was a direct threat to Democratic liberals." Moynihan claimed that the redistributive aspects of the Family Assistance Program threatened those who were adept at manipulating the symbols of egalitarianism for essentially middle- and upper-class purposes. Similarly, Kenneth Boulding (1968, pp. 29-31) speculated that the war on poverty may have helped administrators more than it did the poor. Agriculture and social security programs also benefited primarily those with the greatest assets (Shultze, 1971; Branch, 1972, p. 202), or those with higher earnings; and public housing policies failed to solve the shelter problem. Moreover, tax benefits, such as deductibles for interest on mortgages and local property taxes, went to property owners, many of whom were wealthy (Greenberg, 1974, pp. 202 ff.).

Kenneth Boulding and Martin Pfaff generalize about the era's trans-fer policies, arguing that

> redistribution toward the poor has increased through the effect of some compo-nents of the *explicit* grants economy, but despite this increase the actual distribution of income seems to have changed little, even though the number of poor has diminished, as we have all gotten richer together. On the other hand, the 'perverse effects' of *implicit* public grants, conveyed either through special provisions of the tax laws, public policy, or administrative practices, tend toward *greater inequality:* They help the rich and propertied more than the poor . . . .
>
> The study of the distributive effects of public grants challenges some notions we may have imbibed in the process of accepting prevailing dogma: 'Public' goods, or at

least a sizable share thereof, convey substantial private benefits to some individuals but not to others . . . .

We must examine allocative decisions not only for their stability implications but also for their distributive, integrative (or disintegrative) freedom and security-enhancing and other social welfare effects (Boulding and Pfaff, 1972, p. 2).

Critics on the right agreed with those on the left that benefits had gone to unintended beneficiaries. Bardach (1977), for example, stressed the inefficiencies of public bureaucracies; and Stockman (1975) made a strong case that the inflation practices of "pork barrel" policies benefited a few at the expense of many.[16] Other plausible explanations for the perceived failure of the Great Society have been: (1) politicians either underestimated the magnitude of the social problem and did not plan accordingly, or (2) they overestimated the expected solution, given the level of spending. These, writes Henry Aaron (1978, pp. 2-4), constitute the "common view" of what went wrong with the Great Society. Aaron summarized the "common view" of why the Great Society failed:

Poorly planned, passed in haste, inadequately funded, the programs of the mid-1960s accomplished little according to the common view except to line the pockets of the middle-class professionals hired to dispense services to the poor. Evaluation, a newly developed art, certified the ineffectuality of these programs (Aaron, 1978, p. 4).

Whatever the cause of failure, a major controversy has focused on the extent to which social programs have been redistributive, and the degree to which political power has been devolved to the beneficiaries.

The Census Bureau and the Internal Revenue Service collect income and wealth data, and publish them annually. Families are divided into quintiles according to their reported income. According to these official statistics, there was little change in pre-tax money income between 1963 and 1968.[17]

Letitia Upton and Nancy Lyons analyzed income and wealth data and wrote:

There is startling and continuing inequality in the distribution of income in the United States, and the overall pattern has remained virtually unchanged since World War II (1974, p. 96).

Based on Census Bureau and IRS data, Upton and Lyons concluded that "Governmental programs have had only a marginal impact on the overall distribution of income" (1974, p. 103). Why?

One explanation is that many of the very poor were excluded from some Great Society Programs, for example, rent supplements and public housing (Heineman, 1969, pp. 129-130). A second explanation is that in-kind benefits were not computed as income, and, therefore, real income was underreported by the recipients of this type of aid; but the rich also underreport their income, for example, because a large portion of long-term capital gains are excluded from income. Another explanation is that most of the transfer payments went to the non-poor. For example, by Fiscal Year 1975, federal aid to the poor amounted to $28.1 billion while federal income-security benefits which allocate money on the basis of contributions, not need, amounted to $177.5 billion in 1976 (Bach, 1977: 497-498). Most of the growth occurred in programs like social security and unemployment insurance which benefited people of all socioeconomic classes.

Redistribution of income and wealth was negligible between 1963 and 1968, but what about redistribution of power? Robert Aleshire (1972, p. 437) has observed that community action (CAA) and model cities pro-grams apparently sensitized the poor to their rights and responsibilities, but, with a few exceptions, neither the CAA nor Model Cities actually transferred power to the poor.

David Austin (1972) conducted a study of a randomly selected sample of twenty Community Action Agencies, illustrating some of the difficul-ties of effectively redistributing power. The study compared the par-ticipation of the board members who were target-area residents (about 1 out of every 3) with the participation on non-target area residents. The target area residents had little or no involvement in the initial organiza-tion of the agency and little impact on major program strategies. More-over, the major funding decisions were made outside the board, and, in seventeen of the twenty CAA's studied, organizational functions took priority over advisory functions.

The fact is, the growth of government was real, but the "trickle down" effects of redistribution of income and power were illusory. Moreover, after four years of the Great Society, the problems of unemployment, inflation, poverty, poor nutrition, poor health, poor housing, and inade-quate education and job training were as pervasive as ever, and, because of rising expectations, seemed worse.

During the Johnson administration, the American public came to ex-pect a new heading for the Ship of State. The government was finally going to do *something* about solving the seemingly intractable problems of poverty, unemployment and civil rights, as well as deprivation in housing, health care, education and public services, especially in urban America. New "entitlement" bills were on the legislative agenda. Political scientists, like politicians and members of mass publics, were caught up in the euphoria of the period.

However, their collective elation at the apogee of the Great Society faded to despair at what seemed like its perigee, i.e., in the midst of a congeries of social programs which created many new problems while trying to solve old ones. Families disintegrated as homes were broken and family members migrated to northern cities in search of jobs or subsistence welfare payments; the elderly and the poor discovered that government programs designed to cut the costs of health and medical care actually increased their out-of-pocket expenses. Veterans returning from Vietnam confronted officials who had cheered them on to continue the fight, but who shied away from any commitment to retrain them for peacetime occupations or to treat them for their service-related problems. Out of frustration with a world which seemed to be turning for the worse at a time when they had been promised better, both police and Blacks rioted and shook the very foundations of authority. These were a few of the symptoms of a new malaise of the late 1960s, which had its roots in an imperial misadventure in Vietnam.

At a time when the Great Society reached its apex, political and legal promises filled both the headlines and the pages of scholarly journals and manuscripts. When the smoke cleared in the aftermath of this legislative explosion, social scientists began tallying the results: delays, cost overruns, shoddy services, inequities in the distribution and utilization of benefits, and under-performance characterized the "bottom line" assessment of much program performance (Haveman, 1969, p. 6; Ginsberg and Solow, 1974).

A Search for "Better" Social Policies

Most effective policy lived up neither to the standards of performance which were specified at the time of enactment nor the hopes and expectations of mass publics. When legislation and concomitant government spending for social programs turned out not to be the panacea that many expected and hoped for, policy scientists increased their efforts to search for alternatives to more spending and more programs to improve government performance in the public interest.

They adopted at least five discrete solutions to the problems of delays in program start-up, inflated costs of services and their delivery, inefficiency, inequity and underachievement. The strategies they tried were (1) devoting more time to policy-relevant research; (2) developing and using better tools of analysis; (3) learning more about system and program performance; (4) advising and teaching policymakers and advisors about how to design policy in order to avoid the perils of bureaucratic politics; and (5) relying more heavily on markets, and less heavily on the public sector to solve the nation's social problems.

Solution 1: *Do More Applied Research*

One alternative was advocated by David Easton in his December, 1969 Presidential Address to the American Political Science Association. Reflecting a growing intradisciplinary dissatisfaction with the substance of government programs and their human consequences,[18] and aroused by the realization that he and other members of the profession were contributing little to solving pressing social problems of the day, Easton challenged his colleagues to reorder their research priorities. He was concerned that too much time was being devoted to basic research, too little to applied policy analysis.[19]

Impatient with the slow, deliberate pace of scientific research to come up with quick solutions to immediate problems, Easton called for a better balance between knowledge for the sake of knowledge and knowledge which is "relevant" and "action oriented". In a mood of panic, Easton confronted his colleagues with a dilemma:

> A decision to contemplate revising the image of our discipline and profession places the political scientist in a strange and difficult predicament. Fierce pressures are building up for solutions to immediate problems. Yet the nature of basic research is to shift the focus away from current concerns and to delay the application of knowledge until we are more secure about its reality (Easton, 1969, pp. 1053-1054).

Easton proposed a "Credo of Relevance" which incorporated the canons of the post-behavioral movement: (1) a research strategy which emphasized substance over form; (2) an agenda of research problems which was relevant to human needs in a time of crisis; (3) a more humanistic orientation; (4) an end to the self-deception that behavioralism is value-free, and an assessment of the impact of these values on the research enterprise; (5) an end to incrementalism and system maintenance in favor of more creative speculation about alternative futures; (6) dissemination of knowledge beyond an inner circle of members of the academic elite; and (7) politicization of professional organization and universities.

In the decade of the seventies, more research time and money was devoted to "policy-relevant" studies.[20] That is not to say that there has been a revolution or turning out of the behavioralists. As Easton predicted, the two modes of research have co-existed and flourished.

Solution 2: *Find Better Analytical Tools*

A second alternative to more spending and more government programs to solve the nation's social problems came from the economists. This approach to improve government performance was also aired in a Presidential Address to a professional association—in Wassily Leontif's

December 1970 speech to the American Economic Association in Detroit, Michigan.

Leontif advocated the development and widespread use of better tools to aid policymakers and policy advisors in reaching "better" decisions. Like Easton, the economist noted the criticism of the discipline's teaching and research for its lack of relevance. Although he drew attention to the "splendid isolation" of economics, Leontif was less alarmed about the irrelevance of the economists' research problems than he was about the "palpable *inadequacy* of the scientific means with which they try to solve them" (1971, p. 1). He noted the need to challenge basic assumptions[21] and to collect more and better statistical data in order to match the sophistication of statistical methods. In his closing remarks, he contrasted the academic theorists who are "content with the formulation of general principles" with the more practical private businessmen who have adopted the methods of applied economics to "answer questions pertaining to specific situations" (1971, p. 7).

Solution 3: *Learn More About Actual Performance*

A third strategy for improving the record of performance of government was to give priority to learning more about how the national political system and various policy sub-systems were actually performing before striking out on a new course of policy activity. At the heart of this alternative to more spending and more programs was a commitment to knowing before doing. These analysts argued that to be able to intervene intelligently, in ways which could result in positive social change, governments must first discover what and how they are doing, compared to their own goals, the progress of other nations, and some universal normative standards.

Policy scientists adopted at least two distinct approaches to the quest for greater knowledge about government performance. They approached their subject from two discrete levels of analysis: (1) the political system; and (2) the social program.

At the system level, scholars applied a variety of criteria to evaluate the performance of nations. Ted Gurr and Muriel McClelland (1971), for example, compared the performance of twelve nations; Harry Eckstein (1971) explained the level of system performance in terms of how well the government fares along the dimensions of durability, legitimacy, civil order and decisional efficacy; and Roland Pennock (1966) posited performance measures in terms of "political goods", i.e., order, welfare, justice and liberty. All of these studies confronted enormous conceptual, measurement, and research design problems.

A variant of this approach was to learn more about how governments perform in a particular policy arena—the program "evaluation" study.

As data about the performance of new social programs associated with the Great Society became available, a harvest of evaluation studies cropped up in agency reports, "in-house" evaluation units were established, consulting firms which specialized in evaluation research were formed, and even an evaluation journal (*Evaluation Quarterly*) appeared.

The success of these evaluation studies was dependent on a number of factors, not the least of which was the skill of the analyst in translating policy goals into observable phenomena, finding control groups in order to increase the confidence level of conclusions, and locating the data necessary to draw valid inferences.

Solution 4:   *Avoid the Shoals of Bureaucratic Politics*

A fourth strategy to improve government performance emerged in the early 1970s. In *Essence of Decision: Explaining the Cuban Missile Crisis*, Graham Allison articulated a "bureaucratic politics" model of government decision-making—a bargaining process among powerful actors with their own ideas, interests, organizational loyalties and affiliations and stakes. Each senior player exercised varying amounts of power in a competitive game of "pulling and hauling" in order to win his or her policy preference.[22]

Accepting this mode of government decisionmaking as both what is and what should be, a number of political scientists recognized that if policymakers and advisors could learn to navigate the political shoals of bureaucratic politics, they could enhance their chances of getting their own way (not necessarily a functional equivalent of getting "better" policy). Richard Nelson, for one, argued forcefully for a strategy which took political and economic feasibility into account when making policy recommendations.

> Good analysis requires a savvy appreciation of what is at its root a political problem;
> what is a problem for which it is possible to find proposals that can gain widespread
> and effective support; and, regarding the latter, the location of the political shoals
> so that they can be avoided (1974, p. 379).

In the implementation studies which followed, and which were no doubt influenced by Allison's book and an article which he co-authored with Morton Halperin, there were two recurrent themes which reflected this checklist mentality: the chances of a policymaker getting his or her own way are improved if (1) implementation problems are anticipated; and (2) expectations of prospective clients are not raised by promising more than can be delivered.

These themes are particularly salient in two empirical studies of the policy implementation process: Jeffrey Pressman and Aaron Wildavsky's

Implementation; and Eugene Bardach's *The Implementation Game: What Happens After a Bill Becomes a Law.* Pressman and Wildavsky (1973, p. 143), in their study of a federal manpower training program in Oakland, California, wrote that they learned an important lesson from their case study of an implementation failure: "There is no point in having good ideas if they cannot be carried out." Their prescription for implementation success included advice to the policymaker: make the problems of implementation a part of the initial formulation process, and mold program content to fit the inherent limitations of the implementation process.

In *The Implementation Game: What Happens After a Bill Becomes a Law,* Bardach identified a variety of bureaucratic games played during the implementation period with the avowed purpose of warning the policymaker about them and advising him or her on how to make those games work in the official's favor. Bardach wrote:

> Every policy worth its salt is vulnerable to at least a few of these games. Such risks cannot be avoided. The object of describing these games—and, where possible, certain mitigating strategies—is to help designers calculate their risks more accurately and to design policies robust enough to survive them (1977, p. 58).

Solution 5: *Transfer Administration to the Private Sector*

Bardach's strategy was to limit policy proposals to only those which discount the constraints of implementation, and of political and economic feasibility.[23] It is a conservative one, for it frequently leads to a tactic of scaling down policy goals. Bardach also admonished his colleagues to "become more modest in our demands on, and expectations of, the institutions of representative government," while recognizing that

> government *ought* not to do many of the things liberal reform has traditionally asked of it; even when, in some abstract sense, government does pursue appropriate goals, it is not very well suited to achieving them. Markets and mores are sturdier and more sensible, and government is probably less sensible and less reliable, than liberal reformers have been willing to admit (Bardach, 1977, p. 283).

However, Eli Ginsberg and Robert Solow caution their readers that the private and non-profit sectors have also failed to solve the nation's social problems:

> The last decade has demonstrated that the strengths and weaknesses of the intermediaries through which the federal government must operate determine in considerable measure the success of its program efforts. It is clear that the best-conceived federal program will falter or fail if the agencies charged with implementing

it lack initiative or competence. And the sorry fact is that most state and local governments—with some notable exceptions—are poorly structured and poorly staffed to carry out new and innovative tasks. They have a hard time even meeting their routine commitments.

We must in fairness add that the record of performance of government's contractors in the private and non-profit sectors also leaves much room for improvement. (Ginsberg and Solow, 1974, p. 25)

The move to deconstruct the welfare state by replacing government subsidies or transfers with a free market economy rests on three fundamental assessments of the Great Society: (1) that the purposes of welfare state had been fundamentally redefined as the redistributive state: there was *too much equality;* (2) that the traditional mode of making public choices had been fundamentally redefined to give more control to consumers, and less control to experts and providers: there was *too much democracy;* (3) that the scope of government had been enlarged to incorporate beneficiaries for whom the social policies were never intended: there were *too many entitlements;* and (4) the welfare state had softened the resolve of the American people by making them too dependent on government and unwilling to make material sacrifices to stand up to the Russians: there was *too little fear of the Communists.* These positions have been articulated in the writings of four neo-conservatives or conservatives (e.g., Plattner, 1979; Huntington, in Crozier, et al., 1975; Stockman, 1975; and Glazer and Kristol, 1976).

Too Much Equality

Marc Plattner is convinced that liberals have exceeded the "legitimate" purposes of the welfare state by adopting a policy that "is *explicitly* aimed at reducing inequalities in incomes." He argues that "social insurance and assistance to the needy can be regarded legitimate functions of the public sphere" and that liberals in the 1960s and 1970s have undermined the individual's right to just entitlement to what he or she has earned. In policy formulation and adoption

Increasing attention is being paid to the distributional consequences of government policies and programs; there is a growing sense that the distribution of income is a proper political concern; and there is a tendency to view specific public policies as justified only if—whatever their other effects—they contribute to (or at least do not work against) a narrowing of income inequalities (Plattner, 1979, p. 29).

His argument rests on the assumption that there is a way of differentiating between "legitimate" and "illegitimate" purposes of the welfare state, that there is a line which can be drawn between instances where the government can legitimately take from people what they have earned, i.e., where the recipients of redistribution are deserving, and when the government cannot, where the recipients of redistribution are not de-serving. Plattner believes that in the social policies of the 1960s the line was crossed, and that what occurred in the 1970s was an overemphasis on equality.[24] The ultimate fear of equality is that the promise of equal-ity creates a "revolution of rising expectations" which threatens stability and the existing class-based distribution of wealth and income.

Too Much Democracy

Too much democracy, according to Samuel Huntington (1976), is to be feared as much as too much equality. An apathetic electorate, for example, is necessary because a restive public threatens stability and active members of the public may demand changes which threaten the existing hierarchical system of unequal incomes, power, and social status.

Huntington (1976, p. 10) characterizes the "democratic surge" of the 1960s as both egalitarian and participatory. He evaluates the "demo-cratic surge" in terms of its negative consequences, namely, "a substan-tial decrease in governmental authority" (Huntington, in Crozier, et al., 1975, p. 64).

The theme of democracy as a threat to democracy has been reiterated in Robert Nisbet's *Twilight of Authority* and the Trilateral Commission's *The Crisis of Democracy*. For example, Huntington, in the Trilateral Com-mission Report complains that:

> People no longer felt the same compulsion to obey those whom they had previously considered superior to themselves in age, rank, status, expertise, character or talents (Crozier et al., 1975, p. 75).

Huntington goes on to document the paradoxical situation of an ex-panding government and a declining trust in government. What are the consequences of this "democratic distemper" (Huntington, in Crozier et al., 1975, p. 102)? Budget deficits, strikes by public employees, economic nationalism, and the government's inability to require its citizens to sacri-fice in the face of military and economic threats from abroad are just a few examples of too much democracy. What really seems to bother him most is that an "excess of democracy" has resulted in "the relative down-turn in American power and influence in world affairs" (Huntington, in Crozier et al., 1975, p. 106). "Overindulgence" in democracy has threat-ened democracy, writes Huntington, and needs to be limited.

Too Many Entitlements

David Stockman (1975) articulates the third fundamental assessment of the Great Society: the scope of government has expanded in an irresponsible way so that too many entitlements threaten the existing system. He relies on the assumptions of neo-conservatives in order to argue that programs that were originally intended to benefit the indigent and the deserving have been transformed into subsidies for the non-poor, and that the pluralistic democratic policy-making process has contributed to this inequity.

Stockman presents a very convincing argument that much of the money spent for social welfare did not get into the hands of the most needy, despite much promise to the contrary. The promise–performance gap created disappointment, frustration, and, at times, violence. Rising expectations were unmet because the government had overpromised.

Stockman's article notes the tendency of policymakers to turn social welfare programs designed for the needy into a social pork barrel for all. He argues that much needed future social policies, for example, national health insurance, an incomes proposal, and general aid to education, will not be possible unless existing programs are redesigned to eliminate waste and to weed out present beneficiaries who are not really in need.

After arguing that the defense budget and tax reform are not realistic sources of funds for future social programs, he cites programs which could be eliminated without doing harm to the least advantaged, for example, medical school subsidies, mental health clinics, and vocational education programs. The main obstacle to eliminating these "unjustifiable" beneficiaries is policymakers' interest in getting re-elected, what David R. Mayhew (1974) calls "the electoral connection". Both Stockman and Mayhew point out what is well known, that pork barreling is an act of survival for politicians who are portrayed as utility or vote maximizers. Stockman continues the argument by pointing out that many of the programs of The Great Society and its aftermath have ended up as subsidies to the non-poor. A number of programs share this characteristic, from federal educational aid to impacted areas, Title I of the Elementary and Secondary Education Act, social security, tax reforms, and federal health manpower programs.

While Stockman singles out legislators for criticism, he does not ignore the complicity of special interests: "Possessing tentacles that reach out into every part of the country and having fully mastered the art of legislative log-rolling, the health lobby, the education lobby, and the various organizational arms of state and local officials have in many ways become the real super powers of Capitol Hill" (Stockman, 1975, p. 13). His indictment of "pork barrel" politics was only a veiled criticism of interest group liberalism.

The seeds of distrust in interest group liberalism had thus been planted in the 1970's. By the time Ronald Reagan was elected to the presidency, there was considerable support for a new public philosophy.

In the next section, the Reagan administration's social policy initiatives are examined for the purpose of explicating Reagan's public philosophy.

IV. DECONSTRUCTING THE WELFARE STATE

One of the first opportunities for any new administration to make known its priorities is during the first 100 days in office—the "honeymoon" period with Congress and with the American people. President Reagan articulated what he envisioned as a "New Beginning" in his Inaugural Address and in two proposed changes in President Carter's Fiscal Year 1982 budget. In this section, the Reagan administration's major budgetary proposals for FY 1982 are examined and compared with the Carter budget and with the adopted budget which was signed by President Reagan on August 13, 1981.

In his February 18, 1981 Address to a Joint Session of Congress, President Reagan outlined a "safety net approach" to social welfare:

> We will continue to fulfill the obligations that spring from our national conscience. Those who, through no fault of their own, must depend on the rest of us—the poverty stricken, the disabled, the elderly, all those with true need—can rest assured that the social safety net of programs they depend on are exempt from any cuts.

But the President went on to add that

> government will not continue to subsidize individuals or particular business interests where real need cannot be demonstrated (Reagan, February 18, 1981, p. 31).

This is very similar to Governor Ronald Reagan's testimony before the U.S. Senate Finance Committee about California's welfare "reform." Reagan testifed in 1972,

> We insured adequate aid to the aged, blind, the disabled, and children who are deprived of parental support and reduced aid to the non-needy with realistic work incentives so that funds could be redirected to the truly needy . . . .

> But maybe most important is the fact that the California plan retains most of the administration and responsibility for an efficient and effective program at the level closest to those who benefit and those who must pay the bill (Reagan, in *Welfare Reform in California . . . Showing the Way*, December, 1972, p. 83).

Reagan assured Congress and the American people in 1981 that social security's OASDI benefits, veterans' aid, Medicare benefits, and Supplementary Security Income for the blind, the aged, and the disabled, as well as the Head Start, nutritional programs for the truly needy, and summer youth jobs programs would be preserved.

These seven basic social programs transferred $144.5 billion dollars in cash or in-kind benefits to 80 million Americans. $134.1 billion or 92.1% of these benefits were included in programs which served older people and veterans, regardless of incomes (Donnelly, 1981, p. 665). Only about one of every nine dollars was targeted to the needy, where a "means" test was applied.[25] Thus, while the rhetoric stressed protecting society's least advantaged, budget priorities provided a safety net of programs, most of which were not exclusively for the poor but which, in fact, served categorical groups of people which included both the poor and the non-poor.

Five "entitlement" programs were slated for the fiscal chopping block in President Reagan's February 18th Address to the Joint Session of Congress: (1) the Food Stamp Program was to be cut $1.7 billion by removing from eligibility those who were not in real need or who were abusing the program; (2) in the AFDC Program, eligibility requirements would be stiffened and strong and effective work requirements would be imposed; (3) CETA's public service employment (PSE) program would be eliminated; (4) spending on the Medicaid Program was to be "capped," and the States were to be granted more discretion over how money was to be spent; and (5) in the school breakfast and lunch program, the Federal Government would cut back subsidies for meals for children of families who could afford to pay. These, together with housing subsidies, are the main public aid programs on which poor people depend (Table 4).

According to a study by the Project on Food Assistance and Poverty, 17 programs for poor people were slated for budget reductions of $25 billion. Table 4 summarizes the amounts and types of cuts in five of these social programs. A close examination of the Reagan administra-

Table 4.   Reagan Administration Proposals for Cuts in Social Program Expenditures, FY 1982

Program	Carter Request	Reagan Request	% Cut
	(in billions)		
Food Stamps	$12.9	$11.2	(13.4)
AFDC	5.7	5.0	(12.3)
CETA PSE	4.1	—	(100.0)
Medicaid	18.8	17.5	(6.9)
School Feeding	4.7	2.9	(38.3)
Total	46.2	36.6	(20.8)

Source: *Congressional Quarterly Weekly Report* April 18, 1981, pp. 665–668.

tion's justification for cutting over 20% of these social programs for the needy will illuminate Reagan's public philosophy.

CETA

The Comprehensive Employment and Training Act was enacted in the wake of the 1973–1975 economic recession and the 1973 oil embargo. The public service employment (PSE) provisions of CETA allocated funds for training the chronically unemployed so that they could learn the skills necessary to compete successfully in the unsubsidized private labor market. In 1975, with a budget of $992 million, the program placed 170,000 welfare recipients and disadvantaged youths in jobs.

CETA was transformed during its implementation: by 1978, the budget reached $5.7 billion to fill 765,000 jobs, amendments were added, and eligibility requirements targeted benefits to only the poor and the long-term unemployed (Van Horn, 1979). According to the commentary on its budget revisions, the Reagan team wanted to return CETA "to its original purpose" and criticized "the previous governmental approach of creating make-work jobs in the public sector" as "doomed to failure by wasting public funds without teaching usable skills to participants" (White House Office of Public Affairs, 1981, pp. 66, 84).

The Reagan administration proposed to eliminate the PSE program, and replace it with a $2.4 billion program which provided private sector training. The CETA program had been criticized on several counts: it had become a vehicle for political patronage; it was perceived as just another income distribution program; it had legitimized the philosophy of the Federal Government as "the employer as last resort"; and it had failed to prepare the workers for new jobs in the private sector. The Reagan administration wanted to try a different approach—one that relied on private companies to train one million people in Fiscal Year 1983, and one that would be run by local councils, with the majority of members experienced businessmen.

AFDC

Following the pattern which Ronald Reagan had established as Governor of California, welfare was to be "reformed."[26] Although there were no fewer than twenty-seven proposed changes, the major ones affected eligibility, program administration, and the requirement that able-bodied welfare recipients work for their benefits. With these reforms, $2 billion—$1.1 billion in Federal costs and $900 million in state and local— were to be eventually pared from the original Carter budget.

Eligibility requirements for cash assistance were tightened by changing the amounts that a potential recipient could earn or own. For the first time, a ceiling was placed on gross earnings and the value of other public assistance was to be calculated as family resources. The controversial "30 and one-third rule," where working heads of families could exclude a portion of their earnings, was to be repealed. Moreover, allowable assets were more limited, and there was to be no more $75 per month deduction for work-related expenses and $160 per month deduction for work-related expenses and $160 per month per child for child care.

In an effort to purge the welfare rolls of "able-bodied poor people," the Reagan administration proposed to give States the option of adopting a voluntary "workfare" program, which required AFDC recipients to "work off" benefits in a non-paying community service job. As many as 800,000 people could be placed in community service jobs. These welfare "reforms" would eliminate 408,000 of 3.9 million or 11% of families, and reduce benefits for about 300,000 more. Under this plan, 16,000 families were to actually receive higher benefits.

Medicaid

In an effort to save $1.3 billion in FY 1982, and up to $5 billion annually, the Reagan administration proposed a cap on federal contributions to state Medicaid programs, and promised to keep annual increases in spending for Medicaid to 5%. States would also be given greater control over how Medicaid money could be spent and how rates would be set. Furthermore, the Federal government planned to make savings by reducing fraud and abuse and by reducing billing errors.

With the proposed 1982 budget, the Reagan administration hoped to achieve substantial savings by changing Medicaid eligibility requirements, and by allowing states to limit benefits and the form of payment. This devolution of decision-making would control costs by stimulating competition rather than by regulating markets.

The Omnibus Budget Reconciliation Act of 1981 allowed states to waive the "freedom of choice" rule, and as a result, two thirds of the states opted for providing home or community-based care instead of institutional-based care as a way of reducing spending.

Two other proposed changes in health programs bear mentioning— the elimination of Professional Service Review Organizations (PSRO's) after 1983, and a $24 million reduction in funding for local health planning for 1981, with a complete phase-out of the program by 1984. The significance of these proposals lies not so much in the amount of money to be saved, but in the elimination of regulatory mechanisms which were designed to improve quality and control costs, and which opened up decisions about resource allocations to the public.

Food Stamps/School Lunch

The Reagan administration's budget proposals included a $3.4 billion reduction in funding for food-welfare programs. The Food Stamp Program reforms included stricter eligibility requirements, the elimination of outreach, a cap on spending for food stamps and a "workfare" provision. Before the Reagan program changes were proposed, a family of four with an income of $14,000 was eligible for food stamps. After the 1982 budget proposals, maximum income for the same family was to be $11,000. This would have eliminated one million people from the program.

Many of the complaints about the Food Stamp Program surfaced during March, 1981 hearings of the Senate Agricultural Committee. Senator Jesse Helms argued that able-bodied workers, strikers, and students were taking advantage of the program, and that the program was riddled with fraud. One of the Administration's main arguments was that the original purposes of the Food Stamps Act was to subsidize food and nutrition for needy families; another was to improve farm income by "priming the pump." As eligibility requirements broadened and the economy worsened, a program which aided 425,000 people in 1964 provided subsidence to 22 million people by 1981.

Alarmed by the rapid growth of the program, President Reagan proposed reforms which included a gross income eligibility cutoff of 130% of poverty, a disposable assets test, and a work requirement for able-bodied persons. Another proposal, which was not approved by Congress, was to eliminate overlapping subsidies for school meals and food stamps. What was approved were administrative changes which would help minimize payment errors and food stamp fraud, with resultant cuts in administrative costs.

Reagan also requested a $1.6 billion cut in the school meals program, hoping to achieve this reduction primarily by changing procedures for determining eligibility. The Agriculture Department proposed reducing the amount of food served to children, but amidst public outcry, this idea was withdrawn. The administration has tried to refocus the school lunch program on the poor, and eliminate subsidies to middle- and upper-income families.

V. REAGANISM: THE NEW PUBLIC PHILOSOPHY

The social policies of the welfare state were expanded during the 1960s and 1970s—in the amount of money expended and the number of services provided, as well as the number and type of people served. According to the Reagan administration's 1984 budget (1983, p. 3-5), "incre-

mental expansion of [entitlement programs] over 1963-1981 resulted in
a nearly five-fold increase in constant dollar costs." As a percentage of
GNP, social contract programs increased from 2.7% of GNP in 1963 to
6.8% of GNP in 1981.

Interest group liberalism, as the operative mechanism for dividing up
an expanding economic pie, worked reasonably well. When, in the
1970s, inflation shrank the real size of the economic pie and local tax
revolts heralded a new era of cutbacks and retrenchment,[27] the philosophy which had dominated public thinking for forty years seemed sud-
denly outmoded. Political leaders like President Jimmy Carter and California Governor Jerry Brown realized this and sought to shrink the size
of government, offered no new major social policies, and asked the
American people to lower their expectations. Turning inward, liberals
began an endless search for self-expression, self-fulfillment, and liberation, eschewing a duty to one's fellow man for a search for private
pleasure (Bresler, 1977, p. 115). However, personal freedom without
social responsibility was not a viable alternative to interest group
liberalism.

Some conservatives and neo-conservatives tried to articulate an alternative set of principles to guide public choices: restore the hierarchical,
meritocratic system of unequal rewards based on contribution; restore
authority to those who are superior by virtue of their claims to expertise;
reduce the size of government; reduce the number of entitlements and
restore America's international economic and military leadership.
Ronald Reagan has continued in this tradition.

His approach to public policymaking has been to outline a set of
criteria which his administration will use in order to determine the legit-
imacy of "claims for Federal support" (Executive Office of the President,
OMB, March, 1981, pp. 8-9). From this set of principles and from the
Reagan administration's actual policy behavior, as indicated by their
March and April 1981 social welfare expenditure proposals (Executive
Office of the President, OMB, March 1981, April 1981), we can infer
Ronald Reagan's public philosophy. "Reaganism," as we shall call it, is a
set of principles which attempts to interpret and delineate what social
policy is about and what it aims to achieve. Reagan's social policies imply
a social theory, or a set of principles to guide action. The theory consists
of four propositions.

Proposition I: *Put the Federal Government on a Diet*

The fundamental assumption of the Reagan administration is that the
social policies of the Federal government for the past twenty, if not fifty,
years have been inappropriate. Their purposes are not only misplaced,
but also they have maximized neither justice, nor freedom, nor equality,

nor social welfare. In his March 10, 1981 speech to Congress (Executive Office of the President, OMB, 1981, p. M-1), President Reagan promised to "move America back toward economic sanity" and made as the new administration's first priority cutting the growth of government spending in areas other than defense.

According to President Reagan, previous Democratic and Republican administrations had expanded the role of government into areas which were no longer "legitimate."[28] This was a recurring theme during Reagan's 1980 campaign for President, and a charge which he reiterated in a number of major Presidential messages. A frequently-cited metaphor is that the Federal government has become "overweight" and has to go on a diet (Goggin, 1982, p. 12). Related to the principle that the Federal government itself has lost its legitimacy is the argument that some social programs, and some benefits and beneficiaries, have also lost their support. Some current recipients of public aid should, therefore, lose their entitlements to government transfer payments.

The first of the nine "criteria for claims for Federal support" (Executive Office of the President, OMB, March, 1981, pp 8-9) is the preservation of the federal safety net. From this criterion and from the list of programs which were spared major budget cuts in FY 1982, we know that OASDI of Social Security, Veterans programs, Head Start, Medicare, Supplementary Security Income, and Summer Youth Jobs Programs constitute this social safety net. These help define the "legitimate" role of the Federal government. Apparently, "legitimate" Federal social programs also: (1) fulfill the original purpose for which they were intended; (2) can be proven to be effective; (3) are administratively efficient; (4) are politically attractive, and (5) are assigned to either state or local governments or the private sector. Above all, "legitimate" social programs are *those which do not deliberately try to redistribute income.* They have limited purposes, limited benefits, and limited beneficiaries.

Proposition II: *Purge Programs of Illegitimate Benefits and Beneficiaries*

Programs have become "illegitimate" because they have overstepped their original purposes. In the eyes of members of the Reagan administration, the CETA public service employment programs had become one of the "nonproductive job programs" which apparently was part of a set of subsidies which "contribute to rather than help solve our national economic problems" (Executive Office of the President, OMB, March, 1981, p. 9). CETA's public service employment program was eliminated and a replacement program given to the private sector partly "in order to return CETA to its original purpose" (Executive Office of the President, OMB, April, 1981, p. 235). OMB's *1982 Budget Revision* charac-

terized CETA as part of a "drift towards universalization of social benefits programs" (Executive Office of the President, OMB, March 1981, p.
9).

The food stamp program had also expanded beyond its original purposes. It had "moved toward a generalized income transfer program,
regardless of nutritional need" (Executive Office of the President, OMB,
April, 1981, p. 21) and, in the opinion of the Republicans, needed to be
restored to its intended purposes. Changes "will help refocus the food
stamp program on its original purpose—to ensure adequate nutrition
for America's needy families" (Executive Office of the President, OMB,
April, 1981, p. 37).

Likewise, the school meals and Medicaid programs had provided subsidies which went well beyond original program intent. "Legitimate"
benefits, then, seemed to be those that were included in the original
statutes. "Legitimate" beneficiaries were those who were "deserving"—
minimally, the elderly, the unemployed, the poor, the disabled, and
veterans. These are the people who, through no fault of their own, have
become dependent on the Federal government for subsistence. These
are the people whom society does not expect to earn their benefits.
However, according to this proposition, there are poor people who do
not deserve government subsidies *because* they are poor. These "un-
deserving" poor are people who, in some way, have deliberately chosen
to be poor, for example, able-bodied adults who are not working but
collecting AFDC cash payments, students and striking workers who receive food stamps, the "medically indigent" whose incomes are above the
poverty line, and middle income families who have benefited from re-
duced-price school meals.

It is the elderly, veterans, and the organized middle class who are to be
protected under the "safety net." It is the working poor or "near poor,"
the unorganized, and young people who are most affected by the proposed deep cuts in the budgets of the welfare, food stamp, CETA, school
lunch, and Medicaid programs. "Reaganism" has identified these as the
people who are the recipients of benefits to which they are not really
entitled, and the proposed budget cuts outline a "sink or swim" strategy
for these poor: if these people who *can* provide for themselves were cut
off from the federal teat in the "grants" economy, they would survive in
the market place, exchanging their labor for income (Gilder, 1981, p.
127).

Proposition III: *Make People Work for Their Benefits*

A corollary to the "sink or swim" strategy is the principle of making
people earn their benefits. The argument is based on the perception of
the recipients of food stamps, job training, and AFDC cash payments,

for example, as able-bodied men and women who are malingers out to take advantage of government beneficence. Moreover, there is a firm belief that dependency leads to a loss of diginity and self-respect, that paternalism leads to self-contempt. Underlying this argument is the hint that a dependent population will not be strong enough in character to stand up to the communists or make sacrifices in times of military crises (Huntington in Corzier, et al., 1975, pp. 105-106).

What is really at the heart of the "workfare" provisions of the AFDC and Food Stamps programs is the belief that those who have become dependent on cash or in-kind transfers from the Federal government have lost their incentives to work and to become self-sufficient. The fear is that the redistributive function of the welfare state will lead to a situation where the rich lose their incentives to expend extra effort and the non-working poor lose their incentive to find a job. The Reagan administration has reduced marginal tax rates for the rich in order to reward them for their extra effort, and has attempted to coerce the able-bodied poor, who only are a small fraction of the 31 million people who now live in poverty, into working by tying non-paying community jobs to welfare.

The Reagan administration's proposed 25% tax reduction was the instrument to reduce marginal tax rates for everyone, but especially the families with earnings over $20,000. Table 5 demonstrates that by 1984, only 3 percent of the tax cut would go to those with incomes below $10,000, whereas the 37.1% of the people who report incomes over $20,000 would get over 80% of the benefits as a result of tax reductions.

In spite of these facts, Reagan continues to believe that his proposals do not benefit the wealthy. For example, in a June 16, 1981 press conference, he said

> I've heard these charges about our supposedly being an administration for the wealthy. I don't see where they fit. We have watched the so-called "social reforms" for three or four decades now fail in trying to lift people that are not in the mainstream and that don't have their foot on the ladder of opportunity and they failed.
>
> As a matter of fact, what they've created is a kind of bondage in which the people are made subservient to the government that is handing out the largesse and the only people who prosper from them is the large bureaucracy that administers them. And I believe that our economic package is aimed at stimulating the economy, providing incentive, increasing productivity so as to create new jobs, and those jobs will make it possible for those people who are now economically below the norm to get a foot on the ladder and improve themselves (Reagan, 1981, p. 1107).

The economic package, in favoring the rich, created the necessary incentives for greater productivity. In order for incentives to work, however, a perpetual underclass has to be maintained and their circumstances kept considerably worse than the conditions of the poorest worker. The rewards for pulling oneself up by ones own bootstraps must be

Table 5.   Distribution of Proposed Tax
Cut

Adjusted Gross Income (1981)	% Returns	% Tax Cut
Under $5,000	19.5%	.2%
$ 5,000–$ 9,999	17.3	3.2
$10,000–$14,999	14.4	6.5
$15,000–$19,999	11.6	8.7
$20,000–$34,999	24.2	31.4
$35,000–$49,999	8.5	20.8
$50,000–$99,999	3.7	17.8
above $100,000	.7	11.3
	100.00	100.0

Source: "A Program for Economic Recovery," Section V,
    p. 14.

sufficient to motivate able-bodied people to work for a better life. In order for this strategy to work, social programs should subsidize the poorest members of society, the subsidies should be at subsistence level, and those who have jobs must be able to keep more of what they earn.

Paradoxically, the "notch" effect of eligibility requirements, and the proposed income and assets tests for eligibility in the food stamps, school lunch, and AFDC programs will probably have the opposite effect: there are now higher tax rates on earnings for welfare recipients. Moreover, in the economy of the early 1980s, and as the economy is reindustrialized, either jobs are not available for all who can work or workers lack the skills to fill those jobs.

Proposition IV: *Implement the "New Federalism"*

A major theme of Reaganism is the transfer of power from the Federal government to State and local governments and to the private sector, a strategy which is explicated in Ronald Reagan's "New Federalism" proposals. With the exception of Medicaid, which the Reagan administration has proposed be federalized, all the programs under study were slated for decentralization. The Food Stamps and AFDC programs were to be part of a swap, where State and local governments were to take responsibility for them in exchange for the Federal take-over of Medicaid. Turning over CETA's public sector employment program to the private sector also underscored the Reagan's administration's faith in the free market, and its preference for it rather than regulation and administration by the Federal government. Devolving decision-making about Medicaid benefits and beneficiaries, as well as payment formats to the States, is also consistent with the principle of reduced responsibility for the Feds.

Many of the proposed health "reforms" also involve replacing federal regulation with market competition. The effort of liberalism to use public power to discipline the power of businesses has been seriously challenged. For example, it is well known that the Reagan administration prefers a health voucher system and Consumer Choice Health Plan, and deregulation of advertising of medical services. This market strategy also includes the dismantling of mechanisms for public control of private decisions: the Professional Standards Review Organizations (PSRO's) are slated for elimination and Health Systems Agencies (HSA's) are viewed as ineffective means of controlling costs. The public role in these programs, as well as in the CETA job training programs, is to be replaced by more professional expertise, underscoring the conservative belief that democracy will kill democracy.

VI. CONCLUSIONS

In this essay, social policies are treated as conditional hypotheses: *if* the government does "x", *then* the preferred outcome "y" will follow. Upon occupying the White House in January of 1981, the Reagan administration perceived the government as *the* problem, not the solution to the nation's problems. The administration was convinced that the government had grown too large, too adversarial in its relations with business, and too parternalistic towards its citizens. Moreover, the Federal government was helping those who did not deserve assistance; the resultant dependency contributed to economic decline both at home and abroad, and military inferiority vis-a-vis the Soviets. According to President Reagan, the problem was created by the growth of entitlement programs and the relative neglect of national defense, beginning in the mid-1960s. This practice continued under both Democratic and Republican administrations in the 1970s. Rather than an attack on the social insurance and incomes strategies of the New Deal, the Reagan initiatives in public service employment, welfare, health care, and nutrition represent an attempt to deconstruct the services strategy of the Great Society.

President Reagan's proposed solutions of cutting non-defense spending and stripping the Federal government of some of its power are consistent with his diagnosis of the problem. Many of his specific proposals have been adopted by Congress and signed into law. Does this mean that there has been a new philosophical realignment in the United States? Is there an end to interest group liberalism?

Answers to these questions vary, as do the analyses of what the Reagan social policies signify.[29] Cynthia McSwain, for one, (1981, pp. 2-3) fears that the administrative state has gone out of control, but believes that the Reagan administration's economic and social policies do not constitute a true alternative to interest group liberalism. Francis Fox Piven and Richard Cloward (1982) recognize the continued importance of private business interests in the making of public choices in the 1980s, and interpret the Reagan policies as a serious effort to reverse a social philosophy which developed since the Great Depression. Piven and Cloward characterize Reagan's policies as an assault on the welfare state for the purpose of increasing business profits: the new public philosophy is designed to redistribute income upward (Piven and Cloward, 1982, pp. 7, 13). The Piven and Cloward interpretation of the Reagan administration policies as an attack on the welfare state and an attack on the poor is consistent with the thesis of several recent books which have also sought to analyze Reagan's economic, social and foreign policies (for example, Champagne and Harpham, 1984; Gartner, Greer and Riessman, 1982; and Ellwood, 1982).[30] The focal question which is raised by these volumes, and which will now be addressed in the concluding paragraphs of this essay is: To what extent do Reagan's social policies represent a public philosophy which is *qualitatively different* from interest group liberalism?

"Reaganism" differs from interest group liberalism in two important respects. One difference in the Reagan administration's approach to the authoritative allocation of the burdens and benefits of government is that the emphasis has shifted from a belief in a *process* to a messianic commitment to a *product*. Interest group liberalism emphasizes the means to make public policy—through bargaining, compromise, and coalition formation among organized interest groups. "Reaganism" represents a philosophical commitment to the ends of a weaker Federal government in domestic affairs, and a stronger military.

Once wedded to these ends, the administration is left with few options. It has become increasingly clear that the nation cannot have the "guns" which the Reagan administration wants and the "butter" which the Congress and previous administrations have spread, without mortgaging the country to future generations with growing deficits. Because the Reagan administration prefers more "guns" to more "butter," it has raided controllable budgets of social programs in order to finance the military build-up. Because the uncontrollable portions of the budget are more difficult to cut and because this administration had, until early 1983, declared off limits several programs which service that portion of the electorate which holds political power, it has sought to modify most of the entitlement programs for the poor. The administration has sought to redefine eligibility requirements, reduce benefits, and ask for contributions in exchange for benefits, and has installed regressive tax cuts.

"Reaganism" differs from interest group liberalism in a second important way. According to the pluralist view of policymaking, power is widely shared. Diverse interests are party to the compromises and bargains. Since Reagan's election to the Presidency, a more homogeneous team of loyalists who share the Reagan philosophy has dominated policymaking in Washington. A faltering economy has also weakened the bargaining power of some interest groups, especially organized labor. Ronald Reagan's personality has contributed to the distribution of power as well. His commitment to conservative principles and his unwillingness to compromise during his first two years in office (Goggin, 1982) have prevented him from nurturing the public philosophy of interest group liberalism; and his insistence on loyalty to the conservative cause as a major qualification for many staff and Cabinet appointments has kept to a minimum open policy differences with fellow-Republicans in Congress and with members of his own White House staff.

However, the mid-term elections of 1982 have given the opposition renewed strength and the administration's faltering economic policies have been abandoned. Although proposals for deep cuts in social programs have been made, Congress has protected many programs, and restored funding to others. In sum, the effects of the Reagan cuts have not been as dramatic as they would have been if the President had proceeded on the course he set for the Ship of State in the first two years of office. Nonetheless, in just three and one-half years Ronald Reagan has fundamentally reordered national priorities. According to Martin Feldstein, spending on non-defense programs other than Social Security and Medicare is 12.5% below what it was in 1980. At the same time, defense spending has risen nearly 40% since 1980. Together with the tax cut, this reordering of priorities and resultant record-high budget deficits constitute the legacy of the Reagan administration and Reagan's public philosophy.

Interest group liberalism is still viable, in spite of the fact that the consensus that the federal government should be the protector of the disadvantaged and the promotor of the public interest is breaking down; it is being replaced with the pre-New Deal conflicts between liberals and conservatives over what the appropriate roles are for public and private interests, and for government regulation and the free market. "Reaganism" is essentially an attempt to return to capitalism and the free market as a guide to public choice, and an effort to install a two-tiered system of social benefits—one set for the rich and another for the poor. A conservative ideology of less equality, less democracy, fewer entitlements, and world economic and military strength has been Ronald Reagan's guide to the deconstruction of The Great Society. His new public philosophy is not only an ideological statement but also a political strategy to build a new conservative coalition at the expense of the poor, minorities, and city dwellers.

The question which remains is whether or not Reagan's public philosophy will become "the" public philosophy. Is his policy rationality only transitory, or is it likely to gain widespread support and become the national doctrine for the conduct of public affairs? If Reagan's "world view" were to be embraced by a broad coalition of interests and supported by a majority of Americans, not only would he win re-election in 1984, but his public philosophy also would become "the" public philosophy.

NOTES

1. The classical formulation of "the" public philosophy is Walter Lippmann's (Lippmann, 1955). What Lippmann meant by a public phlosophy was doctrine—a bill of rights and natural law—which was generally shared by nations of the Free World and which acted as a guide to action. Political scientists Theodore Lowi and Samuel Beer have defined public philosophy in a more limited way, confining the term to mean the United States' set of guiding principles. Lowi (1967, p. 5) defines "public philosophy" as a nation's "political formula" or set of principles and criteria which guide public choices, and which can shift from time to time. This public philosophy, according to Lowi, can be reconstructed by analyzing the prevailing policies of government and their effects on society. Beer (1978, p. 5) defines public philosophy as an "outlook on public affairs" that helps government to define problems and formulate choices for solving them. A public philosophy is a view which not only is shared by a broad coalition of interests, but also has popular support.

2. This strategy was articulated in the economic writings of Lord John Maynard Keynes. In economic hard times, the Federal government "primed the pump" by increasing the level of government spending, by reducing interest rates and taxes, and by stimulating production. Deficit spending characterized these "bust" periods. In "boom" times, the government gradually withdrew from the economy, thus allowing the law of supply and demand to bid up taxes and interest rates as a way of cooling off the economy. Keynesian economic principles worked for a time, until Richard Nixon, in 1970, identified inflation as the country's most important problem and adopted a deliberate policy of slowing growth and productivity as a way of slowing the growth of inflation. This led to increasing rates of unemployment. Margaret Thatcher implemented the identical strategy in Great Britain.

3. Pluralism, as a model of American public policymaking, is characterized by competing centers of power, numerous opportunities for access, active participation by individuals and groups, elections, and a consensus on the "democratic creed". Robert Dahl (1970, pp. 132-134) defines pluralism as "rule by minorities," in contrast to the elite model of politics which describes decision-making as a process dominated by only a few, with power concentrated rather than dispersed throughout the polity. For an elaboration of the pluralist model, see Darryl Baskin (1971).

4. Public opinion polls of American adults tend to reveal a bifurcated mode of positive and negative attitudes about social welfare: if beneficiaries tend to work for and earn their benefits, the program is acceptable; if the benefit is perceived as an entitlement which is not earned, the program receives less public support. However, one should be careful in interpreting public opinion and translating supports and demands into specific policy preferences. For example, although a majority of the public supported government intervention to help society's least fortunate members in the mid-1960s, it does not mean that the public *demanded* the War on Poverty. In fact, this set of Great Society programs was concocted by a small group of academics. See Gettleman and Mermelstein (1967, pp. 173-179).

5. Martin Landau, (1977, p. 423) describes policy as "a statement of fundamental principle." In this essay, I treat policy as theory, made up of conditional hypotheses of the "if . . . then" variety.

6. For an analysis of the 1981 reconciliation, see "Reconciliation Round-up" (1981) and Svahn (1981). I have chosen these policies because they represent what appear to be the administration's major priorities as part of a deliberate strategy to cut non-defense federal spending, to restore more control over spending to State and local authorities, and to replace public choices with market choices.

7. See note 1.

8. *Social policies* involve unilateral transfers of cash or in-kind services to individuals with no expectation that there will be a return or an "exchange". Therefore, social policies are part of the "grants" economy, and not part of the "exchange" economy (Boulding, 1967; Boulding and Pfaff, 1972; Boulding, Pfaff and Pfaff, 1973; and Heclo, 1974). Boulding (1967) is critical of the haphazard, ad hoc nature of social policymaking and suggests a council of social advisors to help establish an integrative system. *Social programs* are the instruments to carry out social policies (Kroll, 1962; Moynihan, 1970).

9. The Poor Law of Elizabeth—"An Act for the Relief of the Poor"—recognized poor relief as a public concern and responsibility. Poor people were divided into three classes—children, the able-bodied, and the infirmed—and assistance was provided for each. Children were apprenticed until their twenty-first or twenty-fourth birthday; able-bodied men were put to work; and the infirmed were sent to poorhouses. Compared to earlier poor laws, the Poor Law of Elizabeth took on a civilizing mission.

10. Although by World War I liberals were calling themselves progressives, they proposed to use a powerful government to curb private, usually corporate, power.

11. In fact, it was probably the Second World War, rather than the policies of the Roosevelt administration, that finally pulled the nation from the depths of the Depression.

12. For background on the design of the Democrats' anti-poverty strategy and Walter Heller's role in it, see Sar A. Levitan, 1969, pp. 3-47, especially pp. 12-18.

13. In an earlier paper (1976) I identify Johnson's margin of victory in the 1964 Presidential election, and the effects that this victory had on the distribution of power within the 89th Congress, as principal reasons for such a productive Congress. Using transcripts of closed door sessions of the House Ways and Means Committee, I reconstructed the health policymaking process of the 89th Congress and concluded that in the case of Medicare and Medicaid the most critical factors in shaping those 1965 amendments to the Social Security Act were: (1) the House Democrats, a group which included what Jeff Fishel (1973) calls the "critical minority" of freshman Congressman; (2) the testimony of and expert role played by Wilbur Cohen of the Department of Health, Education, and Welfare; (3) pressure from private interests; and, most importantly, (4) Wilbur Mills, Chairman of the House Ways and Means Committee. Mills was director, writer, producer and leading man in Committee mark-up hearings in which a political bargain was struck that made it politically possible for key Democrat *and* Republican committee members to support the compromise.

14. Compare, for example, Feder (1977 and 1978) with Harrell Rodgers, Jr. and Charles Bullock III (1972 and 1976).

15. For different perspectives on the failure of the social policies of the 1960s to deliver on their political and legal promises, see Ginsberg and Solow, 1974; Wilensky, 1975; and Aron, 1978. According to Steinfels (1979, p. 6), the idea of failure was widespread, working its way from evaluation studies to scholarly articles to the mass media.

16. The "pork barrel" has become synonymous with legislation that distributes public works money in amounts in excess of what needs would justify, but Stockman extends the concept to include any program that distributes benefits excessively or widely. For contrasting views of what the "social pork barrel" means, see Brian Barry (1965, pp. 250-256) and James Buchanan and Gordon Tullock, (1962, Chap 10). Stockman raises the politically troubling question of how to dismantle a "pork barrel" program which has outlived its

usefulness or is badly in need of reform. Apparently the 1970s Republican strategy of dismantling an unproductive program by impounding funds for it (e.g., OEO and the anti-poverty program) has been abandoned, and replaced with a 1980 Republican strategy of eliminating programs through fiscal starvation. Numerous cases of this are incorporated in the 1982 budget revision proposals.

17.   There are two questions which are central to a debate about the distributional consequences of social policy. First, the empirical question: Has there been income re-distribution? and second, the normative question: Has economic growth meant a better life? While there has been an upward shift in the income structure, there has been little change in income distributon. Some have argued that this does not take into account sizable transfers of in-kind benefits which are not reported as income; others (e.g., Paglin, 1975) contend that current calculations do not take differences in "life cycle" needs into account when deciding whether or not distribution patterns are fair. There is the illusion (Milner, 1972, p. 36) that economic growth automatically brings with it more equality, and more social justice; but a number of scholars who have studied modernization cross-nationally have concluded that economic development breeds both inequality and in-stability. A number of comparativists (Huntington and Nelson, 1975; Adelman and Mor-ris, 1973; Hirschman and Rothschild, 1973) point to a curvilinear relationship between growth and equity. Hirschman's and Rothschild's (1973, p. 560) metaphor of a "tunnel effect" demonstrates how the most disadvantaged members of society are often left behind as a nation modernizes. The fundamental argument is that "more" does not necessarily mean "better": an increase in the abundance of goods cannot be equated with their equita-ble distribution. Writing his 1976 edition of *The Affluent Society,* John Kenneth Galbraith reiterates the point: "The thrust of this book is that increased production is not the final test of social achievement, the solvent for all social ills" (Galbraith, 1976, p. xxiv). This is the failure of Keynesian economics.

18.   The concern of political scientists took two forms. First, there were direct attacks on behavioralism and pluralism (McCoy and Playford, 1968), and, second, there were more reasoned arguments for alternative strategies for research, for example, the essays on the study of public policy collected by Austin Ranney (1968).

19.   This debate neither started nor ended with Easton. For example, in the Summer, 1947 volume of *Public Administration Review,* Robert Dahl (1947, pp. 1-11) and Herbert Simon (1947, pp. 200-203) addressed the question of the merits of basic and applied research, and James Coleman's *Policy Research and the Social Sciences* provoked further discussion of the issue.

20.   One indicator of this is of the increase is the number of professional journals that have been published since Easton's Presidential address; another is the increased number of graduate schools of public policy that have developed in some of the most prestigeous universities around the country.

21.   Most economic analysis is conservative. In accepting the values and goals of others as given and demonstrating how those values can be maximized, most analysts support and maintain the existing social, political and economic arrangements. Economic analysis has been criticized on a number of grounds. One of the most scathing critiques (Tribe, 1972) is that economic analysis only masquerades as science; it is, in fact, an ideology which entails commitments to substantive conclusions. Echoing the sentiments of critics of economics for its pretentions at value-free science, John Kenneth Galbraith (1973) pleads for more normative economics which challenges fundamental assumptions and questions values and goals.

22.   For a comprehensive review of the "bureaucratic politics" literature, see Caldwell, (1977).

23.   In a 1982 paper which was delivered at the American Political Science Association annual meeting in Denver, I argued that policies can be designed in order to take into

account the political and economic constraints of the implementation system, but these "feasibility estimates" are conservative. A bolder approach to implementation problems involves "capability estimates"—strategies to improve the capacity of the system to implement optimal policies rather than formulating satisficing policies which meet the needs of implementing actors (Goggin, 1982, p. 45).

24. For contrasting views of egalitarianism, see Cobbs (1975 a,b,c) and Gans (1968). Compared to other social welfare states, the United States is a "laggard" (Wilensky, 1975). In Europe, social programs are generally broader, and include more classes of people as beneficiaries. Costs are controlled not by limiting beneficiaries but by rationing benefits. As a consequence, comparable programs in Europe tend to be more regressive than in the United States, but do not need the costly bureaucractic apparatus to sort out eligibles from ineligibles, and to enforce eligibility requirements. Moreover, social welfare programs in Europe are not stigmatized, as they are in the U.S.

25. Elsewhere (1983) I have argued that President Reagan has revived the 1950's and early 1960's issue of health as a right versus health as a privilege, with the debate revolving around the issue of who should be entitled to subsidized health and medical care. If the "means" test were eliminated, as it is in virtually every other industrial democracy's health care financing program, citizens' rights to health care, regardless of income, would be recognized.

26. When Ronald Reagan was Governor of California the welfare system was reformed to cut benefits to the working poor, to require others to work for their benefits, and to raise payments to a few. It is no accident that Reagan has brought in his chief California architect, Robert Carleson, to repeat the "reform" at the federal level of government.

27. See, for example, Behn, 1980; Levine, 1978, 1980; and Levine, Rubin and Wolohojian, 1981.

28. One might say that this is a new version of the "legitimation crisis," one that casts political elites, not members of mass publics, as the skeptics about government and the role that it plays in society.

29. Shortly after the Reagan proposals were outlined in a series of fiscal year 1982 Budget revisions, Richard Nathan (1981), a Princeton University urban policy specialist, described the Reagan program as "domestic and social policy changes of historic character . . . the most radical shift in domestic policy since the New Deal." Others have called his economic policies revolutionary, comparing them with the bold initiatives of the Second New Deal.

30. These are the latest books to analyze the Reagan administration proposals and their preliminary impact. Palmer and Sawhill (1982, p. 24) characterize Reagan's social policies as experiments which constitute a "counter-revolution"; and most authors agree that the first year tax and spend proposals hurt the poor and middle class most of all. Writing the introductory essay for John W. Ellwood's edited volume, Samuel H. Beer (in Ellwood, 1982, p. xv-xvi) argues that the Reagan public philosophy was an attack on the Great Society, and not the New Deal, with the philosophical goal of restoring individualism over interventionism. In this regard, I concur with Professor Beer.

REFERENCES

Aaron, Henry J. *Politics and the Professors: The Great Society in Perspective,* Studies in Social Economics Series. Washington, D.C.: The Brookings Institution, 1978.

Adelman, Irma, and Morris, Cynthia Taft. *Economic Growth and Social Equity in Developing Countries.* Stanford, Ca.: Stanford University Press, 1973.

Aleshire, Robert A. "Power to the People: An Assessment of the Community Action and Model Cities Experience." *Public Administration Review.* 32 (1977): 428-443.

Allison, Graham T. *The Essence of Decision: Explaining the Cuban Missile Crisis.* Boston: Little, Brown, 1971.

————. "The Place of Principles in Policy Analysis." *American Political Science Review.* 73 (1979): 711-723.

Aron, Raymond. *Progress and Disillusion: The Dialectics of Modern Society.* New York: Frederich A. Praeger, 1968.

Austin, David M. "Resident Participation: Political Mobilization or Organizational Cooptation?" *Public Administration Review.* 32 (1972): 409-420.

Bach, George Leland. *Economics: An Introduction to Analysis and Policy,* ninth edition. Englewood Cliffs, N.J.: Prentice-Hall, 1977.

Bardach, Eugene. *The Implementation Game: What Happens After a Bill Becomes a Law?* Cambridge, Ma.: MIT Press, 1977.

Barry, Brian. *Political Argument.* New York: Humanities Press, 1965.

Baskin, Darryl. *American Pluralist Democracy: A Critique.* New York: Van Nostrand Reinhold Co., 1971.

Beer, Samuel. "In Search of a New Public Philosophy." In *The New American Political System,* pp. 5-44. Edited by Anthony King. Washington, D.C.: American Enterprize Institute, 1978.

Behn, Robert D., ed. "A Symposium: Leadership in an Era of Retrenchment." *Public Administration Review.* 40 (1980): 603-626.

Boulding, Kenneth. "The Boundaries of Social Policy." *Social Work* 12 (1967): 3-11.

————. "The Many Failures of Success." *Saturday Review,* November 23, 1968, pp. 29-31.

————. and Pfaff, Martin, eds. *Redistribution to the Rich and the Poor: The Grants Economics of Income Distribution.* Belmont, Ca.: Wadsworth Publishing Co., 1972.

————. Pfaff, Martin, and Pfaff, Anita, eds. *Transfers in an Urbanized Economy: The Grants Economics of Income Distribution.* Belmont, Ca.: Wadsworth Publishing Co., 1973.

Branch, Taylor. "The Screwing of the Average Man: Government Subsidies: Who Gets the $63 Billion?" *Washington Monthly.* 4 (1972): 9-27.

Bressler, Robert J. "A Cultural Counterrevolution." *Intellect.* 106 (1977): 115.

Buchanan, James M. and Tullock, Gordon. *The Calculus of Consent.* Ann Arbor: University of Michigan Press, 1962.

Caldwell, Dan. "Bureaucratic Foreign Policy Making." *American Behavioral Scientist.* 2 (1977): 87-110.

Chambers, Clark A., ed. *The New Deal at Home and Abroad 1929-1945.* New York: The Free Press, 1965.

Champagne, Anthony, and Harpham, Edward J., eds. *The Attack on the Welfare State.* Prospect Heights, Ill.: Waveland Press, 1984.

Cobbs, John. "Egalitarianism: Threat to a Free Market." *Business Week,* December 1, 1975, pp. 62-65.

————. "Egalitarianism: Mechanisms for Redistributing Income." *Business Week,* December 8, 1975, pp. 86-90.

————. "Egalitarianism: The Corporation as Villain." *Business Week,* December 15, 1975, pp. 86-88.

Coleman, James. *Policy Research in the Social Sciences.* Morristown, N.J.: General Learning Press, 1972.

Cohen, Toby. "Reagan's New Deal." *New York Times.* August 19, 1981, Sec. 1, p. A23.

Conkin, Paul K. *The New Deal,* second edition. Arlington Heights, Ill.: AHM Publishing Corporation, 1975.

Crozier, Michel, Huntington, Samuel P., and Watanuki, Joji: *The Crisis of Democracy: Report on the Governability of Democracies to the Trilateral Commission.* New York: New York University Press, 1975.

Dahl, Robert. *Preface to Democratic Theory.* Chicago: University of Chicago Press, 1970.
———. "The Science of Public Administration: Three Problems." *Public Administration Review.* 7 (1947): 1-11.
———. *Who Governs? Democracy and Power in an American City.* New Haven, Conn.: Yale University Press, 1961.
Demkovich, Linda E. "Medicaid for Welfare: A Controversial Swap." *National Journal.* February 27, 1982, pp. 362-369.
Donnelly, Harrison. "What Reagan Budget Cuts Would Do to the Poor: 'Safety Net' Not Much Help, Critics Charge." *Congressional Quarterly Weekly Report.* 39 (April 18, 1981): 665-668.
Douglas, Paul H. *Real Wages in the United States—1890–1926.* Boston: Houghton Mifflin Co., 1930.
Easton, David. "The New Revolution in Political Science." *American Political Science Review.* 63 (1969): 1051-1061.
Eckstein, Harry. *The Evaluation of Political Performance: Problems and Dimensions.* Beverly Hills, Ca.: Sage Publication, 1971.
Edelman, Murray. *The Symbolic Uses of Politics.* Urbana, Ill.: University of Illinois Press, 1974.
Edwards, R.C. "Who Fares Well in the Welfare State?" In *The Capitalist System.* Edited by R.C. Edwards. Englewood Cliffs, N.J.: Prentice-Hall, 1972.
Ellwood, John William, ed. *Reductions in U.S. Domestic Spending: How They Affect State and Local Governments.* New Brunswick, N.J.: Transition Books, 1982.
Executive Office of the President, Office of Management and Budget. *Budget of the United States Government, Fiscal Year 1984.* Washington, D.C.: U.S. Government Printing Office, March, 1983
———. *Fiscal Year 1982 Budget Revisions.* Washington, D.C.: U.S. Government Printing Office, March, 1981.
———. *Fiscal Year 1982 Budget Revisions: Additional Details on Budget Savings.* Washington, D.C.: U.S. Government Printing Office, April, 1981.
———. *The United States Budget in Brief: Fiscal Year 1982.* Washington, D.C.: U.S. Government Printing Office, 1981.
Feder, Judith M. "Medicare Implementation and the Policy Process." *Journal of Health Politics, Policy and Law.* 2 (1978): 173-189.
———. *Medicare: The Politics of Federal Hospital Insurance.* Lexington, Ma.: D.C. Heath and Co., 1977.
Fishel, Jeff. *Representation and Responsiveness in Congress: The Class of Eighty-nine.* Beverly Hills, Ca.: Sage Publications, 1973.
Free, Lloyd A., and Cantril, Hadley. *The Political Beliefs of Americans: A Study of Public Opinion.* New York: Simon and Schuster, 1968,
Galbraith, John Kenneth. *The Affluent Society.* Boston: Houghton Mifflin, 1976.
———. *The New Industrial State.* Boston: Houghton, Mifflin Company, 1967.
———. "Power and the Useful Economist." *American Economic Review.* 63 (1973): 37-50.
Gans, Herbert. *More Equality.* New York: Vintage Books, 1968.
Gartner, Alan, Greer, Colin, and Riessman, Frank, eds. *What Reagan is Doing to Us.* New York: Harper & Row, 1982.
Gettleman, Marvin E., and Mermelstein, David, eds. *The Great Society Reader: The Failure of American Liberalism.* New York: Random House, 1967.
Gilder, George. *Wealth and Poverty.* New York: Basic Books, 1981.
Ginsberg, Eli, and Solow, Robert M., eds. *The Great Society: Lessons for the Future.* New York: Basic Books, 1974.
Glazer, Nathan, and Kristol, Irving. *The American Commonwealth- 1976.* New York: Basic Books, 1976.

Goggin, Malcolm L. "Policy Design and Implementation Politics: A Plausibility Probe of a Candidate Theory." Paper presented at the Annual Meeting of the American Political Science Association, Chicago, September, 1982.

———. "Presidential Behavior: Ideologues and Pragmatists." Paper presented at the Annual Meeting of the Northeastern Political Science Association, New Haven, November, 1982.

———. "Presidential Beliefs and Policy Behavior: Ronald Reagan and the Presidential 'Marriage Cycle'." unpublished manuscript, 1982.

———. "Reagan's Revival: Turning Back the Clock in the Health Care Debate." In *The Attack on the Welfare State*. Edited by Anthony Champagne and Edward Harpham, pp. 61–86. Prospect Heights, Ill.: Waveland Press, 1984.

———. "Toward a Theory of Non-incremental Public Policy Development: A Multivariate Model to Explain Medicare." Stanford, CA., unpublished manuscript, 1976.

Gordon, Robert Aaron. *Economic Instability and Growth: The American Record*. New York: Harper & Row, 1974.

Goulet, Denis. *The Cruel Choice: A New Concept in the Theory of Development*. New York: Atheneum, 1971.

Greenberg, Edward S. *Serving the Few: Corporate Capitalism and the Bias of Government Policy*. New York: John Wiley & Sons, 1974.

Gurr, Ted, and McClelland, Muriel. *Political Performance: A Twelve Nation Study*. Beverly Hills, Ca.: Sage Publications, 1971.

Guzzardi, Walter, Jr. "Who Will Care for the Poor?" *Fortune* 105, June 28, 1982: 34-42.

Hansen, W. Lee, and Weisbrod, Burton. *Benefits, Costs and Financing of Public Higher Education*. Chicago: Markham, 1969.

Harrington, Michael. *The Other America: Poverty Amid Plenty in the United States*. Baltimore Md.: Penguin Books, 1962.

Haveman, Robert H. "An Analysis and Evaluation of Public Expenditures: An Overview." In *The Analysis and Evaluation of Public Expenditures: The PPB System*. Edited by the Joint Economic Committee, Congress of the United States. Washington, D.C.: Government Printing Office, 1969.

Heclo, Hugh. *Modern Social Politics in Britain and Sweden: From Relief to Income Maintenance*, Yale Studies in Political Science, vol. 25. New Haven, Conn: Yale University Press, 1974.

Heineman, Ben W., ed. *Poverty Amid Plenty: The American Paradox: The Report of the President's Commission on Income Maintenance Programs*. Washington, D.C.: U.S. Government Printing Office, 1969.

Hirschman, Albert O. and Rothschild, Michael. "The Changing Tolerance for Income Inequality in the Course of Economic Development." *Quarterly Journal of Economics*. 87 (1973): 544-566.

Hofstadter, Richard. *The Age of Reform: From Bryan to FDR*. New York: Vintage Books, 1955.

———. ed. *The Progressive Movement— 1900–1915*. Englewood Cliffs, N.J.: Prentice-Hall, 1963.

Huntington, Samuel P. "The Democratic Distemper." In *The American Commonwealth-1976*, pp. 9-38. Edited by Nathan Glazer and Irving Kristol. New York: Basic Books, 1976.

———. and Nelson, Joan. *No Easy Choice: Political Participation in Developing Countries*. Cambridge, Ma: Harvard University Press, 1976.

King, Willford I. *Wealth and Income of the People of the United States*. New York: McMillan, 1915.

Kroll, Morton. "Hypotheses and Design for the Study of Public Policies in the United States." *Midwest Journal of Political Science*. 11 (1962): 363-383.

Landau, Martin. "The Proper Domain of Policy Analysis." *American Journal of Political Science.* 21 (1977): 423-427.

Leontif, Wassily. "The Theoretical Assumptions and Non-observable Facts." *American Economic Review.* 61 (1971): 1-7.

Leuchtenburg, William E. *Franklin D. Roosevelt and the New Deal: 1932-1940.* New York: Harper & Row, 1963.

Leven, Maurice, ed., assisted by Kathryn Robertson Wright. *The Income Structure of the United States.* Washington, D.C.: The Brookings Institution, 1938.

Levine, Charles H., ed. *Managing Fiscal Stress: The Crisis in the Public Sector.* Chatham, N.J.: Chatham House, 1980.

————. "Organizational Decline and Cutback Management." *Public Administration Review.* 38 (1978): 315-325.

————. Rubin, Irene, and Wolhojian, George. *The Politics of Retrenchment.* Beverly Hills, Ca.: Sage Publications, 1981.

Levitan, Sar A. *The Great Society's Poor Law: A New Approach to Poverty.* Baltimore, Md.: The Johns Hopkins Press, 1969.

Lippman, Walter. *Essays in the Public Philosophy.* Boston, Ma.: Little, Brown, 1955.

Lowi, Theodore. *The End of Liberalism: Ideology, Policy and the Crisis of Public Authority,* second edition. New York: Norton, 1979.

————. "The Public Philosophy: Interest-Group Liberalism." *American Political Science Review.* 61 (1967): 5-24.

Mayhew, David R. *Congress: The Electoral Connection.* New Haven, Conn.: Yale University Press, 1974.

McCoy, Charles Allan, and Playford, John, eds. *Apolitical Politics: A Critque of Behavioralism.* New York: Crowell, 1968.

McSwain, Cynthia J. "The Conservative Anarchist Alternative to Humanist Liberalism." Paper prepared for delivery at the Annual meeting of the American Political Science Association, New York, 1981.

Milner, Murry, Jr. *The Illusion of Equality: The Effect of Education on Opportunity, Inequality, and Social Conflict.* San Francisco, Ca.: Jossey-Bass, 1972.

Moynihan, Daniel P. "Policy vs. Program in the '70's." *The Public Interest.* 20 (1970): 90-100.

————. *The Politics of the Guaranteed Annual Income: The Nixon Administration and the Family Assistance Plan.* New York: Vintage Books, 1973.

Nathan, Richard. "National Health Policy Forum." George Washington University, Washington, D.C., May 19, 1981.

Nelson, Richard R. "Intellectualizing about the Moon-Ghetto Metaphor: A Study of the Current Malaise of Rational Analysis of Social Problems." *Policy Sciences.* 5 (1974): 375-414.

Nisbet, Robert A. *Twilight of Authority.* New York: Oxford University Press, 1975.

Owen, John. "Inequality and Discrimination in the Public School System: Some Empirical Evidence." In *Economics: Mainstream Readings and Radical Critique.* Edited by David Mermelstein. New York: Random House, 1970.

Paglin, Morton. "The Measurement and Trend of Inequality: A Basic Revision." *American Economic Review.* 65 (1975): 598-609.

Palmer, John Logan, and Sawhill, Isabel V., eds. *The Reagan Experiment: An Examination of Economic and Social Policies under the Reagan Administration.* Washington, D.C.: The Urban Institute, 1982.

Pennock, Roland. "Political Development, Political System, and Political Goods." *World Politics.* 18 (1966): 415-434.

Piven, Francis Fox, and Cloward, Richard A. *Regulating the Poor: The Functions of Public Welfare.* New York: Pantheon, 1971.

————. *The New Class War: Reagan's Attack on the Welfare State and its Consequences.* New York: Pantheon, 1982.

Plattner, Marc F. "The Welfare State vs. the Redistributive State." *The Public Interest.* 55 (1979): 28-48.

Pound, Edward T. "U.S. Fraud Unit to Start Inquiry in New York City." *New York Times.* September 3, 1981, Sec 1, p. 21.

Pressman, Jeffrey, and Wildavsky, Aaron. *Implementation.* Berkeley, Ca.: University of California Press, 1973.

Ranney, Austin. *Political Science and Public Policy.* Chicago: Markham Publishing Co., 1968.

Reagan, Ronald. "Budget Proposals: A Program for Economic Recovery." February 18, 1981, as quoted in *Congressional Quarterly Weekly Report.* February 21, 1981: pp. 360-363.

————. *Third Press Conference.* June 16, 1981, as quoted in *Congressional Quarterly Weekly Report.* June 20, 1981: pp. 1105-1108.

"Reconciliation Roundup." *Congressional Quarterly Weekly Report.* 39, August 15, 1981: 1461-1520.

Rodgers, Harrell R., Jr., and Bullock, Charles S., III. *Law and Social Change: Civil Rights Laws and Their Consequences.* New York: McGraw-Hill, 1972.

————. *Coercion to Compliance.* Lexington, Ma.: Lexington Books, 1976.

Runciman, Walter Garrison. *Relative Deprivation and Social Justice: A Study of Attitudes to Social Inequality in Twentieth Century England.* Berkeley, Ca.: University of California Press, 1966.

Schultze, Charles. *The Distribution of Farm Subsidies.* Washington, D.C.: The Brookings Institution, 1971.

Simon, Herbert A. "A Comment on the Science of Public Administration." *Public Administration Review.* 7 (1947): 200-203.

Spahr, Charles B. *An Essay on the Present Distribution of Wealth in the United States.* Boston: T.Y. Crowell, 1896.

Steiner, Gilbert Y. *The State of Welfare.* Washington, D.C.: The Brookings Institution, 1971.

Steinfels, Peter. *The Neoconservatives: The Men Who are Changing America's Politics.* New York: Simon and Schuster, 1979.

Stockman, David A. "The Social Pork Barrel." *The Public Interest.* 39 (1975): 3-30.

Svahn, John A. "Omnibus Budget Reconciliation Act of 1981." *Social Security Bulletin.* 44 (1981): 3-24.

Tribe, Lawrence H. "Policy Science: Analysis or Ideology?" *Journal of Philosophy and Public Affairs.* 2 (1972): 66-110.

Upton, Letitia, and Lyons, Nancy. "Basic Facts: Distribution of Personal Income and Wealth in the United States." In *Exploring Contradictions: Political Economy in the Corporate State,* pp. 96-115. Edited by Philip Brenner, Robert Borosage and Bethany Weidner. New York: David McKay Company, Inc., 1974.

Van Horn, Carl E. *Policy Implementation in the Federal System: National Goals and Local Implementors.* Lexington, Ma.: D.C. Heath and Co., 1979.

Weinstein, James. *The Corporate Ideal in the Liberal State, 1900-1918.* Boston: Beacon Press, 1968.

Welfare Reform in California . . . Showing the Way. Sacramento, Ca.: State of California, December 1972.

White House Office of Public Affairs. *The Reagan Presidency: A Review of the First Year, 1981.* Washington, D.C.: White House Office of Public Affairs, 1982.

Wilensky, Harold L. *The Welfare State and Equality: Structural and Ideological Roots of Public Expenditures.* Berkeley, Ca.: University of California Press, 1975.

Wolfe, Alan. *America's Impasse: The Rise and Fall of the Politics of Growth.* New York: Pantheon Books, 1981.

Part III

THE IMPACT OF PUBLIC PHILOSOPHIES AND POLITICAL STRUCTURES

CONTROLLING HEALTH CARE COSTS:

A CROSS NATIONAL PERSPECTIVE

Howard Leichter

I. INTRODUCTION

Even for Americans, who have come to view inflation as an almost natural and inevitable part of life, the growth in health care costs must still seem breathtaking. Consider some of the evidence. In 1981, national health care costs alone increased almost $40 billion: from $247.2 billion to $286.6 billion. This 15.1 percent increase came on the heels of a 15.8 percent increase in the previous year and represented a two year increase from 8.9 percent to 9.8 percent of the Gross National Product spent on health care. And, it should be noted that in 1982 health care costs rose 11 percent, while the overall inflation rate was just 3.9 percent, the lowest rate in a decade. In fact, over the last decade hospital care costs, which comprise the fastest growing and largest part of the national health care bill, rose more than twice as fast as the consumer price index. Finally, between 1952 and 1982, the daily per patient cost of a hospital stay increased from $18 per day to $476, while the average cost of a stay in a hospital rose from $670 in 1971 to $2119 in 1981.

One could go on but the point should be clear. Health care costs are rising at a rate that appears to be both politically and economically untenable. Reflecting what has to be a consensus among most observers of all political persuasions, former Secretary of Health and Human Services Richard Schweiker recently said: "We cannot allow health costs to keep climbing, because we simply cannot afford to pay the bill" (*New York Times* June 12, 1982).

In the strictest sense, of course, we can "pay the bill." The national government could devote more of its resources to health care—currently about 11 percent of the Federal budget. But as a practical matter, individually, in terms of our own personal budgets, and collectively, in terms of local, state and national budgets, there appears to be a sense that a critical threshold has been or is soon to be reached. Americans want other things besides health care: libraries, schools, roads, protection, and so on. There is certainly the feeling on the part of policy makers that something has to be done to control the spiralling costs of health care, so that other demands can be satisfied—and budgets balanced.

This chapter examines the issue of health care cost containment. The chapter begins with a discussion of the merits of a cross-national perspective on the study of health care policy, including cost containment. Following this, I will document the rise in health care costs over the past several decades. Next, I will outline the demographic, economic, political and technological reasons why health care costs have risen so rapidly, continuously and persistently over the last few decades. Following this, I will examine the experiences of other Western nations. Here we shall see that the United States is not alone in contending with steeply rising health costs. In addition, I will examine the different policy strategies which these nations have adopted to deal with the problem. These experiences will provide the basis for examining, in the next section, the proposals by liberals and conservatives in the United States for dealing with the health cost explosion. The chapter concludes with an evaluation of the various proposals for and experiences with health care cost containment at home and abroad.

II.   A COMPARATIVE PERSPECTIVE ON HEALTH CARE POLICY

The comparative study of health care policy is one of the most rapidly growing of all academic enterprises (See Elling, 1980; Leichter, 1979; Roemer, 1977). While there are a number of reasons for this, the most important is that a comparative perspective reflects the reality of the health care policy-making process itself. Policy makers in the United

States routinely look toward the policy experiences of other nations when formulating American health care policy. This cross-national perspective is manifested in periodic Congressional studies (e.g., "Medical Care Systems in Industrialized Countries," 1974; "National Health Insurance Resource Book," 1974) and in the work of the Fogarty International Center. The Fogarty Center, which is part of the Department of Health and Human Services, is devoted to the international study of the health sciences including health care policy.

While I have suggested elsewhere (Leichter, 1977) that the inclination to look toward the experiences of other nations is characteristic of most areas of public policymaking, nowhere is it more widely used than in health care. As in other policy areas, a comparative perspective offers policy makers a convenient, inexpensive and expeditious opportunity to: (1) gather information; (2) make rhetorical points for or against a proposed policy idea; (3) engage in quasi-experimental research—i.e., compare the experiences of nations which have adopted a particular policy with those that have not. In short, a comparative policy perspective simply makes good policymaking sense.

It makes the most sense, however, and has been applied most frequently, in the field of health care policy. The reason for this is quite simple. For the past 70 years the experiences and example of other nations with national health insurance (and to a lesser extent the British National Health Service since 1948) has provided the touchstone for the health care policy debate in this country. Starting around 1912 when it first appeared on the policy agenda, until the present day, national health insurance has dominated the national debate over health care policy. It has been *the* standard—either to be emulated or avoided—upon which American policy makers, academicians and journalists have measured our own health care policy efforts.

And because national health insurance originated and developed in Western Europe, and later spread to Canada, Japan, and other parts of the world, it has been to these countries that Americans have turned for policy guidance. Thus, describing the early (1912-1917) health insurance movement in the United States, Tishler (1971, p. 165) notes that "both opponents and proponents of health insurance relied primarily upon the experience in Germany and England for evaluating the specific machinery under which the system would operate. . . ."

The national health insurance model continues to be the basis for American health care policy debate. It is instructive in this regard that in a book devoted to examining NEW DIRECTIONS IN PUBLIC HEALTH CARE: A PRESCRIPTION FOR THE 1980s (Lindsay, 1980), virtually every chapter deals with either a defense of, or an attack upon, national health insurance. In sum, in no other policy area has a single, non-American policy model so influenced the thinking and debate over U.S. public policy than in health care.

There are, of course, certain practical and theoretical problems involved in taking a comparative approach to studying health care policy. While there are several potential problems to the approach (See Stone, 1980-81), perhaps the most obvious is the one of policy transferability. The question of what, if anything, one can learn from the policies and policy experiences of other nations, is often resolved in one of two, diametrically opposite, ways. The first is to uncritically embrace the policy examples of other nations and urge their adoption in this country. This typically is done without any regard for the comparability of national social, economic and political circumstances. Illustrative of this is the obsession that liberals have for Sweden and conservatives for Hong Kong (See Friedman and Friedman, 1980) in the area of social and economic policy. In neither case is there any acknowledgement of how extraordinarily different these systems are from our own. What may work well in relatively small, homogenous, politically peripheral nations, may not work well in the United States.

There is, however, the danger of being overly impressed and immobilized by such differences. This is what Stone (1980-81, p. 279) calls "The Assumption of Uniqueness," and is the second approach to and problem with the transferability issue. Here the problem is the claim that we are so different, in our culture, history, values and so on, than other nations that what they do could not possibly be relevant here. American public policy, in this view, must be home-grown.

Clearly what is called for in comparative health policy research to minimize the transferability problem, in both of its manifestations, is to: (1) recognize and admit the problem; (2) be more careful in selecting cases for comparison, and; (3) recognize that it is not necessary to engage in wholesale borrowing from others in order for a comparative approach to be useful. Thus, it may be that selected borrowing, coupled with appropriate adaptations for the American system, is the most valid approach to both policy research and actual policymaking. With this background on the comparative approach in mind, we can now turn to the first substantive concern of the chapter, namely the growth in health care costs.

III.   THE GROWTH IN HEALTH CARE COSTS

It has become commonplace in discussions of health care policy to refer to the "crisis" in American health care (See Riska 1980-81; Dolbeare 1982). The crisis is reputed to have several dimensions. Among these is the quality of health care. On the issue of quality, particular concern has been expressed about the overuse of surgical procedures and drugs, as well as sheer incompetence as measured by mounting malpractice claims. But the dimension of the crisis which is most frequently described is the cost explosion. In his 1983 State of the Union address, President Reagan promised to "act to improve the quality of life for Americans by curbing the skyrocketing cost of health care that is becoming an unbearable financial burden for so many." What exactly is the magnitude of this burden? Table 1 documents the rise in health care spending in absolute and relative terms over the past three decades.

There are several points worth underscoring with regard to the trends revealed in Table 1. The first is that while health care costs have risen at immodest rates throughout the period 1950-1981, it is only in the last 15 years (1966-1981) that they have really taken off. Thus, for example, the annual average rate of increase for the period 1966 to 1981 was 13.1 percent compared to the 8.3 percent increase from 1950 to 1965. The period of 1975 to 1981 is particularly noteworthy because of the increase of the GNP spent on health care from 8.6 to 9.8 percent. It is important to note that public spending has risen more sharply than private spending for health care. This, as we shall see shortly, is mainly attributable to the introduction in 1965 of the Medicare and Medicaid programs. The relatively more rapid growth of public as compared to private spending on health is also reflected in the proportion of total spending on health care from the public and private sectors. Public sector spending has increased from approximately 27.2 percent in 1950 to 42.7 percent in 1981.

Table 1.   The Growth of Health Care Costs (1950–1981)

	1950	*1960*	*1965*	*1975*	*1981*
Total Health Expenditures					
In $ billions	$12.7	$26.9	$41.7	$132.7	$286.6
As % of GNP	4.4%	5.3%	6.0%	8.6%	9.8%
Per capita	$81.86	$146.30	$210.89	$603.57	$1225.00
Annual % increase	12.2%	8.7%	9.2%	14.0%	15.1%
Public Expenditures					
In $ billions	$3.4	$6.6	$10.8	$56.2	$122.5
Per capita	$22.24	$36.10	$54.57	$255.49	$524.00
Annual % increase	15.5%	7.8%	10.2%	19.2%	16.2%
Private Expenditures					
In $ billions	$9.2	$20.3	$20.9	$76.5	$164.1
Per capita	$59.62	$110.20	$156.32	$348.08	$701.00
Annual % increase	11.2%	9.0%	8.8%	9.7%	14.3%

Source: Health Care Financing Review, September 4, 1982.

Another point to be noted about the rise in medical costs is that it has been going up at a rate faster than other goods and services. In 1982, for example, while the Consumer Price Index for all items rose just 3.9 percent, the smallest increase in a decade, medical care costs increased 11 percent.

There is one final issue concerning the nature of health cost increases which is not reflected in the data in Table 1, namely, the relationship between hospital care costs and physician and other medical care costs (e.g., dental services, drugs, etc.). Three points need to be made in this regard. First, hospital costs constitute the largest proportion of health care expenditures. In 1981, 41.2 percent of all money spent on health care went to hospitals compared to 19.1 percent for physicians' services.

Second, that proportion has increased over the years: 30.4 percent in 1950 compared to 41.2 percent in 1981. The third point is a function of the first two. "Since hospital care has accounted for an increased share of the total health care dollar, it has been responsible for a disproportionate share of the relative growth of the health care sector during the past 15 years" (Goldfarb et. al. 1980, p. 101). The significance of this will be discussed later in the chapter when I examine proposals for containing health costs.

The profile of health care spending that emerges then is one of rapid and accelerated increases in absolute and relative spending on health care, with the public sector portion increasing more rapidly and accounting for a larger portion of the bill, over time, than the private sector, and hospitals consuming an increasing proportion of the resources allocated to the health care sector. It is now time to try to account for these extraordinary cost increases.

IV. WHY HEALTH CARE COSTS HAVE RISEN

There are several reasons which explain the rapid rise in health care costs in the United States and in other nations as well. For purposes of analysis, it is useful to organize these into the three categories suggested by the Department of Health and Human Services. These factors are: price-related, utilization-related and technology-related.

Price Factors

Among the more prominent factors explaining the increase in health care costs, and especially hospital costs, is the impact of the inflationary rise in the prices of goods and services used by the medical industry. These increases account for about one-half of the total rise in health costs. The medical industry is, of course, a highly labor intensive enterprise. Increases in wages and salaries have played an important role in the increase in health costs. In addition, over the last decade the industry has become even more labor intensive. Thus, in 1971 there were 272 hospital personnel per 100 patients, whereas by 1978 the number had increased to 323 per 100 patients (Goldfarb et. al. 1980, 105-106). Increased labor intensity, combined with increased labor costs, are major factors in health cost inflation. It must be remembered, however, that medical cost increases have been running at a rate two to three times as high as overall inflation and, therefore, one has to look beyond general inflation to fully explain these increases.

A second price-related factor is the nature of the medical financing mechanism. It is this factor that many policy makers and academic observors have identified as the chief culprit in the health cost crisis. There are actually three facets of the medical market mechanism that need to be identified. These are: "third party" and "fee-for-service" reimbursement and the unique market arrangement between the major actors in the medical marketplace. I will examine each of these.

By 1976 ninety percent of the American people had some form of health insurance. Today approximately 90 percent of all hospital costs and 60 percent of all physician fees are paid by either private (e.g., Blue Cross/Blue Shield) or public (e.g., Veteran's Administration, Medicaid, Medicare) "third party" insurance carriers. A majority of Americans never see or touch the money (or at least not very much of it) which goes to physicians or hospitals. Hence, it is argued, there is no incentive for either the patient, the physician or the hospital to be cost conscious because the insurance company, or the government, not the individual, is paying the bill or most of it. Doctors order, hospitals perform and patients have come to expect more tests, more amenities (e.g., private rooms, color TVs) and more attention because it will be paid for by some unseen "third party." As former Congressman Al Ullman put it: "With an invisible 'third party' insurer paying more than 90 percent of the cost, the consumer and the doctor rarely spare the expense" (Quoted in Demkovich 1979b, p. 1998).

Doctors and hospitals rarely "spare the expense" not only because of the intervention by third party insurers but also because of the fee-for-service reimbursement procedures which dominate American medical practice. Basically, doctors and hospitals are paid a fee for every service they perform or provide—every office visit, every test, every injection. The more they do, the more they earn. This, combined with third party payments, leads to little cost consciousness on the part of consumers or providers of health care. Alain Enthoven, a severe critic of the system, says it "is a totally inappropriate way to finance medical care" (*Health Policy* 1980, p. 36).

Another facet of this third party mechanism is that the tax system tends to encourage even more generous and, critics charge, inflationary coverage. Under current Federal tax laws, employers can deduct from their taxable income all health insurance costs paid on behalf of their employees. Offering employees more generous health insurance coverage—i.e., plans that cover more, cost more, and push the nation's health bill up even higher—is good for employee morale and a very attractive tax incentive. Of course, ultimately someone has to pay the bill. General Motors estimates that health care costs for their employees (which in 1980 cost $1.5 billion) added about $315 to the cost of every GM car and truck. Finally, it also should be noted that these benefits are not calculated as part of the employee's taxable income—although in 1983 President Reagan proposed just such a tax. Hence it is to both the employer's and employee's advantage to increase coverage.

Yet another feature of the financing of medical care which contributes to its' spiralling costs is the nearly unique nature of the medical marketplace. In most economic relationships cost is typically a function of supply and demand. In general, the greater the demand by buyers, the higher the cost. In medical care, however, the supplier (i.e., the physician) also determines the demand. It is the physician, not the patient, who orders the tests, determines if and for how long patients will stay in the hospital, prescribes medication and so on. The functional equivalent would be if the local Ford dealer determined that every family needed three automobiles (and Fords at that). The typical restraints that supply and demand impose on costs in other areas are simply absent in the American health care market.

There is one final price-related factor which has contributed to the rapid increase in health care costs, namely the mushrooming of malpractice suits against American physicians. To give just one example, in 1960 the average malpractice insurance premium paid by surgeons was $229 per year; in 1972 it was $2037 and in 1979 it had reached $7190. Several factors, other than increasing incompetence by the medical profession, explain these extraordinary increases—although incompetence and carelessness cannot be ruled out. Among the more prominent factors are: (1) a general increase in consumer willingness to hold "sellers" accountable for actual or perceived poor service; (2) an increase in skepticism toward all social institutions; (3) greater use of medical services, and particularly high risk procedures; (4) a changing legal environment that has facilitated, and perhaps encouraged recourse to litigation and; (5) a bandwagon effect produced by the publicity given to malpractice suits and, particularly, highly celebrated large settlements.

Whatever the reason, the increased recourse to malpractice suits and the resulting increase in malpractice insurance costs have contributed to the health cost explosion in two ways. First, physicians pass along the increased costs of insurance to their patients. Second, and most importantly, physicians are increasingly practicing "defensive medicine;" that is, they order more tests and use more sophisticated (and costly) diagnostic procedures in order to protect themselves from charges of malpractice. Defensive medicine then can be added to the list of factors which have boosted up national health care costs.

Utlization Patterns

The second category of factors contributing to health cost inflation is changes in utilization patterns. In particular increases in the number, relative proportion, and health care usage of three groups—women, non-whites, and the elderly—each of whom tends to use medical services more than their opposites, have contributed to the problem of soaring costs. Of the three, however, the elderly have had the most profound impact on the system.

To begin, there are over 13 million more Americans 65 years old or over today than there were in 1950—25.2 million compared to 12.5 million. Furthermore, this represents an increase in the proportion of older Americans of from 8.1 percent of the population in 1950 to 11.3 percent in 1980. By the year 2030 it is estimated that there will be 50 million elderly people comprising 17 percent of the population. Not unexpectedly, the elderly make greater demands upon the health care system and account for a disproportionate share of the health care bill. (Gibson and Fisher 1979, p. 12), in examining age differences in health expenditures for fiscal year 1977 found that: "Total per capita spending [for the elderly] was more than two and one half times that for persons aged 19-64 and nearly seven times that for those under age 19. Thus, expenditures for the aged, comprising 11 percent of the population, totaled 29 percent of personal health care spending." The elderly become ill more frequently than other age groups. They see physicians more often and take up more of their time when they do. It has been estimated that it takes three times longer to x-ray an elderly person than a younger one (Demkovich 1979a, p. 222). They are hospitalized more frequently and stay longer when they are. They are more likely to require costly medical procedures than other age groups and the demand for these more costly procedures is going up faster for the elderly than other age groups. Surgery rates for the country as a whole rose by 25.5 percent between 1965 and 1978; but for people 65 years of age and over, the rate increased 64.7 percent (Goldfarb, et. al, pp. 106-107).

The reasons for the rapid growth in the consumption, and hence costs, of medical care by the aged are not hard to find. First and foremost was the introduction of Medicare in 1965 which had as its purpose the removal of financial barriers to acquiring necessary medical care. The impact of Medicare on the government's health bill was immediate and profound: in 1967 the Federal government spent $4.5 billion on Medicare; in 1981 the cost was $44.8 billion. The increase in demand (and coincidentally the costs) for health care by the aged is in no small measure the result of deliberate and benevolent government policy.

The increased demand is also a function of the success of the medical/scientific community in preserving life and conquering illness. For example, between 1950 and 1979 the death rate for people between 65 and 74 years old declined from 4931 per 100,000 to 4018. In addition, the proportion of those 75 years of age and older is also increasing—making the demands on health care even greater.

In sum, what has happened is that American society's success, in terms of better and more accessible health care for the elderly, improved nutrition, greater health awareness among its people, and scientific advances in dealing with such diseases as hypertension, arthritis, etc., have combined to increase demands made upon the health care system and increase the costs of running it.

Technological Change

Another factor which has contributed to the cost explosion in health care is the revolution in medical technology. This technology has introduced in just the last few decades extraordinary, sophisticated, *and costly,* life-saving and life-sustaining diagnostic equipment, drugs, and procedures into American medical practice. In fact, Victor Fuchs, one of the foremost students of the American health care system, has argued that: "The most important thing that drives up costs, over time, is new technology" (*New York Times* March 28, 1982). Such diagnostic procedures/equipment as the CAT scanner (Computerized Aerial Tomography), colonscope and stress tests, surgical procedures such as heart bypass and kidney transplants, the use of treatments like kidney dialysis and the introduction of Intensive Care Units in hospitals all have contributed to the ability of the medical profession to sustain life and treat illnesses that were beyond the reach of medical science just a few years ago. But the cost of this technology has been enormous. Consider some of the following examples: (1) In 1982 it cost approximately $1.056 billion for kidney treatments, dialysis and transplant operations for the 59,125 kidney patients enrolled in a special Federal program. This group constituted just .025 percent of the U.S. population. (2) With the introduction of Intensive Care Units to treat premature infants, the mortality rate for those born earlier than seven months declined from 80 percent to 20 percent—while the cost for such care increased from $10,000 per care to $120,000 per care (Demkovich 1979a, p. 223). (3) CAT scanners are modern medical miracles which allow physicians to observe any part of the body, in three-dimensional detail, and to locate medical problems which heretofore could only be found, if at all, through surgery. Currently CAT scanners cost about $1.2 million to buy and about $300-$400,000 a year to operate. As more and more hospitals, physicians and patients utilize these technological innovations the cost of health mounts higher and higher—and so does consumer demand. Herein lies the last, and in some sense most important, explanation for the continued explosion in health care costs.

Health—At Any Cost

It is difficult to conceive of anything more important or basic to human happiness, dignity and freedom than good health. The importance which Americans, individually and collectively, attach to maintaining and regaining good health and preventing ill-health is reflected in the billions of dollars ($287 billion in 1981 or more than $1225 per person) we spend on health care and in our expressed opinions on the subject. A 1981 Gallup Poll (*Report#198* March 1982) found that among the social values prized by Americans, the two most frequently cited as being most important were a good family life (82 percent mentioned this) and good physical health (mentioned by 81 percent).

On an individual basis the attitude seems to be that illness should be cured and life sustained "at any cost". It is the extraordinary value we attach to good health and the often emotional atmosphere within which medicine is practiced that make any effort to effectively contain costs so very difficult. As David Mechanic (1981, p. 3) has noted:

> The psychology of illness, and the importance that consumers give to their own medical care, make policy formulation particularly difficult. Reasonable consumers can see the logic of more efficient distribution and organization of services, more parsimonious use of laboratories and technologies, and allocating resources in some relation to expected benefits, but when sick, they want the best that medical sciences make possible.

In effect, when it comes to our own and our family's health, none of us are "reasonable" consumers. Cost, particularly since most of it is paid by third parties, is no object.

From a macro-economic or societal perspective, of course, cost is a matter of concern. How much can we as a nation afford to spend on health care? In 1950 4.4 percent of the GNP was devoted to health care, while in 1981, it was 9.8 percent. How much is enough to do the job, or is politically acceptable? Alain Enthoven is quoted in the *Congressional Record* (February 3, 1981, p. 845) as conceding "There is no magic number. The right number is the number people want it to be." Thus far the American public seems not to have reached the point where they are willing to concede that "enough is enough."

Price factors, utilization patterns, technological advances and the extraordinary value attached to health care combine to make for a seemingly unabated and uncontrollable explosion in health care costs. While consumers appear, at least for the time being, willing to pay the bill, policy makers who must set priorities each year, and suffer the consequences of their decisions, see the issue as an intolerable one. Before we examine some of the cost containment policy proposals, it would be useful to place the American experience in a comparative context. It is hoped that by broadening the geographic basis of the analysis, we might learn some useful lessons about what may or may not work in the battle against rising health care costs.

V. LESSONS FROM ABROAD

The Worldwide Explosion in Health Care Costs

For whatever comfort it may offer, data from other industrialized nations during the 1960s and 1970s indicates that the United States was by no means alone in suffering the burdens of increased health care costs. In fact, a recent study by Joseph Simanis and John Coleman of the Social Security Administration found that among nine industrialized nations during the period 1960-76 (See Table 2), the United States, in

Table 2. Health Care Expenditures as a Percentage of GNP Nine Industrialized Nations, Selected Years 1960–76

Country	1960	1965	1970	1975	1976
Australia	5.0	5.2	5.6	7.0	7.7
Canada	5.6	6.1	7.1	7.1	7.1
France	5.0	5.9	6.6	8.1	8.2
West Germany	4.4	5.2	6.1	9.7	NA
Netherlands	NA	5.0	6.3	8.6	8.5
Sweden	3.5	5.8	7.5	8.7	NA
United Kingdom	3.8	3.9	4.9	5.6	5.8
United States	5.3	5.9	7.2	8.4	8.6
Finland	4.2	5.2	5.9	6.8	7.2

Source: Joseph Simanis and John R. Coleman, "Health Care Expenditures in Nine Industrialized Countries," *Social Security Bulletin* 43 (January 1980), p. 5.

unadjusted expenditure figures, "had the lowest average annual rate of increase in actual expenditures during the entire study period" (Simanis and Coleman 1980, p. 4).

When the authors adjusted the annual rate of growth for change in the consumer price index for the nine countries, the U.S. ranked next to last. The annual rate of increase for each country (in percent) for the period 1969–76 was:

West Germany	11.30%
The Netherlands	9.69%
Australia	9.55%
France	7.39%
Finland	7.31%
Canada	6.65%
Sweden	6.29%
United States	5.93%
United Kingdom	5.13%

Finally, it should be noted that Simanis and Coleman found that as in the case of the United States, in each country the annual growth of health care costs exceeded both the overall rate of inflation and the growth rate of GNP. Although the relative rank-order of these countries may have changed since 1976, the problem of rapid increases in health care costs has not. And, while there undoubtedly are some idiosyncratic factors which might account for some of the increase, for the most part they are attributable to the same sources as in the United States: fee-for-service and third party reimbursement, expanded coverage, overall inflation, aging populations, increased use of new and expensive medical technology, and the importance attached to health and health care.

While they share a common problem, and for similar reasons, the various industrialized countries have tried a variety of policy approaches to deal with the problem. Because U.S. policy makers undoubtedly will look to the experiences of these countries, either to imitate their successes or avoid their failures, it would be useful to examine their experiences before turning to policy proposals being considered here in the United States.

Approaches to Cost-Containment

There are basically two approaches to containing health care costs (Roemer 1978, p. 104). The first seeks to control patient consumption of medical services through cost-sharing. In other words, it tries to influence the demand or consumer side of the equation. The second is geared toward making the medical establishment more economical in providing these services and products—i.e., supply side restraints.

Cost containment through cost-sharing (an important facet of the health care policy changes urged by American conservatives) is based upon the assumption discussed earlier that health care costs have risen as rapidly as they have, in part, because in most industrialized countries consumers (i.e., patients) do not feel the economic consequence of their consumption patterns. In every Western European country, in Japan and in other industrialized countries such as Canada, Australia, and New Zealand, health care costs for 90 percent or more of the population are paid for by third party, public carriers (i.e., either national health insurance or, in the case of Great Britain, a national health service). Because there is little or no direct financial impact on the consumers at the time of receiving medical care there is little or no incentive to be more economical in consuming medical services.

Most countries have adopted or experimented with some form or degree of cost-sharing but few view it as a major vehicle for cost control. Either patients pay a fee for physicians' (or less frequently hospital) services (e.g., Sweden, Japan, France, the Netherlands, Norway, Belgium, Australia) or for some ancilliary services like drugs or medical and dental appliances or eye glasses (e.g., West Germany, Great Britain, Canada). In many countries charges are not sufficiently high to have very much of an inhibiting effect on consumer behavior. In Sweden, for example, patients pay a net fee for each physician visit regardless of the amount of laboratory, x-ray, or other services provided. The fee, which is periodically revised, is calculated at 10 percent of a nationally determined "average" physician visit. When it was first adopted in 1970 the fee was seven kroner (or crowns) or about $1.48. In 1973 this was raised to 12 kroner which, according to its defenders, made an office visit still cheaper than a haircut (Shenkin 1973, p. 559). These increases do not appear to have had a profound affect on health care costs (see Table 2). In Germany, in which cost-sharing for physician and hospital services has never been used, there has been a minimal charge for prescription drugs. But even here large groups of people such as students, pensioners and war injured are excluded.

The evidence from most of the industrialized nations which have tried cost-sharing is that it does not constrain costs (Blanpain, Delesie and Nys 1978, p. 218). Milton Roemer, however, suggests there is one exception to this pattern. "There is evidence that co-payments selectively reduce the doctor's utilization [sic] by low-income families but not others, and for this reason is often waived for pensioners or other presumably poor persons" (1978, p. 104). Thus, for example, while there is a 20 percent cost-sharing provision in the Norwegian system for physician care and prescription drugs, these fees are waived for pensioners and the very poor (Roemer 1977, pp. 212-13). Because cost-sharing runs contrary to one of the fundamental principles underlying national health insurance systems, that is ensuring equal access to health care for all citizens, most nations have been reluctant to use it as a major mechanism for cost control. Instead, primary emphasis has been placed on controlling the supply rather than demand side of the health care system. While it is not possible to review all such efforts, some of the more popular, although not necessarily effective, policy efforts are examined below.

One approach that has been attempted, with some apparent success in Great Britain and West Germany, is to limit the amount of money available to the health care system each year. This strategy, called "global budgeting," was a major feature of the West German "Health Care Cost Containment Act" of 1977. The act provided for, among other things, annual cost ceilings on physician and dental services as well as prescription drugs. The decision on the ceiling for each year is made by a National Health Commission consisting of sixty representatives of the medical, insurance, employee, employers and governmental sectors. The law provided that the allowable rate of growth is to be pegged to certain economic indicators. Although it was somewhat early to determine its long-term impact, Deborah Stone (1979) found that initially the effort was succeeding in holding down the growth of health expenditures. Somewhat later on, Schrijvers (1981, p. 309) reported that global budgeting had been "rather successful in containing the total development of costs."

A related cost control effort is aimed at hospital costs. In Canada, New Zealand and many European countries officials have used a reimbursement procedure called prospective budgeting. As described by Roemer (1978, p. 107), " 'Prospective Budgeting' pays the hospital a global sum each month for the total operations, based on budget review, application of sound standards of staffing, and a reasonable occupancy level." Hospitals must then work within their budget—although, in Canada, supplemental grants can be made for justifiable extra expenses. The purpose of this approach is to encourage hospital administrators to use their resources more economically. Roemer (Ibid.) reports that ". . . Canadian hospitals are basically happy with the system and their costs have risen less than those in the United States."

Still another, and by far more popular, prospective cost control mechanism is the use of nationally set physician fee schedules. In countries such as Canada, France, West Germany, Great Britain and Japan, the amount of money physicians receive for their services is set through negotiations between various interested parties (e.g., insurance carriers, government, physicians, consumer groups, etc.). These negotiations have often been acrimonious since under a national health insurance system, this is the major opportunity for physicians to influence their income level and for government negotiators to contain costs.

In addition to the size of physicians' fees, the mode of remuneration has been the object of governmental attempts to control health care costs. The principal mode of physician reimbursement in non-Communist countries is fee-for-service whereby, as the name suggests, the physician is paid a set fee for each medical service performed. The more they do, the more they earn. In some countries, for example, Great Britain, Sweden, the Netherlands, and in parts of Denmark, physicians are salaried. Thus, there is no personal financial incentive to "over doctor." Salary levels, like fee schedules, are set in negotiations between concerned parties. One of the major innovations of the 1970 Swedish "Seven Kroner Reform" law was to change the Swedish system from a fee-for-service to a salary system. Indeed this was viewed as one of the major cost-containment provisions of the reform.

The approaches to cost control mentioned above all deal with the direct manipulation of the amount of money going into the health care system. Another approach has sought to limit the utilization of the system. The focus of this has been on physicians and hospitals, not the consumer. The starting point of this effort is the fee-for-service mechanism. Since, as described above, physician and hospital incomes are a function of how much they do, not only is there no incentive to conserve resources, there is a strong incentive to use those resources with abandon. Thus a number of countries, including the Netherlands, Belgium, Canada, and West Germany monitor the performance of physicians in terms of their rates of medical activity—e.g., how frequently they order blood tests, x-rays, certain drugs, etc. Although the systems differ, there is typically a peer review committee which establishes average or normal profiles for medical activity and reviews deviations from the norm. In West Germany, for example, this system is supported by a rather sophisticated and elaborate computer system. In addition, there is typically some form of disciplinary procedure—e.g. warnings, penalties, and even expulsion from health insurance practice (Roemer 1978, p. 105). In Canada errant physicians can "be charged the cost of procedures ordered beyond that which might be normally considered justifiable" (Armstrong 1978, pp. 98-99), while in Germany, where 90 percent of the population is covered under national health insurance, physicians can be prohibited from practicing in the system.

Yet another way governments have tried to control costs has been to manipulate, usually through limitation, the availability of health resources. Studies have shown, for example, that the use of surgery is positively correlated with the availability of surgeons; the more surgeons there are the more surgery performed. Thus several studies have found that the United States, with one of the world's highest proportion of surgeons among its physician population, has the highest rate of surgical procedures among industrialized nations (McPherson et. al. 1982; McPherson et. al. 1981).

In addition, hospital occupancy rates are positively correlated with the availability of hospital beds; the more hospital beds per population in a given area, the more likely a person is to be hospitalized. By placing national limitations on the availability of health resources, government officials hope to control unnecessary use of some of the more costly procedures such as surgery, recourse to hospitalization and high technology diagnostic procedures. Specific efforts along these lines have included government controls of: (1) The number of medical school students and limiting the number of places available in medical schools for certain specialties in order to encourage more general practitioners—e.g., France, the Netherlands, Sweden and West Germany (Blanpain, Delesie, Nys 1978, p. 251). (2) Hospital contruction and bed-to-population ratios—e.g., Canada, Japan, Belgium, West Germany, France and the Netherlands (Roemer 1978, p. 106; Glaser 1980, p. 108), and (3) Expensive medical technology through formal planning, certification of need, and licensing—e.g., France, the Netherlands, and West Germany (Blanpain, Delesie, Nys 1978, p. 251).

It is impossible to generalize about the effectiveness of these cost control mechanisms. In many instances the programs have only been recently introduced, while in others data are simply not yet available. In a recent study comparing the different approaches to the problem in West Germany, Canada and France, Uwe Reinhardt (1980, p. 156) concluded:

> At this time neither the 'classical market' approach favored in the United States, nor the 'quasi market' approach favored in West Germany, nor the more centrally directed systems of Canada and France can safely be judged a resounding success. For neither model has yet had a chance to be fully operative. Whatever approach one favors, however, one may find it instructive to keep an eye on the others.

It should be remembered that Stone and Schrijver's assessments of the West German "Health Cost Containment Act", which included expenditure ceilings and scrutinizing of physicians' utilization records, was that it seemed to be effective. Whatever the case, Reinhardt's recommendation that it may be instructive to monitor these efforts is well taken. At a minimum, it should certainly make us aware of the policy alternatives available to U.S. policy makers as they come to grips with the issue of cost containment.

VI. TO REGULATE OR DEREGULATE?

For the reasons developed in the beginning of this chapter, health cost containment has become a major policy issue and cause for academic debate in the United States since the early 1970s. Policy proposals generally have paralleled ideological lines. Liberals have recommended government regulation and conservatives deregualtion and increased reliance on market mechanisms. The major proposals of each side will be examined here and evaluated in the concluding section.

In the area of health care policy, as in others, liberals have favored the intervention of government to protect the interests of the public. In this case, two specific proposals have emerged. The most publicized and persistent is the recommendation that the United States adopt national health insurance, including a cost containment provision. While there have been several such proposals, the best known of these is that of Senator Edward Kennedy. Kennedy's proposal for a national health insurance program has known several cosponsors and formulations over the years. In one of its more recent incarnations it was cosponsored by Representative Henry Waxmen (D-California) and developed in conjunction with the labor coalition Committee for National Health Insurance. The bill, (The Health Care for All Americans Act) whose non-cost related details need not be discussed here, contained several proposals for reducing health care costs, many of which have been used abroad. Specifically, the bill proposes the following cost control mechanisms. First, Congress would set an overall annual budget for the national health care system—i.e., "global budgeting." Annual increases in the budget could not exceed the growth rate in the GNP—something which they have done for a decade or more.

Second, physicians' fees which would be paid by the health insurance system, would be negotiated between the medical profession and a national advisory board. These fees, like all other components of the health care system, would be part of, and limited by, the annual budget for the entire system. Third, hospital budgets would be set a year in advance and physicians and hospitals would be held responsible for exceeding those budgets. Fourth, the federal government would reimburse capital expenditure outlays only for *approved* medical projects. This latter provision is aimed at unnecessary increases in hospitals and hospital bed expansion. Finally, restrictions would be placed on the use of certain high risk and costly medical procedures. The Kennedy approach, which would mandate health insurance for everyone, is the most comprehensive proposal for dealing with all facets of the cost crisis. It is also the most difficult to "sell" politically.

A more modest, but ultimately no more successful, proposal was introduced by President Carter in 1977 and again in 1979. The Carter proposal was aimed at the largest and fastest growing facet of the health care bill namely, hospital costs. The original Carter-sponsored bill contained two major provisions. The first would have limited hospital cost increases in fiscal year 1978 to nine percent and to smaller increases in subsequent years. Any hospital that exceeded the nine percent limit would have to put the exceeded amount in escrow and reduce its following year's budget by the appropriate amount. The second provision would have set a limit of $2.5 billion a year for new hospital construction. The money would be allocated among the states based upon population and need (*Health Policy,* 1980, p. 23). The bill met with strong opposition from the hospital industry and had only lukewarm support among members of Carter's own party within Congress. Some, like Senator Kennedy and Congressman Paul Rogers (D-Florida), felt the bill did not go far enough. In any event the bill died in committee in both houses.

The bill was revived and revised in 1979 and made more attractive to the medical industry by including certain voluntary cost control efforts. Voluntary controls would be replaced by mandatory controls if the industry could not hold down costs. This bill proved no more popular than its predecessor and suffered a similar fate. In 1980 the Democrats lost control of the White House and the Senate. The regulatory path to health cost containment now appeared less likely, but not impossible.

Another regulatory effort, aimed at both cost and quality control, was the introduction in 1972 of professional standards review organizations (PSROs). These organizations were intended to encourage doctors within a geographical area to monitor the professional practices and procedures of their colleagues in dealing with Medicaid or Medicare patients. If the PSRO determines that the physician is not conforming with the treatment standards set by the organization, it may warn the physician and, if there is no behavioral change, exclude him/her from participating in Medicaid and Medicare. The original law (PL 92-603) provided that if local physicians did not voluntarily set up their own PSRO, the government would designate a group. The medical profession vigorously opposed the system and was able to win postponement of its implementation. Even today, a decade after its passage, the PSRO law has not been fully implemented and in the areas where it has, the results have been mixed in terms of improved quality of care and decreased costs.

The advent of the Reagan Presidency and strong conservative support within Congress opened the prospect that a quite different approach to health cost containment might be taken. Indeed, in June, 1981 then Secretary of Health and Human Services Richard Schweiker announced that: "This Administration is committed to trying something new. We intend to loose the forces of the market to make the health care system more competitive" (*New York Times* June 12, 1981).

How would increased competition and reliance on the marketplace help bring health care costs down? Reagan Administration officials such as Schweiker and Budget Director David Stockman, a number of Congressional advocates, and academic economists like Alain Enthoven argued that the main problem lies in the system's financing mechanism and particularly third party carriers. It will be recalled that the major criticism of this mechanism is that consumers and providers have no incentive to be economically prudent because the tab is picked up by the third party—Blue Cross, Blue Shield, Medicare, etc.

The Reagan Administration developed a package of legislative plans, the essential parts of which were already embodied in the "Health Incentives Reform Act (1981)" sponsored by Senators David Durenberger (R-MN), David Boren (D-OK) and, John Heinz (R-PA) and proposed two years earlier by Professor Alain Enthoven for the Carter Administration. Enthoven's plan, called Consumer-Choice Health Plan, was rejected by President Carter. In 1981, the essence of the plan was resurrected in the Heath Incentive Reform Act, and contained a three-pronged attack on health costs. First, the Act would limit the amount that employers could deduct as a business expense for their employees' health benefits package. Such a ceiling would discourage employers from increasing employee health care benefits. Second, it would encourage employers to offer employees a choice of competing health care plans. Here it is hoped that employees, who would be allowed to choose among plans each year, would shop around for the best buy in medical coverage. Theoretically health care insurance providers would have to offer plans with good coverage, at reasonable rates, to attract and keep members. Third, each employee would get a fixed and equal amount toward his/her health care plan. Thus, if a person chooses a plan more costly than covered, he/she would have to pay the difference themselves. On the other hand, if he/she chooses a plan that costs less than the employer's contribution he/she could keep the difference. The assumption is that employers will offer and employees will choose less costly and, therefore, less comprehensive plans in which there would be more out-of-pocket payments—and more cost-consciousness when seeking medical care.

In a related plan, the Reagan Administration proposed the introduction of a voucher system whereby Medicare recipients would be given a voucher equal to the amount for which they were eligible. Recipients would then shop around for medical coverage. If they choose a plan that costs less than their allocation, and undoubtedly would require greater out-of-pocket expense, they would keep the difference. If they choose a more costly and comprehensive plan they, not the government, would pay the difference. Here too the assumption is of greater frugality, more out-of-pocket payments and greater cost consciousness.

The final part of the package was a proposed tax credit to employers who offered low-cost, group health plan options. These plans, called Health Maintenance Organizations (HMOs), are prepaid medical programs in which members pay a set monthly fee regardless of the actual medical services provided. HMOs provide an alternative to the fee-for-service approach. When individuals need medical attention they go to the HMO medical center, where they are seen by one of the staff physicians from a wide variety of medical specialities. The fees paid to the HMO become, in effect, its' budget. It is in the interests of the HMO to keep costs within budget to avoid deficits and enjoy a profit. Theoretically there will be no unnecessary tests, office visits or hospitalization because the physicians and staff have an interest in keeping costs down.

The Reagan proposals were not well received either in Congress or among various interest groups. In a rare show of agreement, almost all the participants—major businesses and organized labor, medical groups, and the insurance industry—attacked some or all of the proposals. No action on any of these was taken in the 97th Congress, although the Administration resubmitted parts of the program to the 98th Congress.

The sense of frustration that the Administration felt and their perception that the continuing problem required some action, even if that action was ideologically obnoxious, is reflected in a statement by an Assistant Secretary in the Department of Health and Human Services. "The health-provider industry is betting that if we cannot get competition, we're going to do nothing. They are making an error. If we have to make a choice between regulating or deficit financing, we're going to go to regulation" (*The Oregonian*, March 14, 1982). Similar sentiments were being expressed at the time by Senate Finance Committee chairman Robert Dole (R-Kansas) who said that Congress may have "made a mistake in not supporting President Carter's mandatory cost containment bill. Maybe we should go back and take a look" (Quoted in Richards, 1982, p. 82).

In the latter part of 1982, the Reagan Administration proposed yet another cost containment plan—and one which seemingly abandoned a free-market approach to controlling health care costs. The plan was in response to a Congressional mandate that the Secretary of Health and Human Services propose a cost containment program for Medicare by December 31, 1982. Congressional and Administration concern with Medicare stems from the fact that it has become one of the most expensive and fastest growing of all Federal programs. Begun in 1966, Medicare cost $4.7 billion in its first full year of operation. By 1981 the program cost $44.8 billion. The 1981 figure represented a 21.5 percent increase over the previous year! "The primary reason for this increase is the rapid escalation of outlays for hospital care" (Gibson and Waldo, 1982, p. 11).

The Reagan proposal to contain Medicare hospital costs is based upon two practices widely used in countries with national health insurance:

prospective budgeting, and diagnostic-related group (DRG) reimbursement. Under the proposal, the Federal government would pay all hospitals treating Medicare patients the same amount, fixed in advance, for
particular diagnoses. The Department of Health and Human Services
proposed establishing 467 DRGs—e.g., heart attack, hip replacement,
cataract removal, etc.—and each hospital would be paid a predeter-
mined fee for each procedure, although some regional variation in
charges would be allowed. Currently hospitals and physicians treating
Medicare patients are reimbursed for the "customary, prevailing and
reasonable charges" with no limits on procedures or tests. This system
has led to both rapidly rising and virtually uncontrollable cost increases,
and remarkable national variation. For example, Medicare has been
charged as little as $2100 for a hip replacement and as much as $8200; it
has paid $450 for a cataract removal at one hospital and $2800 at another—and all of this with no apparent difference in the quality of
health care provided.

By standardizing reimbursement for specific diagnoses, the Reagan
Administration hoped to eliminate such disparities, as well as control the
growth of health care costs. Each hospital in the country would receive,
for example, $3200 for a heart attack patient covered by Medicare,
regardless of how long the patient remained hospitalized—currently the
range for treating heart attack patients is $1500 to $9000. If a hospital's
costs were less than $3200, it would keep the difference; if higher, they
would swallow the loss. Under no circumstances could a hospital bill a
patient if his costs exceeded the Medicare fee. Hospitals, it was argued,
would have a strong incentive to control costs under this system.

The Reagan proposal for prospective budgeting, which was approved
by Congress in April 1983 and went into effect on October 1, 1983,
represents a retreat from the free market approach to Medicare cost
containment represented by the voucher system and to which he has
been so philosophically attached. That he would swallow his ideological
pride and accept what is essentially a regulatory approach to health cost
control is a measure of his (and others) frustration toward this seemingly
intractable problem.

VII. EVALUATION AND CONCLUSIONS

Assuming for the moment that the major alternatives available to American policy makers are either government intervention in the form of
mandatory cost controls or the encouragement of greater competition
within the medical marketplace, what can we expect from these policies?
Let us look first at the case for regulation.

There is no doubt that health care costs can be limited by imposing annual ceilings either on all expenditures, as proposed by Senator Kennedy, or on hospitals, as proposed by President Carter, or on Medicare. This is not to say that costs would not rise. In most such proposals the growth of health expenditures is pegged to some economic indicator such the Consumer Price Index or growth rate of the GNP. Thus, health costs would continue to rise but not, as they have over the past decade, at a rate exceeding that of other goods and services.

The real issue in the use of mandatory global or sector cost controls is not their economic or technical feasibility but rather their political acceptability. First, there is now, as there has been for decades, the prospect of strong and typically successful opposition from the medical industry which has long opposed both national health insurance and mandatory cost restraints. To achieve mandatory expenditure ceilings, either within the framework of national health insurance, or even a more limited effort aimed at hopital costs only, would be a legislative achievement of rather significant proportions.

Second, it should be recognized that setting and maintaining fiscally prudent health expenditure ceilings will require legislative statesmanship of the highest order. Public pressure for more and better health services, not curtailment of those services, will be enormous. In this effort the public will find, of course, a ready ally in the medical industry. The experiences of such nations as West Germany, Canada, Japan and Great Britain demonstrate that the medical establishment, especially when it has public support, can be a formidable adversary when it comes time to negotiate fees for medical services.

Finally, it should be recognized that truly effective cost containment may result in a decline in the quality of medical care in the United States. The industrialized nation that has been most successful in containing the growth of health care costs is Great Britain (see Table 2). However, the British National Health Service has been criticized, on both sides of the Atlantic, for the long lists of patients waiting to see specialists, or for a bed in a hospital for non-critical surgery. It is not at all unusual for someone to wait months to see a specialist and years for a vaccant bed in a hospital. It would be wrong to suggest that successful cost containment in the United States would result in the medical resource problems experienced by the British. There are too many differences between the two countries, which we can not go into, to make such a conclusion valid. Nevertheless, global or sectoral cost-containment would require some adjustments in the medical resource consumption patterns of Americans—e.g., fewer diagnostic tests, greater use of semi-private rooms or wards, shorter hospital stays, etc.

In addition, some critics of the Reagan Administration's prospective reimbursement program argue that it might encourage hospitals to specialize either in private patients, or Medicare/Medicaid patients. The latter group of publicly insured patients might end up with access only to less expensive, and perhaps less attentive and competent, health care. In effect, the country would have a two-track health care system: one for the poor and elderly, and one for the rest of the people. Even worse, some argue that hospitals simply may turn away Medicare patients who require costly and long term care because it would be unprofitable to treat them.

It is somewhat more difficult to evaluate the conservatives' competition/marketplace approach to cost containment for unlike liberal proposals these have not been tried by any nation in this century. Indeed much of the attraction of this approach is that it has not yet been tested and found wanting. Thus a recent *New York Times* (March 6, 1982) editorial while advising caution in this area still concluded that: "The economy cannot long endure runaway medical costs. It's time to find out whether a competitive health care market will make the bill more affordable." Despite the absence of direct experience with cost containment through competition, some speculative comments can be offered.

To begin, as the *New York Times* editorial noted, a limitation on tax deductability for health care benefits will not have as dramatic an impact as supporters predict because it will not affect that many employers. "Merely limiting tax deductability would not alter the behavior of nonprofit and public agencies, employing 40 percent of workers; they have no liability to begin with."

Second, competition advocates assume that, if given the choice, Americans will opt for less extensive and expensive health care coverage with more out-of-pocket payments. The evidence on this, however, is at best mixed. A *New York Times* (March 29, 1982) national health survey found that 45 percent of the people were willing to enroll in less expensive plans even if it meant more out-of-pocket payments. Forty-four percent, however, were unwilling to do so and the remainder had no opinion. In theory then there does appear to be some support for purchasing less costly insurance. Actual experience with Medicare, however, casts some doubt on this hypothetical commitment. The House Committee on Aging found that in 1978, 15 of the 23 million older Americans covered by Medicare spent nearly $4 billion to supplement their coverage. Furthermore, the desire for more health care security, in the form of more comprehensive insurance, is not restricted to the elderly. A study of federal employees found "that many younger people, too, would rather pay high premiums for high-option health coverage than pay medical costs out of their own pockets" (*Health Policy*, p. 37). The evidence does not appear to give strong support to the theory that if given a choice among programs, people will opt for the less costly ones.

In addition, one may question the average citizen's ability to make a rational economic choice among competing health plans. Clearly, the bottom line dollar figure is not the only relevant factor in making a decision about health insurance. The House Committee on Aging found that "Nearly $1 billion of the $4 billion Medicare recipients spent on supplementary coverage in 1978 went for overlapping coverage, with the elderly purchasing double or triple coverage for some things while omitting others completely . . ." (*Health Policy,* p. 37).

In short, there is some reason to question the purported effectiveness of the market/competition approach to containing health care costs. This, combined with the resistance of the key actors in the health care system, makes adoption of the approach as problematic as that of cost control within the context of national health insurance. Where then does one go from here? I do not presume to have an answer, but I would suggest that at this point we may not yet have reached the point where anything has to be done. The reason for this lies in the nature of health and health care as a policy issue.

The problem with devising an appropriate and acceptable health care policy is that in many respects it is a politically, economically and psychologically unique issue area. While it is true, for example, that health costs are rising more rapidly than other goods and services, that is not the same as saying they are rising too rapidly or that we are spending too much on health care. Is 9.8 percent of the GNP too much or is 12 percent too much? The right number *is,* as Alain Enthoven has said, the number people want it to be. Thus far there does not appear to be as much public concern as there is elite concern over the size of the nation's health care bill. Until the time that health care costs so crowd expenditures in other areas, so that other goods and services must be sacrificed, it is not likely that policy makers will be able to overcome the resistance of organized interest groups like the AMA or the American Hospital Association. As long as Americans give a "higher priority to the growth of medical investment than to expenditures for education, transportation, or urban problems" (Mechanic 1981, p. 2), a fundamental assault on health care costs is unlikely.

REFERENCES

Armstrong, Robert A. "Canadian Lessons About Health-Care Costs." *Bulletin of the New York Academy of Medicine* 54 (1978): 84-101.

Blanplain, Jan; Delesie, Luc, and Nys, Herman. *National Health Insurance and Health Resources: The European Experience.* Cambridge, Ma.: Harvard University Press, 1978.

Demkovich, Linda. "Who Can do a Better Job of Controlling Hospital Costs?" *National Journal* 11 (1979a): 219-223.

———. "Cutting Health Care Costs—Why Not Let The Market Decide." *National Journal* 11 (1979b): 1796-1800.

Dolbeare, Kenneth M. *American Public Policy*. New York: McGraw-Hill, 1982.

Elling, Ray. *Cross-National Studies of Health Systems*. New Brunswick: Transaction Books, 1980.

Enthoven, Alain C. *Health Plan: The Only Practical Solution to the Soaring Cost of Medical Care*. Reading, Mass.: Addison-Wesley, 1980.

Friedman, Milton and Friedman, Rose. *Free To Choose*. New York: Harcourt Brace Jovanovich, 1980.

Gibson, Robert M., and Fisher, Charles R. "Age Differences in Health Care Spending, Fiscal Year 1977." *Social Security Bulletin* 42 (1977): 3-16.

Gibson, Robert M., and Waldo, Daniel R. "National Health Expenditures, 1981." *Health Care Financing Review* 4 (1982): 1-35.

Glaser, William A. "Politics of Cost Control Abroad." *Bulletin of the New York Academy of Medicine* 56 (1980): 107-114.

Goldfarb, Marsha G.; Hornbrook, Mark C.; Kelly, Joyce V., and Monheit, Alan C. "National Health Expenditures." In *Health United States, 1980*, pp. 101-106. Hyattsville, Maryland: Department of Health and Human Services, 1980.

Health Policy: The Legislative Agenda. Washington, D.C.: Congressional Quarterly, 1980.

Leichter, Howard. *A Comparative Approach to Policy Analysis*. New York: Cambridge University Press, 1979.

———. "Comparative Public Policy: Problems and Prospects." *Policy Studies Journal* 5 (1977): 583-595.

Lindsay, Cotton, ed. *New Directions in Public Health Care*. San Francisco: Institute for Contemporary Studies, 1980.

McPherson, K; Strong, P.M.; Epstein, A., and Jones, L. "Regional Variations in the Use of Common Surgical Procedures: Within and Between England and Wales, Canada and the United States." *Social Science and Medicine* 15A (1981): 273-288.

McPherson, K.; Wennberg, J.; Hovind, O., and Clifford, P. "Small-area Variation in the Use of Common Surgical Procedures: An International Comparison of New England, England, and Norway." *New England Journal of Medicine* 307 (1982): 1310-1314.

Mechanic, David. "Some Dilemmas in Health Care Policy." *Health and Society* 59 (1981): 1-15.

Reinhardt, Uwe E. "Health Insurance and Cost-Containment Policies: The Experience Abroad." *American Economic Review* 70 (1980): 149-156.

Richards, Glenn. "Cost Containment: The Heat is On and Up." *Hospitals* 56 (1982): 82-86.

Riska, Eleanor. "Paradigms in the Study of Health." *Policy Studies Journal* 9 (1980-81): 198-205.

Roemer, Milton. "National Health Insurance as an Agent for Containing Health-Care Costs." *Bulletin of the New York Academy of Medicine* 54 (1978): 102-112.

———. *Comparative National Policies on Health Care*. New York: Marcel Dekker, 1977.

Schrijvers, Guus. "Cost Control: A Multi-disciplinary Approach." *Social Science and Medicine* 15A (1981): 307-311.

Shenkin, Budd N. "Politics and Medical Care in Sweden: The Seven Crowns Reform." *New England Journal of Medicine*. 11 (1973): 555-559.

Simanis, Joseph G., and Coleman, John R. "Health Care Expenditures in Nine Industrialized Countries." *Social Security Bulletin* 43 (1980): 3-8.

Stone, Deborah A. "Obstacles to Learning from Comparative Health Research." *Policy Studies Journal* 9 (1980-81): 278-285.

————. "Health Cost Containment in West Germany." *Journal of Health Politics, Policy and Law* 4 (1979): 173-199.

United States Congress-Senate. *Congressional Record* 127: 845. Washington, D.C.: Government Printing Office, Feb. 3, 1981.

United States Department of Health and Human Services. *Health United States, 1980.* Washington, D.C.: Government Printing Office, 1980.

WOMEN AND PUBLIC POLICIES:
COMPARATIVE PERSPECTIVES ON
WELFARE MOTHERS

Ellen Boneparth

I. INTRODUCTION

Why, in the mid-1980s, twenty years after the emergence of the second wave of feminism in the United States, should it be necessary to include a chapter especially devoted to women in a new collection of policy studies? It is not as if women's policy demands are new items on the policy agenda. To the contrary, over the past two decades the contemporary women's movement has not only become more and more vociferous, but also more and more sophisticated in making public policy demands (Bernard, 1971; Boneparth, 1982; Cardin, 1977; Gelb and Palley, 1982; Freeman, 1979). Moreover, some of these demands have been incorporated into policy and others, although ignored or rejected by policy-makers, nevertheless remain topics for debate.

The answer to the question of why a chapter on women is needed lies in the fact that while some modest gains have been made by women in their struggle for policy change, the status of women in the United States has not only *not* improved dramatically but, rather, has remained unchanged in some areas, and has deteriorated in others.

Why have past approaches to public policy not achieved greater progress toward ameliorating the condition of women? It is not sufficient to argue that progress has been impeded by male policymakers who are insensitive to women's needs. While there is no question that demands have often fallen on deaf ears, it is also clear that women, themselves, whether acting as lobbyists, legislators, administrators or activists have also failed to avoid many of the pitfalls of the policymaking process. A brief survey of past approaches to public policy illustrates some of these pitfalls as well as the need for a fundamentally different approach to policymaking.

II. PAST APPROACHES

It is both obvious and yet necessary to reiterate that historically women's interests as workers, wives and mothers have been invisible to policymakers who, even with the best intentions, have cast issues in terms which fail to acknowledge women's stake in them. A good illustration of this phenomenon is the effort to achieve a national system of child care in the late 1960s and early 1970s (Norgren, 1982). The demand for child care centers in the United States has historically been based on the needs of children who are socially, economically or educationally deprived. When other aspects of child care have been discussed at all, the benefits have been seen as making better use of women's labor, as in World War II when women were needed as workers in defense industries, or as solving some other policy problem, such as the escalating costs of welfare for mothers who might work if child care were available. Neither of these justifications is likely, however, to generate sufficient support for the establishment of a national child care system. Why not? Because, in the latter case, child care centers are more expensive to establish and maintain than the present system of welfare and, in the former case, the need for female labor is only acknowledged in crisis situations.

The point is that child care has never been promoted by policymakers in the United States as a *right* of working mothers, or, more appropriately, as a right of working parents. When President Nixon vetoed the Comprehensive Child Care Act of 1972 because of its "family-weakening implications" and Congress failed even to attempt to override that veto, the losers were perceived to be the childrens' and public educational lobbies rather than the millions of working and nonworking mothers and fathers who were suffering from the inability to integrate work and family roles.

Even when women's interests in public policy are visible and correctly represented, women can, nevertheless, be made scapegoats for policy failures. A good example is the issue of pregnancy and employment rights. No less a body than the Supreme Court has taken a punitive view of pregnancy, arguing in the *General Electric v. Gilbert* case that is is not discriminatory to exclude pregnancy from company health plans, even if exclusively male illnesses are covered, because not *all* women get pregnant (Huckle, 1982). The clear implication is that female workers who get pregnant are doing their employers a disservice. Nowhere in the court's holding is it suggested that women are serving society by producing the next generation. Moreover, a more liberal Congress in trying to rectify the Supreme Court's injustice by amending legislation to include pregnancy as grounds for non-discrimination put its own stamp on the policy by making it possible to exclude abortion from health insurance coverage. Thus, if a woman becomes pregnant, she can get insurance coverage for having a child, but not for terminating a pregnancy. Under present law, she is a scapegoat not for choosing motherhood, but for *not* choosing motherhood.

III. THE NEED FOR A FEMINIST PERSPECTIVE

Given past approaches to women and public policy, a feminist policy perspective is sorely needed to assure that women's interests are visible and properly represented, and to counter attempts to make women scapegoats for public policy failures. What are the key ingredients of a feminist perspective? First, a feminist perspective must account for the variety of women's interests, that is, for the needs of women from various ethnic, socioeconomic, family, and occupational backgrounds. The white, middle class biases of women's policy successes in the last twenty years reveal how limited past policy approaches have been (Freeman, 1982; Gittell and Naples, 1982). While white working class and middle class women have benefitted somewhat from anti-discrimination policies championed by liberal reformers, poor women, third world women, and older women have only rarely been the target of public policy change and then, relatively unsuccessfully.

Second, a feminist perspective would not only encompass women from all social categories but would also examine the costs and benefits of policy change for men as well as women. Past efforts have fallen into the trap of identifying issues as "women's issues" implying that if there are *benefits* for women, there must be *costs* for men. A feminist perspective, however, does not view policy change as a zero-sum game but rather demonstrates that where there are direct policy benefits for women, there are direct or indirect benefits for men. As seen above, child care is not uniquely a woman's issue but an issue for working parents.

Violence against women is not only a pressing problem for women but also a pressing problem for the male friends and family of female victims. A feminist policy perspective, therefore, would reorient cost/benefit analysis from female versus male, to costs versus benefits for women *and* men.

Lastly, a feminist perspective would move beyond the short-term benefits of policy change for women to assessing the long-term impact of policy on sex roles. The issue of occupational segregation provides a useful example of the need for analysis of long-term impacts. A considerable amount of time and money in the 1970s went into apprenticeship programs designed to train and employ women in nontraditional jobs. Yet, by the end of the 1970s, the workforce was more sex-segregated than ever before. In fact, the most successful attempts to eliminate occupational segregation based on sex occurred as a result of men moving into traditionally female jobs rather than the reverse.

Why were these apprenticeship programs unsuccessful? They failed in part because they did not recognize the durability of traditional sex-role socialization and the limited potential of training programs to overcome it. Indeed, policy to reduce the sex-segregation of the workforce might be more successful if aimed at youth through the educational process as is done in Sweden, even though this policy is long-term, than at adults whose attitudes are less susceptible to change (Organization for Economic Cooperation and Development, 1975: 45). What is needed, then, is a kind of sex-role impact analysis as an element of a feminist perspective in order to assure that short-term policy objectives are compatible with and likely to achieve long-term goals.

The area of public policy most frequently tackled by activists seeking to change the status of women has been employment (Freeman, 1975, 1982). A case study of employment policy illustrates all of the problems associated with traditional approaches to policy change for women as well as all the potential benefits of approaching issues from a feminist perspective.

IV. EMPLOYMENT POLICY

From the end of World War II until 1963, female workers were virtually invisible to public policymakers. This was true despite the fact that rising rates of female employment have been the most dramatic aspect of change in the labor force in the postwar period. How do we explain this invisibility? First, American society during the 1950s was caught up in the ideology of female domesticity and, while women's lives were rapidly changing, there was a considerable time lag before myths about women's fulfillment in the home were replaced by more realistic assessments of the rewards of homemaking compared to other pursuits (Friedan, 1963). Secondly, and more importantly, it was impossible to recognize the role of women in the workforce without alerting society to the oppressed position of women workers. Thus, it was functional to ignore women, relegating them to the ranks of marginal workers, either concentrated in part-time jobs where they lacked access to fringe benefits and were victims of discriminatory pay, or segregated into full-time but low-paying, low-status clerical and service jobs.

When women workers were ultimately recognized in the 1960s, efforts to effect policy change were, for the most part, biased on behalf of middle class women. The bias occurred because of the emphasis on the elimination of discrimination in pay and hiring and promotion through equal opportunity legislation and affirmative action. These policies affected women who not only already were working, but who also worked for firms employing a maximum number of employees. Women in the most vulnerable economic positions—pink collar workers, unemployed women or women marginally employed in small businesses—were not covered by the new legislation. Thus, while some middle class women benefitted from equal opportunity policies, the largest proportion of women, women who needed help the most, were untouched by them. Since many of the women in the lowest paying, lowest status jobs are minority women, the emphasis on anti-discrimination policy as opposed to full employment or higher pay can be seen as racist as well as classist.

Two policies did address the needs of unemployed women or women at the bottom of the occupational scale, CETA (the Comprehensive Training and Employment Act), which was designed to train economically disadvantaged, unemployed workers for jobs (Women's Bureau, 1980a), and Social Security for household workers (U.S. Department of Health, Education and Welfare, 1979), were important initiatives but insignificant compared to the dire needs to expand job opportunities and to improve pay scales.

An equally serious failure of public policy on female employment in the 1960s and 1970s was its inattention to the problem of women's dual burden of work inside and outside the home. Public policy dictated that women entering the work force should pattern themselves after male workers, keeping the same schedules, seeking the same benefits, and adapting to the world of work in the same manner. Once again, women's interests misrepresented as being the same as those of men when, in fact, the greatest need of women in the workforce is to resolve the home/work split (Bernard, 1974, 1975; Boneparth and Stoper, 1983). Rather than developing policy which eases the burden of childbearing and childrearing on women workers as has been done throughout Europe (Cook, 1978), U.S. policy has made clear, both explicitly and implicitly, that women who combine motherhood and employment are expected to shoulder all responsibility for the two activities. While other industrial democracies have instituted paid maternity and paternity leaves, systems of child care centers, family allowances and flexible work schedules for parents, the U.S. lags far behind in assisting parents to adapt to the world of work (Kamerman and Kahn, 1978).

V. SINGLE FEMALE HEADS OF HOUSEHOLDS

All of these policy failures converge in the case of the single female head of household. She has been relatively invisible to policymakers except as the negative stereotype of the irresponsible, promiscuous welfare recipient. Furthermore, she has been consistently misrepresented as seeking greater dependency through increased government benefits rather than a measure of independence through employment. She has been made the scapegoat for many other policy concerns—rising rates of divorce, illegitimacy and juvenile delinquency and rising costs of welfare—at the same time that she has been the target of budget cuts for family planning, child care, Social Security, food stamps, medical services and basic support payments (Ross and Sawhill, 1975).

The single female head of household is at the heart of the problem when we examine the failures of employment policy affecting women. She is neither seeking promotion to a managerial position nor work as a plumber. She simply wants a job or, if she is working, to make enough money to support herself and her family. She wants to work *and* care for her children, and she wants to climb out of the grinding poverty which makes her the largest population category—35 percent—below the poverty line (*Newsweek*, January 17, 1983, p.27). Moreover, her numbers are escalating. The National Advisory Council on Economic Opportunity predicts that "all other things being equal, if the proportion of the poor in female-households families were to increase at the same rate as it did from 1967 to 1978, the poverty population would be composed solely of women and their children before the year 2000" (Ehrenreich and Stallard, 1982: 217).

In the post World War II period, the plight of the single female head of household worsened dramatically, especially in light of rising rates of divorce, desertion, teenage pregnancy and female unemployment. In the last half of the 1970s single female heads of households became the fastest growing population group of workers as noted by the Women's

Bureau in its report on the U.S. Employment Goals in the World Plan of Action:

> The labor force participation rate of mothers who had ever been married remained stable at the last half of the decade (the 1970s) at about 50 percent. After 1975, however, there was rapid growth in the number of women whose husbands were absent (divorced, deceased, or separated) and who had children of school age or pre-school age. The number grew from 2.7 million to 3.3 million, or over 19 percent, from 1975 to 1979.
>
> Although married women with husbands present were the fastest growing group earlier in the decade, by the mid-decade they were displaced by the more rapidly increasing number of single women who maintain families (Women's Bureau, 1980b: 4).

Women who maintain families have the highest levels of female participation in the labor force. Because they are generally poor and less well-educated, "they are overrepresented in occupations associated with higher unemployment rates compared with other segments of the labor force" (Women's Bureau, 1980b: 4). In 1979, the unemployment rate for single mothers was approximately 21 percent; typically the family had no other employed person when the mothers were out of work (Women's Bureau, 1980b: 4).

What are the specific needs of the single female head of household? First and foremost she needs financial support for herself and her family. The more fortunate of these women receive child and/or spousal support from divorced husbands. However, the delinquency rate on court-ordered support payments is extremely high and rising (Ross and Sawhill, 1975: 175–177). Even those women who do receive support payments are disadvantaged as few divorce agreements include escalator clauses to keep pace with inflation. There has been some discussion in recent years of utilizing the federal bureaucracy to collect support payments, a proposal which was included ironically, in the New Right's legislative package, the Family Protection Act. In California, Assembly Bill 3693 was introduced in 1982 to raise court ordered child support payments seven percent annually. Neither of these proposals, however, has met with any groundswell of enthusiasm.

Many single heads of households whether divorced, separated or never married, do not receive private support of any kind and rely on public welfare payments (in the form of Aid to Families with Dependent Children) which create as many problems as they solve. First, they institutionalize dependency by removing the immediate necessity for employment or education and training. Second, they support families at such modest levels that they perpetuate the cycle of poverty. Third, they stigmatize the recipient as "needy" which in American culture translates to "unfit" and which explains why some of the eligible do not apply for benefits (Rodgers, 1982: 11; Ross and Sawhill, 1975: 103–4). Thus, government benefits, rather than improving the status of women, have made single female heads of household the least able of any population group to alter their social situation.

The alternative to government benefits is, of course, employment. A successful employment program for single heads of household must involve two elements—a new supply of decent-paying jobs and child care. The obstacles to achieving full employment in the U.S. are many, given its long standing antipathy toward public employment and its contemporary aversion to spending for social programs. To make matters worse, the technological revolution presently occurring in the world of information-processing may, in the near future, create an even greater shortage of jobs in technical and clerical fields, women's greatest source of employment (Stein and Brown, 1982).

Even if job opportunities were to expand, single heads of households with young children would be unable to avail themselves of these opportunities without child care. This obvious truth has been taken into account throughout Western and Eastern Europe where child care has been incorporated as a key element of economic policy (Cook, 1978: 31–36; Kamerman and Kahn, 1978; Organization for Economic Cooperation and Development, 1975: 75–87). Ironically, the United States which has one of the highest proportions of single to married parents of any industrialized democracy has one of the least developed systems of child care. Until child care is acknowledged as an inseparable element of employment policy, employment policies of any kind will *ipso facto* disadvantage women.

A last critical policy need of single female heads of households is housing and transportation. Single women pay a far greater proportion of their income (57 percent) for housing than single men (30 percent) or married couples (22 percent), both because their incomes are low and because their housing needs—safe neighborhoods and rental units which accept and are suitable for children—are relatively costly (Diamond, 1982; National Council of Negro Women, 1975). The housing problem is compounded by the single head of household's need for transportation to work, child care facilities, schools, and shopping. While not as imminently related to employment policy as child care, housing and transportation are crucial elements of any policy specifically designed to alleviate the dual burdens of work and family. Many observers have noted the interrelationship of family, employment and housing needs for women in advocating urban design which integrates residential and commercial areas (Hayden, 1980). While some countries, particularly Scandinavia, have developed new communities based on these principles (Nordstrom, 1981), social considerations have yet to become paramount in urban planning in the U.S.

VI. COMPARATIVE PERSPECTIVES

The plight of the single female head of household in the United States is even more vivid when viewed in comparative perspective. While in other industrialized countries the needs of unmarried women with children are addressed in varying degrees, very few countries have relegated these women to the situation of dependency found in the United States. An examination of public policy in several other countries highlights both the potential to enable single female heads of households to participate as productive members of society, and the obstacles to achieving such a goal in the American society.

Family Policy in Sweden

The best example of a society which has utilized public policy to assist women (and men) in integrating their productive and reproductive functions is Sweden where family policy has had an explicit governmental focus since the 1930s when it was developed in response to the need to increase the population and the labor force (Liljestrom, 1978: 19). Today, the goals of Swedish family policy include protecting unmarried mothers and their children, increasing population, equalizing family incomes and achieving sexual equality within and outside the family (Liljestrom, 1978: 19–20). Moreover, the definition of the family has been adapted to changing lifestyles with the result that, unlike most other industrialized nations, the traditional nuclear family is no longer either the explicit or implicit model for public policy.

The specific premise underlying policy toward single-parent families in Sweden is that the state must assume the role of the missing parent in order that the family may function effectively (Liljestrom, 1978: 23). This goal has almost been achieved. While single-parent families do not enjoy as high a standard of living as two-parent families, they neither suffer the social stigmas associated with divorce or illegitimacy in other countries nor are they maintained by a system of governmental handouts (Liljestrom, 1978: 23).

Before examining the specific efforts made in Sweden to support the single parent, it is necessary to understand in a general way the extent to which Swedish social policy provides for family needs. Income maintenance policies include family, rent and maintenance allowances. Parenting receives explicit support through paid "child leaves" equal to 90 percent of income for nine months after birth which are available for *either* parent, as are 15 days of paid leave per year for caring for sick children. In addition, childminders (babysitters) are employed by child care centers to care for sick children when parents cannot or do not choose to take time off from their jobs (Ruggie, 1981: 174).

Child care centers, including after-school centers, are heavily subsidized; center fees account for a smaller percentage of female wages than in most other industrialized countries (Kamerman and Kahn, 1982, p.192). The state's heavy investment in child care in Sweden is viewed not simply as a benefit for working parents but also as a benefit for the whole society by providing high quality early childhood education (Darling, 1980: 54). Moreover, the Governmental Family Policy Committee has elected to support child care centers over child care allowances in order to encourage mothers of small children to remain in the workforce (Liljestrom, 1978: 40).

The support for families in Sweden is, of course, in line with the extensive provision of public services found in a highly developed welfare state. While family policy has evolved in response to the changing needs of families in society, it has also, interestingly enough, stimulated change in family patterns. For example, rapidly rising rates of divorce and children born outside of marriage have not been accompanied by rising rates of remarriage, leading one observer to wonder whether support for the family in Sweden might not eventually make marriage, or even cohabitation, obsolete (Herman, 1976: 397).

What specific policies ameliorate the situation of the single parent? In a concern for maintaining the standard of living of single-parent families and rectifying the "new poverty" brought on by escalating costs of family maintenance, single-parent families receive higher income maintenance payments than two-parent families as well as priority placements for housing and childcare. Moreover, parents of small children may opt for shorter workdays (without compensation) in order to give them more time for nurturing and, specifically, to alleviate the time burdens of single parents managing family and work roles alone (Kamerman and Kahn, 1982: 233). While labor unions have expressed concern that parents of young children having shorter workdays might experience discrimination in the workforce, advocates agree that participation by both parents in shorter workdays may mitigate this problem by not segregating female heads of households off from the larger population of working parents (Liljestrom, 1978: 46).

Swedish public policy illustrates the benefits to working mothers of an explicit governmental recognition of their roles as workers and mothers. As early as 1962, a Governmental Family Welfare committee established a goal to:

> Spare the woman from having to choose between children and occupation, but
> make it possible for her to have both so that she can satisfy herself both as a woman
> and as an individual (Liljestrom 1978: 28).

While Swedish family policy has not yet produced a utopia for single female heads of household, or for women generally, there is no doubt that the neutrality of the state toward varying lifestyles and the commitment to productive labor and family life yield women more life options than in other industrialized socieites. Moreover, the Swedish commitment to use public policy to break down sex stereotyping by enabling men to play an equal role in parenting and by encouraging women to move into nontraditional jobs distinguishes Sweden as the country most advanced in dealing with the various burdens of motherhood and employment.

Family Policy in Israel

Israel provides an interesting contrast to Sweden in its approach to single mothers, both in terms of public policy and in terms of Israel's unique social institution, the Kibbutz. Israel is similar to Sweden in its pronatalism and full employment policies, as well as its fairly well-developed welfare state. Unlike Sweden, the nuclear family is an established social value, bolstered by religious tradition and the Jewish search for security in an unstable world. Challenges to the nuclear family deriving either from the collectivist ideology of the kibbutz, or from the extended family pattern of immigrants from Middle Eastern, North African and Asian countries are waning as Kibbutzniks and non-European immigrants alike are, for different reasons, adopting more and more the values and behavior of the nuclear family.

While Israel does not have an explicit policy on the family as an institution, the family is aided through family allowances, housing assistance and widespread kindergarten and part-time child care facilities. Motherhood is promoted through a maternity program including leaves of three months at nearly full pay, extensive maternity and pediatric care, payment for hospital births, infant clothing, and postnatal work leaves of three months covering 75 percent of wages (Honig and Shamai, 1978: 406–426).

Likewise in Israel, working mothers, although not fathers, receive numerous special benefits, including tax credits, work leaves for sick children, either a one-year job guarantee after childbirth or shorter working hours of one hour per day for the year following childbirth. In the civil service, women with two or more young children also have reduced workdays. Interestingly, since employers absorb the costs of these programs, they acknowledge a reluctance to hire women starting families, although there is no similar discrimination against men serving in the military, who are absent on average 1½ months per year (Honig and Shamai, 1978: 412). While the goal of meeting the needs of all working mothers for full-time day care is often espoused in Israel, unlike Sweden, less than half the need is currently being met (Honig and Shamai, 1978: 416). Moreover, while some leaders of the Israeli women's movement support the goal of extending the same benefits provided working mothers to fathers, there is little likelihood of such policy innovation in the near future.

The single parent family is not a well-defined policy concern in Israel, although single parents are included with young couples as having the highest priority needs for housing. Beyond housing, Israeli policy is its most innovative in dealing with the problem of delinquency in alimony and child support payments. Women who have received court orders for support payments, whether divorced or not, are guaranteed these payments by the National Insurance Institute, which, in the case of delinquency, makes the payments directly to the mother, using its own resources to collect from the father (Honig and Shamai, 1978: 421). In the absence of any other special policy provisions for single parents, however, the support payment policy, while admirable, may be seen as being motivated as much to inhibit divorce as to prop up the single-parent family.

The similarities between Sweden and Israel in policy on working mothers contrast with the two countries' differing approaches to single-parent families. While many cultural and historical factors contribute to the willingness of a society to recognize alternative family patterns, a critical factor as well is the degree to which the policy-making establishment addresses the changing family as a social issue. Whereas in Sweden definitions of and social services to the family have changed as a result of government-initiated concern, in Israel the government has reinforced the ideal of the nuclear family. While in Sweden benefits are extended to both working men and women in an effort to effect role change through parenting, Israeli policy is directed at mothers only in order to help them achieve equity in work roles while maintaining their primacy in family roles.

The Israeli Kibbutz and the Single Parent

The Israeli kibbutz is perhaps the longest-surviving modern social institution which challenges the traditional nuclear family. As such, it has been studied from almost every conceivable perspective. Thus, it is curious to find that the single-parent family has not been a major concern for kibbutz research, although the reasons for this may become clear in the discussion which follows. While systematic study of single-parent families is lacking, interview material and anecdotal evidence together provide enough data to draw some tentative conclusions regarding single parents, particularly mothers, on the kibbutz.

A brief history of the kibbutz suggests that in the early year of the Kibbutz movement family issues were insignificant as kibbutzniks were typically unmarried young people, immersed in a struggle for economic survival who channeled the bulk of their energy into agriculture, road building and construction. In addition, the secular and revolutionary values of many of the first pioneers made them view the marriage ceremony and the institution of marriage with disdain. As the kibbutzim became established, Kibbutzniks set about creating institutions which would foster sexual equality by collectivizing family functions such as childrearing, food preparation and laundry. The goal, in line with kibbutz egalitarian ideology, was to liberate women from traditional roles so that they might participate as equals in the economic, social and political responsibilities of kibbutz life.

There is considerable debate regarding the extent to which the early kibbutzniks achieved their goal of sexual equality. While much of the literature of the kibbutz applauds the successes of the pioneers in breaking down sex roles, as well as lauding pioneer women in their struggle for equality, there is also considerable evidence from the writings of the pioneer women that they experienced sex discrimination in work assignments, self-defense and military activities and leadership roles (Azaryahu, 1977; Maimon, 1962; Shazar, 1975). As one woman pioneer, later to become a leader of many women's organizations and the wife of Israel's second President wrote:

> In the thick of that passionate movement toward the land the women workers suddenly found themselves thrust aside and relegated once more to the ancient tradition of the house and the kitchen. They were amazed and disappointed to see how the cleavage was opening, the men comrades really uniting themselves with the land, but they, though on it, not becoming part of it (Rachel Janaith in Shazar, 1975: 137).

What is evident is that as the kibbutz developed, a sexual division of labor became clearly apparent in which men assumed the major responsibility for production and economic and political decisionmaking, while women were concentrated in services, serving only minor roles in the decision making structures of the community. This change, whether evolutionary or counterrevolutionary, depending on how one evaluates the early kibbutz experience, has been the subject of much analysis and debate with explanations deriving from sociobiology (Tiger and Shepher, 1975; Spiro, 1979), structural functionalism (Blumberg, 1976) or social change theory stressing the impact of external societal changes on kibbutz life (Honig and Shamai, 1978: 411). Without entering into the debate, it is sufficient for our purpose here to note the tendency of the kibbutz to become more familial over time with a lessening commitment to collective social structures and an increasing commitment to individualized family patterns. While communal institutions are still the norm on the kibbutz, they are, on many kibbutzim, being modified to accommodate the desires of the nuclear family for a home-centered family life. Sex role stereotyping occurs not only in work roles but also in the home. As one kibbutz researcher has observed, "private domestic and child-care work of women is lighter than the average burden of married men and mothers outside, yet heavier than that of married men and fathers inside the kibbutz" (Buber-Agassi, 1980: 122).

How does the single-parent family fare on the kibbutz? The great proportion of single parent families are headed by women—widows, divorcees and a very small number of unmarried women—whose situations vary somewhat depending on their marital status. Yet, in every case, the most unequivocal benefit of kibbutz life for these women and their children is economic security, with not only the necessities of life, but also the opportunities for personal development, educationally, socially, and culturally provided by the kibbutz community. In fact, single mothers seeking to advance themselves with study or activities off the kibbutz or requesting new housing often get preferential treatment in having their needs met (interview with Dr. Moshe Talmon, Seminale Kibbutzim, February 1983).

The economic benefits extend beyond security to a situation of economic equality in which the standard of living of single-parent families on the kibbutz is no different from that of two-parent families. In particular, women who experience widowhood or divorce suffer none of the decline in their standard of living which typically accompanies a similar change in marital status in modern society. Finally, because the kibbutz is organized to provide a thorough integration of family and work roles by relieving women of individual responsibility for childcare and many domestic chores, the single mother on the kibbutz does not experience conflict between her work and family roles to anywhere near the degree of the single parent elsewhere managing a job and an individual home. As one single mother put it in an interview:

> The two biggest advantages go hand in hand. One is guaranteed, high level, no-cost child care and the other is job security and flexibility with a guaranteed median income (Interview, February 1983).

The kibbutz also provides the single parent with a social network—a community—which takes an interest in her/his children and which provides children with a wide range of adults to serve as role models and to relate to. The kibbutz protects single-parent families from social isolation and, in the best situations, provides social support. One kibbutz widow described her situation in the following way:

> I have not experienced widowhood outside the kibbutz but I think it's probably easier here than elsewhere. My children are well taken care of and economically we have no worries whatsoever. We have a socially supportive system, with holidays, celebrations and cultural activities organized by the kibbutz. Although I'm frequently sad on these occasions, I know it's good for the children to sit together with all the families in the presence of the whole community so that they know we are not alone (Lieblich, 1982: 210)

On the other hand, as the nuclear family ideal becomes more and more enshrined on the kibbutz, the single-parent family may experience increasing social deprivation by virtue of comparison with two-parent families. Particularly for widows who have not chosen singleness, the loss of a spouse may be exacerbated in a setting where couples are the prevailing norm, as seen in the words of a woman widowed in the 1973 Yom Kippur War:

> The thing which makes being a widow so difficult here is the fact that such a large proportion of our life is communal. . . . I accompany my children every evening, each one to his or her children's home, and I'm observed by all the other parents. Every evening I see other children accompanied by their fathers and I'm alone. . . . At every party or holiday . . . . I always felt different, odd among all the happy families. . . . In town, I'd probably not go; I'd be able to lead my life in the way most appropriate for me. . . . It's obvious that a woman might feel more protected economically in the kibbutz. But the ministry of Defense takes very good care of widows in town, too, and these widows have the further advantage of freedom to form their own lifestyle (Lieblich, 1982: 228–230).

While some kibbutzim have made efforts to aid new widows in their social isolation by providing them with private telephones or by giving them driving lessons to provide greater social mobility, the kibbutz has not been especially sensitive to the problems of these women in adjusting to a new life situation, although one kibbutz movement is now beginning a series of psychological support groups for single parents (interview with Dr. Moshe Talmon, Seminale Kibbutzim, February 1983).

For the divorced or separated mother on the kibbutz, the situation is somewhat different from that of the widow as she receives less sympathy and social approval. If her former spouse remains on the kibbutz, there is the advantage of close contact between the offspring and their father but also the disadvantage for the mother of having to have regular contact with her ex-spouse. As one kibbutz mother described the situation:

> Kibbutz life is really advantageous for my son because there is no conflict with being with either parent—he can choose where he wants to be at any point. He's in a much freer situation while we (the parents) are in a confined situation because we have to see each other all the time (interview, February 1983).

If the former spouse lives off the kibbutz, the divorced mother experiences less social strain but still has to deal with the fact that she is not part of a couple and may, in some cases be perceived as a threat to the stability of other couples (interview with Dr. Moshe Talmon, Seminale Kibbutzim, February, 1983). Yet, as seen from the following table prepared by a kibbutz researcher comparing divorce situations in an American urban environment with the kibbutz, the kibbutz environment is far superior in maintaining economic status and social stability for the children.

It is not clear whether the kibbutz today provides a more or less congenial environment than the kibbutz of the past for the woman who *chooses* to be a single parent. It may be argued that in the past when the kibbutz environment was more radical and sexually permissive, and the family was less well established, the social atmosphere was more accepting of non-conformist lifestyles. Certainly early kibbutz lore contains many stories of men fathering children by single women in addition to their wives. Observations of kibbutz life today, however, also suggest that single parenting is countenanced on the kibbutz, despite the nuclear family pattern, as seen in the following comment from a female Kibbutznik:

> Nowadays it's quite common for a single woman to bear a child and the kibbutz is supportive, not in the least bit critical of this phenomenon. Children of single mothers are raised as the other children are. Just a few months ago a child was born to a single woman and people came to celebrate with her and make a toast, just as if they were a traditional family (Lieblich, 1982: 224).

And, on some kibbutzim, support for single parents even extends to agreements by the kibbutz to pay the alimony or child support payments of separated or divorced male members whose ex-wives and children live off the kibbutz.

Structurally, the kibbutz provides an enviable solution to the problems of the single parent as family economic needs are underwritten by the community and role strain between work and family is greatly reduced. What may be missing in the kibbutz environment is some form of orga-

Table 1. Comparison Between Divorced Families in Kibbutzim and in Urban Cities

The Issue	Urban–American	Kibbutz–Israeli
Economic Stability	Divorce increases the possibility of downward economic movement, (Bane, 1976). Factors such as the need of mothers to go back to work; change in standards of housing and neighborhood and socio–economic status is experienced by mothers as stressful issues in coping with their every day life following the divorce (Colletta, 1978; Hodges, et al., 1978).	As long as parents stay in the kibbutz their economic status undergoes no change following divorce. Vast majority of divorced parents continue to work in the same occupation, live in the same neighborhood and enjoy the same benefits as before.
Child Care and Household Routines	Divorced mothers and their children, when compared to intact families have erratic bedtime, the children are read to less often, both parents are less likely to eat dinner with their children and the children are more likely to come back from school to an empty house, (Hetherington, Fox and Fox, 1978). Change in babysitter and periods of seeing one of the two parents. Hetherington, et al, associated this period of disorganization and lack of stable child care routines with the child's mental and behavioral problems.	The availability of the two parents remains as before the separation (unless one of the parents decide to leave the kibbutz) and the structure of the playtime, meals and bedtime stays unchanged. Child care arrangement remains largely stable. The only change is that sometimes the parents choose to divide the afternoon and weekend hours half and half between the father's home and the mother's home.
Lifestyle	Divorced parents are likely to change their schedule and priorities, e.g., change jobs, go back to school, meet new friends; join new social or civil activities.	Changes in lifestyle are less intense and rapid. Rarely, jobs are changed, or social activities are new. There is only a slight shift from "married friends" to "single friends" and somewhat more free–time (since the children spend half of the time with the other parent).

(continued)

Table 1. (Continued)

The Issue	Urban–American	Kibbutz–Israeli
Custodial Arrangements	Although there is a slight increase in father–custody and joint–custody cases, in 91 percent of divorced families, custody is given to mothers. In most cases, each spouse hires his/her own lawyer and the agreement is reached through family court; in cases of more compatible couples, by negotiation between the two lawyers.	Most kibbutz educators and parents favor co–parenting arrangements (unless one of the parents leaves the kibbutz or the divorce is extremely hostile). Some parents continue to spend the early evening hours (called the children's hours) jointly with their children. Others divide it equally between the two households. In cases of disagreements, the legal aspects are handled by one lawyer (representing both spouses), and the psycho–educational aspects are handled by one kibbutz educator or counselor. Cases rarely reach the court.
Public Opinion and Values	In large urban cities like Philadelphia, divorce is a very common phenomenon. A divorcee can easily find social and therapeutic activities addressed to single and divorced parents. Children can find many other children in their school and neighborhood, who are from divorced families. The mass media, books and movies, address the issue quite often and most people seem to be familiar with the phenomenon.	Divorce is regarded as an inalienable right, but people feel that it should be exercised only in cases of very serious and persistent estrangement. Divorced couples with children are in the small minority and are sometimes condemned by public opinion. Divorced parents often find less flexibility to explore new networks of friends, to change their internal image, and to date single people (since kibbutz is largely family–oriented and the families are, on the whole, cohesive and stable).

Source: Moshe Talmon, Divorce in Crosscultural Perspective: Family Structure and Individual Adjustment. Unpublished doctoral dissertation, University of Pennsylvania, 1982.

144

nized psychological support for single parents, who have emotional, as well as physical, needs which must be addressed. As an illustration of just how far the kibbutz has come in promoting the nuclear family, the widow or divorcee receives considerable emotional support for finding a new mate, but far less for adapting to her aloneness and establishing a rewarding set of social interactions with other adult members.

Despite its evolution to a more traditional family structure, the kibbutz presents an alternative social setting where single mothers experience neither the low social and economic status nor the dependency on government support commonly found in most industrialized countries. While the kibbutz lifestyle clearly lacks appeal not only to non-Israelis, but also to the vast majority of Israelis, it does stand as a significant example of a community in which membership for the single parent and her/his children means equal opportunities for economic and social participation. Perhaps the most important message to be gleaned from the kibbutz experience is that, unlike Sweden, where the family has been redefined to incorporate single parenting, the kibbutz promotes more and more traditional family structures, and yet provides enormous institutional support for single parenting, which, whether brought on by tragedy or choice, remains a viable, if atypical, lifestyle.

VII.   POLICY CHANGES IN THE U.S.

What are the prospects in the United States of utilizing public policy to improve the status of the single female head of household? Before discussing specific possibilities, it is necessary to examine in a comparative perspective the factors which facilitate or inhibit policy change in this area.

Several environmental factors are of critical importance in analyzing the prospects for change. A major consideration is the extent of the society's commitment to the welfare state, specifically, the state's responsibility for the economic and social well-being of its citizens. In both Sweden and Israel the welfare state is firmly established and has not been dislodged to any significant degree, despite recent accessions to power by non-socialist political parties. Thus, efforts to attend to the welfare of single mothers and their children occur in a context in which public policy has historically been used to assure the security, mobility and even dignity of its less advantaged members.

The United States obviously presents a different case in point. Despite the creation of a wide variety of income transfer programs and social services over the last fifty years, the prevailing political ideology refrains from embracing social welfare as the overriding public policy goal, stressing instead remedial solutions to a changing array of politically identified social problems. Moreover, as we have seen recently, changes in the political regime can, indeed, result in the dismantling of long established distributive and redistributive social programs.

Within the broad social policy framework, two other environmental factors are significant. The first involves the extent to which the state is concerned with the family as an institution, as compared to its concern for individuals who happen to be family members. The development of a coherent family policy is typically generated by other social and economic goals such as stimulating population growth or full employment; once in place however, policy on the family *qua* family may encompass many other social issues, including housing, education, health, transportation and child care. The experiences of Sweden and Israel reflect this pattern of family policy evolving out of pronatalist and labor market goals. In Sweden, family policy has become explicit as well as innovative in its definition of family; in Israel, family policy is less well-defined, but family welfare is a recognized objective of policies in the employment, educational, health and welfare fields.

Again, the United States presents a very different picture. Not only is explicit family policy lacking, but family welfare is rarely identified as an objective of policies in other realms (Dempsey, 1980). The failure to address the family in public policy is not surprising, of course, given the fierce ideological and moral conflict between left and right over the nature of the family, its needs and appropriate directions. The irony, however, is that the American family as an institution appears to be undergoing more rapid change today than at any previous time and the failure to agree on a definition of the problem, no less public policy solutions, is perhaps the most destabilizing force of all.

A third environmental factor affecting prospects for policy change is the state's ideological commitment to sexual equality. The Swedish approach to sexual equality extends beyond issues of role equity to those of role change, in other words, breaking down traditional sex roles so that women and men not only have the same rights, but also the same responsibilities in society. Efforts to expand men's roles in the family have been institutionalized through education and employment policy and are seen as the complement of efforts to expand opportunities for women outside the home. In Israel, the ideology of sexual equality is not well supported by public policy, clashing as it does with religious and cultural traditions prescribing clearly defined sex roles.

The rebirth of feminism in the United States in the mid-1960s brought demands for sexual equality under law, in public and in private spheres. While the political system partially recognized these demands with equal rights legislation providing for role equity, the more radical demands of the women's movement for role change, that is, liberation from traditional sex roles and sex role stereotyping, and for productive and sexual freedom have met with stiff resistance from a coalition of right wing forces which has, in most cases, successfully stymied the drive for sexual equality (Gelb and Palley, 1982; Boneparth, 1982).

Thus the barriers in the United States to achieving policy change for single female heads of households stem not only from a narrow conception of the state's role in providing for social welfare, but also from the failure to identify the family as an explicit, or even implicit, policy concern and from opposition to demands for sexual equality. The policymaking process further impedes efforts to assist single mothers and their families by favoring incrementalism over comprehensive policymaking and by relegating most public policy concerning the family to the state, rather than the federal, governments with the result that policies vary considerably, with progressive approaches in a few states more than offset by the conservative biases of most state governments. In comparison to Sweden, where policy initiation on the family is assigned to a government ministry and to high-level national commissions of experts, which provide ongoing surveillance of the state of the family or to Israel where women's concerns have been promoted for over fifty years by powerful extragovernmental women's groups such as the Working Women's Council and Working Mothers Organization (Maimon, 1962, pp. 145–216), policy recommendations in the United States, whether generated by White House Conferences on the Family or by women's advocacy groups such as the Women's Bureau or Commissions on the Status of Women, lack any clear institutionalized channels for consideration or implementation.

VIII.   POLICIES FOR THE UNITED STATES IN THE 1980s

Given the lack of an ideological or policymaking focus on single female heads of households in the United States, public policies or social institutions serving single parents and their families, such as found in Sweden or Israel, will not be easily introduced into American society. Moreover, the policy changes necessary to address the problems confronting the single female head of household in the 1980s will, unfortunately have to be aired and debated in a political environment generally hostile to women and to social welfare programs. Despite the gains made by the Democratic Party in the 1982 congressional elections which suggest some public disillusionment with Reaganomics, fiscal conservatism including taxpayer revolts will doubtless continue to characterize the

American political economy in the 1980s. Resistance to public spending and to the use of tax revenues for social welfare programs makes policy change on the order of programs found either in Sweden or Israel an unlikely prospect for the near future.

Yet, all the same current demographic trends in the workforce are expected to persist in the near future: by 1990 it is predicted that 60 percent of all women (most of them mothers) will be working as compared to 80 percent of all men (Women's Bureau, 1980b: Appendix, Table 14). Moreover, rising divorce rates and birth rates among unmarried women (Parachini, 1982, p.1) will create an even larger group of single female heads of households.

How will these women maintain themselves and their families? Given the present political climate, what kinds of public policies are possible to alter the status of the single female head of household who, if she continues to remain ignored or made the scapegoat for other social problems, will not only cause the status of all women to stagnate but will also drain off enormous resources of money, time and human potential from all society?

The most immediate need for the single female head of household is a job. Since the creation of new public jobs, particularly in the service fields where women workers are concentrated, is not likely in the foreseeable future, job creation, specifically for single heads of households, must be approached indirectly. One way to expand the number of jobs would be to reduce workers' hours in existing jobs and hire additional workers to perform those jobs. Experiments with decreasing work hours have shown that many workers, especially women, prefer working fewer hours even for less pay than a 40-hour week (Best and Stern, 1977: 9; Stewart, Kennedy, Sierra and Gosset, 1975: 14). Since shorter hours for women workers would yield more "women's" jobs, the beneficiaries of such a policy would, more likely than not, be single female heads of household.

The obvious objection to such a policy is that not many single women would be able to support their families on reduced pay. Thus, a policy decreasing work hours must be accompanied by comparable worth policies in which "women's work" is compensated according to its actual worth as opposed to its worth as dictated by a discriminatory labor market. While equal pay for work of equal value will not be easy to achieve in the present policy environment, the advantage of such a policy is that it does not require major federal legislation but can be fought for in lawsuits, in labor negotiations or in state and local governments where women are increasingly better represented (Grune and Kahn, 1980).

An additional means of boosting the income of single female heads of households would be to introduce child allowances for single parents.

While such a policy approach is not new—most European countries have provided children's allowances for decades (Kamerman and Kahn, 1978)—the limiting of child allowances to single parents or even to single parents *first* entering the work force would be far less costly than providing them for all families. Realistically, however, child allowances in any form may be anathema to policymakers bent on budget-cutting, and child allowances to single parents would be vociferously opposed by the New Right as rewarding the breakdown of the traditional nuclear family.

Another approach is expanding employment opportunity for single female heads of households would be to treat them as a special category of workers with all the benefits provided to target groups, such as minorities and veterans, in the past: subsidized training programs and apprenticeships, tax benefits to industries employing these workers, coverage through affirmative action, and even preference points on civil service exams. While such an approach also smacks of special treatment for women who are violating traditional norms, the object of these policies is to eliminate the need for government support rather than increase it. A further advantage of this approach is that, as policies utilized in the past, only incremental changes are needed to extend them to single parents.

Increasing the number of jobs available for working mothers and increasing the level of pay for "women's work," while necessary short-term initiatives, will not alleviate the dual burdens of work and family for single heads of households. In order to tackle this issue, creative long-term strategies must be developed to adapt the world of work to the needs of mothers.

The technological revolution occurring in post-industrial societies may provide just such a strategy. The computer age makes possible two adaptations to the world of work of enormous value to working parents: flexible work schedules and neighborhood work or work-at-home. While flex-time is becoming a more common feature of the workforce, its current use is limited, for the most part, to minor adjustments in the opening and closing times of the traditional eight-hour day (Stoper, 1982: 91–93). Its potential, however, is far greater: combinations of day and evening work, weekday and weekend work, alternating longer and shorter work weeks adjusted to the cycles of the work setting. Experience with these approaches in Europe indicate that they go a long way toward allowing workers to accommodate the needs of the job and the family; as well as meeting the needs of employers for an adjustable work force.

Bringing more work into the home or neighborhood is a second adaptation of great potential value to working parents. A home terminal would allow technical and clerical workers to accomplish much of their work at home during hours which are normally devoted to television-viewing or household tasks and would free up other hours during the day or week for child care and family needs. Moreover, the home terminal in combination with televised instruction provides enormous possibilities for job training and upgrading of technical skills (Toffler, 1981: 194–207).

An excellent example of the potential of computer technology to provide new employment opportunities for mothers is found in an ultra-orthodox religious community outside Tel Aviv where 20 women, restricted by religious tradition from working outside their community, have trained as computer programmers and are working in a neighborhood apartment for a Tel Aviv computer company. Initial assessments of this experiment suggest that the new workers are highly productive, have high levels of job satisfaction and experience few conflicts between their work and family roles (interview with Professor Ilan Salomon, Hebrew University, February, 1983).

Clearly, there are also possible disadvantages for women in such arrangements including segregation from the world of the office and isolation in the home (Stein and Brown, 1982). These disadvantages can be avoided, however, by having both men and women participate in neighborhood work or in work-at-home and by utilizing work-at-home as a partial rather than full-scale work mode. Particularly for parents of pre-schoolers, work-at-home presents a viable means of remaining in the workforce while raising young children.

In the final analysis, the need to address the issue of women and employment reflects the need to develop family policy in the United States. Changing family patterns are highlighted in government statistics, analyzed in research reports, noted in social commentary and decried in the rhetoric of the New Right seeking to preserve the traditional, patriarchal nuclear family. Moreover, existing welfare programs are clearly inadequate to maintain the family both because of dwindling levels of budgetary support and because of their failure to interrupt the cycle of poverty. Even the women's movement, which has done the most to identify the problems of women who maintain families, has failed to generate policy proposals which confront the issue of female dependency, if not on male breadwinners, then on government handouts.

Policy on single family heads of households must, therefore, be informed by a feminist perspective which would focus on women at the lowest social and economic levels, which would legitimize and foster changing sex roles in the home and in the workplace, and which would promote new approaches as *family* policy, benefitting women, men and children, rather than women exclusively. Lacking such a perspective, the policy gains of the 1960s and 1970s will continue to effect the status of only a select group of women, and then only marginally, while the needs of the great majority of women and their families remain unattended.

REFERENCES

Azaryahu, Sarah. *The Union of Hebrew Women for Equal Rights in Society: A Selected History of the Women's Movement in Israel (1900–1947)*. Translated by Marcia Freedman. Haifa: Women's Aid Fund, 1977.

Bernard, Jessie. *Women, Wives and Mothers: Values and Options*. Chicago: Aldine Publishing Company, 1975.

Bernard, Jessie. *The Future of Parenthood*. New York: The Dial Press, 1974.

Bernard, Jessie. *Women and The Public Interest: An Essay on Policy and Protest*. Chicago: Aldine, 1971.

Best, Fred, and Stern, Barry. "Education, Work and Leisure: Must They Come in That Order? *Monthly Labor Review*, July, 1977 pp. 3–10.

Blumberg, Rae Lesser. "The Erosion of Sexual Equality in the Kibbutz: Structural Factors Affecting the Status of Women." In *Beyond Intellectual Sexism: A New Woman, A New Reality*, pp. 320–329. Edited by Joan Roberts. New York: David McKay & Company, 1976.

Boneparth, Ellen, ed. *Women, Power and Policy*. New York: Pergamon Press, 1982.

Boneparth, Ellen, and Stoper, Emily. "Work, Gender and Technology." In *Families, Politics and Public Policy: A Feminist Dialogue on Women and the State*. Edited by Irene Diamond. New York: Longman, 1983.

Buber-Agassi, Judith. "The Status of Women in Kibbutz Society." In *Integrated Cooperatives in the Industrial Society: The Example of the Kibbutz*, pp. 118–130. Edited by Klaus Bartoelke et.al. Assen: Van Gorcum, 1980.

Carden, Maren Lockwood. *Feminism in the Mid 1970s*. New York: Ford Foundation, 1977.

Cook, Alice H. *The Working Mother: A Survey of Problems and Programs in Nine Countries*. Ithaca, New York: Cornell University, 1978.

Darling, Martha. *The Role of Women in the Economy*. Paris: The Organization for Economic Co-operation and Development (OECD), 1980.

Dempsey, John. *The Family and Public Policy: The Issue of the 1980s*. Baltimore: Paul H. Brookes Publishing Company, 1981.

Diamond, Irene. "Women and Housing." *Women, Power and Policy*. Edited by Ellen Boneparth. New York: Pergammon Press, 1982.

Ehrenreich, Barbara, and Stallard, Karin. "The Nouveau Poor." *Ms*, August, 1982.

Freeman, Jo. *The Politics of Women's Liberation*. New York: David Mackay, 1975.

Friedan, Betty. *The Feminine Mystique*. New York: Dell Publishing Co., 1963.

Gittell, Marilyn, and Naples, Nancy. "Activist Women: Conflicting Ideologies." *Social Policy*, Summer 1982, pp. 25–27.

Gelb, Joyce and Palley, Marian Lief. *Women and Public Policies*. Princeton, N.J.: Princeton University Press, 1982.

Hayden, Dolores. "What would a Non-Sexist City Be Like? Speculations on Housing, Urban Design, and Human Work." *Signs Supplement* 5, No. 3 (Spring 1980).

Herman, Sondra R. "Sweden: A Feminist Model?". In *Women in the World: A Comparative Study*, pp. 391–400. Edited by Lynne B. Iglitzin and Ruth Ross. Santa Barbara: Clio Books, 1976.

Honig, Marjorie, and Shamai, Nira. "Implicit and Reluctant Family Policy: Israel." In *Family Policy: Government and Families in Fourteen Countries*, pp. 400–421. Edited by Sheila Kamerman and Alfred J. Kahn. New York: Columbia University Press, 1978.

Huckle, Patricia. "The Womb Factor: Pregnancy Policies and Employment of Women." *Women, Power and Policy.* Edited by Ellen Boneparth. New York: Pergamon Press, 1982.

Johnson, Beverly L. "Women Who Head Families, 1970–77 Their Numbers Rose, Income Lagged." *Monthly Labor Review,* Feb. 1978, pp. 32–37.

Kahn, Wendy and Grune, Joy Ann. "Pay Equity: Beyond Equal Pay for Equal Work." *Women, Power, and Politics.* Edited by Ellen Boneparth. New York: Pergamon Press, 1982.

Kamerman, Sheila B. and Kahn, Alfred J. *Child Care, Family Benefits and Working Parents: A Study in Comparative Policy.* New York: Columbia University Press, 1981.

Kamerman, Sheila B. and Kahn, Alfred J., eds. *Family Policy: Government and Families in Fourteen Countries.* New York: Columbia University Press, 1978.

Kanowitz, Leo. *Women and the Law: The Unfinished Revolution.* Albuquerque: University of New Mexico Press, 1969.

Lieblich, Amia. *Kibbutz Makom.* New York: Pantheon, 1982.

Liljestrom, Rita. "Explicit and Comprehensive Family Policy: Sweden." In *Family Policy: Government and Families in Fourteen Countries,* pp. 19–48. Edited by Sheila Kamerman and Alfred J. Kahn. New York: Columbia University Press, 1978.

Maimon, Ada. *Women Build a Land.* New York: Herzl Press, 1962.

Murphy, Irene L. *Public Policy on the Status of Women.* Lexington, Mass.: D.C. Heath and Company, 1973.

National Council of Negro Women, Inc. *Women and Housing: A Report on Sex Discrimination in Five American Cities.* Washington, D.C.: U.S. Department of Housing and Urban Development. 1975.

Newsweek, January 17, 1983.

Nordstrom, Maria. "Sex Differences and the Experiences of the Physical Environment." Paper read at the International Interdisciplinary Congress on Women, December 28, 1982, at Haifa, Israel. Mimeographed.

Norgen, Jill. "In Search of a National Child-Care Policy: Background and Prospects." *Women, Power and Policy.* Edited by Ellen Boneparth. New York: Pergammon Press, 1982.

Organization for Economic Co-operation and Development (OECD). *Women and Employment: Policies for Equal Opportunities,* 1975.

Palley, Marian Lief and Preston, Michael B. *Race, Sex and Policy Problems.* Lexington, Mass.: D.C. Heath and Company, 1979.

Parachini, Allan, "Husbands Optional? Birth Rate Rising for Unwed Women," *The San Jose Mercury.* December 8, 1982, p. 1A.

Rodgers, Harrell R., Jr. "Ending Poverty in America: A Comparative Policy Perspective." Paper read at the Western Political Science Association Meetings, March 1982, at San Diego, Ca. Unpublished.

Ross, Heather L. and Sawhill, Isabel V. *Time of Transition: The Growth of Families Headed by Women.* Washington, D.C.: The Urban Institute, 1975.

Ruggie, Mary. "Public Day Care in Britain and Sweden: A Sociological Perspective." In *Women and World Change,* pp. 159–182. Edited by Naomi Black and Ann Baker Cottrell. Beverly Hills: Sage Publications, 1981.

Shazar, Rachel Katznelson, ed. *The Plough Women: Memoirs of the Pioneer Women of Palestine.* New York: Herzl Press, 1975.

Spiro, Melford. *Gender and Culture: Kibbutz Women Revisited.* Durham, North Carolina: Duke University Press, 1979.

Stein, Barry and Brown, Jane Covey. "Home Computers: Life in the 'Electronic Cottage.'" *Ms.,* Dec. 1982, pp. 22–25.

Steward, Cheryl A., et al. *Job Sharing in Municipal Government: A Case Study in the City of Palo Alto.* Stanford, Ca.: Action Research Liaison Office, 1975.

Stoper, Emily. "Alternative Work Patterns and the Double Life." *Women, Power and Politics.* Edited by Ellen Boneparth. New York: Pergamon Press, 1982.

Talmon, Moshe. *Divorce in Crosscultural Perspective: Family, Structure and Individual Adjustment.* Unpublished doctoral dissertation, University of Pennsylvania, 1982.

Tiger, Lionel, and Shepher, Joseph. *Women in the Kibbutz.* New York: Harcourt, Brace and Jovanovich, 1975.

Toffler, Alvin. *The Third Wave.* New York: Bantam Books, 1981.

U.S. Department of Health, Education and Welfare. *Social Security and the Changing Roles of Men and Women.* Washington, D.C.: U.S. Department of Health, Education and Welfare, 1979.

U.S. Department of Labor. *Employment in Perspective: Working Women.* Washington, D.C.: U.S. Department of Labor, 1980.

Woman's Bureau. *CETA Journey. A Walk on the Women's Side.* Washington, D.C.: U.S. Department of Labor, 1980.

Women's Bureau, *Employment Goals of the World Plan of Action: Developments and Issues in the United States.* Washington, D.C.: U.S. Department of Labor, 1980.

AMERICAN HOUSING POLICY IN A COMPARATIVE CONTEXT:
THE LIMITS OF THE POSITIVE STATE

Harrell R. Rodgers, Jr.

I. INTRODUCTION

For some fifty years the federal government has been formulating, financing and implementing policies designed to provide Americans with housing assistance. Most would agree that the government's housing programs have had many positive impacts on the amount, quality and affordability of housing. In fact, by the standards of most of the world, Americans are quite well housed and government programs have clearly played a role in this accomplishment. Currently, over 60 percent of all American families own their own homes, and the vast majority of all Americans live in decent housing. Still, most would also agree that America has some serious housing problems. There are three problems that are most often identified:

1. Millions of Americans live in poor quality housing and/or decaying and disrupted neighborhoods. Citizens who live in these houses or neighborhoods often receive inadequate public services, and little or no housing assistance.

2. High inflation and high interest rates have increased the price of housing to the extent that many first-home buyers have been priced out of the market.
3. American housing tends to be segregated by both race and socio-economic status.

The evidence suggesting that America's housing stock has improved greatly during the 20th century is impressive. The Department of Housing and Urban Development (HUD) classifies housing as sub-standard when it lacks hot running water, or a private bath or shower, or is grossly dilapidated. In 1940, 49 percent of all housing was judged to be sub-standard. By 1960 only 16 percent was so classified, and by 1978 only 7.8 percent (CBO, 1978, Tables 1 & 8). However, for some groups housing problems are still severe. Among families earning less than $10,000, 25 percent of all black families and 10.6 percent of all white families live in sub-standard housing. In rural areas 32 percent of all black families with incomes below $10,000 live in poor quality housing. President Reagan's Commission on Housing estimated that 5.6 million households lived in deficient housing in 1977 (U.S. Census, 1977, Part E).

Not only do millions of families live in poor quality housing, they tend to pay a disproportionate percentage of their total income for shelter. In 1976, 61 percent of all renter households with yearly incomes below $10,000 spent more than 25 percent of their income on rent. Nineteen percent spent more than half of their income for rent (CBO, 1978, Tables 3 and 4). Kristof reported that of the families living in poverty pockets, between 25 and 33 percent could not afford to pay the cost of adequate housing (1973, p. 171). Because public programs do not fill this gap, most of these families must pay to live in housing that is deteriorating and poorly maintained.

While much more difficult to quantify, millions of Americans live in undesirable neighborhoods. The nation's major cities all contain poverty pockets, some of which contain several hundred thousand people. Some of the worst of these communities are called ghettos and are characterized by squalid housing, severe crime and many other problems. Some of these communities—the South Bronx, large sections of St. Louis, Detroit, and Cleveland—represent some of the most frightening ruins in America. These neighborhoods provide extremely unwholesome environments for residents. Not only are they plagued by crime and poor and abandoned housing, they are isolated from job markets, generally provide poor quality schools, and usually are inadequately served by the city. Most would agree that families living in such environments are disadvantaged in dozens of ways.

The second major problem noted above is the increasing cost of buying and financing a home. By 1982 the average new home in America was selling for $88,200. Most of those Americans who are not already home owners cannot afford to buy a house in this price range. The freezing out of first-time home buyers is a reversal of post-World War II trends and expectations in America. In the mid-1970s, over 80 percent of all families earning more than $20,000 a year owned their own homes (Smith, 1981, p.105). In fact, home ownership is the major investment for most Americans. Goodman reports that by 1979 Americans owned $1.6 trillion in housing equity (net of mortgage). This investment is larger than the value of all stocks and bonds listed on the New York Stock Exchange (Smith, 1981, p.104). For many Americans, then, a home is not only a place to live, it is their chief asset; an asset they expect to grow and provide security in their retirement years.

But the dream of home ownership that Americans long could depend on is becoming more elusive. In 1981 and 1982 new housing starts numbered 1.08 million and 1.06 million respectively, the lowest number since 1946. During the late 1970s about 2.0 million new houses a year were built. High interest rates have even made it difficult to sell existing housing. In 1981 only about two million houses a month were sold, compared to an average of about four million a month in 1978. The nation's housing slump created a 22 percent unemployment rate in the construction trades by 1982, and forced thousands of construction firms and subcontractors to declare bankruptcy (CQ, April 1982, p. 852). With recent declines in interest rates, most analysts expect substantially more homes to be built and sold in 1980s, but hardly at 1970s levels.

The nation's housing problems are occurring just when the demand for housing is rapidly increasing. During the 1980s more than 40 million Americans will turn 30, creating record demands for housing (CQ, April 1982, p. 848). Some housing specialists think that by the mid-1980s housing will become a volatile political issue (CQ, April 1982, p. 848).

The last major problem is residential segregation by race and socio-economic status. Housing segregation is the result of past and present racial discrimination in both housing and employment. America only developed the laws and legal apparatus to attack housing discrimination in the late 1960s and early 1970s, It is widely conceded that less change has occurred in this area of civil rights than any other. Indeed, housing has been called the last frontier of the civil rights movement (U.S Commission on Civil Rights, 1974, p.10). But while racial discrimination in housing continues, it is widely conceded that economic barriers are the most important obstacle to neighborhood integration. Here we examine the economic policies designed to make it easier for any citizen, regardless of race, to purchase a home.

We begin our analysis by reviewing the nation's existing housing policies. Emphasis is placed on why the government developed specific housing programs, and the major criticisms of these policies by both conservatives and liberals. We then examine European housing policies to determine if these nations are using any approaches that might inform housing policies in the United States. This analysis requires us to examine the limits of comparative policy analysis and policy adoption. Last we compare conservative and liberal proposals to deal with the nation's most pressing housing needs, and then contrast these proposals with those policies currently in effect in other western nations.

II. AMERICAN HOUSING PROGRAMS: ASSISTANCE TO LOW-INCOME AND POOR CITIZENS

Compared to the other Western industrialized nations, America does not have a comprehensive policy on housing. This is a fact of which European scholars often make note. For example, Headey (1978, p. 242) observes that:

> As for the United States, it scarcely even makes sense to talk about policy objectives and priorities since policy formulation is essentially a process in which diverse groups agree to disagree about objectives, but sometimes manage to put together pork barrel, omnibus programmes which command just enough support to pass Congress.

Headey's observations reflect the typical European dismay at the inability of America's fragmented power structure to develop comprehensive public policies. As Headey notes, public policy in America is often a short-term compromise between competing interest groups to meet only limited, and sometimes conflicting, goals.

Essentially the philosophy of the United States is that the market should determine the quality and quantity of housing. However, market forces often have not been adequate to produce enough good quality housing to meet the public's needs. The primary response of the federal government has been to pass policies that subsidize the private market. The major housing assistance policies of the United States are devoted to helping middle and upper-income citizens purchase homes. A series of much less expensive and comprehensive programs are designed to allow some low-income citizens to live in better housing than their own purchasing power would permit. This is a perfect example of the type of policy that Furniss and Mitchell (see Chapter 2) would predict the Positive state to adopt.

Like most of America's social programs, housing policies date back to the Great Depression. The nation's greatest economic calamity caused millions of Americans to lose their homes, and threatened to force millions of additional families to forfeit their mortgages. Millions of other Americans were simply ill-housed. The nation's public leaders were reluctant to intervene in the housing market, but as the depression and its consequences deepened, they began to fear the political consequences of failing to act. The result was a series of programs designed to provide decent housing for some low-income citizens, and assistance programs to help homeowners maintain their mortgage payments, while insuring mortgage lenders against losses.

The more radical reformers of the 1930s hoped to convince Congress to build a great deal of publicly-owned housing that would be available to a wide range of income groups. The home building associations were intensely opposed to such a policy, however, because they believed that it would seriously undermine the private enterprise housing sector. The result was that the Congress decided to limit publicly-owned housing to poverty-level families and let the states decide if they wanted to build the housing with federal subsidies. In the Wagner Housing Act of 1937, Congress established subsidies and regulations for local governments that wanted to build and run housing projects for low-income citizens. As these policies have evolved the federal government pays up to 100 percent of the initial cost of building the project and continues to subsidize it if the local government follows federal guidelines.

The Wagner Act created an approach that precluded a national public housing policy. Public housing is a local option program, based on federal funds and standards. There have been several obvious results of this approach. First, the amount of public housing varies considerably by city. Second, limiting public housing to the poor has meant that it is a policy with little public support and considerable social stigma. This has greatly limited the amount of public housing in the nation. By 1978 there were only 1.3 million units of public housing in the United States, composing about 1.5 percent of the nation's housing stock (Statistical Abstract of the United States, 1981, p. 798). This is the smallest amount of public housing of any nation in the western industrialized world. Last, some critics argue that limiting public housing to the poor doomed the policy to failure. They argue that such a policy creates housing which is a collecting point for welfare-dependent, jobless, disrupted families. One, perhaps predictable, outcome has been a proliferation of crime and social disorder in many of these projects, leading in some cases to complete failure. To make matters worse, until the Supreme Court ruled the practice unconstitutional in 1967, most housing projects were located in central cities, often in ghettos (Hills v. Gautreaux, 1967). This policy contributed to racial segregation.

The housing problems of millions of poor and low-income Americans were increased by the Housing Act of 1949. The Act authorized the construction of 810,000 units of public housing over a six year period. This part of the Act was never carried out because Congress did not authorize the necessary funds. However, this same Act authorized an urban redevelopment plan that eventually would be known as "urban renewal." Under this plan the federal government allowed local authorities to use their powers of eminent domain to purchase and clear blighted areas of their cities. The areas cleared were often the homes of the city's poorest residents. The city in turn could sell the land to developers at a loss. The federal government agreed to provide the city with a grant equal to two-thirds of the loss. The city sold the land at a loss to make it economically attractive to private developers. The builders, in turn, were under no obligation to rebuild housing for the poor. In fact, under the program a great deal more housing was destroyed than built.

The poor and their representatives complained vigorously about a program that cost them so many homes. In 1954 Congress made an attempt to modify the program, but failed. The 1954 Act attempted to encourage rehabilitation of existing structures, reserving demolition for only the most irredeemable structures. The distinction amounted to little since in practice the emphasis was still on clearance. Even when units were rehabilitated they were generally too expensive for the former occupants. Still, urban renewal funds were made available until 1974 when the Community Development Block Grant program succeeded it.

In the 1960s Congress passed a number of acts designed to help low-income families either rent or purchase a home. The best known of these programs were amendments to the 1968 Housing Act. Section 236 was a rental housing assistance program. Under the program the Department of Housing and Urban Development (HUD) agreed to pay specified landlords the difference between a low-income renter's payment and the fair market value of the unit. The renter paid at least 25 percent of his/her income toward the rent. Any discrepancy was paid by HUD. This program reached a much larger number of low-income citizens than had earlier programs. In 1977 Section 236 was subsidizing 650,000 units to families with a median income of $6,361 (CBO, 1978, p. 14).

Section 235 of the 1968 Act was a home-ownership assistance program. Much like 236, qualifying families purchased a home on the open market and received subsidies to help pay for it. The purchasing family was required to pay 20 percent of its income toward the mortgage, insurance and taxes, and the government took care of any unmet proportion of these bills. The program also reached a large number of low-income families. In 1977 some 290,000 homes were being subsidized by

235, with the median income of recipient families being $8,085 (CBO, 1978, p. 18). Neither Section 235 or 236 really reached the nation's poorest families. In fact, one study estimated that no more than 10 percent of the families eligible for housing assistance because of low-income actually were receiving assistance under the programs (CBO, 1978, p. 12).

While the government was obligated to continue to finance the families and units previously contracted under Section 235 and 236, the Nixon administration obtained a moratorium on further commitments in 1973. Nixon argued that housing priorities needed to be re-examined. Like earlier programs, the Section 236 program was criticized for giving builders subsidies that were too generous and it often was charged that the homes purchased under Section 235 were overpriced and/or poorly constructed. Housing experts also were beginning to argue that it would make more sense simply to give poor families a grant that they could use to obtain better housing in the existing market. Proponents argued that the nation did not have a housing shortage, rather there existed a shortage of housing that low-income citizens could afford. They also pointed out that it was much cheaper to subsidize rent than home purchases (Carlson and Heinberg, 1978, pp. 46–47).

In 1974 Congress passed the Housing and Community Development Act. Section 8 of this act replaced Section 236. Unlike Section 236, Section 8 is oriented toward very low income families. Qualified renters pay between 15 and 25 percent of their income in rent, and HUD pays the difference between this amount and what it considers adequate rent for the given family. This part of the program works like a housing allowance for selected families, but the grant is paid directly to the landlord. By 1978 almost 500,000 families were receiving rent assistance under the program, but this was only a small proportion of all the families who were income-qualified. The median income of the families receiving assistance was about $3,700 (CBO, 1976, p.14).

Section 8 also has rental programs for newly constructed or substantially rehabilitated housing. Much like earlier programs, HUD subsidizes the rent of low-income families in specific buildings. These subsidies represent grants to designated developers and landlords. In 1978, 92 thousand families were being subsidized by this program. Their median income was almost identical to that of the families receiving subsidies in existing housing. The emphasis of the 1968 act on rental assistance was designed to tailor assistance to household need and, to some extent, to disperse the poor. In actuality, the fair-market rent rule deters most recipients from renting better-quality housing and concentrates recipients in low-income areas. Additionally, landlords have the option of refusing Section 8 renters and many do.

In 1976 HUD revised the Section 235 home-ownership assistance program. The subsidy was lowered and the required family income was raised. This change was designed to orient the program toward families able to meet the mortgage payments. Under the old program the default rate was extremely high. By 1978 about 7,500 families were receiving assistance under the revised program. These families had a median income of about $11,000 a year, well above the median under the original program (CBO, 1976, p. 14).

By 1982 3.4 million low-income to poor families were receiving housing assistance under one of the federal government's housing programs. The recipients of assistance represent about 38 percent of the total of nine million families that are income qualified for assistance. Most of the families receiving aid were in public housing or one of the rent supplement programs. The total cost of the various programs was about $5.3 billion in 1982. Of the 5.6 million families who qualify for assistance but receive no aid, millions are on waiting lists for public housing. In New York City, for example, there is an 18 year wait for a vacancy in public housing. Most of the nation's large cities also have such a shortage of public housing that waiting periods of several years are not uncommon (CQ, 1981, p. 1471).

One other set of federal programs should be noted. The Housing and Community Development Act of 1974 provided grants to local governments to take the place of categorical programs such as Urban Renewal, and Neighborhood Development. Local communities now receive a single grant, to be spent at their discretion, to improve neighborhoods. The allotments under the 1974 Act are almost as expensive as all the funds spent directly on housing for low-income and poor citizens. In 1980 Community Development spending totaled $4.5 billion. There are literally a dozen or so other programs, mostly quite small, which fund some type of housing program. For example, the 1982 budget included $13.5 million for the urban homesteading program, and $75 million for loans and grants to repair rural housing.

III.   AMERICAN HOUSING PROGRAMS:
ASSISTANCE TO UPPER AND MIDDLE-INCOME
CITIZENS

At least from a monetary point of view, American housing policy is oriented more toward assistance to middle- and upper-income citizens than to low-income citizens. As noted above, the federal government's first significant forays into the housing field grew out of the impact of the Great Depression on middle-income citizens, not the poor. During the Depression there was considerable concern about the number of working families who had lost their homes or were in imminent danger of doing so. By 1931, 50 percent of all mortgages were in default and residential construction was in a severe slump (Fainstein, 1980, pp. 215–216). The Hoover administration's response was The Federal Home Loan Act which made loans to the nation's distressed mortgage lenders. The Act assisted the lending institutions but not the nation's jobless home owners who continued to lose their homes at record levels over the next few years. By 1933 foreclosures were running one thousand a day.

To deal with the foreclosure problem, President Roosevelt convinced Congress to pass the Home Owners Loan Act. This act set up the Home Owners Loan Corporation which refinanced mortgages at 5 percent interest. By 1936 one home owner in five had been rescued by this Corporation and the immediate crisis was over.

The Roosevelt Administration also addressed the problem of saving the home construction industry. Thus in 1934 Congress established the Federal Housing Administration (FHA). FHA insured mortgages so that lenders, in effect, could make risk-free loans. This program assisted mortgage lenders but not builders who still did not believe that there was sufficient demand for new housing. Congress again responded by creating in 1938 the Federal National Mortgage Association (Fannie Mae); a government corporation which would buy some lender mortgages. Fannie Mae allowed lenders to sell mortgages so that they could invest in other more profitable ventures. Until the 1950s both FHA and Fannie Mae served middle-income home buyers, but under the Eisenhower administration FHA protections were extended to groups such as the elderly and those displaced by urban renewal. Another middle-income program was the Veterans Administration (VA) housing programs. These programs provided both mortgage insurance and below market interest rates to veterans. FHA, Fannie Mae and the VA program have made very significant contributions to home ownership in the United States.

The major method by which home owners are subsidized by the federal government is through the tax code. Home owners are allowed to deduct all mortgage interest and taxes paid on a home. These provisions considerably reduce the cost of home ownership. The common practice of mortgage lenders is to collect most of the interest incurred on a loan within ten years. The result is that during the first decade of a loan almost the total monthly house payment is tax deductible. Those home owners who receive the largest subsidy are those who can afford to purchase the most expensive homes and those who are in the highest tax brackets. Thus, in America the most heavily subsidized home owners are millionaires who live in mansions. Under this program there is also no limit on the number of houses for which the deduction can be claimed. If a person owns one home or a dozen, the deductions can be claimed for each residence.

This tax policy is so lucrative that it is a major tax shelter. It has become common practice for many Americans to trade up to higher priced homes to protect their income from taxes. The tax program is the most expensive housing policy in America. In fiscal 1982 the mortgage interest deduction will cost approximately $25.3 billion, while the property tax deduction will cost approximately $10.9 billion (The U.S. Budget in Brief, 1982, p. 60). The combined costs ($36.2 billion) represents about six times the amount of housing assistance given to low-income and poor citizens.

IV. LIBERAL AND CONSERVATIVE CRITIQUES OF AMERICA'S HOUSING PROGRAMS

As with many public issues, conservatives and liberals share some concerns about America's housing problems. Both are concerned about the barriers that first-time home buyers and other home buyers and sellers increasingly face, and the slump in housing starts and consequently the construction industry. Both conservatives and liberals tend to agree that the cause of these problems has been high interest rates. As noted above, there are many reasons why both liberals and conservatives are concerned about these problems, but one important reason is that housing is potentially a quite volatile issue. A fundamental part of the American dream is owning one's own home. Of course, it is also generally accepted by both philosophical groups that a slump in the construction industry is bad for the economy.

One other area of general agreement involves public housing. Neither liberals nor conservatives are vigorous advocates of traditional public housing. Both groups tend to believe that the type of public housing that concentrates large numbers of poor, often jobless families in one large project is often doomed to failure. Liberals, however, do generally support public housing for elderly citizens, especially when it can be located away from the slum areas of cities. Liberals also believe that the government should help expand the supply of decent, low-cost housing, but not in the form of inner-city public housing. There is currently no significant support in America for the European-style public housing (discussed below) designed for a broad range of income groups. Indeed, most Americans are probably not even aware that this is a popular housing option in Europe.

Beyond these basic points, the differences between liberals and conservatives are considerable. Conservatives do not support an extensive role for government in the housing area because they believe that the market can meet the housing needs of Americans. Of course, conservatives do support government programs such as FHA, Fannie Mae and tax policies which subsidize and protect the private market. Conservatives in recent years have supported housing programs for low-income and poor citizens, but believe that these programs should be kept modest.

The philosophical concerns of liberals about housing are much broader. The liberal position is that good housing and healthy neighborhoods are critical elements in the promotion of specific social goals. Poor housing and undesirable neighborhoods promote social problems such as cynicism and alienation, public health dangers, poor quality schools, and crime. Liberals believe that good and productive citizenship is promoted (not necessarily guaranteed) by a healthy living environment. Decent housing, a critical part of that environment, should therefore be a public right.

The philosophical and policy concerns of liberals cause them to be quite critical of America's current housing policies. First, they argue, the government provides too little assistance to low-income and poor citizens. Only 3.4 million low-income families receive any assistance, and the cost of that assistance is less than one percent of the total federal budget. Some 5.6 million families who qualify for assistance receive no aid. Second, the primary method that most conservatives support to deal with the housing needs of most low-income citizens is not practical. Conservatives traditionally maintain that the housing needs of most low-income citizens can be met through "filtering." Filtering is the process by which home owners trade up for better housing as their incomes improve, leaving their old housing for lower-income groups. Liberals argue that by the time most housing filters down to low-income groups, it is either in bad repair or located in squalid neighborhoods.

Liberals also contend that it is wrong for federal housing policy to be biased toward middle- and upper-income groups. It is unfair for the tax system to provide assistance to middle- and upper-income groups at four to six times the rate that low-income groups are given housing assistance. Such policies are both unfair and highly dysfunctional. They redistribute wealth toward upper-income groups, while often making housing a tax haven rather than a home. And, they stimulate inflation in the housing market, further pricing lower-income citizens out of the housing market. The tax laws, then, need to be changed to take housing out of the investment speculation market.

Liberals also argue that the past and, to some extent, current policies of the FHA, VA and other government programs have been to segregate housing by race and socio-economic status, while contributing to white flight to the suburbs. The impact of white flight has been to rob central cities of their tax base while isolating those citizens in the city who are too poor to flee.

Evidence supporting these charges is compelling. Until about the mid-1960s both FHA and VA made most of their loans to buyers of suburban housing; housing that was sold almost entirely to white families (Danielson, 1976, p. 242). By the time the official policies were changed, segregated residential patterns were well established. Of course, public housing and rent subsidy programs also played a substantial role in isolating and segregating minorities and the poor in the central city. Well into the 1970s local authorities maintained separate waiting lists for housing applicants, not allowing housing integration. Other federal policies such as the federal highway program encouraged flight to the suburbs, while frequently destroying the homes of the poor. In 1974 the U.S. Commission on Civil Rights pointed out that "Urban freeways have cut through ghettos to facilitate white suburbanites' travel from suburban homes to central city jobs. And the new roads also have uprooted suburban minority communities, forcing minority suburbanites to relocate in the central city" (U.S. Commission on Civil Rights, 1975, pp. 46–48).

Liberals point out that the problems caused by decentralization of authority have served to aggravate these problems. As Headey (p. 177) observes:

> The problems of federalism, of decentralization and local autonomy are everywhere evident in the housing field. Many programs, including public housing and urban renewal, require local authority initiative before any action can be taken and, in cases in which private developers propose building for lower income groups, they can often be effectively blocked by regulations included in housing and building codes and by rigid enforcement of zoning laws. Blocking tactics have been used not only to prevent racial integration, which is now mandatory in public housing, but also to prevent economic integration.

Last, liberals often argue that federal housing policy in America is unplanned and uncoordinated. The federal government has never adopted a philosophy about housing goals or land use policy. Until 1965, with the creation of the Department of Housing and Urban Development, there was no agency in charge of federal housing programs. FHA, VA and Urban Renewal all operated independently, and often in violation of the specific orders of Presidents (Headey, p. 223). The result, liberals argue, has been a set of housing policies that better reflect the policy demands of specific special interests than a rational approach to the nation's housing needs. Another result is that public policies often have been ineffective in meeting public needs. As one critic says:

> In a sense U.S. housing policy is to have no policy and rely on private enterprise. Private enterprise has, however, been stimulated by the increased demand for owner-occupied housing resulting from the tax concessions and mortgage guarantees which the federal government makes available to home-owners. Compared with Sweden and Britain lower income groups have been neglected. However, Congress has enacted diverse unco-ordinated programmes (e.g., public housing and subsidized rental and mortgage interest programmes) intended to assist both these groups and also groups with special needs (e.g. the elderly, war veterans, students, the handicapped). The programs have been launched with great optimism but have failed to serve more than a small proportion of those who, on paper, are eligible (Headey, p.175).

A second effect, liberals say, is that local communities have been allowed to benefit from federal housing policies without any community or land use planning. The frequent result is that urban areas have developed by random sprawl rather than plan, creating numerous social problems. For example, housing is often not thoughtfully related to the job market, thus many urbanites must travel long distances to work. In addition, uncharted sprawl makes it extremely difficult for many communities to provide public services such as garbage collection, police protection, street maintenance, and public transportation.

Both conservatives and liberals, then, have some substantial housing policy concerns. Before the specific proposals of both groups are examined, European housing policies will be reviewed. The emphasis will be on the policy decisions of western nations, the impact of these policies, and the implications of their experiences for dealing with America's housing needs.

V. EUROPEAN HOUSING POLICIES

Government intervention in the housing market is much more extensive in the European nations than in the United States. There are several reasons why this is true. First, during the 20th century Europe has been ravaged by two wars and a major depression. These upheavals either destroyed much of the housing stock or disrupted home building. The critical shortages caused by these events required massive catch-up efforts that were at least partially directed and financed by the government. Once the government became involved in housing, it stayed involved. Second, the European nations, unlike the United States, have viable leftwing political movements, generally represented by labor unions and Social Democratic parties. These leftwing groups have made housing an important policy priority, forcing governments to devote attention and resources to its promotion. These groups have attempted, with some success, to promote the idea that housing is a fundamental right and that government has an obligation to assist all citizens, regardless of wealth, in obtaining decent housing (McGuire, p. 8).

There are at least two other significant reasons why housing is given a high priority in Europe. Most of the Western European nations and even the Eastern European nations believe that housing represents a valuable national resource since it is a durable good. In addition, it provides jobs for those who finance, build and maintain housing. The Western nations also consider good housing to be a critical component of family and social policy. Like family allowances, housing subsidies are designed to promote social well-being and a higher standard of living. In addition to the promotion of healthy families, many Europeans believe that an increasingly technological society will require a more educated and sophisticated public. It is their belief that an elevated standard of living is necessary to produce the type of citizens society will need. Thus, as McGuire (p. 18) says, from this perspective improvement in housing is "not just an adjunct to economic growth but an integral part of it."

There are three major differences between European and American housing policies that provide interesting insights. Each of these policies is worthy of examination in some detail.

Universal Assistance

Direct housing assistance is much more universal in Europe than in the United States. Direct assistance takes a variety of forms including housing allowances, public housing, home purchase grants, rehabilitation loans, and building and savings subsidies. Housing allowances are a common social-welfare benefit in the European nations. In Sweden and West Germany, for example, over 40 percent of the population is eligible for housing grants. In France housing allowances also are extended to a significant proportion of the population. In most countries the allowance varies with family size and income. In some nations the allowances are designed to give special assistance to particular groups, such as single mothers and the elderly. Both socialist and conservative parties in Europe generally have supported housing allowances. The socialists tend to like the redistributive potential of the grants, while the conservatives are comforted by the fact that the grants support the private housing sector (Heidenheimer, Heclo, and Adams, 1975, p. 77).

Publicly-owned housing is also more extensive in Europe than in the

United States. In Britain about twenty percent of all families live in publicly-owned housing. Public housing is not as extensive in any of the other western nations, but it is more common in all the European nations than in America. Both Sweden and France also have a significant amount of quasi-public housing; housing subsidized and financed by the government and run by quasi-public authorities. Public and quasi-public housing in Europe is never limited to low-income families. In France, Britain and Sweden there is no means test for such housing and, therefore, it is common for middle-income families to live in public or quasi-public housing (Heidenheimer, Heclo, and Adams, p. 92).

Another method by which the government promotes housing in Europe is by direct subsidies to builders and purchasers. In most of the European nations the government provides below-market loans to builders, and sometimes buyers, as a method of holding down the costs of housing. In France and Sweden a considerable proportion of all housing is built or purchased with this type of assistance. In Sweden, for example, over 90 percent of all housing construction is financed, at least in part, by the government. In France first-time home purchasers receive special grants, and the state-directed financial institutions finance home construction with a bias toward moderate and low-income housing.

One of the most interesting government subsidies in Europe is the savings bonus. In Britain, for example, there are special savings accounts for citizens who want to save for the down payment on a home. If the citizen saves every month for five years, the government awards the saver a tax-free bonus equal to one year's savings. If the bonus is not withdrawn from the account for two years, it is doubled. In West Germany there is a similar plan. Savers can earn a government bonus equal to as much as 25 to 35 percent of the sum saved (McGuire, pp. 134, 147).

As in the United States, the governments of Europe also promote home ownership by allowing purchasers to treat interest and tax expenses as tax deductions. However, in most European nations there are monetary limitations on these deductions. The limitations are designed to allow about 80 percent of all families (all but those at the highest income levels) to deduct the total cost of yearly mortgage interest and property taxes. In many of the nations the interest and tax deductions are limited to the imputed rental income of the house; the value of the rent that could have been obtained in the market (McGuire, pp. 53, 173). In some countries there is also a limit on the number of years in which the deductions can be taken. For example, in France the deduction can only be taken during the first ten years of the loan. In West Germany the deductions can only be taken by first-home buyers. The reasons for the limitations on deductions are fairly obvious. The governments want to encourage home purchasing without stimulating inflation in the housing market, or unduly subsidizing wealthy citizens.

The Non-Profit Housing Market

A major difference between the American and European housing markets is that in Europe there is a very large non-profit housing construction sector. The non-profit sector has been promoted primarily by labor unions and encouraged and financed by national governments. The non-profit sector consists of building societies, housing associations, and housing cooperatives. The first two organizations operate much like savings and loan associations except that they often directly develop, own and operate housing and commercial property (Fainstein, p.226). Housing cooperatives raise money through bond or equity markets and build housing for their members which is then managed on a joint-ownership basis (Headey, pp. 44–48).

The non-profit sector has a long history in Europe and in most of the nations it accounts for a very significant percentage of all home construction. In Sweden, for example, 65 percent of all post-war housing has been built by housing or consumer cooperatives (Headey, p.45). The Swedish government partly financed this housing, as it did most of the privately built housing.

Land and Development Planning

Unlike the United States, urban planning is common in the European nations. Planning is designed to promote managable, functional, socially desirable growth. Fainstein (p. 221) describes the variety of goals that planning is designed to accomplish:

> European national and regional planning involves restrictions on investment in developed regions, incentives to growth in designated development areas, direct governmental investment in housing and industry, and subsidization of labor costs. Many countries require planning permission of any new construction, and such permission accrues to land only when it conforms to national and regional master plans, which set developmental priorities and seek to contain urban sprawl.

As an integral part of planning, governments often purchase development property in urban areas. This is a common practice in Sweden and the Netherlands and increasingly common in Britain. The government, usually at the local level, purchases development property to make certain that sites for home building will remain available, to limit land speculation, and to retain profits from built-up land for the public. In Sweden, the Netherlands and Britain, the government has used its financing and publicly owned land to develop new towns. New towns are intended to reduce development pressure on urban areas or on the periphery of major metropolitan areas.

It is not our intention here to formally attempt to assess the success of European housing policies. There are, however, a few points with which most observers would probably agree. Certainly after War II the European nations managed to build a great deal of quality housing in a relatively short period of time. Some nations such as West Germany, Sweden, The Netherlands and Britain made very impressive gains. In recent years France also has built a great deal of quality housing. Both public and quasi-public housing, often combined with housing allowances, has provided millions of citizens with decent housing at very low cost. Subsidies for both home builders and purchasers also have served to promote home ownership. The comprehensive policies of Sweden have created the highest ratio of dwelling units to population, and the best housing amenities of any nation in the world (Headey, p. 47). It also should be noted that there are no slums in Sweden.

A major area in which the European nations clearly lag behind the United States, however, is in home ownership. The figures below show the rate of home ownership in selected nations in 1978 (Melton, p.44):

United States 63%
Belgium 56%
Canada 60%
France 45%
West Germany 34%
Sweden 35%
Switzerland 28%
United Kingdom 48%

As the figures show, Sweden, West Germany and Switzerland, particularly, have much lower rates of home ownership than America. Both Britain and France are also significantly behind the United States in making home ownership possible. The reasons why the rate of home ownership varies by nation are numerous, but a major one is that some of the nations have not emphasized this policy. In those nations with generous housing allowances, renting simply has been the most advantageous policy for most families. In more recent years, Britain, France and Sweden have developed policies that make home ownership a more desirable alternative. While home ownership is not as extensive in many nations as it is in the United States, housing costs often take a relatively modest proportion of family income in those nations which emphasize apartment living.

Most observers believe that urban and land use planning has been a valuable method by which European countries have made growth more manageable, and attractive. There is little doubt that most European cities are better designed to accommodate the delivery of public services (including transportation), than are American cities. Most European cities also provide a better mix of industrial, residential neighborhoods and parks and recreational space than do American cities. Additionally, a few nations have used planning as a method of integrating housing by socio-economic status and age. Sweden has been particularly successful in integrating housing along these lines. Of course, this has been made easier by the virtual absence of racial division.

VI. THE LIMITS OF COMPARISON

The major question raised by this review is how applicable European housing techniques are to America's housing problems. The answer is not simple. Some of the policies that have been effective in European nations clearly would not be easily accepted in the United States. The reason is that they would constitute non-incremental policy alterations that often would seriously conflict with prevailing practices or power relationships. For example, housing allowances for middle-income citizens would run counter to the common American practice of trying to adopt policies that help such families purchase, rather than rent, property. Similarly, attempts to build public housing for a broad range of income groups would, as it did in the Great Depression, run into immediate opposition from the real estate and building industries. The real estate and building lobbies would also be a major obstacle to government subsidies to cooperatives or other types of non-profit housing associations. The stigma commonly associated with public housing in America would also make it difficult to broadly promote this kind of policy. Public housing for the poor, the handicapped, or the retired would, if carefully designed, be more politically feasible.

Some of the European policies would fit into the American political and economic framework much more easily. For example, savings bonuses or tax breaks for individuals trying to accumulate the downpayment on a home would probably be quite popular. In fact, in early 1983 Senator John Tower (R., Tex.), a prominent conservative, introduced just such a bill. Financial limits on deductions for real estate taxes and mortgage interest is currently being discussed by both Republican and

Democratic members of Congress. Housing allowances for poor citizens, as opposed to public housing, is already an accepted alternative. The controversy here is, and will continue to be, over how much money should be budgeted for the programs and who should be covered. In Europe, of course, the decision has long been made that all low-income citizens who need housing assistance should receive it. Planning is a more complex issue. Some American cities are more concerned with planning than others. In the last decade, most major cities have shown serious concern about planning, but hardly on the scale considered typical in Europe. In America there is still a great deal of faith in the free market and a belief that planning retards growth. Thus, while some cities plan in modest ways, there is still considerable opposition to anything that might even modestly be called comprehensive planning.

One of the most important lessons of comparison, then, is that political, social and economic patterns may make it difficult or even impossible for policies that have worked quite well in one country to be adopted by another country. This does not mean, of course, that the policy environment is unchanging. A housing crisis, or changes in the age of the population, could create greatly different needs and policy expectations.

VII.   HOUSING REFORMS: CONSERVATIVE PROPOSALS

Conservatives, like liberals, are not entirely united when it comes to proposals to deal with the nation's housing problems. Some conservative proposals have found broader support within conservative ranks than others. We begin by examining the major proposals of the Reagan administration and then discuss a few proposals put forth by conservative members of Congress.

In late 1981, a Commission appointed by President Reagan to study the nation's housing needs made its official report (CQ, November 7, 1981, p. 2190). The Commission's major conclusions and proposals were consistent with recent conservative positions on housing. The Commission concluded that the nation's housing needs could (and should) be met by reliance on the private sector. The Commission noted that the private sector would need some subsidies, but that it could meet the nation's housing needs without major intervention by the government. The Commission also concluded that there is no shortage of good housing in America. The problem, as the Commission saw it, was that many families in America do not have the funds necessary to acquire the serviceable housing that is available.

The Commission's major policy recommendation was that low-income families receive a consumer assistance grant to be used to rent adequate housing. The grant would simply be a housing allowance that the recipient could use to pay for more expensive housing than his/her personal income would allow. The Commission favored this proposal over the Section 8 program which pays a grant directly to landlords. The Commission felt that the allowance would give recipients more freedom in the selection of housing, allowing low-income families to better integrate into the community. In addition, the allowance would stimulate home and apartment construction.

The Commission recommended that the allowance not be an entitlement program open to all eligible families. In fact, it proposed that the program be kept quite small. Priority should be given to low-income families living in inadequate housing, families paying rent in excess of 50 percent of their income, or families suffering involuntary displacement. For these groups, the Commission recommended a first come, first serve program limited by funding. This, of course, is a much more modest proposal than the housing allowance common in Europe.

Some conservatives are uncomfortable with housing allowance programs because they fear that the recipients will not use the money to improve their housing. Like proposals to "cash out" the Food Stamp Program, some are skeptical that the money would be used wisely. For this reason the allowance program is not as popular with many conservatives as the Section 8 program which provides subsidies directly to landlords. Interestingly, some liberals share this fear. In 1970 HUD launched an experimental housing allowance program. Over an 11 year period some 30,000 households in 12 states participated in the experiment (Struyk and Bendick, 1981). Evaluations of the program varied, with some investigators concluding that the program was more effective and much less expensive than traditional housing programs (Struyk and Bendick, 1981; Frieden, pp. 15–35). However, some liberals and conservatives had doubts. They noted that only about half the families that could have qualified under the program even applied. Second, most of the recipients did not use the grants to obtain better housing. Rather they stayed put and used the subsidy to reduce their contribution to housing. To meet federal standards many of the recipients did make modest improvements in their housing, but the repairs were too minor to substantially improve their situation.

Many conservatives and liberals found it difficult to label this type of program a success. They argued that a good program should improve the quality of the housing and neighborhood in which recipients live. Many observers also noted that when recipients stay put, the housing market is not stimulated to build homes or even to substantially renovate existing housing. Of course, a rental allowance program could require recipients to seek better housing, but one implication of the study was that the poor are often quite reluctant to move. They may be reluctant to move because they do not believe that they could obtain substantially better housing with the supplemental grant.

The Commission recommended three other proposals: (1) that local communities be allowed to use Community Development Block Grants to build new housing; (2) that pension funds be allowed to expand their investment in mortgages; and (3) that owners of residential property be given a special tax credit for rehabilitating rental structures. The Commission made no estimate of the impact of these changes on the housing market (CQ, November 7, 1981, p. 2190).

President Reagan had no official reaction to the Commission's recommendations. In his 1983 budget proposal he recommended: (1) the continuation of fundings for the Section 8 program, with assistance budgeted for about 600,000 households; (2) no funding for Section 235 or 236 housing, and (3) a modest increase in the number of families eligible for FHA mortgages, the construction of 70,000 additional units of public housing, easing regulation of mortgage revenue bonds, and allowing pension funds to expand housing investments. In response to critics, who charged that his policies were too modest given the nation's housing problems, Reagan argued that his economic policies would turn the economy around and once it did so, the nation's housing problems would be solved by market forces.

The nation's worsening housing problems stimulated some Republican members of Congress to break with the President and back emergency legislation to give the industry some immediate help. In the late Spring of 1982 Senator Richard Lugar (R-Ind.) sponsored a $5.1 billion mortgage subsidy plan designed to create 700,000 new jobs in housing related fields. Under the Lugar plan, families with incomes of up to $30,000 a year ($37,000 in high-cost areas) would be eligible for interest rate subsidies to help them buy new homes. The government would provide subsidies to cut the mortgage rates by as much as 4 percentage points, but not below 11 percent. Recipients of the grants would be expected to repay them when the house was sold or refinanced. In support of the bill, Senator Lugar argued that legislation was needed to stimulate the housing market. Lugar noted that "Housing has led us out of past recessions, and it can do so again" (CQ, April 17, 1981, p. 847). Lugar's plan was passed by both the House and Senate in June, 1982, but was vetoed by President Reagan.

VIII. HOUSING REFORM: LIBERAL SOLUTIONS

Within Congress, the Democratic and liberal housing proposals pending in 1982 did not differ radically from those supported by moderate and conservative members of Congress. Henry Gonzales (D. Tex.) was the author of the most comprehensive housing recovery proposal (CQ, April 17, 1982, p.847). Gonzales' proposal called for new funding for the Section 235 programs that subsidize mortgages for low- and moderate-income home buyers. Gonzales' bill called for one billion in 235 mortgage subsidies to stimulate the construction of about 10,000 homes for low-income families. The bill would also have authorized $3.5 billion for the 235(q) program which would lower interest rates to 9.5 percent during the first 10 years of a mortgage. Recipients would be required to repay part of the subsidy when the house was sold. The bill also provided $760 million in loans to homeowners faced with mortgage foreclosures because of economic problems. Because of the nation's economic problems there seemed to be little chance that Gonzales' total bill would actually pass Congress or even be given very serious consideration. Some observers believed that some provisions of the bill might attract attention if the housing crisis continued through 1983.

Other moderate Democratic members of the House were proposing that the government provide first-time home buyers with loans for down payments on homes. A bypartisan proposal circulating in the House would give new home buyers a $5,400 tax credit. During a severe housing slump in 1975 a similar plan had given new home buyers a $2,000 tax credit. Last, some Democratic members of the House were proposing that Fannie Mae be authorized to buy up additional mortgage loans to give lenders new funds to lend to home buyers.

The housing proposals being actively supported by liberal members of Congress in 1983 were quite moderate. They were certainly not as extensive as the policies commonly employed in Europe. The difference between American liberal proposals and those of the left in Europe, of course, reflects the much weaker position of the left in the United States. In Europe, the labor unions and the Social Democratic parties are much more powerful and can win support for more egalitarian proposals. American liberals and leftwing scholars have put forth more radical proposals to deal with the nation's housing problems, but at the current time they are not being seriously considered by policy makers. Below we will review some of the major proposals of liberal scholars. There are at least six major housing proposals that are often supported by liberals (Headey, pp. 220–226).

A National Housing Budget

Liberals often argue that the United States subsidizes wealthier home buyers more than moderate- and low-income buyers because the subsidies that go to higher-income groups are hidden within the tax expenditure budget. They believe that if it became common knowledge that the tax deductions for mortgage interest and taxes actually subsidize wealthier groups at several times the rate at which other groups are subsidized, the public would force the government to alter its policies. Thus, liberals recommend that a National Housing Budget should be published each year. This budget would show all government expenditures (including tax expenditures) by income class for housing during that budget year. Such a budget would scandalize the public, it is argued, and force an alteration in housing priorities. As Headey argues, even conservative politicians would be reluctant to say "that it should be an objective of public policy to redistribute resources in favor of the rich" (Headey, p. 254). Liberals, of course, hope that a reduction in benefits for wealthier groups would result in increased assistance for moderate- to low-income families and a reduction in housing inflation.

Tax and Interest Rate Limitations

Liberals say that current laws which allow home purchasers to deduct all mortgage interest and real estate taxes not only discriminates in favor of the rich, but also that the policy creates housing inflation. To deal with both problems, they propose limitations on such deductions. There are a number of proposals along these lines. One idea is to place a limit on the amount of taxes and interest that could be deducted each year. As proposed, most citizens would be allowed the full deduction, with limitations imposed on only the most expensive mortgages. There are some variations on this theme. Some argue that the tax and interest deductions should be replaced by a housing expense deduction that would vary with family income and size. Another option is to place a limit on the number of years in which tax and interest deductions could be taken. A common proposal, along the lines of the West Germans, is that the deductions only be allowed during the first ten years of a loan. The rationale for this is that the deductions should help people purchase a home but that the subsidy should be limited so that government resources could be shifted to low-income and first-home buyers. Last, it is often proposed that subsidies be available only for one home. This proposal is obviously designed to limit government assistance to wealthier citizens. In early 1983, some Republicans in Congress and the executive branch were promoting reforms along these lines.

Housing Allowances

Another liberal proposal would involve government housing allowances to low- and moderate-income earners. These housing allowances would be made available to at least the nation's lowest 10 to 20 percent of all income earners. This proposal would create a housing allowance system similar to those available in many European nations, but it would not be as extensive. The allowances would be given only to families living in decent housing or those families willing to relocate to better housing. The allowances would be grants to the family rather than to the landlords. The intent is for family grants to allow recipients a broader range of housing options, hopefully resulting in better neighborhood integration of low-income families, and the eventual end of America's major slums. Liberals feel that slum neighborhoods have negative social impacts on residents, and eventually on the larger society. Thus, housing allowances and other housing assistance programs should be designed to banish slums from the American scene.

Financing and Savings Proposals

Liberals also favor public policies designed to encourage home purchases and sales. This would require the government to take those actions necessary to hold down interest rates and make available home loan money. When interest rates are very high (as they were in 1981 and 1982) the government could subsidize loans to bring the interest rates down, with a recovery option when the house was sold or refinanced. The government, liberals argue, should adopt the European technique of builder and lender subsidies to reduce the costs of housing.

Furthermore there are a number of things that the government could do to help ensure availability of mortgage money. One option would be the incentive saving plans that are popular in Europe. Families or individuals investing in a savings plan designed to accumulate the funds necessary to finance a home purchase could receive matching grants and tax breaks. Liberals also believe that current laws discriminate against small savers, often making it unprofitable for them to save. Small savers could be given tax breaks to encourage saving rather than spending. Limits on tax deductions for consumer spending also would help to encourage citizens to save rather than spend. Thus, liberals favor a number of policies to give all Americans more incentives to save and accumulate capital for home mortgages and other investments.

Urban and Land Use Planning

From the liberal perspective, it is utter folly for cities to fail to employ building and land use planning. Lack of planning has created a crazy-quilt pattern of municipal development leading to unsightly and wasteful urban spread. In addition to other problems, sprawl makes delivery of standard services such as education and garbage collection more difficult. Property owners frequently are confronted with drainage or even flooding problems caused by hasty housing construction in under-developed areas. Cities usually must bear the cost of water control systems. The failure of cities to control urban property has contributed significantly to inflation in building prices. True, some cities have better growth planning than others, but basically liberals believe that most cities have done a poor job in this area. Liberals accept the fact that most cities are too developed to be transformed by planning, but suggest that the adoption of planning would promote more rational and manageable growth, contributing to better urban environments.

Housing for the Aged

Liberals often argue that the government should build creative communities for retired citizens. Three reasons are offered in support of this policy. First, citizens should have reasonable housing and community options when they retire. The aged should have the option of moving to smaller, yet decent housing located away from the more congested areas of large cities. This housing should provide the support services (e.g. medical care and recreation) that aged citizens need. If such housing were available, the aged would have more manageable, safer, stimulating and companionable environments in which to live. Such communities would provide an alternative to the nursing homes and decaying central city neighborhoods in which America's aged often end up. Liberals favor housing projects created specifically for the aged and located outside central cities.

Second, by providing housing for the aged, the nation's stock of family dwelling would be significantly increased. As the aged moved out of their family residence to retirement communities their homes would become available, thereby increasing the number of residences available for families still in the workforce.

Last, if residence in such a community was based on ability to pay, retirement communities would be cost effective. Nursing home care is extremely expensive and many of the residents of such facilities are there only because they have no where else to go or because they cannot perform some basic services (such as grocery shopping) for themselves. In a supportive environment, many of the aged would remain viable and independent much longer and be happier.

IX. CONCLUSIONS

This paper has examined three of the nation's most pressing housing problems. Current housing policies have been critiqued from both liberal and conservative perspectives. Both liberal and conservative proposals for housing reform have been examined and compared to European housing policies. This review has made several things apparent. First, while America has been quite successful since the end of World War II in housing most of its citizens, current housing problems are substantial. Conservatives and liberals clearly have different priorities, but both groups are concerned about specific problems in the area of housing. One reason for the shared concern is that current housing problems affect a very large proportion of the total population. Even middle-income citizens are having difficulty in purchasing or selling homes, and the construction and related housing industries are in financial difficulty. Conservatives and liberals also share concern for the millions of Americans who are not well-housed. Both agree that the government should sponsor programs to help low-income citizens obtain better housing but, of course, they disagree over the mechanics and magnitude of such programs.

In addition, both conservatives and liberals agree that the policies established and administered by the federal government since the New Deal have played a major role in increasing the quality and affordability of American housing. They also have created public expectations of attractive and affordable housing that policymakers are reluctant to disappoint. For this reason the nation's current housing problems are considered serious enough to become a major issue in future elections. Our review of current housing reforms under consideration in Congress, however, suggests that neither liberals or conservatives support policies that are very radical. Both groups admit that if the policies under consideration were adopted, they would have only a modest impact on the nation's housing problems. Even liberal members of Congress currently support rather modest housing reforms, in part because they seem to think that more comprehensive proposals would not win support during a period in which the nation's economy is in a slump. Of course, the modesty of liberal proposals in Congress reflects the weakness of left wing political movements in the United States, which is itself a reflection of our historical suspicion of government. This suspicion, of course, is the core value of the American public philosophy as described by Furniss and Mitchell (Chapter 2) and Goggin (Chapter 3).

The difference between the housing proposals being supported by liberal and conservative members of Congress, and conservative and liberal scholars reflect the very fundamental differences between these two schools of political thought. Liberals want the government to play a larger role, and want the emphasis of government assistance to be shifted from aid to upper-middle income and wealthy citizens to moderate- and lower-income citizens. Liberals want the government to play a larger role because they have less faith than conservatives in the power of the market to provide equitably for the housing needs of all citizens.

Liberals are more inclined to believe that a wealthy society has an obligation to succor the less fortunate members of society. Thus, they believe that all citizens have a right to decent housing. Conservatives do not totally reject an obligation for the housing needs of low-income citizens. They support more modest programs for the poor on the grounds that extensive programs constitute too large a financial drag on the economy, thus rendering economic forces less capable of meeting public needs.

Liberals tend to have a more global view of the role of housing in society. They believe that citizens who are ill-housed and isolated in squalid neighborhoods are less capable of realizing their full human potential, and thus less capable of being viable, productive members of society. Consequently, society ends up paying a great price for its deprived citizens, in crime, low productivity, welfare expenses and many other ways. Good housing and other preventive social services, liberals believe, are investments that yield social, moral and economic profits.

The differences between conservatives and liberals on issues of housing, then, are consistent with those reflected in debates between these two groups over other policies. Conservatives are more trusting than liberals in the ability of the market to solve social problems. They believe that costly social problems often interfere with the ability of the market to meet public needs. Liberals believe that government is a better friend of most citizens than the market, and that historical evidence shows that the market has been unable to equitably or efficiently meet most public needs. They often point out that the government accepted the obligation of providing many public services only when the market failed to meet public needs.

Conservatives point out that liberal policies are redistributive and expensive, requiring all citizens to pay higher taxes and have less control over their lives. Liberals generally accept this charge. They simply argue that if public services are financed by progressive taxes, moderate- and low-income citizens will receive better services than their personal incomes would provide, and the more equal distribution of income produced by progressive taxes would produce a less class-structured and more egalitarian society.

The housing policies and experiences of other western nations are insightful, but realistically limited in their ability to inform American housing policy or the conservative/liberal debate over housing. Established political and economic priorities (the American public philosophy) substantially limit the type of policies that are likely to be adopted. Thus, unless American's housing problems become substantially more acute, only the more modest European policies are likely to be palatable to American policymakers.

REFERENCES

Carlson, David B. *How Housing Allowances Work*. Washington, D.C.: The Urban Institute, 1964.

Congressional Budget Office. *Federal Housing Policy: Current Problems and Recurring Issues*. Washington, D.C.: Government Printing Office, 1978.

Congressional Quarterly: Weekly Report. Washington, D.C.: Congressional Quarterly, Inc., August 15, 1981.

Congressional Quarterly: Weekly Report. Washington, D.C.: Congressional Quarterly, Inc., November 7, 1981.

Congressional Quarterly: Weekly Report. Washington, D.C.: Congressional Quarterly, Inc., April 17, 1982.

Danielson, Michael N. *The Politics of Exclusion*. New York: Columbia University Press, 1976.

Fainstein, Susan S. "American Policy for Housing and Community Development: A Comparative Examination." In *Housing Policy for the 1980s*. Edited by Roger Montgomery and Dale Rogers Marshall. Lexington, Mass.: Lexington Books, 1980.

Frieden, Bernard J. "Housing Allowances: An Experiment That Worked." *The Public Interest*, 1980, pp. 15–35.

Heidenheimer, Arnold J., Heclo, H., and Adams, Carolyn Teich. *Comparative Public Policy: The Politics of Social Choice in Europe and America*. New York: St. Martin's Press, 1975.

Headey, Bruce. *Housing Policy in the Developed Economy: The United Kingdom, Sweden, and the United States*. London: Croom Helm, 1978.

Heilbrum, James. *Urban Economics and Public Policy*. New York: St. Martin's Press, 1981.

Hills v. Gautreaux. 1967. 425 U.S. 284.

Kristof, Frank S. "Federal Housing Policies: Subsidized Production, Filtration and Objectives: Part II." *Land Economics*, May 1973, p. 171.

McGuire, Chester C. *International Housing Policies: A Comparative Analysis*. Lexington, Mass.: Lexington Books, 1981.

Melton, Caroll. *Housing Finance and Homeownership*. Chicago: International Union of Building Societies and Savings Associations, 1978.

Smith, Adam. *Paper Money*. New York: Dell Books, 1981.

Struyk, Raymond J. and Bendick, Marc., eds. *Housing Vouchers for the Poor: Lessons from a National Experiment*. Washington, D.C.: The Urban Institute, 1981.

The United States Budget In Brief: Fiscal Year 1982. Washington, D.C.: Government Printing Office, 1982.

U.S. Commission on Civil Rights. *The Federal Civil Rights Enforcement Effort: To Provide Fair Housing*. Washington, D.C.: Government Printing Office, 1975.

U.S. Commission on Civil Rights. *Equal Opportunity in Suburbia*. Washington, D.C.: Government Printing Office, 1974.

U.S. Bureau of the Census. *Census of the Population and Housing, 1950, 1960, 1970, and Annual Housing Survey: 1977, Part E*. Washington, D.C.: Government Printing Office, 1978.

U.S. Bureau of the Census. *Statistical Abstract of the United States: 1980*. 101st Edition. Washington, D.C.: Government Printing Office, 1981.

THE ELECTION AND IMPACT OF
BLACK OFFICIALS IN THE
SOUTH

James W. Button and Richard K. Scher

I. INTRODUCTION

The civil rights movement in America was a complex social upheaval whose many goals remain incomplete. It began in the South during the 1950s, but eventually spread to all other parts of the country. And while it initially was seen as primarily a black political, economic, and social movement, it later incorporated other minority groups as well, including American Indians, Hispanics, women and gay people.

The goals of the civil rights movement were as diverse as its geography, ethnic and racial composition. For blacks (who began and perhaps remain the central figures in the movement), the goals ranged from the most concrete to extremely abstract. Blacks hoped to break down traditional and very tangible barriers of discrimination which existed in the South, including the right to enter and be served in restaurants, theaters, hotels, and other public accommodations. They also sought to end dual school systems and to remove discriminatory practices common in public schools. Another key goal was the right to vote. Since the establishment of Jim Crow laws late in the nineteenth century, blacks had not

183

been permitted to register to vote in all but a few areas of the South. Yet the right to vote was seen as crucial to blacks, for they correctly saw that without the franchise they would continue to be regarded as second class citizens. Perhaps most abstractly, the civil rights movement was aimed at legitimizing blacks and enabling them to achieve their rightful place in American society. It was, in a sense, a revolution designed to allow blacks a chance to participate in the American dream which before had been denied to them.

One of the other major goals of the civil rights movement was a corollary of the search for the franchise: the election of blacks to political office. Blacks felt that the exercise of real political power in America could not be limited to voting. If they were to achieve true political capabilities, they could not remain on the outside looking in, but had to insure that blacks became part of political decision making processes at local, state, and national levels. As a result, as blacks began to register to vote (especially in the South), black candidates for political office emerged who, it was hoped, could be elected by black voters and their white allies. These efforts, which began in the mid to late 1960s, were not initially very successful. But by the mid 1970s, substantial numbers of blacks were being elected to public office in the South. Most of these officials occupied positions at local (municipal, county, and school district) levels. Nonetheless, black candidates for state legislatures and even the U.S. House of Representatives also appeared, and it is possible, if past trends continue, that blacks will achieve greater degrees of success at these positions. Indeed it may be that the so-called "New South" will not be fully mature until blacks are able to achieve greater and more equitable levels of representation at all levels of government.

This chapter surveys the rise and impact of black elected officials in the modern South. Available literatures as well as space do not permit a wider analysis. But since most of the civil rights effort to secure the election of blacks to public office occurred in this region, a focus on the traditional 11 southern states is worthwhile (Alabama, Arkansas, Georgia, Florida, Louisiana, Mississippi, North Carolina, South Carolina, Tennessee, Texas and Virginia). After a brief discussion of some theoretical and methodological issues concerning the importance of black representation in office, the chapter examines the history of black elected officials, with emphasis on the change from failure to success in reaching this goal. It next examines the conditions associated with the election of black elected officials: what has to happen in order that blacks be elected to office? Then the impact which black officials have had once elected to office is analyzed: have they accomplished anything, or has their occupation of public office been only a hollow shell? Finally future possibilities for black representation are speculated upon, and some areas for further research are suggested.

II.   BLACK VOTERS AND BLACK REPRESENTATION: THEORY AND METHODOLOGY

The effort by blacks to secure the election of black officials raises theoretical questions that are as important as the practical political ones. Indeed, they are far too complex to be treated here. But two are extremely germane to the election of black officials. First, why is it important that blacks be elected to represent the black community? Second, how is it possible to tell when individuals, especially members of a minority such as blacks, are being adequately or equitably represented?

The first question will be addressed below in the section on the impact of black officials, but a few remarks need to be made about the second. As the discussion which follows will show, blacks have not always been very satisfied with their own elected black officials. There is then a certain qualitative, even subjective, element in considering whether or not representation is "adequate." Nonetheless, as a convenient measure it has been assumed that approximate numerical correspondence between representation and population constitutes at least a minimum level of "equity." That is, where the percentage of blacks in public office begins to approach that of the percentage of blacks in the population, then some degree of adequacy is present. Of course there are numerous problems with this measure. It lends itself to quota systems and to a concern with quantitative measures of representation rather than its quality. But at least in these relatively early days of significant numbers of blacks' occupying public office, this measure continues to be used, especially in assessing black representation in legislative bodies.

In addition to these theoretical considerations, a few methodological issues need to be briefly mentioned as well. While the literature on black elected officials has become substantial in recent years, it is not always comparable, and in some ways it is very fragmented. Even a brief discussion of these methodological problems can help our understanding of the literature on the election and impact of black officials.

In the first place, some of the literature deals only with parts of the South, some with the entire South, some is national in scope, and some includes all regions but the South. There is not even agreement on what states constitute the South. Political data from non-southern regions may actually be significantly different from southern data, and might substantially affect our understanding of the election and impact of black elected officials. Thus extreme care must be taken in interpreting the results of many of these studies, particularly those which have as their focus areas other than the South exclusively.

Next, many of the research designs are not comparable, and variables which seem to be similar in various studies are not always measured in the same way. There are significant differences, for example, in the size and kind of samples chosen for analysis. To mention only two, Karnig and Welch (1980) limited their study to cities over 25,000 persons which were more than ten percent black; Engstrom and McDonald (1982) examined central cities in 224 metropolitan areas, while eliminating 15 cities which have black populations less than one percent and four in which blacks constitute a majority of the population. Some studies focus on counties, while others examine cities, and urban–rural distinctions are often blurred.

Perhaps the most crucial measurement problem concerns the classification of election systems. The two major forms—at-large and district—do not always exist as pure types. Often there are mixed forms, in which there is a combination of the two, and some seats will be selected by districts and others at-large. Sometimes there are residence requirements for candidates, even though the elections may be at-large. As Karnig and Welch observe (1982, pp. 100–103), the way in which different election systems are treated can strongly affect the outcome of individual studies, but there is little agreement in the literature on the best way to categorize them.

There is also difficulty in establishing appropriate standards for interpreting the results of different studies. For example, as already noted, "equity" of representation is usually assumed when the percentage of blacks on a city or county legislative body roughly equals the percent of blacks in the whole population. But other studies subtract the black percentage in the population from the black percentage on the legislative body in order to measure equity. These different approaches lead to rather different views of "equity." A newer approach to the problem regresses seat percentages onto population percentages (Engstrom and McDonald, 1982), leading to yet another standard for "equity." And as noted earlier, each of these methods begs the very basic question of whether equity can really be assessed by a simple quantitative measure.

The problem of appropriate standards is also seen in measuring the impact of black elected officials. Because it is difficult to determine the independent effect these persons have on the political system, subjective measures often have to be employed instead. This is true enough in trying to assess the impact of black officials on relatively substantive areas such as desegregation of schools or hiring of black police and firemen. It is even more difficult in assessing their role in more symbolic areas of politics, such as changing public attitudes on racial issues. And there is little agreement on determining, even in qualitative terms, the impact of black officials; that is, how "effective" are they?

Finally, care must be taken to avoid making causal inferences from incomplete or imperfect research models about the impact of black elected officials, or indeed about the preconditions for their election. In the latter case, correlation analysis allows for reasonably certain levels of predictability; even so, there is no "sure" recipe for successfully electing blacks to office. But in attempting to assess the impact of blacks in office, there are numerous other variables which could also account for changes besides the presence of these individuals. Attempting to isolate their contribution or making causal inferences about the relation between black elected officials and changes in the political system is tenuous indeed.

This brief discussion of the theoretical and methodological issues in the available literature is not meant to be exhaustive. The ensuing discussion will illustrate these points in more detail. Moreover, care will be taken in interpreting the literature to insure that its limitations will not be exceeded. Nonetheless, the research is rich and varied enough to provide a valuable insight into the election and impact of southern black public officials.

III. BLACK ELECTED OFFICIALS IN THE SOUTH: RECONSTRUCTION TO VOTING RIGHTS ACT

Actually there is nothing new in the election of blacks to public office. After the Civil War, during Radical Reconstruction, blacks occupied prominent political positions in the South. Approximately one quarter of the delegates to southern state constitutional conventions in 1867 and 1868 were black. In South Carolina, Blacks constituted a majority of the lower house of the legislature (but not the upper house). In other southern states (especially of the black belt) there were substantial numbers of blacks in the legislature and in local offices. A dozen blacks served in the U.S. House of Representatives during Radical Reconstruction, and two, Hiram Revels and Blanche K, Bruce of Mississippi, went to the U.S. Senate. No black was elected governor of a southern state, although P.B.S. Pinchback did serve as acting Governor of Louisiana for six weeks. Blacks were also elected lieutenant governor in South Carolina, Mississippi and Louisiana, and there were a few others occupying state executive positions in the South (Newby, 1978, pp. 262–3).

Nonetheless, even though blacks constituted a majority of Republican voters in the South, they did not carry corresponding political power. Lacking economic resources and political experience, they were forced to ally themselves with white Republicans. As Newby and other southern historians have observed, few white Republicans in the South were really committed to promoting racial equality, and nowhere did state policies really foster economic, political, and social success for blacks (Newby,

1978, pp. 263–4). As a result, by the end of Reconstruction (1876), blacks were politically isolated. Their white Republican "allies" (both north and south) had disappeared. New governments and constitutions, composed of and by Democrats for Democrats, replaced the Reconstruction regimes. It was only a short step, by the late 1880s, to the institution of Jim Crow laws and the total disenfranchisement of southern blacks (Woodward, 1974).

The sad tale of post-Reconstruction years is well known and requires little elaboration here. Between 1889 and 1902 all of the ex-Confederate states established a poll tax, which was designed as an economic obstacle to voting. It was not finally eliminated until the Twenty-fourth Admendment to the U.S. Constitution was ratified in 1964 (Rodgers and Bullock, 1972, pp. 36–37). The white primary was also established as a means of keeping blacks out of the Democratic party, and hence out of any meaningful electoral participation. It was not overturned until the U.S. Supreme Court in *Smith v. Allwright* (1944) held that political parties could not determine party membership on the basis of race (Key, 1949, pp. 619–25; Rodgers and Bullock, 1972, p. 18).

Other devices also existed to keep blacks away from the polls. Literacy tests were often given to blacks, but not to whites. Local voting registrars had enormous discretion in determining who passed these tests. They often required "character references" for prospective voters, which blacks could not obtain. Registrars also disqualified prospective voters for minor defects on the applications (such as miscalculation of age), and they often limited registration periods to times and places inconvenient for blacks (Key, 1949, pp. 555–77).

Sometimes other mechanisms were used to keep blacks away from the polls. Physical intimidation was not unusual, and occasionally the Ku Klux Klan and other self-proclaimed white vigilantes were aided by law enforcement officers as they beat, tortured, and even murdered blacks seeking to vote (Watters and Cleghorn, 1967). But intimidation was not limited to physical activity. Psychological and economic intimidation were brought to bear against those seeking to vote as blacks were fired from jobs, denied credit or evicted from their farms (Garrow, 1978, pp. 6–30; Salamon and Van Evera, 1973, pp. 1288–1306).

Even in large cities, the only places in the South where blacks could register and vote in significant numbers, mechanisms were found to minimize their impact on the electoral process. Gerrymandering of black residential areas was not unusual. Also, through annexation and the use of at-large elections, the impact of even substantial numbers of black voters could be diluted. These techniques in particular are still used today (Rodgers and Bullock, 1972, pp. 39–49).

The effect of all these practices was to reduce to insignificance the impact which blacks had on southern electoral politics. They were almost totally disenfranchised, and therefore their ability to elect blacks to public office was nil. The onset of the civil rights movement, however, began the process whereby this situation slowly was eroded. As indicated earlier, one of the principal goals of the movement was the search for the franchise. Blacks were aided in these efforts by three pieces of federal legislation: the Civil Rights Acts of 1957, 1960 and 1964, each of which had as a major component mechanisms to try to secure access to the polls for blacks.

As well intentioned as were these acts, however, they were not ultimately very successful in increasing the number of black voters. Several reasons for this could be mentioned, but perhaps most important was their reliance on litigation as a major weapon to force black registration. The process was simply too slow and the ability of the federal government too limited to force implementation in order to bring about much change (Garrow, 1978, pp. 6–30; Lawson, 1976, pp. 179–249; Rodgers and Bullock, 1972, pp. 23–28).

Significant progress came only after the passage of the Voting Rights Act of 1965. Called "the most successful piece of civil rights legislation" (Garrow, 1978, p. xi) in American history, the purpose of the Act was to permit the federal government to intervene directly into southern states which had clearly discriminated against blacks and to force local registrars to add the names of eligible blacks (and poor whites) to voting rolls. It did this by sending federal registrars to targeted areas to ensure that blacks' names were added. Even the threat of a visit by federal registrars seemed sufficient to force many local voting officials to act. Federal observers were also sent to monitor elections to make sure that blacks were actually permitted to vote and their votes counted. Finally, through the so called "preclearance" provisions of the Act, the federal government could assess changes in southern election laws and practices to ensure that no new methods of discrimination were established.

The effect of the Voting Rights Act in the South was both immediate and emphatic. Millions of previously disenfranchised blacks and whites were added to registration rolls. Black registration alone rose from 38 percent of the voting age population in 1964 to 62 percent in 1968. The changes were even more dramatic in deep South states where the Voting Rights Act initially was targeted. Here registration rates among blacks rose enormously: Alabama from 19 percent in 1965 to 52 percent in 1967; Georgia, 27 percent to 53 percent; Mississippi from 7 percent to 60 percent (Matthews and Prothro, 1966; U.S. Census, 1978; U.S. Civil Rights Commission, 1968).

IV. BLACK ELECTED OFFICIALS: WHO ARE THEY?

Table I shows in absolute numbers the extent to which blacks have been elected to public office in the South. The table first shows the number of officials elected in 1968, three years after the Voting Rights Act was passed (prior to that time the number of blacks in office was insignificant). The table next shows the number of black officials in 1982, the most recent year for which data are available. In the 14 year period shown there was more than a ten-fold increase (from 248 to 2,601) in blacks elected in the South. Next, the table breaks down the number of black elected officials according to categories to offices held. Absolute change between 1968 and 1982 is shown for each category. Omitted from the table are state administrators, members of the U.S. House of Representatives or U.S. Senate, and judges. Only South Carolina had a black member of the state executive in 1981, and Texas and Tennessee each had a black member of the U.S. House of Representatives. Not all judges are elected or even subject to voter review and therefore have been omitted from the table.

Several interesting points can be found in the table. First, most black elected officials hold their position at the lowest levels: city councils and school boards. This was as true in 1968 (76 and 52, respectively) as in 1982 (1,097 and 574, respectively). Moreover it is also clear that the percentage of blacks holding these relatively low level positions has increased between 1968 and 1982. In 1968, 30.6 percent of black elected officials occupied city council positions and 21 percent, school board. By 1982, these figures had changed to 42.2 percent for city council and 22 percent for school board. What this means is that while the *number* of blacks elected to office in the South has increased dramatically, they remain relegated to political positions at the lowest rung of the ladder. This is not to imply that these positions are unimportant or to suggest blacks cannot win higher office (Bullock, 1975, pp. 737–8). It is to underscore the difficulty blacks have in entering more politically sensitive offices.

This latter point is emphasized by examining the percentage of blacks in mayoral and state legislative positions. In 1968, only four blacks of a total of 248 elected to office were mayors (1.6 percent); in 1982, 131 out of 2,601 elected blacks were mayors (only 5 percent). But in spite of the low numbers, it is also true that by the 1980s blacks held the mayorship in some of the South's most important cities, including Atlanta, New Orleans, and Birmingham. In 1968, 9.2 percent of black elected officials were in the state legislature. But by 1982 only 127 of 2,601 black elected officials were members of a southern state legislature (a decline to 4.9

Table 1. Black Elected Officials in the South

	Total*		State Legislature		County Governing Body		Judicial or County Law Enforcement		School Board		City Mayor		City Governing Body	
	1968	(1982)	1968	(1982)	1968	(1982)	1968	(1982)	1968	(1982)	1968	(1982)	1968	(1982)
Covered by Voting Rights Act (1965)														
Alabama	24	(269)	0	(16)	0	(26)	3	(37)	3	(32)	2	(24)	12	(118)
Georgia	21	(271)	11	(22)	3	(20)	0	(14)	3	(51)	0	(11)	4	(145)
Louisiana	37	(372)	1	(12)	10	(84)	16	(42)	4	(97)	1	(11)	5	(124)
Mississippi	29	(424)	1	(17)	4	(27)	15	(72)	1	(73)	1	(20)	5	(161)
No. Carolina	10	(266)	0	(4)	0	(20)	0	(10)	1	(73)	0	(15)	9	(142)
So. Carolina	11	(235)	0	(15)	3	(29)	2	(14)	0	(54)	0	(12)	1	(105)
Virginia	24	(93)	1	(5)	2	(29)	1	(3)	0	(0)	0	(5)	12	(44)
Not covered by Voting Rights Act (1965)														
Arkansas	33	(219)	0	(5)	0	(0)	0	(30)	33	(83)	0	(13)	0	(78)
Florida	16	(118)	0	(5)	0	(2)	0	(5)	1	(13)	0	(9)	14	(82)
Tennessee	28	(127)	6	(13)	10	(51)	2	(15)	2	(20)	0	(1)	8	(26)
Texas	15	(207)	3	(13)	0	(6)	0	(21)	6	(78)	0	(10)	6	(72)
TOTAL (all states)	248	(2601)	23	(127)	32	(294)	39	(263)	52	(574)	4	(131)	76	(1097)

Sources: U.S. Commission on Civil Rights, 1968. Appendix VI; and Joint Center for Political Studies, *National Roster of Black Elected Officials* (1982).

*Total includes all black elected officials in the state, not just those categorized here.

191

percent). It may well happen that reapportionment in the early 1980s will aid in the election of more black state legislators. But it is still true that throughout the South, blacks continue to be very much underrepresented, regardless of the particular office considered. Figures indicate that only about 5 percent of all elected officials in the South are black; thus in terms of the "equity" of representation, blacks have a long way to go (U.S. Civil Rights Commission, 1981, pp. 12–15).

Finally, Table I suggests the impact which the Voting Rights Act had on the election of black officials. All but one (Virginia) of the initially targeted states increased the number of black elected officials between 1968 and 1982 by at least ten-fold, and two increased by nearly twentyfold. Only Texas among the non-covered states reached these same levels. Again, however, it must be emphasized that these dramatic increases were not uniform across different levels of political office; the lower the office, the greater the amount of increase in all the states.

In what kind of southern cities do most black elected officials serve? They tend to be found in small communities where blacks are either a majority of the population or a relatively small minority. In a 1975 survey, Campbell and Feagin discovered that nearly two-thirds of all black city council members could be found in cities of populations less than 5,000; indeed, about one-third served in towns of less than 1,000 persons. Another 10 percent served in the largest cities (over 100,000). The figures for mayors are even more dramatic. Almost 87 percent occupied their position in cities of less than 5,000; 54 percent of the total were in towns of less than 1,000. Even more interestingly, they found that most cities having black city council members are less than 50 percent black. Moreover, cities where blacks occupy a relatively small minority of the population (0–39 percent) were more likely to have black city council members than where blacks comprise 40–49 percent of the population. The authors speculate that white resistance is less where blacks constitute a small minority than in those communities where they threaten to become a majority (Campbell and Feagin, 1975, pp. 139–149).

Who are the black elected officials? What are they like? Interestingly, very little research has been done on the backgrounds and attitudes of southern black elected officials. However, available literature suggests similarities in their characteristics.

In a 1978 study of 56 black municipal officials in Florida, Button uncovered a consistent pattern in their background. They tended overwhelmingly to be fairly young (average age 45) and male (only five were women). Their occupational status was also relatively high: 37 percent were businessmen, 30 percent were educators, and 18 percent were in blue collar, service, or semi–skilled jobs. Only four percent were doctors or lawyers, and only four percent were ministers. Their educational status was also reasonably high. All but five were high school graduates, and 54 percent were college graduates. Finally, all claimed church memberships (Baptist predominantly) and 63 percent were officials in their church. Fifty percent claimed some prior civil rights activities: 75 percent were or had been members of the NAACP, and all but two were Democrats (Button, 1978, pp. 5–6). A study of the social status of black school board members also confirmed that these individuals had substantially higher achieved and ascribed status than the general community. The study was nationwide, however, and not strictly southern in scope (Wirth, 1979, pp. 764–5). Finally, other studies of southern black elected officials have also discovered results similar to these (Parker and Jackson, 1982; Salamon, 1973).

V. ELECTING BLACKS TO OFFICE: SOCIAL AND POLITICAL PRECONDITIONS

There can be no denying the importance of the Voting Rights Act as both a stimulus to black voting and to the election of black officials. Without blacks' securing the franchise in such sufficient numbers that they could affect the outcome of an election, and being willing to exercise that franchise (which in some places still means taking risks of a physical, economic or psychological nature), no black officials or even sympathetic whites could have been elected. Historians explaining the rise of black electoral politics in the South will surely point to the Voting Rights Act as one of those watersheds which truly caused a change in southern, and indeed American, society.

But as important as the Voting Rights Act has been and continues to be, it is fair to say that it was only a necessary but not sufficient condition to the election of black officials in the South. Other factors have also been important. An ambitious empirical literature has been developed in recent years which can help explore this key point: what are the conditions associated with the election of black officials? Stated otherwise, what environmental factors must exist before it can reasonably be expected that blacks will be elected to public office? It turns out, of course, that merely providing blacks with access to political resources, especially the ballot, does not automatically ensure black representation. Blacks have to want to participate in the electoral arena before anything can happen. Viable, serious black candidates have to emerge who can attract black voters. Also, except in those areas where blacks constitute a clear majority of voters, black candidates must also seek out white voters. The "dual legitimacy" analyzed by Parker and Jackson, in which black candidates potentially have to appeal to both blacks and whites, does not occur just because of a candidate's position on issues (Parker and Jackson, 1982); socioeconomic and attitudinal changes in the population as a whole must also occur. Finally, the structure of government and the rules of the electoral system seem to have an impact on the extent of black representation in political office. It is to a consideration of each of these factors that we now turn.

One of the most obvious, but important, changes which helped bring about the election of black officials in the South was a shift in black demography (Karnig and Welch, 1980, pp. 1–4). While it is a commonplace fact that central cities in the northern and midwestern United States have had increasing black percentages among their populations, what is not so well known is that in southern cities these same patterns have emerged. Indeed in 1980, Atlanta had a population that was 67 percent black; New Orleans, 55 percent; Jackson, 47 percent; and Montgomery, 39 percent. Where blacks represent increasingly large percentages of the urban population, it becomes mathematically as well as politically easier for them to elect black officials. And when residential patterns are segregated, as is characteristic of most urban places in the South, it is very possible for blacks to elect black officials. These points will be considered below in the discussion of governmental forms and electoral systems.

But numbers and geographic concentration alone do not account for black voting patterns. The voting black community in the traditional South, for example, was often fragmented and easily manipulated (Clubok, DeGrove, and Farris, 1964). To elect black officials requires reasonable cohesiveness, especially where blacks are a minority. The rise of black political consciousness brought about by the civil rights movement apparently has created the requisite degree of cohesion needed to foster "cooperative" voting patterns among blacks. In its most extreme form, black political consciousness gave rise to the "black power" ideology so feared by many whites and blacks. But the great benefit of black power as a political slogan was that it enabled many blacks to see the enormous advantages in electoral solidarity. It also forced them to view government and politics in a new way: instead of passively accepting these as white-dominated and beyond their reach, black power gave cynical and alienated blacks hope. The pride and consciousness it engendered in blacks enabled them to feel more secure about entering the political system, participating in its processes, and especially seeking to elect blacks as their representatives to replace whites (Karnig and Welch, 1980, pp. 7–9).

Two other contributing factors influencing the election of black officials were the media and the federal government. While these institutions did not act in unison, they both served similar purposes for blacks in the South. They provided publicity for the cause and, in a sense, protection as they sought political gains. The media, in particular, served to publicize both the goals of the civil rights movement and white reaction to it. Evidence suggests that TV pictures of southern whites' (including law enforcement officers) brutalizing blacks helped shape national public opinion in such a way that blacks felt less isolated as they articulated political demands. Indeed at a minimum the publicity and sympathy generated by the media elsewhere in the country helped to attract resources in the form of money and manpower to the southern civil rights movement as blacks sought greater levels of equality (Garrow, 1978, pp. 163–66).

Similarly the federal government offered protection to blacks seeking to exercise their civil rights. Many black leaders felt, perhaps correctly, that the federal government was never at the forefront of the civil rights movement, but rather had to be dragged into the struggle. Indeed it did so only after northern and western white elites regarded the black struggle as legitimate. Nonetheless, even if the federal government was late in backing the civil rights movement, its entry did bring significant changes. The Civil Rights Act of 1964, the Voting Rights Act of 1965 and their vigorous enforcement by the Johnson administration indicated to southern blacks that the federal government was willing to view the civil rights movement as a social necessity whose goals were very much in the mainstream of American democracy.

Thus there were changes within white America which helped make the election of black officials possible. Public opinion polls taken during the civil rights movement showed that many whites began to view black political participation not with alarm but as an accepted fact (Karnig and Welch, 1980, p. 9). Perhaps even more important was the change among white elites. "Civil rights" became a "cause," not only among college students (some of whom went South to assist the black struggle), but among the population as a whole, especially its opinion and other political leaders. Thus later on, when blacks began to vote, and even put forward black candidates for office, there was some support for them within the white community, even among moderate southern whites (Mars, 1977; Watters and Cleghorn, 1967). Yet it is also possible to overstate this. By the 1970s, when blacks demanded further electoral changes (such as changing from at-large to district electoral systems, which almost guarantee black representation), even non-southern whites began to resist. As it became clear that these further changes might cost whites political power, their enthusiasm waned (Scher and Button, 1983, p. 27). Hence, while white America undoubtedly accepts the idea of black political participation and black candidates, it is by no means certain how far or how deep the support actually extends.

So far the discussion has considered macro-level changes in America which have aided the election of southern blacks to political office. There are also very important micro-level political forces, behaviors, and institutions which have contributed very substantially and directly to this end. One of these is the existence of organizational or group effort, including previous civil rights activity and federal programs such as OEO and Model Cities. The theory is that where blacks have been well-organized, especially in political as opposed to purely vocational or social activity, it might be relatively easy to elect black officials. Likewise, if blacks demonstrated previous civil rights activity, whether of local origin or under a federal aegis, the same result might be obtained.

Data on these variables show only a slight positive correlation and conclusive evidence is lacking. In a national study of black organizational activity, Miller discovered that since the 1950s blacks have shifted their organizational efforts towards more partisan political activity. He found that the "skill and competence" engendered by these organizations among their members aided in an increase in black political participation, although he did not explore whether this added participation led to the election of black officials (Miller, 1982, p. 83). Support for Miller's findings can be seen in a Mississippi study of political participation among rural blacks by Salamon and Van Evera. They found that the presence of political organizations among relatively poor blacks could mitigate the "fear" caused by economic and psychological vulnerability. The effect was to increase the level of electoral participation above what might be expected among these population groups (Salamon and Van Evera, 1973, pp. 1296–1301). However the extent to which this additional participation led directly to the election of black officials is unclear.

Similarly, Karnig and Welch found only very tenuous correlations between the existence of both civil rights activity and such federal programs as OEO and Model Cities, and elected black officials nationwide. In fact, the presence of civil rights disorders in the 1960s was found to have slight *negative* correlations with black city council representation (Karnig and Welch, 1980, p. 100). It might have been expected that political activity of such a vigorous nature may have been transformed eventually into more conventional electoral arenas. This is not so, however, and it may be that civil rights activity (especially riots) created additional racial antagonism and disillusionment with traditional forms of politics, which prevented higher levels of black representation (Karnig and Welch, 1980, p. 100).

On the other hand, the presence of some federal programs seems to have been slightly positively associated with the rise of black mayors. Interestingly, the correlations are only significant for Model Cities programs, not the more unconventional Community Action and Neigh-borhood Youth Programs (Karnig and Welch, 1980, p. 50). However, the data indicate that the presence of Model Cities programs (probably the most "moderate" and conventional of federal anti-poverty pro-grams) correlates only with the presence of black candidates, not elec-toral success. Whatever the impetus for political activity generated by Model Cities, it did not necessarily carry over into winning elections (Karnig and Welch, 1980, p. 63).

Another variable which scholars anticipated would be positively associ-ated with the election of black officials is partisanship. Local political parties historically have provided avenues for political advancement by minorities (Merton, 1968, pp. 125–126). Non-partisan elections, on the other hand, have been found to be class oriented, even to the point of discriminating against certain minorities (Adrian, 1961, pp. 208–213). Thus one would be more inclined to find black elected officials in "non-reformed", traditional urban political systems.

However, Karnig and Welch found that partisanship was only very slightly positively correlated with the presence of elected black officials. For both mayors and city council members, partisanship had only a small impact on black electoral chances (Karnig and Welch, 1980, pp. 61, 85). But they did discover that partisanship does have a small positive effect on the "equity" issue of representation (the extent to which the percentage of black representation on city councils begins to approach that of the city's black population). They conclude, "(p)olitical parties, then, probably do not harm the electoral chances of blacks and may actually promote their chances of winning council seats" (Karnig and Welch, 1980, p. 85). These findings were generally corroborated in O'Loughlin's 1979 study (O'Loughlin, 1979, p. 84). Moreover, in a study of 36 cities with substan-tial black minorities, Bent found that large partisan cities were generally more "responsive" to the issues raised by blacks in the mid 1960s than were non-partisan cities (Bent, 1982, p. 310). The cities studied, however, were all non-southern.

Demographic indicators for both black and white populations con-stitute another set of variables thought to be associated with black elected officials. In fact, they turn out to be very powerfully correlated with black representation. A number of studies indicate that as levels of in-come and education rise among whites, the number of black elected officials increases (Karnig and Welch, 1980, pp. 74, 106). Why this is true remains a matter of speculation. Banfield and Wilson suggest that whites become more tolerant of blacks as whites enter the middle class (Banfield and Wilson, 1963). Key and Karnig each argue that, in the South particularly, it has been poor whites who are most threatened by blacks. As levels of education and income increase among whites (and correspondingly, levels of urbanization rise), whites feel less vulnerable and not only can accept the idea of black representation, but can even vote for "acceptable" black candidates (Key, 1949; Karnig, 1976, p. 235). However it should also be indicated that the impact of increasing socioeconomic indicators among traditional, often rural, southern whites, in terms of their willingness to support black candidates, is not necessarily as certain as it is among whites elsewhere (Karnig and Welch, 1980, p. 77).

What is very clear is the strong positive correlation between increasing levels of black income and education and the presence of black elected officials. This relationship far exceeds that between white socioeconomic indicators and black officials. Karnig and Welch are unequivocal about the impact of greater levels of black resources on black electoral success: "Where the black population is better developed socioeconomically, it is more capable of vying with whites for elective office" (Karnig, 1976, p. 235; Karnig and Welch, 1980, p. 64). These findings hold true for both black mayors and black city council representation (Karnig and Welch, 1980, pp. 66, 106). Importantly also, increasing black resources affects not merely the presence of blacks on the city council but black equity, that is, the extent to which the percent black representation on the city council approximates that of blacks in the whole city (Karnig and Welch, 1980, p. 103).

Even more important than black resources, however, is the percentage of the total population that is black. This finding is not surprising. Where blacks form substantial portions of the population, it can naturally be expected that black population strength can be translated, at least in some measure, into electoral strength. Karnig and Welch estimate that almost 38 percent of the variance in black council representation can be accounted for by the size of the black population alone (Karnig and Welch, 1980, p. 106). Combined with black resources, it explains 52 percent of the variance, and, in the case of black mayors, they conclude, "As black populations grow larger, better-educated and less poor, the chances of having a black mayor improve" (Karnig and Welch, 1980, p. 66). These findings appear to hold for both the South and the rest of the country.

And yet the relationship between the size of the black population and the presence of black elected officials is not quite so simple. Several other scholars have observed that the relationship is not a linear but rather a curvilinear one (Bullock and Dennis, 1982; Collins, 1980; O'Loughlin, 1979). This means that increases in the percentage of blacks within the population are not automatically and directly reflected in increases of blacks in public office. Rather, there is probably a "take-off" point below which blacks are under-represented, and above which they can approach and possibly exceed their percentage in the population. For example, it is theoretically possible for a black population of, say, 30 percent to elect no or only one representative on a five-member city council (0–20 percent). When blacks constitute a "mid-range" of the population (30–49 percent), whites apparently feel threatened, and resist black demands, possibly making election of black officials more difficult (Button and Scher, 1979; Keech, 1964; Key, 1949). But a 65 percent black community might be able to elect three to five members (60 percent to 100 percent). More commonly, however, there may be a "threshold" or "plateau", beyond which black representation does not seem to increase. O'Loughlin found that this curvilinear relationship exists not only for city council but for congressional, state senate, and state house contests; however, his was a national, not purely southern, study (O'Loughlin, 1979).

Bullock and Dennis have attempted to refine these findings of a complex, curvilinear relationship between population size and black elected officials. In a study of county black officeholders in Louisiana and South Carolina, they found that the size of the black population was less important than the size of black voter registration. Moreover, the "threshold" levels at which election of black officials to county offices becomes both theoretically and actually possible has declined since the impact of the Voting Rights Act was first felt. Thus, they conclude that to elect more black officials requires not simply substantial black populations, but rather actual increases in the voter registration of black citizens (Bullock and Dennis, 1982, p. 29).

The last variable to be considered in conjunction with the election of black elected officials is the nature of the electoral system, specifically the impact of at-large versus district systems. Perhaps no other issue concerning the election of blacks to office has created as much controversy as this one, probably because it goes to the very heart of traditional American values about the utility and democratic impulse of each method of electing representatives. The issues involved are not easily resolved empirically, but rather rest on fundamental assumptions and values about American democracy. Those favoring at-large systems argue that they promote consensus politics, prevent parochial interests from being injected into politics, and insure "majority rule"; they also contend that district lines can easily be drawn and maintained. Those favoring district elections, in contrast, argue that they protect minority interests (because their vote is not diluted as in at-large election systems), enhance articulation of individual and community level concerns in decision centers, and insure that the "one man–one vote" rule of the U.S. Supreme Court is maintained.

The question of whether one form of representation is "better" than the other cannot be resolved here. But one aspect of this matter is extremely relevant to this chapter: namely, does one form of electoral system promote the election of black officials or, put another way, is there evidence that it is easier to elect blacks to public office under one of these systems than the other?

In their most recent study, Karnig and Welch (1982) carefully review the most sophisticated literature on the subject. They observe that much of it is contradictory, for the reasons noted above in the section on methodological issues. The authors seek to overcome these difficulties by analyzing the effect of at-large versus district elections using all of the different indices of black representation, and by considering each of the major forms of electoral systems, including the so-called "mixed" forms which combine district and at-large systems. Their analysis leads to un-equivocal results. Regardless of the measures used or the classification of electoral systems, district elections favor the success of blacks running for office over at-large systems (Karnig and Welch, 1982, p. 112; Karnig and Welch, 1980, pp. 85, 95). Moreover, not only are district elections important for the success of black candidates, but also for improving the level of equity of representation. At-large elections, then, tend to have a depressing effect on the ability of blacks (and other minority groups) to win elections (Karnig and Welch, 1982, p. 113). Finally, as one might expect, since in the South at-large election systems are found frequently, in many areas blacks are substantially under-represented even in juris-dictions of significant black population aggregations (Karnig, 1976, p. 229; Latimer, 1979, p. 82).

The Karnig and Welch research corroborated earlier studies by Jones (1976) and Latimer (1979) on the impact of local election systems on black representation. They, however, were also able to show that the nature of the council itself can affect the degree of black representation. Thus not only are district elections important for this goal, but so are increasing the number of council seats and decreasing the size of dis-tricts (Jones, 1976, p. 354; Latimer 1979, p. 82). Increasing the number of council seats may permit whites to feel more secure about the pres-ence of "some" black council members, and if it is combined with smaller districts, it may allow the black community, especially a residentially segregated community, to exert its political muscle (Karnig and Welch, 1980, pp. 81–83). This is not to say that blacks cannot win in at-large electoral systems (Karnig and Welch, 1982, p. 113). Indeed, if black candidates can establish "dual legitimacy", and successfully appeal to both blacks and whites, then their task is not impossible. But in at-large elections, if blacks are to be successful, it seems clear that they must unite behind one candidate, pool their political resources, and seek out the endorsement of key white groups, especially the media (Parker and

Jackson, 1982, pp. 18–19). Otherwise, a successful electoral outcome is questionable.

Earlier it was noted that more than fifty percent of the variance in black representation on city councils can be demonstrated by the combined variables of the size of the black population and available black resources. A recent study by Engstrom and McDonald (1982) attempted to discover whether black resources or electoral systems (at-large or district) are more important in influencing black representation. In an analysis of 224 central cities in Standard Metropolitan Statistical Areas, they conclude that at least in the South, district elections have a much greater direct impact on black representation than' do socioeconomic resources. However, this seems to hold mainly when the black population is greater than ten percent. When the black population passes thirty percent, the "difference in impact" between changing socioeconomic conditions and changing to district elections becomes "quite striking" (Engstrom and McDonald, 1982, p. 1098).

Is it possible to summarize, briefly, all of the relevant factors which seem to contribute to the election of black officials? Available research does not provide a "recipe" which will guarantee success, but it can point the way to some minimum prerequisites. Perhaps the most crucial factor is a substantial percentage of blacks in the population, especially among the population of registered voters. Only slightly less important is the presence of district election systems, particularly in those areas where segregated residential patterns can potentially be translated into electoral power, Next is a black population increasingly affluent, educated, and willing to use its resources and knowledge for political activity. The presence of a significant white middle class may also be helpful in this regard, not only because of possibly greater levels of tolerance but a willingness to use some of its resources to aid black candidates. Finally, where at-large elections prevail, black candidates have to emerge who are perceived as legitimate and acceptable to both black and white citizens.

VI. IMPACT OF BLACK ELECTED OFFICIALS

As we have seen, there has been much scholarly focus on the kinds of blacks who have been elected to office and under what conditions. Thus far there has been considerably less attention given to the consequences or impact of having blacks in public office. Part of this lack of attention is probably due to the fact that in many parts of the South, blacks have not held elected office for very many years. Moreover, measuring political impact is often difficult, as we shall see. There are various kinds of effects an official might have and empirical data on impact are not always readily available. Even with available data, it is often difficult to separate out the independent effects of black officials because a variety of other factors may also be important in any process of policy change.

Yet it would seem of crucial importance to ask what difference black representation has made. Given the history of racial inequalities and discrimination in the South, the election of blacks to public office is a remarkable change. But the larger and more significant question is whether black representation has had any effect on public policy and on the socioeconomic conditions of blacks. Whatever the answer to this question, it should be noted that the possibility for black political power and change is greater in the South than in any other region of the country. Only in the South, for example, is the size of the black population and black voting strength significant at the state, county, and municipal level. Furthermore, as of 1982 the South had a majority of blacks elected to office in the nation.

This political power and representation does not mean much, however, if it cannot be translated into political rewards for blacks. Although theories of representation are complex, a useful and generally accepted definition of representation is "acting in the interest of the represented, in a manner responsive to them" (Pitkin, as quoted in Karnig and Welch, 1980, p. 108). Pitkin goes on to discuss two distinct kinds of representation: descriptive and substantive. Descriptive representation refers to the racial, social class, religious, or other distinctive characteristics of the representative. This form of representation emphasizes the symbolic aspects of winning office and has been the focus of most ethnic scholars. Substantive representation looks at the degree of similarity between the policy preferences of the representative and those of his or her constituents. While a black elected official clearly provides descriptive representation for blacks (at least in regard to race although not necessarily social class), if the official does not share the policy views of most black constituents, there is no substantive representation.

Nevertheless, even with substantive representation there is no guarantee that the policy needs of the black community will be met. As we shall see, there are a variety of constraining factors, both formal and informal, which may limit the ability of substantive representatives to effectively fulfill the policy preferences of blacks. Thus, although the descriptive and substantive dimensions of representation are significant, it is even more important to investigate the aspects of representation which attempt to link elected officials with policy benefits for constituents. By looking at policy impact, the emphasis is clearly on the dynamic aspect of representation whereby one is "doing something" rather than simply "being something" (Eisinger, 1982, pp. 380–81).

A prerequisite to favorable policy impact, however, is that the general views of black officeholders reflect those of most of their constituents. Hence initially we must ask to what extent black officials are substantive representatives of the black community. In general, elected officials show basic agreement with the policy orientations of their constituents, and this seems to hold for black representatives as well. Yet the empirical evidence here is somewhat sparse. As in the case of white officials, black officeholders are usually of higher socioeconomic status and educational attainment than their constituents. Studies in Alabama (Campbell, 1976), Florida (Button, 1978; Parker and Jackson, 1982), and Mississippi (Salamon, 1973) concluded that black candidates and/or elected officials were usually professional or white collar in occupation, middle-class in income, and college-educated. Indeed, other nationwide and non-southern studies have discovered a greater gap between the educational and occupational level of black officeholders and the black public than among comparable white officials and the white community (Cole, 1976; Conyers and Wallace, 1976). Moreover, this disparity between black elected officials and constituents is probably greater in the South than elsewhere because of the relatively low income and education levels of southern blacks. Yet Ippolito, Donaldson, and Bowman (1968), and Kronus (1971) reported that there is a basic congruence between policy preferences of blacks of various social classes. Thus we would expect to find that the basic policy orientations of black representatives parallel those of their constituents.

Black officeholders are indeed aware and concerned with the problems experienced by lower-class blacks, and these officials tend to advocate social welfare policies. In the Cole study (1976, p. 94) of black and white elected officials in 16 New Jersey cities, 68 percent of the blacks saw themselves as liberal or radical (only 34 percent of whites perceived themselves as liberal). Furthermore, in a nationwide survey of black and white officeholders, Conyers and Wallace (1976) reported that blacks were much more likely than whites to favor social programs. In terms of the South, studies of black elected officials in Alabama (Campbell, 1976) and Florida (Button, 1978) found that more than half of these officials reported that one of their main reasons for seeking office was to help blacks. Moreover, most black officeholders in Florida municipalities claimed that one of the main problems confronting blacks in their communities was lack of basic public services such as paved streets, employment, and water or sewage (Button, 1978). Lack of such services was reportedly raised as a campaign issue by the majority of those black officials who perceived it was a serious problem. Hence many blacks in public office in the South tend to feel a sense of mission to help others of their race.

Thus it seems that black officials generally reflect the policy views of the black community and are clearly sympathetic to the plight of most blacks. To what extent have these officials been able to modify policies aimed at improving conditions for southern blacks? In attempting to answer this question, we shall look at two general ways black officeholders have been able to help their constituents: *material* benefits and *symbolic* benefits. The former refers to new or changed policies (usually public policies) which tend to favor blacks more than whites. The paving of streets in the black community or the hiring of a black policeman would be examples of material benefits. Symbolic kinds of improvements would include the psychological, attitudinal, and educational benefits of having blacks in elected office. Increasing the affective orientation of blacks toward government, for example, would be a symbolic benefit of black officeholding. Such kinds of benefits are usually more subtle and difficult to ascertain than material ones, but are certainly no less important.

VII.   MATERIAL BENEFITS

For a long time most southern blacks have endured inequalities in housing, employment, education, and basic public services such as street paving, water and sewage, recreation, and police protection (Keech, 1968; Matthews and Prothro, 1966; Myrdal, 1944). These issue areas have also been among the major policy concerns of blacks. Therefore when blacks were first elected to office, there were high expectations among constituents about the changes in policies that would take place. Although some of these expectations proved to be optimistic, most black officials have played an important role in modifying policies favorable to the black community.

Several studies indicate that southern black officeholders have been moderately effective in increasing social welfare expenditures and in improving basic public services for blacks (Button, 1978; Button and Scher, 1979; Campbell, 1976; Campbell and Feagin, 1975; Jones, 1976; Karnig and Welch, 1980; Sanders, 1979). Since most black officials are found at the local level, studies have primarily focused on black mayors and city council members. In perhaps the best of the limited studies thus far, Karnig and Welch (1980, Ch. 6) tested the effect of black representation on early 1970s city budgetary changes for 139 cities nationwide with more than 50,000 population. Utilizing multivariate statistical procedures, the authors found that the presence of black mayors was positively related to spending on social welfare (health, housing, welfare, and education), but negatively related to spending for amenities (parks and libraries), protective services, and most physical facilities (streets, sanitation, sewage, and hospitals). Black council representation, on the other hand, was not consistently related to any expenditure categories. In terms of region, however, Karnig and Welch found that in the South black council members did seem to have a small positive influence on total city expenditures and on social welfare and physical facilities expenditures. A regional analysis of the impact of black mayors was impossible because of the lack of big city black executives in the South.

Other studies, using different approaches from that employed by Karnig and Welch, have reported similar conclusions. Interviews with large numbers of black elected municipal officials in Florida (Button, 1978) and Alabama (Campbell, 1976, Chs. 6–7) indicated that these officials perceive they have been most effective in improving basic public services for blacks. The improved services mentioned by black officials included streets, water and sewage, parks and recreation, garbage pick-up, and police and fire protection. Both studies also found that black officials in predominately black communities reported greater effectiveness in improving public services than did their counterparts in cities where blacks were a minority. As would be expected, in majority black municipalities where black officials were often in political control of city government, they found it easier to change public service priorities than did black council members who were in the minority in city hall.

In addition, Button (1978) reported that black officeholders claimed they were more effective in improving capital-intensive services such as streets, parks, and water and sewage than in changing human resource services such as public employment and police and fire protection. Thus, it was less threatening to whites and therefore easier politically to implement a policy of paving roads in black areas rather than to change a policy so that more blacks are hired to work alongside whites in city hall. The latter policy required racial integration, as opposed to the equal distribution of public goods, and was therefore more strongly resisted by many southern whites.

Another intensive, longitudinal study (Button and Scher, 1979; Button, 1982) of black municipal service changes in six Florida cities asked knowledgeable citizens (white and black) to evaluate the effectiveness of nine political factors which may have influenced such changes. The results showed that having blacks in public office was consistently the most important political variable, even more significant than voting, protesting, or federal action. The study suggested, however, that the influence of political factors varied depending on the kind of municipal service and the type of community. Thus service improvement and the role of black officials was somewhat greater in majority black communities and in newer, more affluent, and more pluralistic communities which lacked the cultural and legal traditions of racial discrimination.

Few studies have explored the impact of black elected officials in positions other than at the municipal level. But these few investigations tend to concur that black officeholders have been moderately effective in providing services and programs for blacks. Studies involving black county commissioners in the South (Campbell, 1976, Ch. 8; Coombs et al., 1977; Jones, 1976; Sanders, 1979) concluded that the presence of such officials was often important to program expansion in public housing, welfare (AFDC), and roads and bridges. Southern black state legislators, a rare breed until relatively recently, have generally been found to be strong supporters of redistributive policies in areas such as education and social welfare (Bullock and MacManus, 1981; Campbell, 1976, Ch. 8; *New York Times*, 1977, p. 14). Only black school board members seem to be relatively ineffective in changing policies, perhaps because they have been preoccupied with the issues surrounding school desegregation (Jones, 1976; Meier and England, 1982), but the evidence here is particularly sparse.

Another major policy area, in addition to social welfare and public services, where black officials have been effective is public employment (Button, 1978; Button and Scher, 1979; Campbell, 1976; Campbell and Feagin, 1975; Coombs et al., 1977; Dye and Renick, 1981; Eisinger, 1982; Jones, 1976). Black mayors both nationwide and in the South have been instrumental in promoting increases in government jobs for blacks (Eisinger, 1980; Levine, 1974; Nelson and Meranto, 1977). Such mayors have typically appointed black personnel administrators, ordered special recruitment efforts, pushed for changes in employee examination procedures, or appointed a number of black department heads. But black city council representation, too, is related to increases in minority employment, particularly in high-level administrative, professional, and police and fire department positions (Button, 1982; Dye and Renick, 1981).

No doubt federal affirmative action regulations have been helpful in furthering black employment as well. Yet the implementation of affirmative action programs has often been a result of the efforts of black officials. Southern black council members, moreover, have frequently served as an invaluable conduit to the black community, informing citizens of government job vacancies and actively encouraging blacks to apply. Further, black officeholders have been important in having black citizens appointed to governmental advisory boards which historically had no or few minority representatives (Button, 1978; Jones, 1976).

Attracting federal and state revenue has also been a significant material benefit provided by southern black officials (Button, 1978; Campbell and Feagin, 1975; Coombs et al., 1977; Karnig and Welch, 1980). Especially in poor, rural areas, blacks in office realized the desperate need for outside funds because of the low tax base. Federal grants proved to be particularly important in helping to improve municipal services and provide jobs for blacks (Button, 1978). The kinds of grants most frequently obtained by black officials included public works, community development, public housing, and CETA, while federal revenue sharing funds were also sometimes used to provide improved services in the black communities. Moreover, in majority black towns and cities where basic services were most lacking, black officials seemed to have secured proportionately more federal grants and outside funding than in other communities with black officeholders (Button, 1978; Campbell, 1976, Ch. 6).

However, in terms of improving economic conditions for blacks in the long run, most officials realized that they could not become overly dependent on federal funds but had to attempt to increase industrial and commercial growth. This was especially the case in the poor, predominately black communities. Yet black elected officials in Alabama (Campbell, 1976) and Florida (Button, 1978) claimed they had not been very successful in such ventures. Unfortunately it is often the impoverished conditions themselves in predominately black cities, especially the inadequacy of basic services such as sewage, education, police and fire protection, which strongly deter industrial and commercial businesses from relocating there. Nevertheless, in other Florida communities with blacks as a minority of the population, almost one-third of black officeholders claimed that they had been able to help bring in industry or retail stores and thus improve the local tax base and provide more jobs (Button, 1978).

VII. SYMBOLIC BENEFITS

In addition to material or policy changes, black elected officials have had impacts of a symbolic nature as well. Symbolic benefits include the psychological, attitudinal, and educational dimensions of black officeholding. Although few studies have focused on the symbolic aspects, this is not to say that these kinds of effects are unimportant. Indeed, in the long run symbolic impacts may be the most important function of having blacks in office. This is particularly true with regard to their influence on race relations and on black affect toward government. As yet, however, evidence on the symbolic benefits of southern blacks in office is very fragmentary.

Black officeholding does seem to increase the knowledge and awareness of government among blacks in the community. In a study of black school childrens' views toward their mayors in two midwestern cities,

Foster (1978) found that more black children could name their mayor when the mayor was black. Likewise, the study of Cole (1976, p. 109) in New Jersey reported that 87 percent of blacks in communities with black mayors could identify their mayor, compared with 72 percent of the blacks in cities with white mayors. This finding is especially important, Cole claims, because low socioeconomic status blacks ordinarily would be expected to exhibit low political cognition, but the effect of having a black mayor reduces the influences of socioeconomic characteristics.

Similarly, black officeholders in Florida (Button, 1978) reported that they believed they had been able to help educate their black constituents on how the local political system works and how to become politically effective. In a typical response, one black representative from a rural town claimed: "I've been able to enlighten blacks on government procedures. They knew so little about government before" (Button, 1978, p. 10). This role of educator was especially prevalent in poor, rural areas where blacks traditionally had been totally excluded from politics, and where politics was generally perceived by blacks as "white man's business."

Another significant symbolic benefit of blacks in office seemingly has been to increase the affective orientation of blacks toward government. Most local black officials meet regularly with black civic leaders, ministers, youth groups and others to inform them of government activity and to bring their complaints back to city hall. This activity seems to have forged a new black trust in government and may have helped reduce feelings of political alienation among blacks (Cole, 1976). Further evidence is reported in the nationwide survey of Conyers and Wallace (1976) which found that one major impact of black elected officials was to develop within the black community "confidence in politics and government as potential instruments of black progress" (p. 137). Moreover, Foster (1978) reported that black school children were not only more aware of, but also evaluated more favorably, a black mayor as opposed to a white mayor. As yet, however, it is impossible to determine whether this increased affective orientation is due more to the material benefits provided by black officials or simply to the fact that the officeholder is black.

Having blacks in office also seems to stimulate increases in black political participation. The expectation of putting a black into office, as well as the increase in awareness and favorable feelings toward government, would suggest an increase in black political involvement. Abney (1974), for example, found that black voter turnout in Mississippi was positively related to the presence of black candidates for office, even when other variables were controlled. Black council members in Florida (Button, 1978) also claimed that once the racial barrier was broken and the first black elected, more blacks became candidates and this whole cycle encouraged greater black participation at the polls.

Psychologically, having black officeholders has been beneficial because they seemingly provide a "sense of legitimacy and normalcy" about blacks serving in public office (Cole, 1976, p. 223). Traditionally there has been the feeling, particularly in the South, that blacks were not capable of holding public positions, that they lacked ability, were too lazy, or would perceive issues only from a black perspective. The service of blacks in office tends to reduce this feeling by providing both whites and blacks with a recognition that blacks can govern in a competent and fair manner (Button, 1978; Cole, 1976; Jones, 1976). As one black councilman in Florida expressed it, having a black elected official "proved to the general public that a black person can sit on the council and be real objective, that whites can trust blacks to work out problems without hatred, and that blacks are not inferior" (Button, 1978, p. 11). Further, the more blacks are elected, the greater is the acceptance of their serving. As proof, black officials usually draw increased white support in re-election bids. Moreover, black representatives often serve as models with whom other blacks might identify (Button, 1978; Cole, 1976). In the words of one black mayor: "I feel I've provided a role model for other blacks, especially young blacks, and increased confidence in the black community that they really can do something in the system" (Button, 1978, p. 11).

The symbolic impact of black representatives has affected the white community in other ways as well. Certainly it seemed to sensitize white officials to black problems (Cole, 1976). As a black councilman in a large Florida city claimed: "Blacks in office have caused government officials to be more empathetic about the needs of poor blacks and whites. It has provided greater moral fiber in government" (Button, 1978, p. 12). The proposals of elected blacks, and often simply their mere presence, made white citizens and officials more aware of black concerns.

Having blacks in office, moreover, has tended to modify racial stereotypes and generally improve race relations (Button, 1978; Cole, 1976; Davidson, 1972). Interviews with white elites in four Florida cities with black officeholders found almost one-third of the whites claiming that having blacks in city government improved race relations in their communities (Button, 1978). Such a condition also seemed to help whites accept other racial changes. Black citizens, too, noticed the improvements in black-white relations. In a survey in one Mississippi community asking what changes had been noticed following the election of black officials, black respondents claimed the following: "more freedom", "more respect", "white folks know they are not going to run over us", and "less fear and more pride" (Jones, 1976: 406). Similar responses were noted among blacks in a Louisiana parish and in an Alabama county. Thus the racial atmosphere of the South is changing and the presence of black elected officials seems to be an important catalyst in this transformation.

IX. CONSTRAINTS ON BLACK OFFICIALS

It is clear from the limited studies thus far that black elected officials in the South have been moderately beneficial to blacks, both materially and symbolically. Some observers, however, anticipated more dramatic socioeconomic changes to follow from increases in black voting and the election of black officeholders. Yet the degree of change resulting from the election of blacks has been limited by a variety of constraining factors. Some of these factors are peculiar to the U.S. political system generally, especially local governments, while other limitations seem special to blacks in office.

In American politics, policy change usually occurs slowly. Most policies and patterns of expenditure are well established and incrementalism is the norm for budgetary and many other kinds of changes. Moreover, policy alterations are most difficult to achieve at the local level where most black officials still operate. Cities and counties are essentially creatures of state government, and their taxing, borrowing, and spending programs are limited by the state. Other programs, such as welfare, education, and public housing, are basically state and federal programs or are administered by independent special districts. In addition, most local governments have a poor record in developing innovative policies in the area of social reform (Karnig and Welch, 1980). Their policies are most apt to be distributive, rather than redistributive, in nature.

Thus regardless of who is in office, particularly at the local level, change is usually slow. But black officials in the South face a host of special problems in addition to these normal institutional constraints. First, black officeholders almost always constitute a small minority of elected officials whether at the state, county, or city level. As a result, they are unable to make unilateral decisions or change policy priorities by themselves. Further, most elected blacks, having won office relatively recently, have little experience in government. This lack of experience, especially in the "give-and-take," informal aspects of politics, often hampers the effectiveness of blacks as a numerical minority on various governing bodies.

Second, blacks in office sometimes find it difficult to serve as "substantive" representatives of blacks. This is especially true when elected in at-large systems, the dominant electoral arrangement at the local level in the South. Under this system, black candidates face the problem of "dual legitimacy," or the need to appeal to whites as well as blacks in order to win and stay in office, and therefore they are less committed to serving blacks (Button, 1978; Karnig and Welch, 1980; Nelson and Van Horne, 1974; Parker and Jackson, 1982). In the Florida study (Button, 1978), for example, 53 of 56 interviewed black council members were elected at-large and thus could not ignore the white community. Predictably those council members discussed representation in terms of "all the people" (not just blacks), and they usually refrained from supporting controversial pro-black issues like public housing and affirmative action so as not to alienate whites.

A third factor which seriously limits black officeholders is unduly high expectations and lack of continued cooperation and participation by blacks. There is often a great deal of black criticism of black representatives for not accomplishing everything that is expected. In the words of one black councilman in Florida: "Black expectations are high when a black is elected. They want us to change the world in one day, and when we don't do this they brand us as 'Uncle Toms'" (Button, 1978, p. 14). Raised black expectations which are not fulfilled often lead to loss of hope and alienation of black constituents (Nelson and Meranto, 1977; Preston, 1976). Lack of a high level of black participation is also due to continued weak organizational strength at the local level and to the lingering belief by some blacks that politics is still "white man's business' (Button, 1978; Preston, 1976). Moreover, as more black candidates within the same jurisdiction compete for office, conflict and internal divisions develop within the black community. This may lead to reduced black support for particular black officials who once had enjoyed almost unanimous endorsement from the black community.

Fourth, lack of support, and in some cases outright resistance, from whites is another problem for many black representatives, particularly in the South (Button, 1978; Campbell, 1976; Karnig and Welch, 1980; Nelson and Meranto, 1977). White officials especially have proved uncooperative, often thwarting black attempts to reorder priorities or redistribute public services. Resistance to black demands is usually greatest when racial integration is called for, or when whites perceive the demand as a zero-sum issue (blacks win, whites lose). But lack of white support outside the public sector can also hinder black officials. Whites usually control major businesses, banks, the media and other important institutions which blacks must depend upon for policy change.

Finally, but perhaps most importantly, black officeholders are constrained by a lack of financial resources (Bullock, 1975; Button, 1978; Campbell, 1976; Colburn, 1974; Karnig and Welch, 1980; Walton, 1972). Surveys of black officials in Alabama (Campbell, 1976) and in

Florida (Button, 1978) both concluded that lack of revenue at the municipal level was the most serious problem faced by these officials. Moreover, this financial situation was most critical in predominately black towns and cities which were overburdened with low tax rolls, lack of industry, and high rates of poverty. Despite federal and state assistance, these poor communities often remain disadvantaged because of their great needs. Furthermore, the recent policy of fiscal retrenchment at the federal level (and often state level) is beginning to diminish revenues even more in financially distressed cities where black representatives are numerous. Thus it may be, as Hanes Walton predicted, that many black officials will soon be "governing ghost towns" (1972, p. 200).

X.   CONCLUSION

One of the major goals of the black civil rights movement in the South was the achievement of the franchise and the ultimate election of blacks to office. To this extent the movement can be considered a moderate success. As we have seen, federal intervention in the form of civil rights legislation, especially the Voting Rights Act of 1965, was crucial to southern blacks' being able to register and vote in large numbers. This intervention, plus changes in black demography, the efforts of civil rights organizations, greater attention from the media and federal government, increased support from whites, and possibly other factors, all served to create conditions favorable to the election of blacks to public office. While these conditions produced a favorable environment, they were not always sufficient in themselves for electing blacks. Other preconditions were usually necessary, and the most important of these included substantial percentages of blacks in the population (especially among registered voters), the use of district election systems, a black population which is relatively affluent and well educated, and a sizable and tolerant white middle class.

Although environmental conditions have improved in the South and are generally conducive to the election of black officeholders, blacks do not always enjoy the requisite preconditions necessary for electoral success. Thus blacks still have relatively low income and educational levels, lack white support (particularly in rural areas), and must usually contend with at-large election systems. But despite these relatively unfavorable conditions, more than 2,600 blacks held elected office in the South in 1982, an increase of more than ten-fold since 1968. To say the least, this has been a dramatic change in a region of the country where few blacks were even registered to vote a generation ago. Nonetheless this electoral success must be tempered by the fact that most blacks have won office at the lowest levels (city councils and school boards) in relatively small cities and towns. These are positions and places with the least amount of political clout and financial resources. Moreover, despite the tremendous gains in numbers of black officeholders, southern blacks are still far from achieving representational equity, and increases in elected blacks have begun to level off.

While the election of a number of blacks to office in the South was indeed a milestone, the more important question perhaps is whether this achievement has resulted in improved conditions for blacks. The issues here are two-fold: what has been the quality of representation of black officials, and what has been the degree to which they have been able to influence policies and thereby improve the socioeconomic situation of their black constituents? Unfortunately southern blacks have been in office for relatively few years, in most cases not sufficiently long to gauge policy impact. Yet evidence suggests that elected black representatives, though often of significantly higher socioeconomic status than their black constituents, are usually concerned with the problems of most blacks and tend to support social welfare policies. Moreover, southern black officeholders seem to have played an important role in providing material benefits such as basic public services, social welfare, and public employment for blacks. These officials have also been able to attract federal and state revenue to help finance these material benefits. In addition, studies suggest that blacks in office have been more effective in improving capital-intensive rather than human-intensive services, in majority black rather than minority black communities, and in more affluent, "New South" communities.

Southern black officials have seemingly had impacts of a symbolic nature as well, although evidence here is indeed fragmentary. Symbolic benefits include increasing blacks' knowledge and affective orientations toward government, stimulating increases in black political participation, providing a sense of acceptance of blacks' serving in government, sensitizing white officials to the problems of blacks, and generally improving race relations. Our knowledge of how effective black officeholders have been in a symbolic sense is still tentative, but in the long run, improvements in black and white attitudes and psychological dispositions may be an extremely important function of having black representation. It may indeed happen that, given the constraints faced by black elected officials, their greatest contribution will be in this symbolic realm.

Thus it seems that black elected officials in the South have been moderately beneficial to blacks. However, as we have pointed out, the effectiveness of these officials has been limited by several factors including the lack of financial resources, being outvoted by white officials, having to serve as "dual representatives" of whites as well as blacks, lacking support from blacks, and sometimes experiencing resistance from whites. While these constraints are specific to black officials, there are more general limitations which serve to restrict the influence of those in political office. For a variety of reasons, public policy, especially re-distributive policy, is slow to change in American politics, particularly at the local level. Hence more time may be necessary before one can ade-quately judge the impact of those in public office.

A more serious limitation, however, is the indication that the ultimate resolution of many problems in our society, including those faced by blacks, lies outside the political arena. Economic factors, even more than political variables, may be most influential in bringing about policy change and development, especially policies of a socioeconomic nature (Dye, 1966; Sharkansky and Hofferbert, 1971). If this is so, it may be that the vote and electing blacks to office has about fulfilled its potential for policy change and that further improvements in black living condi-tions in the South will have to depend on factors external to the political process.

Yet these generalizations about the election and impact of southern black officials are tentative for a variety of reasons. As we have shown, many of the studies of black representation do not focus on the South or deal with only parts of the South. There are also relatively few scholarly investigations of the consequences (especially those of a symbolic nature) of electing blacks to office. In addition, there are measurement prob-lems; some variables need to be measured more rigorously while in other cases there is no consensus on the appropriate standards to be used in measuring variables. This latter problem is especially acute in attempting to measure forms of electoral systems. The final issue is one of incomplete or poorly developed models of causality, a particular problem thus far in studies of the impact of black officials.

What of the future of black elected officials in the South? Given the problems blacks face both in getting elected and in serving in office, is there any reason for optimism? Forecasting is always dangerous, but we can point to at least three factors which suggest that the election and impact of black officials may well continue to grow.

First, as blacks remain in public office, they acquire more political skills and knowledge. This experience in learning "the ropes" of the system can only serve to aid them as they work with other public officials in promoting black concerns. The time when whites can no longer prey on the political inexperience, even naivete, of black officials to thwart their goals may well be rapidly approaching. Second, throughout the South there are increasing challenges to at-large elections. These chal-lenges are being fought in both legal and political decision centers and they have often been successful. The result is that district (or, in some cases, "mixed") electoral systems are replacing at-large ones. The ultimate outcome of this development is likely to be the election of more blacks to public office. Finally, as the black middle class continues to grow, it is likely that more blacks will be "electable," because more resources will be available for black candidates and because whites may well be increasingly tolerant of middle class black candidates. More important, however, some of these black candidates, if they can establish "dual legitimacy," might be elected to higher political offices: state legislative and executive positions and even Congress. In these places it might be possible for blacks to have an impact at the macro, system-wide level which now they cannot, since they are largely confined to lower, often small town political offices.

More research is most certainly needed to improve our understanding of the election and impact of black officials. Longitudinal studies are essential to determine if, over time, there are changes in the "electability" and impact of black officials. It is also necessary that longitudinal studies be done on the impact of black elected officials on intra-city (or intra-county) resource allocation. In other words, it is not enough to know that more funds for local services are available; how are they distributed, are blacks getting a fair share, and do black elected officials have any effect on the way these resources are allocated? Finally, we know very little about how black elected officials actually do their job. What are the political dynamics of black officials at all levels and positions? How do they interact with white officials and other white elites? How do they try to represent black interests and concerns in very sensitive arenas of political decision making? These questions become especially important for black officials who have substantial numbers of white, as well as black, constituents. In short, until we know how black officials actually behave in office, our knowledge of their significance will be limited.

REFERENCES

Abney, Glenn F. "Factors Related to Voter Turnout in Mississippi." *Journal of Politics* 36 (November 1974): 1057–63.

Adrian, Charles A. "Some General Characteristics of Nonpartisan Elections." In *Urban Government*. Edited by Edward C. Banfield. New York: The Free Press, 1961.

Banfield, Edward, and Wilson, James Q. *City Politics*. Cambridge: Harvard University Press, 1963.

Bent, Devin. "Partisan Elections and Public Policy: Response to Black Demands in Large American Cities." *Journal of Black Studies* 12 (March 1982): 291–314.

Bullock, Charles S., III. "The Election of Blacks in the South: Preconditions and Consequences." *American Journal of Political Science* 19 (November 1975): 727–39.

————, and Dennis, Christopher. "A Diachronic Analysis of Black Registration and Officeholding in Two Southern States." Paper presented at the Southern Political Science Association meeting in Atlanta, Georgia, November, 1982.

————, and MacManus, Susan A. "Policy Responsiveness to the Black Electorate: Programmatic Versus Symbolic Representation." *American Politics Quarterly* 9 (July 1981): 357–68.

Button, James. "Impact of Black Elected Municipal Officials: A Descriptive Analysis." Paper presented at the Southern Political Science Association meeting in Atlanta, Georgia, November, 1978.

————. "Political Strategies and Public Service Patterns: The Impact of the Black Civil Rights Movement on Municipal Service Distributions." In *The Politics of Urban Public Services.* Edited by Richard C. Rich. Lexington, Mass.: D.C. Heath, 1982.

————, and Scher, Richard. "Impact of the Civil Rights Movement: Perceptions of Black Municipal Service Changes." *Social Science Quarterly* 60 (December 1979): 497–510.

Campbell, James David. *Electoral Participation and the Quest for Equality: Black Politics in Alabama Since the Voting Rights Act of 1965.* Doctoral Dissertation. University of Texas at Austin, 1976.

————, and Feagin, Joe. "Black Politics in the South: A Descriptive Analysis." *Journal of Politics* 37 (February 1975): 129–59.

Clubok, Alfred B., De Grove, John M., and Farris, Charles D. "The Manipulated Negro Vote: Some Pre-Conditions and Consequences." *Journal of Politics* 26 (February 1964): 112–29.

Colburn, Kenneth S. *Southern Black Mayors: Local Problems and Federal Responses.* Washington, D.C.: Joint Center for Political Studies, 1974.

Cole, Leonard. *Blacks in Power.* Princeton, N.J.: Princeton University Press, 1976.

Collins, William P. "Race and Political Cleavage: Ten Positions in a Local Election." *Journal of Black Studies* 11 (September 1980): 121–36.

Conyers, James E., and Wallace, Walter L., *Black Elected Officials: A Study of Black Americans Holding Governmental Offices.* New York: Russell Sage Foundation, 1976.

Coombs, David W., Alsikafi, M. H., Bryan, C. Hobson, and Webber, Irving L. "Black Political Control in Greene County, Alabama." *Rural Sociology* 42 (Fall 1977): 398–406.

Davidson, Chandler. *Biracial Politics: Conflict and Coalition in the Metropolitan South.* Baton Rouge, La.: Louisiana State University, 1972.

Dye, Thomas R., *Politics, Economics and the Public: Policy Outcomes in American States.* Chicago: Rand McNally, 1966.

————, and Renick, James. "Political Power and City Jobs: Determinants of Minority Employment." *Social Science Quarterly* 62 (September 1981): 475–86.

Eisinger, Peter K., "Black Employment in Municipal Jobs: The Impact of Black Political Power." *American Political Science Review* 76 (June 1982): 380–92.

————. *The Politics of Displacement: Racial and Ethnic Transition in Three American Cities.* New York: Academic, 1980.

Engstrom, Richard L., and McDonald, Michael D. "The Underrepresentation of Blacks on City Councils: Comparing the Structural and Socioeconomic Explanations for South/Non-South Differences." *Journal of Politics* 44 (November 1982): 1088–99.

Foster, Lorn S. "Black Perceptions of the Mayor: An Empirical Test." *Urban Affairs Quarterly* 14 (December 1978): 245–52.

Garrow, David J. *Protest at Selma.* New Haven: Yale University, 1978.

Ippolito, Dennis, Donaldson, William, and Bowman, Lewis. "Political Orientation Among Negroes and Whites." *Social Science Quarterly* 49 (December 1968): 548–56.

Joint Center for Political Studies. *National Roster of Black Elected Officials,* Vol. 12. Washington, D.C.: Government Printing Office, 1982.

Jones, Clinton. "The Impact of Local Election Systems on Black Political Representation." *Urban Affairs Quarterly* 11 (March 1976): 345–54.

Jones, Mack. "Black Officeholding and Political Development in the Rural South." *Review of Black Political Economy* 6, no. 4 (1976): 375–407.

Karnig, Albert K. "Black Representation on City Councils." *Urban Affairs Quarterly* 12 (December 1976): 223–42.

———, and Welch, Susan. *Black Representation and Urban Policy.* Chicago: University of Chicago, 1980.

———, and Welch, Susan. "Electoral Structure and Black Representation on City Councils." *Social Science Quarterly* 63 (March 1982): 99–114.

Keech, William. *The Impact of Negro Voting: The Role of the Vote in the Quest for Equality.* Chicago: Rand McNally, 1968.

Key, V. O., Jr. *Southern Politics.* New York: Knopf, 1949.

Kronus, Sidney. *The Black Middle Class.* Columbus, Ohio: Charles Merrill, 1971.

Latimer, Margaret K. "Black Political Representation in Southern Cities: Election Systems and Other Causal Variables." *Urban Affairs Quarterly* 15 (September 1979): 65–86.

Lawson, Steven F. *Black Ballots.* New York: Columbia University, 1976.

Levine, Charles H. *Racial Conflict and the American Mayor.* Lexington, Mass.: D. C. Heath, 1974.

Mars, Florence. *Witness in Philadelphia.* Baton Rouge: LSU Press, 1977.

Matthews, Donald, and Prothro, James. *Negroes and the New Southern Politics.* New York: Harcourt, Brace and World, 1966.

Meier, Kenneth J., and England, Robert E. "Black Representation and Educational Policy: Does It Make a Difference?" Paper presented at the American Political Science Association meeting, Denver, Colorado, September, 1982.

Merton, Robert. *Social Theory and Social Structure.* New York: Free Press, 1968.

Miller, Philip L. "The Impact of Organizational Activity on Black Political Participation." *Social Science Quarterly* 62 (March 1982): 83–98.

Myrdal, Gunnar. *An American Dilemma.* New York: Harper and Brothers, 1944.

Nelson, William E., and Meranto, Philip J. *Electing Black Mayors.* Columbus, Ohio: Ohio State University, 1977.

———, and Van Horne, Winston. "Black Elected Administrators: The Trials of Office." *Public Administration Review* 34 (November–December 1974): 526–33.

Newby, I. A. *The South: A History.* New York: Holt, Rinehart and Winston, 1978.

New York Times, February 21, 1977, Sec. 1, p. 14.

O'Loughlin, John. "Black Representation Growth and the Seat-Vote Relationship." *Social Science Quarterly* 60 (June 1979): 72–86.

Parker, Paige Alan, and Jackson, Larry R. "The Southern Black Candidate in At-Large City Elections: What Are the Determinants of Success?" Paper presented at the Southern Political Science Association meeting, Atlanta, Georgia, November, 1982.

Preston, Michael. "Limitations of Black Urban Power: The Case of Black Mayors." In *The New Urban Politics.* Edited by Louis H. Masotti and Robert L. Lineberry. Cambridge, Mass.: Ballinger, 1976.

Rodgers, Harrell R., Jr., and Bullock, Charles S., III. *Law and Social Change: Civil Rights Laws and Their Consequences.* New York: McGraw-Hill, 1972.

Salamon, Lester M. "Leadership and Modernization: The Emerging Black Political Elite in the American South." *Journal of Politics* 35 (August 1973): 615–46.

———, and Van Evera, Steven. "Fear, Apathy, and Discrimination: A Test of Three Explanations of Political Participation." *American Political Science Review* 67 (December 1973): 1288–1306.

Sanders, M. Elizabeth. "New Voters and New Policy Priorities in the Deep South: A

Decade of Political Change in Alabama." Paper presented at the American Political Science Association meeting, Washington, D.C., September, 1979.

Scher, Richard, and Button, James. "The Voting Rights Act: Implementation and Impact." In *Implementing Civil Rights*. Edited by Charles S. Bullock, III, and Charles Lamb. Monterey, CA.: Brooks/Cole, 1983.

Sharkansky, Ira, and Hofferbert, Richard. "Dimensions of State Politics, Economics, and Public Policy." *American Political Science Review* 63 (September 1969): 112–32.

U.S. Bureau of the Census. Current Population Reports, Series P-23, No. 74. "Registration and Voting in November, 1976—Jurisdictions Covered by the Voting Rights Act Amendments of 1975." Washington, D.C.: U.S. Government Printing Office, 1978.

U.S. Commission on Civil Rights. *Political Participation*. Washington, D.C.: U.S. Government Printing Office, 1968.

———. *The Voting Rights Act: Unfulfilled Goals*. Washington, D.C.: U.S. Government Printing Office, 1981.

Walton, Hanes. *Black Politics*. Philadelphia: Lippincott, 1972.

Watters, Pat and Cleghorn, Reese. *Climbing Jacob's Ladder*. New York: Harcourt, Brace and World, 1967.

Wirth, Clifford J. "Social Bias in Political Recruitment: Ascribed and Achieved Status of Black and White School Board Members." *Social Science Quarterly* 59 (March 1979): 758–66.

Woodward, C. Vann. *The Strange Career of Jim Crow*. New York: Oxford University Press, 1974.

POLITICAL RESPONSES TO POPULATION STABILIZATION AND DECLINE IN THE UNITED STATES AND WESTERN EUROPE:
IMPLICATIONS FOR POPULATION POLICY

Michael E. Kraft

I. INTRODUCTION

One of the most striking developments in industrialized societies in the last several decades has been the transition to sustained low fertility of the population. Fertility is now at or below replacement level in some 23 developed nations, including the United States, Canada, Japan, and most of Western and Northern Europe, and it is widely expected to remain low if not decline even further.[1] In a number of European countries, the growth rate is now negative; death rates exceed birth rates, and the size of the population is declining. In other developed nations the immediate implications are less dramatic but nevertheless of historic importance. After a variable period of continued slow growth, these nations face the prospect of a stationary or nongrowing population, and in some cases one of slow decline in population size. These trends are especially notable when juxtaposed with the high rates of growth characteristic of the developing nations.

Reaction to these developments has ranged from expression of concern about possible adverse social and economic consequences of a non-growing population to enthusiastic endorsement of population stabilization as a contribution to solving problems of resource scarcity and environmental quality. The concern has been more evident in Europe where the process of change has been underway for a longer period of time. Some Eastern European nations have adopted strong pronatalist policies in an effort to reverse the decline in fertility, and there has been speculation that the liberal democracies of Western Europe might find such a course of action appealing as they approach stabilization. In the United States there has been increasing debate in the scholarly literature and in the popular press over the implications of slowing rates of growth, and some effort to formulate public policies to enhance governmental capacity to plan more effectively for the consequences of a changing population.

Because these issues are now reaching the social and political agendas of developed nations, it may be useful to examine initial responses to them in anticipation that the future will see sharply increased levels of concern and political activity. Demographers and economists have dominated research on the implications of population stabilization, but political scientists and policy scholars have a quite different contribution to make. I hope this paper suggests some useful lines of inquiry.

The focus here is on the United States, and to a lesser extent on Western Europe. I explore several questions: How have nations experiencing sustained low fertility in recent years responded to this condition? In particular, how have such population changes been perceived and assessed by political elites, and what efforts are made to reverse these trends or to accommodate them? What public policies have been seriously considered and/or adopted, and what alternative policies have been proposed that might become the objects of greater attention in the future? What explains the differences among nations in the type and manner of their responses to population changes and to proposed policies? The chapter begins with an overview of population trends and consequences in the developed nations. It then considers what governments might do in response to such trends (a policy repertoire), actual policy actions to date, and possible future actions. In addition to the United States, attention is given to policy activity in three European nations: West Germany, France, and Sweden. There is special emphasis on the need for innovation in population policy to deal effectively with emerging problems not well addressed by the present array of public policies.

II. POPULATION TRENDS AND CONSEQUENCES

Any assessment of the implications of population change, particularly as regards probable future conditions, rests upon a number of assumptions about demographic projections, and about our knowledge of the way in which population changes affect other significant social, economic, political, and environmental variables. For present purposes these methodological complexities need not concern us greatly (but see Kirk, 1979; Demeny, 1979; and Keyfitz, 1982). However, the most widely used projections of population change in the next several decades should be reviewed, and in the process the reasons why one ought to have some faith in the numbers. The relatively poor track record of previous attempts to project future population conditions may well incline many to dismiss the very notion that we can know much of anything about our demographic future, much less plan for it in any systematic fashion. While some skepticism is warranted, that position is unreasonably pessimistic about the tools and methods of modern demography.

As of mid-1982, 25 nations in the world had a total fertility rate (TFR) at or below the replacement level of about 2.1 lifetime births per woman.[2] Of the 29 industrialized nations in Europe and North America, 20 were at or below replacement-level fertility. In six nations, the natural rate of increase is now at or below zero; these include Austria, Denmark, East and West Germany, Hungary, and Luxembourg.[3] Great Britain, Sweden, Norway, Switzerland, Italy, and Belgium are very close (.2 percent or lower), and if present trends continue, the population of Europe as a whole would begin to decrease by the year 2000 (Population Reference Bureau, 1982; Westoff, 1978).

Were these changes to be merely a short-term deviation from previous patterns of population growth, they would be of no great interest. But there are good reasons to assume they represent something close to a permanent alteration in the conditions that characterized the period immediately following World War II. The high fertility rates of the so-called "baby boom" years (1946–1964 in the United States) appear to have been an aberation. The long-term change in the population characteristics of developed nations has been a demographic transition from previously high rates of fertility and growth to a period of sustained low fertility and slowing rates of growth (van de Walle and Knodel, 1980). Most demographers seem to agree with Charles Westoff that "nothing on the horizon suggests that fertility will not remain low. All the recent evidence on trends in marriage and reproductive behavior encourages a presumption that it will remain low." (Westoff, 1978, p. 54).

As a result of later marriages, higher divorce rates, an increase in the number of women in the labor force, the popularity of smaller families and childfree lifestyles, and the widespread availability of reliable means to prevent the birth of unwanted children, some expect a further decline in the TFR, possibly to 1.5 children per woman. Others, most notably Richard Easterlin, have called into question some of these assumptions. Easterlin suggests that fertility rates are likely to rise in the next two decades as a consequence of the less restrictive social and economic conditions under which today's younger cohorts are being raised; subjected to less competition for life's rewards, members of these smaller cohorts, he argues, are likely to adopt a more optimisitc outlook on the future (especially on their own futures) and return to higher levels of fertility as a result (Easterlin, 1980). Of course, economic recessions and high rates of unemployment in the early 1980s weaken Easterlin's argument to some extent.

Despite the dissenting opinion, the level of agreement among those demographers expecting continued low levels of fertility is impressive, and it suggests the validity of near-term to medium-term population projections based on these low rates. Indeed, even the cautious U.S. Census Bureau has apparently become convinced of that fact. In October 1982, the Bureau released its latest projections for U.S. growth through 2050, basing its middle-range Series II figures on a sustained TFR of 1.9, the current level in the U.S. Previously, only the lowest-level Series III projections were based upon such a low fertility assumption (U.S. Bureau of the Census, 1982).

Given these expectations of continued low fertility in the United States and Western Europe, a number of interesting projections can be made. Table 1 indicates expected population size and growth rates for the United States and selected Western European nations through 2020. Population size for 1940 is provided to allow comparison of growth in the last four decades with anticipated changes over the next four decades. The pattern is clearly one of a gradual movement toward a stationary or slightly declining population by 2020. The United States will continue to grow at a substantial but declining rate (partly attributable to an unusually high rate of immigration), and is expected to reach a population of about 309 million in 2050 (U.S. Bureau of the Census, 1982; Bouvier, 1981). Several nations—most strikingly, West Germany—will face a future of sharply declining population size. The West German population is expected to decrease from the current 61.7 million to 49.3 million by the year 2020.

Estimates of the policy consequences of such low fertility are more difficult, but the demographic implications have been studied thoroughly (U.S. Congress, 1978b; Bouvier, 1980). The major finding is that there will be a dramatic change in the age composition of the population. Most of the social, political, and economic consequences of note are

Table 1. Population Size and Growth Rates for the United States and Selected Western European Nations: 1940–2020

Nation	Total Fertility Rate 1982	Annual Rate of Natural Increase (1982)	Population in 1940 (in millions)	Population in 1982 (in millions)	Projected Population[a] (in millions)	
					2000	2020
United States	1.9	0.7	133.1	232.0	259.0	274.1
Austria	1.7	0.0	6.7	7.6	7.3	6.8
Belgium	1.7	0.1	8.3	9.9	9.9	9.3
Denmark	1.5	0.0	3.8	5.1	5.1	4.8
France	2.0	0.5	41.3	54.2	56.4	56.6
Netherlands	1.6	0.5	8.9	14.3	14.9	14.2
Norway	1.7	0.2	3.0	4.1	4.1	4.0
Sweden	1.7	0.1	6.4	8.3	8.0	7.4
Switzerland	1.5	0.2	4.2	6.3	6.2	5.6
United Kingdom	1.9	0.2	48.2	56.1	57.1	56.5
West Germany	1.5	-0.2	43.0	61.7	59.9	49.3

Source: Population Reference Bureau, "1982 World Population Data Sheet." PRB's data are drawn chiefly from the United Nations *Demographic Yearbook* and the *Population and Vital Statistics Report* of the UN Statistical Office.

[a] Projections by PRB were made by applying the growth rates incorporated in the projections prepared by the U.N., the World Bank, or the U.S. Bureau of the Census. Projections for 2020 are subject to a wider range of error.

assumed to follow from this outcome and from the absence of growth itself. Table 2 illustrates these demographic effects for the United States. It shows expected changes by age group for the period 1990 to 2050. At current fertility levels, the average age of the population will increase from 30.3 in 1981 to 36.3 in the year 2000 and to 41.6 by 2050. The percentage of the population over age 65 will increase markedly from 11.4% in 1981 to 21.7 by 2050, and the percentage under age 18 will decline slightly from 25.5 in 1982 to 19.8 in 2050. With a lower level of fertility the increase in the proportion over age 65 would be appreciably higher.

The consequences of these demographic shifts cannot be stated with any precision because of the uncertainty of long-term projections and other relevant developments (e.g., technological invention) and because there is no direct relationship between demographic conditions and quality of life in a nation; the influence of demographic changes is mediated through a complex set of social, economic and cultural conditions. Despite these uncertainties, it is quite clear that persistent low fertility in the developed nations can have major effects on the type and level of demands citizens make upon governments, on the capacity of governments to respond to those demands, and on the distribution of political power both within a given nation and in relations among nations. The effects are likely to be greatest for age-sensitive public policies (e.g., retirement programs, education, and health care for the elderly), but may well be significant for the rate of economic growth; energy use and environmental quality; national security; and society, politics, and

Table 2.   Estimates and Projections of the U.S. Population in Selected Age Groups: 1900–2050

Estimates	*Percent Distribution*				
	Under 18	18–24	25–44	45–64	65 and over
1900	40.4	13.6	28.2	13.8	4.1
1930	34.9	12.6	29.5	17.5	5.4
1982	25.5	13.1	29.1	19.2	11.6
Projections					
1990	24.2	10.3	32.6	18.6	12.7
2000	23.8	9.2	29.9	22.7	13.1
2025	20.9	8.5	26.0	24.0	19.5
2050	19.8	8.3	25.0	24.0	21.7

Source: Thomas J. Espenshade, "Zero Population Growth and the Economies of Developed Nations," *Population and Development Review* 4 (December, 1978), and U.S. Bureau of the Census, Current Population Reports, Series P-25, No. 922, "Projections of the Population of the United States: 1982–2050 (Advanced Report)." Figures for 1990–2050 are calculated from the Census Bureau's Series II projections.

government more generally (Espenshade and Serow, 1978; Campbell, 1979; and Council of Europe, 1978).

While research to date has been modest, there is nevertheless substantial consensus in the research community on the overall consequences of low growth rates. Consider two representative assessments offered in the 1970s concerning economic consequences of slowing growth rates. In 1972, the Commission on Population Growth and the American Future concluded that

> in the long run, no substantial benefits will result from further growth of the Nation's population, rather that gradual stabilization of our population through voluntary means would contribute significantly to the Nation's ability to solve its problems. We have looked for, and have not found, any convincing economic argument for continued population growth. The health of our country does not depend on it, nor does the vitality of business nor the welfare of the average person. (Commission on Population Growth and the American Future 1972, p. 4)

In 1978, Espenshade published a major review of recent research on economic consequences, including studies conducted between 1972 and 1978. He concluded that although many research questions remained unanswered, the overall consensus among economists "would appear to be positive, in terms of a per capita measure of economic well being."

> Is the cessation of growth that has been projected for most European countries by the end of this century and for the majority of other developed countries by some time early in the twenty-first century a cause for alarm? . . . [T]his review of the recent literature on the economic implications of slowing population growth in the industrial countries suggests that the health of a nation depends far more on the wisdom of its economic policies than on its underlying demographic trends. (Espenshade, 1978, p. 667)

Espenshade correctly noted that the question is not merely whether population stabilization is desirable or not, but over what time period and with what type of public policies or other actions a country can move toward such a future state of affairs while minimizing social and economic disruptions resulting from a changing age structure: "A transition to zero population growth will require some readjustments, but with proper anticipation and planning, there need be no insurmountable problems." (p. 668) An important question is whether governments will recognize the need for that anticipation and planning, and develop appropriate public policies.

These studies—and many others that have reached similar conclusions for Western Europe as well as for the United States (e.g., Council of Europe, 1978; Kirk, 1981b; Campbell, 1979; and Day, 1972 and 1978)—may not allay the "fear of falling" or the persistent anxieties about social and economic stagnation that slowing rates of growth or nongrowth seem to generate. Public perception of the "problem," as is often the case, may be in sharp contrast to scientific findings. Thus, myths are perpetuated about the characteristics of a future stationary population (e.g., "old people ruminating over old ideas in old houses") that bear little resemblance to the reality (e.g., the present age structure in Sweden and England is very nearly that of a stationary population). Political responses, of course, can be shaped far more by misperception, myths, and emotional reactions than by sound evidence and logic.

III. POLICY ALTERNATIVES IN RESPONSE TO SLOWING GROWTH RATES

What might governments do about these population trends and consequences? Presumably there are two broad reactions possible. A nation might approve of the changes and either formulate policies for accommodation to them over time or leave any such adjustment to individual and private sector initiative. Alternatively, a nation might disapprove of the changes and either formulate policies to increase fertility and/or immigration levels (to postpone the arrival of stabilization or slow the rate of decrease) or choose not to attempt intervention because the financial and political cost of any such effort would be too great. Depending on which of these two postures prevails, a range of policy alternatives may be considered, from a fairly low level of governmental intervention to a quite substantial role for government. The range of possible political responses to population stabilization is indicated in Figure 1.

This figure and the discussion below reflect a broad definition of population policy. For present purposes the most useful definition is simply what governments choose to do or not to do about population conditions and trends, either to shape them or to respond to them. Decisions (or "nondecisions") to take no action are included because they represent a preference, or at least a willingness, to allow other influences such as prevailing personal and private sector decisionmaking to determine population events.

Most of the literature on political responses to population stabilization has focused on the case of negative assessment of stabilization and the possibility of governmental intervention through adoption of pronatalist fertility policies. This reflects the historical experience of many Western nations with low fertility during the economic depression of the 1930s as well as their belief that sustained low fertility will have adverse impacts on the economy, national prestige, and national power (Finkle and McIntosh, 1978; Council of Europe, 1978). This analytic focus may be

Figure 1. A Typology of Political Responses to Population Stabilization

Preferred Level of Governmental Intervention

	Low	Moderate	High
Positive	Stabilization may be desirable, but minimum governmental role is preferred. There will have to be accommodation to the changes over time, but decisionmaking can be left largely to individuals and the private sector.	Stabilization is clearly desirable, and government should keep present policies facilitating maintenance of low fertility. But no major policy changes are needed to achieve stabilization or to plan for the consequences of continued low fertility. Accommodation to the changes can occur over time by "muddling through" and with a moderate governmental role.	Early achievement of stabilization is desirable and requires government policy declaring it as a national goal, and increased support for anti-natalist policies. New policies and new governmental offices are needed to strengthen institutional capabilities for long–term, integrated planning for the consequences of population change.
Negative	Stabilization may be undesirable, especially if it arrives too quickly. But fertility behavior should be left to individual decisionmaking. Any adjustments to changing social and economic conditions should also be left largely to the private sector.	The negative consequences of stabilization outweigh the benefits and careful monitoring of population trends and analysis of the consequences are necessary. Government may have to consider measures to increase fertility or immigration levels. A major goal is to minimize oscillations in fertility to create a smoother transition to a stationary population, and thus less fluctuation in demands for education, jobs, pensions, etc. A moderate governmental role is preferred.	Stabilization is clearly undesirable. The costs of slowing rates of growth (or of population decline) are so great that government should act to increase fertility or immigration levels. Major policy change to increase growth rates is favored. Government should play an active role.

Assessment of the Trend Toward Stabilization

227

justified by current political reality in some European nations, but it ignores the other quite different responses indicated in Figure 1. What nations have done in the past may not be a very useful guide to what they are likely to do in the future. There is an emerging perspective on the interrelationship of population, resources, and environmental quality that may well influence policymakers to shift from a negative to positive assessment of low growth (Council on Environmental Quality and Department of State, 1980; Dunlap, 1980; Pirages, 1977). Also, recent survey data indicate increasing public support for building a "sustainable society" in nations entering a post-industrial era of development (Inglehart, 1977; Milbrath, 1983). A stationary population is likely to be viewed very favorably in such a society.

Even a supportive stance on slowing rates of growth does not necessarily eliminate a need for new public policies. Governments will have to plan for the remaining years of continuing growth and help manage a smooth transition to an era of nongrowth in order to minimize the inevitable disruptions that would otherwise occur. Public attitudes supportive of a stationary population and demands that governments become more efficient in their use of scarce public funds suggest the relevance of innovative population policies that increase governmental capabilities toward these ends.

There is no shortage of policy typologies that may be used to generate a wide range of specific alternatives for each of the positions identified in Figure 1, including these innovative planning policies. Any number of texts in public policy would readily reward the reader with a bewildering array of possibilities (e.g., Anderson, 1979, pp. 125–150). Some political scientists have applied the more common schemes to population issues. Stetson (1973) develops a policy repertoire using Theodore Lowi's typology and distinguishes regulative, symbolic, and distributive policy alternatives for changing the environment of fertility behavior from pronatalist to antinatalist. She applies it to three categories: contraceptive policy, abortion policy, and sterilization policy, and distinguishes three levels of "capability performance" to indicate the extent of governmental power or effort involved. In a similar analysis, Miller and Godwin (1977) propose four categories of policies: distributive, redistributive, self-regulatory and regulatory. They go on to review policies that range from informational programs to basic research, and offer a set of evaluative standards that include familiar normative concerns such as individual freedom, equity, procedural fairness, efficiency, and effectiveness.

The level of public policy intervention favored will reflect the way policymakers assess the seriousness of the problem faced and their view of the need for governmental action. The benefits and costs of population stabilization will be judged according to whatever criteria are deemed relevant. For some such evaluation will reflect largely economic calculations such as the impact on future labor force needs and economic growth. For others it will turn on evaluation of the social impacts such as an aging population and its effects on the vitality of a culture. And for still others it will be a matter of the effects on resource consumption, environmental quality, national security, or some other important values. There may also be some consideration of what constitutes an "optimum" population size or growth rate.

In all of these calculations, policymakers face the difficult job of examining a diverse and complex set of data, sorting through conflicting arguments of variable quality, and rendering some overall judgments about where the national interest lies. Such decisions will take place in institutional settings not necessarily well equipped for the assessments and will be subject to a variety of political pressures. In some nations the decisions will be largely in the hands of high-level professional administrators (common in Europe) and in others they will rest with elected policymakers and political appointees (the American case). It is conceivable that one approach will yield technically superior decisions that are less directly influenced by political pressures and the other will produce technically weaker decisions that are heavily influenced by political forces. Ideally, one would want decisions that are technically sound as well as politically legitimate. In such a system there would be a substantial capacity for data gathering, long-range projections, and sophisticated analysis suitable for the complexity of the task. Professionally qualified analysts would provide the best data and projections possible and address the factual issues embodied in alternative courses of action, but there would also be a representative political process in which competing claims and arguments receive consideration. Such a political process would facilitate assessment of the data in terms of a wide range of important perspectives and interests, and may be essential to producing an acceptable, effective, and administratively feasible policy. Comparison of the political responses to population stabilization and decline in the United States and Western Europe allows exploration of these questions and suggests some possible innovations in population policy to meet needs not well addressed by present policies.

IV. POLITICAL RESPONSES TO POPULATION STABILIZATION AND DECLINE

In a recent review of low fertility and liberal democracy in Western Europe, C. Alison McIntosh argues that "low population growth has reached the political agenda in virtually all the advanced industrialized nations." Throughout Europe, in particular, she says a majority of governments have established or revitalized population commissions to monitor population trends and advise on policy; national and international conferences have proliferated; public discussion in many countries has become intense; and a number of countries have adopted explicit or implicit population growth targets. (McIntosh, 1981, p. 182).

Eastern European nations have shown a much greater willingness to adopt pronatalist policies than have the liberal democracies of Western Europe, where there is much talk but not much action (David, 1982). In the United States there has been considerable talk about selected aspects of low fertility (such as the aging of the population) but not as much evident concern with stabilization as such.

Because policy responses to population stabilization have been quite limited outside of Eastern Europe, any review and assessment must necessarily focus on the early stages of the policy cycle, that is, on agenda-setting and policy formulation. Most of the focus below is on the United States, but attention is given to three nations in Western Europe: West Germany, France, and Sweden. The selection reflects an attempt to have at least some variation in fertility patterns, political cultures, and institutional structures. This account, then, is one of the comparative politics of agenda-setting and policy formulation.

The United States

While McIntosh and others have written about low population growth having reached the agenda in Europe, one might better characterize low growth in the United States as something of a nonproblem or nonissue at the national level. It may be "on the agenda," but it is certainly not near the top of the agenda. The low salience of these issues—combined with the uncertainty about long-term effects—has constrained rational assessment of population trends and inhibited development of national policy to deal directly with the problems associated with slow growth and stabilization. In part as a consequence, political responses to date have been influenced more by ideologies and short-term political considerations than by the collected findings and recommendations of research studies and government commissions and reports on the subject. The fragmented nature of policymaking in the American political system, the lack of any natural organizational setting for population policy, and the absence of a strong, organized constituency pressing for policy change are further reasons for a minimal policy response. Thus one can suggest that the United States falls on one side of the continuum noted above: The American political system excels at political representation and incremental adjustments in public policy but fails at assessment of long-term population trends and consequences and comprehensive policy development.

Table 3 lists the most notable policy activities since 1969 (something of a watershed year) and offers a modest assessment of their significance for population policy. No single activity or decision represents public policy, although many of these activities are the ingredients of what might be called an informal or implicit population policy, particularly when there is an identifiable and consistent course of action over time. State and local actions and policies are omitted from the table. While there have been a number of highly innovative policies setting limits on local growth (Rosenbaum, 1978; Whisler, 1978), the focus of this analysis is on the national level.

The activites summarized in Table 3 indicate a varied set of governmental responses to growth issues. There has been a moderate expression of interest in the issues in a variety of institutional settings, including national commissions on population growth and on immigration policy, several subcommittees and select committees in both houses of Congress, study groups in some administrative agencies and departments, and the Office of Management and Budget. This attention and activity, though, has been sporadic and is attributable largely to a small number of congressional and bureaucratic policy entrepreneurs, an especially favorable political climate (e.g., in the early 1970s), and to the pressures from nongovernmental interest groups and professional associations (e.g., the Global Tomorrow Coalition, Zero Population Growth, the American Public Health Association, and the Population Association of America). Some would add that another influential force has been the so-called "population establishment" (the Population Council, Planned Parenthood/World Population, the Ford Foundation, the Rockefeller Foundation, and certain prominent individuals such as John D. Rockefeller 3rd, identified with federal population activities since the early 1960s (Piotrow, 1973; Bachrach and Bergman, 1973).

All of this activity has had very little evident impact on formal governmental responses to population stabilization or development of national population policy. There is no policy statement that can be said to represent authoritatively the position of the U.S. government on growth rates or population size, and no reliable empirical data on elite perception and response to slowing rates of growth. Nor has the government established any of the offices or agencies recommended to correct the institutional deficiencies noted as far back as the 1972 Population Commission report. Thus one must draw tentative conclusions from the disparate activities noted in Table 3 and posit an informal or de facto policy based on the course of action over the last decade.

Given these qualifications, the U.S. government would have to be

Table 3. Policy Activities Related to Population Stabilization in the United States: 1969 to 1982

Date	Activity	Major Recommendations or Actions	Impact on Population Policy (weak, moderate, strong)
1969	Presidential message to Congress on population (Nixon, 1969)	Asks for establishment of a Commission on Population Growth and the American Future; creation of a family planning office in Dept. of Health, Education & Welfare; and budget increases for population research. Included a statement on the importance of better data and analysis of population impacts and greater foresight and planning by government.	Moderate—recognition of the impact of population growth on nation's quality of life and environmental quality. Led to establishment of the Commission and a large body of research on the impact of growth. A strong expression of support for availability of family planning services. However, little presidential activity beyond initial message.
1970	Congress creates the Commission on Population Growth and the American	Approval of the President's request with slight modification.	Moderate—indicated congressional concern with population change, but little additional activity followed.
1970	Passage of the Family Planning Services and Population Research Act of 1970, Title X of the Public Health Service Act (the "Tydings Act")	Created Office of Population Affairs in H.E.W.; provided grants for family planning projects; funds for research, training, and education.	Moderate—represented expansion of governmental support for family planning services and consolidation of previously established programs. No explicit demographic goals and no government–wide coordination of programs and goals dealing with population.
1971	Senate hearing on a population stabilization resolution, SJ Res. 108, by the Special Subcommittee on Human Resources of the Senate Labor and	Resolution was endorsed by Population Commission. Stated that the policy of the U.S. would be to "develop, at the earliest possible time, voluntary pro-	Weak—represented the first time in U.S. history that a committee of Congress considered legislation to declare a national population policy. 25 witnesses

	Public Welfare Committee (U.S. Congress, 1971)	grams, consistent with human rights and individual conscience, to stabilize the population size of the Nation"	heard on five days of the hearings, and 30 statements submitted for the record, but resolution was not reported out of committee. No other hearings on similar legislation over the following ten years.
1972	Report of the Commission on Population Growth and the American Future (Commission on Population Growth, 1972)	Stated that the nation should "welcome and plan for a stabilized population," and that there are "advantages of moving now toward the stabilization of population." Extensive documentation of the impact of population growth in six volumes of commissioned research. Recommendations included moving "promptly and boldly to strengthen the basic statistics of research upon which all sound demographic, social, and economic policy must ultimately depend" by creating a National Institute on Population Sciences, an Office of Population Growth and Distribution in the Executive Office of the Presidet, a Joint Committee on Population in Congress, and strengthening the Office of Population Affairs in HEW, among other organizational changes, to "improve the federal government's capacity to develop and implement population–related programs." Also, recommended that immigration levels not be increased and that immigration policy be assessed to reflect "demographic conditions and considerations."	Weak—report was largely ignored by the president and Congress, President Nixon criticized recommendations on abortion and teenage contraception and took no action on the rest of the report. Major impact of the report and research findings was educational, primarily within the population community. There is no evidence of any significant impact on policy elites more generally, and there has been no significant policy change as a result of the report.

(continued)

Table 3. (Continued)

Date	Activity	Major Recommendations or Actions	Impact on Population Policy (weak, moderate, strong)
1977–78	Select Committee on Population, U.S. House of Representatives established by House Res. 70 in late Sept., 1977; authorized to act only during the 95th Congress. An investigative committee, not legislative. Directed to investigate, among other things, the causes and consequences of changing population conditions in the U.S., and approaches to population planning that would be most effective in coping with unplanned population change.	Held 37 days of hearings, supported by a staff of 30–40 people, between February and August, 1978. Released extensive reports in 10 volumes covering four areas, including domestic consequences of U.S. population change and fertility and contraception in the U.S. Major recommendations included: that there be substantial increases in funding for population research and for family planning services, comprehensive review of immigration policy, stronger commitment to population activities at the highest levels of American government, expanded research on the consequences of a changing U.S. population, and increased attention to methods of planning for the consequences of population change. Special emphasis was given to improving federal capacity for analyzing the impact of demographic change on federal programs and policies and for developing alternative policies and programs for planning for future population change. (U.S. Congress, 1978a, 1978b)	Weak—no change in policy occurred. The chairman of the committee, James Scheuer of New York, described the work of the committee as "consciousness-raising." Little coverage of the hearings and reports in the mass media. Committee failed to gain approval for another two years of existence, during which inquiry was to be more directly policy-relevant.
1978–1981	Select Commission on Immigration and Refugee Policy. Created by Congress in 1978 to provide comprehensive review	Work began in August, 1979 and continued through February, 1981. Staff of 25 arranged 12 hearings nationwide,	Moderate—impact on immigration policy was strong, although at this writing the Congress is still deliberating on im-

234

	of immigration policy, assess past and present immigration and its consequences, and recommend policy change. (U.S. Congress, 1981)	but did not compile extensive research reports similar to previous population–related commissions and committees. Commission sharply divided on immigration issues and recommendations. Supported additional funds and staff for enforcement of immigration laws and administrative reforms, establishment of civil and criminal penalties for employers hiring illegal aliens, amnesty for most illegals currently in the U.S., and an increase in legal immigration levels. (U.S. Congress, 1981)	migration reform. A major impact on the visibility of immigration issues. However, commission did not consider immigration within the context of population policy. Little concern with stabilization of U.S. population and more concern with limiting illegal immigration for other reasons (e.g., impact on U.S. labor force).
1979	Office of Management and Budget includes in the budget for fiscal year 1980 a six–page statement on "Population Change and Long Range Effects on the Budget." Represented the first time the budget message included any assessment of long–term population change (Executive Office of the President, O.M.B., 1979, pp. 52–57)	The statement focused on "probable changes in the age profile of American society and some possible results of those changes, particularly on the budget." Noted fertility changes; impact on education; labor force; armed forces; relationship of age structure and crime rate; housing demand; savings, credit, and investment; retirement and medical programs for the aged; and federalism.	Weak—no evidence of the effect on budgetary policymaking. No specific demographic goals implied. Primary impact was to demonstrate the possibility of incorporating long–term population impact analysis into such routine governmental policymaking.
1980	Global 2000 Report to the President. Represented the first federal effort to project long–term changes in population, resources, and environmental conditions on a global basis. Strong emphasis given to role of population growth.	Recommended establishment by law of a permanent office in the Executive Office of the President to "institutionalize the coordination of long–term global and holistic consideration of population, resources, environment	Weak—several hearings in Congress, but no legislation reported from committee. Reagan administration indicates very little interest in the study and the recommendations. Coalition of environmental groups (Global Tomorrow

(continued)

Table 3. (Continued)

Date	Activity	Major Recommendations or Actions	Impact on Population Policy (weak, moderate, strong)
	Follow-up report, *Global Future: Time to Act* (January, 1981) enumerated policy recommendations. (Council on Environmental Quality and Department of State, 1980, 1981).	and their related issues." *Global Future* concluded that U.S. should develop a national population policy addressing issues of stabilization, availability of family planning programs, improved information needs and a capacity to analyze impact of population change in the U.S., and new institutional arrangements to insure continued federal attention to domestic population issues. Improved "foresight capacity" was the key theme.	Coalition) becomes the major force for policy change. Emphasis is on viewing population issues in a broader context of environmental and resource problems and on improving institutional and analytical capabilities of U.S. government to deal with these problems.
1982	Hearings in the House of Representatives on National Population Policy, H.R. 907. Subcommittee on Census and Population of the Committee on Post Office and Civil Service, March 10 and 11. (U.S. Congress, 1982).	16 witnesses and 14 statements submitted for the record on the establishment of a national population policy introduced by Rep. Richard Ottinger of New York. The bill declared a "national policy of coordinated planning for the Nation's approach to population change, and to establish a goal of eventual stabilization in the United States as a keystone of a national population policy." Similar legislation was introduced in the Senate (S. 1771 by Senator Mark Hatfield of Oregon), but with a stronger emphasis on "coordinating planning for changes in population characteristics" and improving long-range foresight capability.	Weak—Subcommittee in the House took no action following the hearing and no hearing was held in the Senate. Only one member of the Subcommittee (Chairman Garcia) attended the two days of hearings, indicating little interest on the part of other subcommittee members.

placed in the upper left corner of Figure 1; it has demonstrated a moderately positive position on the desirability of stabilization and prefers a relatively low level of governmental intervention. Endorsement of the goal of stabilization can be found most directly in the report of the Population Commission, congressional testimony during the 1971 and 1982 hearings on policy proposals, and the *Global 2000* and *Global Future* reports. While no explicit policy emerged, those actions and documents do indicate widespread perception that a slowing rate of growth is beneficial or at least not harmful. Scholarly literature in the United States is predominantly supportive of the same position (Espenshade and Serow, 1978; Campbell, 1979), although there is little agreement on an optimum population size for the United States (Petersen, 1978; U.S. Congress, 1978a, p. 43). Reaction seems to depend largely on the rate of change; a precipitous decline in fertility—or a sharply fluctuating fertility rate—creates a more difficult problem for public policy than does a slow rate of decline. It is difficult to find any significant group in the U.S.—or any political leader—that adopts a strongly negative position at this time on slowing rates of growth and urges an increase in fertility or immigration to reverse present conditions; there is, however, a contingent of scholars and popular commentators who dissent from the mainstream view (Petersen, 1978; Simon, 1981; and Weber, 1977).

Intervention to raise fertility is very unlikely in the United States. There is little organized opposition to slowing rates of growth and there is strong support for reproductive freedom; individual choice in setting family size is assumed to be nearly inviolate (Nash, 1971). Although there is increasing criticism of federal family planning programs and liberal abortion policies, it comes largely from conservative religious groups and the political right more concerned with the morality of family planning and abortion than with demographic goals per se (Kantner, 1982). Moreover, these efforts represent a minority viewpoint and are unlikely to reverse the predominant pattern of low fertility or the prevailing ideology of reproductive freedom.

While there appears to be substantial support in general for population stabilization and a very low probability of either pronatalist or antinatalist intervention, most of the commissions, committees, and study groups reviewed in Table 3 do call attention to the possibly adverse policy implications of slowing rates of growth, especially to the impact of a changing age structure. The most extensive commentary on those implications can be found in the reports of the Select Committee on Population (U.S. Congress, 1978a). The major conclusions that emerge from the Select Committee parallel those of the *Global Future* report. Emphasis is given to the present institutional weaknesses of the federal government that limit its ability to identify policy implications and to deal with them. For example, the Select Committee concluded that the federal government "has no capacity to plan systematically for population change" even though changes in the size, age composition, and geographical distribution of the population "can, and often do, have profound effects" on federal policies and programs and those programs often influence the direction of population change "unintentionally." It also noted that the government has "no explicit policy outlining goals related to the overall size, growth, and distribution of the population" and that "policymakers at all levels of government and the American public have limited understanding of the long-term consequences of population change for individuals and society as a whole." To correct some of these deficiencies, the Select Committee recommended an extensive array of actions. The Committee does not reflect an official government position, but its views can be described as a professional assessment based on extensive hearings and study that included a broadly representative process for soliciting diverse perspectives and opinions on population problems and institutional needs. The recommendations, then, are both important and representative of the professional population community in the United States.

The major recommendations dealing with responses to population stabilization included the following: (1) that Congress should investigate more fully "the effects of the population size and growth rate of the United States on the well-being of our people"; (2) that there be continuing analysis of the interrelationships of demographic change and federal programs and policies; (3) that there be greater coordination of programs and policies that will be affected by population change or that may affect population; (4) that Congress undertake a thorough investigation to identify "all population-sensitive programs and policies, to assess their impact on population, and to consider alternative mechanisms" for improving the capacity of the federal government to conduct continuing analysis of the interrelationship of demographic change and federal policies, coordinate policies and programs which will be affected by population change, and develop alternative policies and programs for "planning for future population change and assess the short-term and long-term costs and benefits of each course of action." (U.S. Congress, 1978a, pp. 50–55).

Many of these recommendations were incorporated into legislation introduced in the 97th Congress in 1981 (H.R. 907 and S. 1771), but as noted in Table 3, little activity occurred in the Congress beyond two days of hearings before the Subcommittee on Census and Population in March, 1982 (on national population policy) and a joint hearing of two subcommittees of the House Energy and Commerce Committee in early December, 1981 (on global issues and national strategic planning related to the *Global 2000 Report*). Thus it is difficult to assess the impact of these more recent study groups and to speculate on what will become of their recommendations on improving institutional capacity for population planning. Given the way policy innovation typically occurs in the American political system, one would expect a fairly long period of incubation or gestation for these recommendations rather than a rapid change in national policy. As Nelson Polsby has suggested, a slower pace of development is characteristic of policy innovation when there is "no widespread acknowledgement of the existence of a problem" and no consensus that governmental action is required. Policy invention or formulation is typically the work of people removed from policymaking settings (e.g., the population community and staffs of interest groups), and the resulting proposals must be incubated until sufficient support develops or favorable political conditions emerge. This incubation is especially likely to be found on Capitol Hill, where

> political actors—Senators, Congressmen, lobbyists or other promoters—take the idea up, reshape it, adapt it to their political needs, publicize it, and put it into the ongoing culture of decision-makers that endures in Washington and in national politics. . . . (Polsby, 1982).

In short, policy innovation of the type recommended by the Select Committee and the Global 2000 Report is not likely to be forthcoming in the near term. The American political system requires substantially greater awareness and concern about population trends and consequences to support policy change. Consensus in the professional population community is not sufficient. Policy change in the future will depend on the accumulation of reliable scientific data on the effects of slowing rates of growth, persuasive arguments on the need for institutional changes or expanded governmental authority, mobilizatin of those who favor the policy change, leadership by highly placed policy entrepreneurs, and effective political action on the part of policy advocates. Until such change, the United States is likely to "muddle through," making incremental adjustments in policies and programs when and where the necessity of doing so is obvious.

Western Europe

If the trend toward sustained low fertility has been a low visibility problem in the United States in the last decade, Western Europe stands in stark contrast. In a 1978 *Wall Street Journal* article reporting West European anxiety about low birth rates, the director of the French National Institute of Demographic Studies, Gerard Calot, spoke clearly of the concern:

In almost every country, the fertility index is falling dramatically, at speeds never before seen and to levels never before reached in peacetime. In the next 10 years, population will undoubtedly be recognized as one of Europe's major problems. (Otten, 1978)

Not every country in Europe has responded negatively to these changes. For example, in the Netherlands, a 1977 report of the Population Commission recommended that the government "aim at ending natural population growth as soon as possible" and the Dutch government itself said that the end of population growth is "viewed positively." (Heeren, 1982). Like the United States, the Netherlands has a relatively high rate of natural increase and thus in a sense can afford to be unconcerned. But most West European nations have expressed at least some concern about the demographic trends and some have altered social policies in a modest attempt to increase fertility rates. My concern here is to review prevailing perceptions of low fertility rates and the actions considered and/or taken by West Germany, France, and Sweden. This analysis will be much less detailed than that provided above for the United States. The purpose is to compare the United States with these three nations to put the American responses into a useful cross-national context, and to suggest factors explaining the nature of these differential political responses to low fertility.

West Germany. The concern over low fertility in most European nations focuses on slowing rates of growth and possible stabilization in the near term. In West Germany, the rate of growth is already negative and the population is declining. In some respects, then, it represents a test case of how nations might respond to the most extreme demographic scenario. The evidence is that even in such an extreme set of circumstances democratic nations are reluctant to intervene with strong policy measures.

Evidence of an official point of view on the part of the Federal Government is hard to come by. In response to a United Nations Population Inquiry in 1978, the Federal Government stated that its birth rate was "too low." Heeren (1982) examined replies to questions posed by opposition parties in the *Bundestag* in 1977 and 1978, prior to completion of the government's review and response to the United Nations, and found a moderate assessment of the situation. In response to questions about negative effects on the economy, health care, national defense and other sectors, the government said that "the present development of population and the changes in population structure give rise to adaptation problems in certain areas," but it did not agree that the problems were as severe as the opposition alleged. On another occasion, it said that "on the basis of the available investigations, the government cannot agree to a negative evaluation of present trends nor to a dramatic estimation of its consequences." These questions were not asked out of mere curiosity; the opposition was using the population problem as a political weapon. Therefore, interpretation of the significance of the government's response is difficult. However, the government did deny the severity of the problem and, as Heeren (pp. 140–141) puts it, "refused to set any quantitative targets for German or foreign population growth."

McIntosh notes that the Germans were very sensitive about population issues and especially hard to interview on the subject. Fears of governmental intervention seem to be based to a large extent on the Nazi experience of the 1930s and 1940s, and are understandably difficult to study. There is evident concern about the effect of negative growth rates on the economy and the impact of age structure changes on social security, but fears of declining national power are harder to find. As McIntosh notes, Germans tend toward silence on the subject. The impact of immigration and the maintenance of a cultural identity are also among the concerns identified in most accounts, and McIntosh found that immigration was "totally unacceptable" as a solution to the problem of population decline (1983, p. 191).

At the national level, there has been only a modest alteration in fertility-related policies. Existing policies involving housing, maternity leaves, education, aid to families with dependent children, and the like have been maintained. There have also been some increases in post-maternity leaves and family allowances, especially for a third child, but these are not explicitly pronatalist in intent (McIntosh, 1981, p. 191; Heeren, 1982, p. 147). In contrast, several German *Laender* have gone further and do have an explicit pronatalist intention. However, the measures they have adopted are fairly weak incentives for increased fertility; they have provided low interest rates to young couples at marriage and have reduced payback requirements for each child born within seven years of the granting of the loan.

Writing in 1974, Schubnell noted that while numerous measures that directly and indirectly influence population could be found,

> population policy has not yet been developed. The concept of 'population policy' is still encumbered by overtones of the National Socialist ideology. Current consciousness of demographic facts and population studies has hardly been awakened.

German concern over low growth has increased since the early 1970s, but the reluctance to adopt explicit population policy evidently continues. The capacity of West Germany to adapt to the consequences of its remarkable demographic situation may well be in doubt. To reverse low fertility would be a massive task with a great deal of behavioral change required. There is an obvious hesitancy to attempt to do so. But there seems to be little effort to improve information about the implications of these demographic changes that would facilitate a smooth transition over time.

Schubnell called attention to the "backwardness of West Germany in the field of demography" despite its having established a new Institute for Population Research. There were only two university professors teaching demography, and none of the German universities had a special research institution (1974, p. 702). As McIntosh correctly observed, information on population changes falls far short of what is provided in the national fertility studies conducted in the United States, leaving the German government with little knowledge of how to devise an appropriate policy to alter fertility rates even if it wished to do so (1983, p. 193–196). To further complicate matters, the German political system is highly fragmented and decentralized, with weak coordination among ministries involved with population matters, making the development and implementation of a comprehensive population policy difficult.

France. In France there has long been a belief that the population growth rate is a matter of national prestige, power, and national security. Not surprisingly, then, debate over the impact of the current low growth rate has been considerably more open and visible than in Germany, Sweden and the United States. Nevertheless, the French government has been unable to translate concern over low growth into a strong pronatalist policy and is unlikely to do so in the near future.

The level of interest in low growth rates is perhaps best illustrated by the national debate sparked by a 1976 statement by President Valéry Giscard d'Estaing. On New Year's Eve he warned that no country with a middle-sized population could realistically aspire to greatness (*The New York Times,* 1976), and he later ordered a high-level, national conference to discuss measures beyond a recently increased family allowance. Former premier Michael Debré came out for policies to increase the birth rate sharply and also equated the size of the French population with national power. However, President Mitterand's government has greatly downplayed such pronatalist policies.

Recent public opinion surveys indicate that the French public is not unduly concerned. In one poll, 65 percent of those questioned favored keeping the population at its present level; only 23 percent were in favor of a population increase (*The New York Times,* 1976). Surveys conducted by the National Institute of Demographic Studies (INED) found 39 percent of respondents in favor of governmental measures to increase fertility (in 1975), increasing to 59 percent by 1978 (Heeren, 1982, p. 143).

These results may indicate only that a majority of the French public would welcome additional family allowances and the like. Any vigorous pronatalist policies are still likely to be opposed. Political and academic debate about the peril of a declining birth rate, including warnings about the growing disparity in population size between developed and less developed nations, have not convinced the French public that a severe problem exists or that strong remedial measures are required.

One cannot say very much about national attitudes toward low growth based on a few opinion surveys and occasional comments by politicians, but systematic data are limited. Perhaps the most extensive data come from the new study by McIntosh, which relied on a series of semi-structured interviews with government officials, politicians, research personnel and "other influentials most closely involved in the formulation of population policy." Asked about their perceptions of low fertility (in their official capacity), most responded negatively and saw the consequences as serious. Discussions with policymakers, she noted, "inevitably included remarks about its consequences for national power and international influence." This was typically noted at the beginning of the interview, although the rest of their remarks often bore little relationship to the early statements. Concern also focused on the cost of pensions and health and social care services for the elderly. National security continued to be mentioned, especially by those on the extreme right, based on the fear that an aging population will be unable to defend itself. There was some expression of concern over the loss of vitality in an aging population. She found less concern with the dislocations arising from a changing age structure, such as the loss of opportunities for occupational mobility, and concern over the economic consequences was expressed only in "vague and generalized terms in which national and international economic and non-economic aspects of power appeared to be confused." She concluded that "there is no doubt that fear of a declining population runs deeper in France" than in other West European nations, and yet there has been a "remarkable tolerance of low fertility and low population growth" (McIntosh, 1983, p. 131).

This mixed set of beliefs helps to explain policy actions taken in France. Like Germany and the United States, France has no explicit population policy. As Jean Bourgeois-Pichat observed, "there is in France no population policy if we mean by that a set of coordinated laws aimed at reaching some demographic goals." (1974, p. 545). There is a complex array of legislation protecting the family (enacted chiefly to achieve social justice), legislation on immigration adopted largely for economic reasons, and contraceptive and abortion policies which are related only in part to demographic goals (Bourgeois-Pichat, 1974; McIntosh, 1983). In 1975, the Central Planning Council, acting under the direction of President Giscard d'Estaing, adopted the objective of a "stable fertility rate close to, and preferably slightly higher than, one needed to ensure the replacement of cohorts." As always, the most important question is the extent to which such goals can be, or actually are, translated into specific policy actions that promise to have a significant impact on the birth rate.

Most attention has focused on French family policy. Its family policy is the most comprehensive and generous in Western Europe, with sizeable increases approved in 1978 and 1979. It includes aid to working mothers with a child less than three years old; long maternity leaves (up to two years without pay for civil servants); educational leaves for personnel of large firms for either the mother or father, with a return to the former job guaranteed; and substantial allowances for families with more than three children (an additional FF 1000 per month over the normal French child allowance). There is also a guaranteed minimum income for unmarried mothers, and exemption from military service for young fathers in some cases (Westoff, 1978). But the impact of these measures on fertility is less clear than their generosity.

The major principle behind their enactment, as noted, has been social justice rather than demographic goals and the level of assistance has declined in real terms since the measures were first introduced (McIntosh, 1981, p. 190). There is also a paucity of research in France on the economic consequences of population stabilization and decline that constrains population policy formation. In 1945, the French government established INED to assist in formulation of population policy. However, like most demographic research institutes, it concentrates on rigorous basic demography to the neglect of policy-relevant studies and produces reports that nonspecialists would find difficult to read and understand. While vastly superior to comparable organizations in Sweden and West Germany, critics of INED have suggested that even its studies of the determinants of fertility are insufficient as a guide to possible formulation of pronatalist policies (McIntosh, 1981, pp. 193–194).

Like West Germany, France disperses the work of formulating and implementing what now passes for population policy among several divisions and ministries. This practice makes coordination difficult, and suggests the challenge that would be posed by attempts to develop a more explicit population policy in the future. Moreover, McIntosh's interviews with policymakers indicate that as concerned as they are with the consequences of low growth, they doubted the "possibility of intervening successfully to reverse the demographic trend." (1983, p. 124). Prevailing ideology about the limited authority of the state to intervene in personal reproductive decisions is at the heart of this pessimism. Thus, they were "at a loss to identify pronatalist measures that are at the same time acceptable to the public and likely to encourage fertility." (1983, p. 124). While the officials believed governmental intervention was justifiable to promote France's long-term national interest, they also believed their hands were tied; action was not possible given public attitudes, available knowledge, and the costs of strong pronatalist measures.

Sweden. Writing in 1974, Lena Johnson observed that "the birth rate in Sweden is one of the lowest in the world. Today, there is little public concern about a possible eventual decline in the Swedish population, and there is no official population policy." (Johnson, 1974, p. 113). There has been a higher level of concern in the press and parliament in recent years, but the Swedes appear to be much less anxious over sustained low fertility than the Germans and the French. No new legislation intended to increase population growth has been enacted, and there is little likelihood of strong pronatalist measures being adopted. Sweden would be severely handicapped if it were to attempt to do so by a very weak base of demographic information on which population policy of any type must be formulated.

In her interviews with Swedish policymakers, McIntosh found that they were surprised in 1977 at the appearance of low fertility on the political agenda, and somewhat alarmed at the lack of information about the causes of the low birth rates and their consequences for Swedish society. That the Swedes were slow to respond to these population changes is not too surprising. The nation has lacked much interest in domestic population issues, and as some writers have noted, Swedish support for international population assistance programs makes them somewhat embarrassed to argue that Swedish growth rates are too low. The predominant attitudes of antinatalism evidently created a disinclination to inquire into the impact of long-term low fertility in Sweden or to develop an explicit population policy. Moreover, unlike France and Germany, there is little equation of population size with strong feelings of nationalism.

The main focus of present concern in Sweden is the consequence of sustained low fertility for the proportion of elderly people who would have to be supported and the role that might be played by immigration in future population growth. A 1977 study on the economic consequences of a declining population focused attention on the problem of supporting the elderly at the levels anticipated in the social plan. It was apparently influential in "awakening political elites to the realization that declining population growth could jeopardize the broad social goals agreed upon by the society." (McIntosh, 1981, p. 187). According to Gendell (1980), Swedes are somewhat divided on the severity of the problem and what, if anything, needs to be done. Those concerned with declining fertility tend to favor broadly pronatalist measures that would decrease the burden of childrearing by providing additional financial assistance. Those less convinced that there will be serious adverse consequences see "no good reason to try to reverse" the trend toward low fertility; they believe the impacts can be handled effectively through planning.

The immigration issue is easy to understand. Sweden has a fairly homogenous culture, and there are concerns that high levels of immigration might lead to a weakening of that culture and to racial tensions and social problems. As McIntosh puts it, a desire to preserve Swedish "cultural integrity, and the security that is seen to derive from it, has surfaced as one of the most fundamental determinants of support for a pronatalist policy." (1983, p. 151). Policymakers and "influentials" interviewed were "unanimous that increased immigration is out of the question." At a minimum there is a strong desire to "slow down the rate of transition to a more pluralistic society." Her respondents were quick to suggest that their views on immigration were not racially or ideologically motivated but were based on practical considerations.

Like most European nations, Sweden has long had a variety of social welfare measures concerning children and families, including financial assistance to parents and protection of children's rights. There are paid leaves for either the mother or father of a new baby (for nine months) that can be taken over an eight-year period. And in 1979 the new center-right government introduced a number of changes in family policy, including increased child allowances and uncompensated leave after the birth of each child. Most of these policies were adopted not for demographic purposes, however, but out of concern for sexual equality and sharing the burden of child rearing. McIntosh concludes that there is some agreement on the need to increase fertility, but no agreement on the means to do so. While bills concerning fertility have been introduced in the Riksdag, the near-term outlook is for little positive action. If the rate of natural increase turns negative, however, additional policy change may be forthcoming.

Any further development of Swedish population policy will be constrained by the very limited demographic information available to the government. Lacking the equivalent of the French and American studies of reproductive attitudes and behavior (from national fertility surveys), there is no clear way to determine what type of incentives would be necessary to increase the birth rate. However, there have been recent commissions studying the economic aspects of families and proposing additional financial assistance (e.g., for families with three or more children). Curiously, the Swedish government seems much less constrained than the French, German and American governments in considering innovative population policies that involve major changes in present institutional arrangements or even mildly coercive fertility measures. McIntosh reports that policymakers interviewed did not seem to be unduly concerned about such action being an illegitimate exercise of governmental authority (perhaps because of the high level of trust in government and the opportunities that exist to change a government that goes too far):

> Particularly striking was the apparent lack of awareness and concern that the introduction of pronatalist measures might infringe the liberty of the individual in a private and personal area of decision making. . . . None of the people interviewed appeared to question the state's right to attempt to intervene in this area." (1983, p. 168).

The Swedish political system has the capacity to develop the kind of innovative policies discussed above for the United States, but has not yet shown a desire to do so. Departments of government are free from many of the day-to-day administrative responsibilities that limit involvement with longer-term issues in the United States. There is also greater emphasis on rationality in policy formation, more reliance on relevant experts, and a greater degree of consensus and cooperation in policy development, particularly in informal arrangements. Those characteristics may be important in any future policy change. Of course, considerable improvement in the nation's capacity to produce and analyze demographic data would be a prerequisite for any population planning policy.

V. COMPARING POLITICAL RESPONSES TO POPULATION STABILIZATION

As limited as this review of Western European nations is, what conclusions are appropriate regarding reasons for the different political responses to low growth in the four nations considered? Clearly as McIntosh suggests, demographic conditions alone do not determine population policy, although the low saliency of population stabilization in the United States can be explained in part by its unique demographic conditions—a continuing substantial rate of growth attributable to high immigration levels and demographic momentum from the baby boom years. National responses to population change are influenced by a wide range of other variables. Among those most frequently mentioned are the quality and salience of demographic information available to policymakers, political culture and ideology, the structure and capability of policymaking institutions, constitutional and budgetary constraints, and the structure and influence of the interest group system. Each merits brief discussion.

Policymakers cannot be expected to respond in a timely and rational manner to population changes they are unaware of or about which they are poorly informed. The adequacy of information available and the manner in which it is presented to them seem to be important variables. Sweden has a particularly poor record of developing sufficient and reliable information about the consequences of demographic trends, and this omission has been an important factor in its response to low growth. But even in the United States, with an apparent abundance of superb demographic studies, policymakers are poorly informed about population change. The mere creation of demographic institutes and population commissions or the expansion of population research is not sufficient. The information must be "policy-relevant" and presented in a manner conducive to its use in a variety of decisionmaking arenas.

A number of writers make much of the differences in political culture and ideologies among nations. How population problems are perceived is in part a function of prevailing cultural values such as nationalism (France) or social equality (Sweden). The value placed on individual rights in reproductive decisionmaking is obviously important in shaping policymaking as is a willingness to tolerate some degree of governmental intervention. It is quite understandable, then, that nearly every commentator on the policy implications of low fertility argues that the liberal democracies are very unlikely to imitate the socialist nations of Eastern Europe in adopting strongly pronatalist policies (Frejka, 1981; Heeren, 1982; McIntosh, 1981; and Kirk, 1981).

Among the four nations discussed in this chapter, Germany and the United States seem to be the most suspicious of governmental intrusion in the setting of population targets or development of explicit population policies, and European nations on the whole are friendlier to the idea of national planning in social policies than is the United States (Sundquist, 1975 and 1978). The degree of social consensus on such matters is also quite important. Thus Sweden possesses a greater capacity for future action in part because of its more homogeneous culture and consensus on social issues. It should be noted that in Europe (and especially in France and Germany) attitudes toward population growth policy tend to divide along ideological lines. There is a very clear left-right split, and thus policy responses to these issues will vary depending on which party controls the government at any given time.

The degree of fragmentation or centralization in governmental structures and the capability of governmental agencies to engage in population planning also make a considerable difference. McIntosh in particular places a great deal of emphasis on the fragmentation of the German political system in comparison to France and Sweden. Power is more decentralized in Germany, and coordination among governmental departments and agencies is more difficult. Similarly, Sundquist (1978) argues that the pluralistic American political system makes policy formulation and adoption difficult even when consensus on policy goals exists in the executive branch. Michael Teitlebaum, staff director of the Select Committee on Population in the United States, offered a parallel criticism of the enormous difficulty of coping with fragmentation and dispersion of authority in the U.S. Congress (Population Reference Bureau, 1979). On the other hand, many have argued that American pluralism and highly dispersed power in Congress facilitate entrepreneurial activity by congressional staff and politicians seeking new problems and issues on which their careers can be built (Davidson, 1981 and Malbin, 1981). Thus the American political system scores well on agenda-setting activity and policy invention even while it is often hard to move quickly to policy adoption.

All nations face budgetary constraints on adoption of expensive pronatalist measures or development of population planning policies that might require new agencies and/or expanded budgets for population research and long-range planning. Several writers (e.g., McIntosh and Westoff) doubt that European nations will adopt stronger pronatalist measures in the future in large part because of their cost. At some point expansion of family allowances and financial incentives for childbearing may become prohibitively expensive. Similarly, opposition in the United States to proposed population policies that create new offices and agencies has been based in part on hostility to any expansion of governmental activity in a time of large budget deficits.

Policy change is often supported or blocked by organized interest groups. Governmental response to population stabilization and the formulation and adoption of population policy is heavily influenced by the political pressures exerted by interest groups concerned with women's rights, abortion, family planning services, immigration, and environmental quality. In the United States group activity is one of the most important variables shaping governmental response on population issues, whereas in Europe policy professionals in the bureaucracy seem to be more influential. In the United States family planning groups and the "population establishment" were major forces behind the adoption of international population assistance programs in the 1960s and the expansion of domestic family planning programs in 1970 (Piotrow, 1973; Bachrach and Bergman, 1973). Conservative religious groups and the right-to-life movement have been very active in opposition to family planning and abortion services in the early 1980s, although the outcome is still hard to predict. Similarly, groups like the Global Tomorrow Coalition and Zero Population Growth have been instrumental in building support for innovative policies on long-term planning and in arranging congressional hearings on population policy and global foresight capability in the early 1980s.

The pervasiveness of group influence on policymaking is both a strength and a weakness for the American political system. It is a strength in terms of helping to insure a broadly representative policymaking process in a sensitive and controversial policy area. It is also a weakness because the building of public consensus for policy adoption is made much more difficult than in those European nations less influenced by a wide range of interest groups.

VI. CONCLUSION

The arrival of low fertility rates in the 1970s and the expectation that they will continue indefinitely pose new and significant political issues for developed nations. While most nations have been slow to recognize the importance of the shift to sustained low fertility and eventual population stabilization, it is most certainly among the more consequential social developments of recent years. Arguments about the inevitability of stationary populations in a world faced with finite limits to growth do not eliminate concern about the ability of nations to cope with slowing rates of growth. Political responses to low growth in Europe—if not in the United States—indicate preoccupation with the negative consequences, particularly the effect of a changing age structure on social security systems and other age-sensitive public policies. In a few nations, concern extends to possible impact on national power and prestige.

Both public discussion of these issues and scholarly attention have focused on possible adoption of measures to halt or reverse the trend toward stabilization. However, fears over low growth rates have not been great enough to support such major policy change and the consensus among scholars seems to be that this kind of action is unlikely in the liberal democracies (McIntosh, 1982 and 1983; Heeren, 1982; Frejka, 1981). Why? Perhaps because population changes are too subtle to attract widespread attention, the consequences too uncertain, and possible policy actions too controversial for democratic nations to consider without a broader base of popular concern.

Given the political responses to date, one can suggest the importance of a quite different perspective on slowing rates of growth: a more positive and accommodationist attitude toward an early achievement of population stabilization. If nations choose not to intervene to halt or reverse low birth rates, they may well have to consider innovative public policies to facilitate planning for accommodation to new demographic conditions. Moreover, population changes should be considered in a broader context than typically the case in the United States and most European nations. They have effects on a wide range of public problems and public policies and cannot be restricted to the domain of ministries or departments involved only with family policy and other social policies. As recent studies in the United States have argued, population size and growth rates are intimately related to resource use and environmental quality, both within nations and globally (Council on Environmental Quality and Department of State, 1980 and 1981). Yet one is hard put to find any nation fully prepared to develop long-range integrated analyses of these conditions and trends. The development of such an institutional capacity lies at the heart of proposals for policy innovation in this area (Kraft, 1982).

The purpose of such policies is to enable nations to develop a reliable base of information about probable future developments and to ensure that such information is made available in a usable form to policymakers and the interested public. Those recommending such policies believe the end result would be a more rational process of long-range planning and decisionmaking than now possible. It would not be necessary as part of such a policy to declare that a particular population size or growth rate represents some magical "optimum" for a given nation. Nor could governments realistically aspire to setting and maintaining particular rates; experience has shown that fertility rates are not subject to such fine tuning.

Policy innovations commonly require a substantial period of time for formulation and adoption. In the meantime, the likelihood is that most nations will choose to do little to alter present policies and will attempt to muddle through. Economic and social policies affected by population changes may be adjusted as needed when the impact is too obvious to ignore, as has happened with Social Security in the United States. Providing that these changes occur slowly enough, such an incrementalist response may prove to be sufficient. Should the changes be more rapid, such adjustments may not be possible or will come only at a substantial cost. That is the primary concern of those supporting innovation in population policy and the development of "foresight capability" in the United States. Given the increasingly severe economic constraints on governments in the developed nations, they make a strong case for new policies promising to reduce the incidence of poor planning and decisionmaking so evident in social security, education, and health care policies in the last decade.

ACKNOWLEDGMENTS

I would like to thank C. Alison McIntosh for her comments on an early draft of this chapter. The University of Wisconsin-Green Bay Research Council provided a release time in the 1982–83 academic year that made work on this chapter possible.

NOTES

1.   Replacement-level fertility refers to a fertility rate which, if maintained, would result eventually in a stationary or nongrowing population. Each generation would replace itself, but there would be no net growth.

2.   The total fertility rate (TFR) refers to the average number of children that would be born to each woman in a population if each were to live through her child-bearing years (15–49) bearing children at the same rate as women of those ages actually did in a given year. In simple terms, the TFR answers the question: How many children are women having at present? In developed nations with low mortality rates, a TFR of 2.1 indicates replacement-level fertility. Migration is not considered in calculating the TFR. It should also be said that a stationary population does not result immediately after achievement of a TFR of 2.1. The reason for the lag is the natural population momentum due to previous high levels of fertility.

3.   The natural rate of increase is the birth rate minus the death rate, with no account taken of immigration levels. It is usually expressed as the annual percentage change in the rate of growth. A negative rate implies a declining population.

REFERENCES

Anderson, J. E. *Public Policy-Making*, 2nd ed. New York: Holt, Rinehart and Winston, 1979.

Bachrach, P., and Bergman, E. *Power and Choice: The Formulation of American Population Policy*. Lexington, Mass.: Lexington Books, 1973.

Berelson, B., ed. *Population Policy in Developed Countries*. New York: McGraw Hill, 1974.

Bourgeois-Pichat, J. "France." In *Population Policy in Developed Countries*. Edited by B. Berelson. New York: McGraw-Hill, 1974.

Bouvier, L. F. America's Baby Boom Generation: The Fateful Bulge. *Population Bulletin* 35, no.1 (1980): 1–35.

————. *The Impact of Immigration on U.S. Population Size*. Washington, D.C.: Population Reference Bureau, 1981.

Campbell, A. A., ed. *Social, Economic and Health Aspects of Low Fertility*. Washington, D.C.: U.S. Government Printing Office, 1979.

Commission on Population Growth and the American Future. *Population Growth and the American Future*. Washington, D.C.: U.S. Government Printing Office, 1972.

Council of Europe. *Population Decline in Europe: Implications of a Declining or Stationary Population*. New York: St. Martin's Press, 1978.

Council on Environmental Quality and Department of State. *The Global 2000 Report to the President: Entering the Twenty-First Century*. Washington, D.C.: U.S. Government Printing Office, 1980.

_____. *Global Future: Time to Act.* Washington, D.C.: U.S. Government Printing Office, 1981.

David, H. P. "Eastern Europe: Pronatalist Policies and Private Behavior." *Population Bulletin* 36, No. 6 (1982): 1–47.

Davidson, R. H. "Subcommittee Government: New Channels for Policy Making." In *The New Congress.* Edited by T. E. Mann and N. J. Ornstein. Washington, D.C.: American Enterprise Institute, 1981.

Day, L. H. "The Social Consequences of a Zero Population Growth Rate in the United States." In *Demographic and Social Aspects of Population Growth.* Edited by C. F. Westoff and R. Parke, Jr. Washington, D.C.: U.S. Government Printing Office, 1972.

_____. What Will a ZPG Society be Like? *Population Bulletin* 33 (1978): no. 3:1–43.

Demeny, P. "On the End of the Population Explosion." *Population and Development Review* 5 (1979): 141–62.

Dunlap, R. E., ed. "Ecology and the Social Sciences: An Emerging Paradigm." *American Behavioral Scientist* 24 (1980): 1–151.

Easterlin, R. A. *Birth and Fortune: The Impact of Numbers on Personal Welfare.* New York: Basic Books, 1980.

Espenshade, T. J. "Zero Population Growth and the Economies of Developed Nations." *Population and Development Review* 4 (1978): 645–80.

_____. and Serow, W. J., eds. *The Economic Consequences of Slowing Population Growth.* New York: Academic Press, 1978.

Executive Office of the President, O. M. B. *The Budget of the United States Government: Fiscal Year 1980.* Washington, D.C.: U.S. Government Printing Office, 1979.

Finkle, J. F., and McIntosh, A. "Toward an Understanding of Population Policy in Industrialized Socieites." In *Population Policy Analysis.* Edited by M. E. Kraft and M. Schneider. Lexington, Mass.: Lexington Books, 1978.

Frejka, T. "Can Pro-Natalist Policies in Western Europe be Potent? (A Comparative Analysis of Conditions Conducive to Pro-Natalist Policies in Western and Eastern Europe)." Paper presented at the annual meeting of the Population Association of America, Washington, D.C. April, 1981.

Gendell, M. "Sweden Faces Zero Population Growth." *Population Bulletin* 35, no. 2 (1980): 1–43.

Haub, C. "Beyond the Demographic Transition: The Case of West Germany." *Intercom* 10 (May/June 1982):8–10.

Heeren, H. J. "Pronatalist Population Policies in Some Western European Countries." *Population Research and Policy Review* 1 (1982): 137–52.

Inglehart, R. *The Silent Revolution: Changing Values and Political Styles Among Western Publics.* Princeton, N.J.: Princeton University Press, 1977.

Johnson, L. "Sweden." In *Population Policy in Developed Countries.* Edited by B. Berelson. New York: McGraw-Hill, 1974.

Kantner, J. F. "Population, Policy, and Political Atavism." *Demography* 19 (1982): 429–38.

Keyfitz, N. "Can Knowledge Improve Forecasts?" *Population and Development Review* 9 (1982): 729–51.

Kirk, D. "World Population and Birth Rates: Agreements and Disagreements." *Population and Development Review* 5 (1979): 387–403.

Kirk, M. "Population Policies in Non-Socialist Societies." In *International Population Conference: Solicited Papers,* Vol. 1, pp. 373–85. Liege, Belgium: International Union for the Scientific Study of Population, 1981a.

_____. *Demographic and Social Change in Europe, 1975–2000.* Liverpool, England: Liverpool University Press, 1981b.

Kraft, M. E. "Innovation in U.S. Population Policy." Paper presented at the annual meeting of the American Public Health Association, Montreal, Canada, November, 1982.

Malbin, M. J. "Delegation, Deliberation, and the New Role of Congressional Staff. In *The
New Congress*. Edited by T. E. Mann and N. J. Ornstein. Washington, D.C.: American
Enterprise Institute, 1981.

McIntosh, C. A. "Low Fertility and Liberal Democracy in Western Europe." *Population and
Development Review* 7 (1981): 181–207.

————. *Population Policy in Western Europe: Responses to Low Fertility in France, Sweden, and
West Germany*. Armonk, New York: M. E. Sharp, 1983.

Milbrath, L., ed. *Environmentalism and Social Change*. Albany, New York: State University of
New York Press (in press).

Miller, W. B., and Godwin, R. K. *Psyche and Demos: Individual Psychology and the Issues of
Population*. New York: Oxford University Press, 1977.

Nash, A. E. K. "Population Growth and American Ideology." In *Population, Environment
and People*. Edited by N. Hinrichs. New York: McGraw-Hill, 1971.

New York Times. "Declining Birth Rate is Troubling French." *New York Times,* December
5, 1976, p. 6, Sec. 1.

New York Times. "West Germans, Births Down, Ponder Future, or Lack of It." *The New
York Times,* April 28, p. 2, Sec. 1.

Nixon, R. M. "The Population Problem—Message from the President." *Congressional Record* (daily edition), July 18, 1969, pp. S8229–32.

Otten, A. L. "West European States See Economic Troubles as Birth Rates Decline." *Wall
Street Journal,* August 23, 1978, p. 1.

Petersen, W. "Population Policy and Age Structure." In *Population Policy Analysis*. Edited by
M. E. Kraft and M. Schneider. Lexington, Mass.: Lexington Books, 1978.

Piotrow, P. *World Population Crisis: The United States Response*. New York: Praeger, 1973.

Pirages, D. C., ed. *The Sustainable Society: Implications for Limited Growth*. New York: Praeger,
1977.

Polsby, N. W. *Political Innovation in America: The Politics of Policy Initiation*. Unpublished
manuscript. Berkeley, Calif.: Department of Political Science, University of California,
1982.

Population Reference Bureau. *1982 World Population Data Sheet*. Washington, D.C.: Population Reference Bureau, 1982.

————. *Intercom,* May 1979, p. 12.

Rosenbaum, N. "Growth and Its Discontents: Origins of Local Population Controls. In *The
Policy Cycle*. Edited by J. V. May and A. B. Wildavsky. Beverly Hills, Calif.: Sage
Publications, 1978.

Schubnell, H. "West Germany." In *Population Policy in Developed Countries*. Edited by B.
Berelson. New York: McGraw-Hill, 1974.

Simon, J. *The Ultimate Resource*. Princeton, N.J.: Princeton University Press, 1981.

Stetson, D. M. "Population Policy and the Limits of Governmental Capability in Developed
States." In *Population and Politics*. Edited by R. L. Clinton. Lexington, Mass.: Lexington
Books, 1973.

————. "Family Policy and Fertility in the United States." In *Population Policy Analysis*.
Edited by M. E. Kraft and M. Schneider. Lexington, Mass.: Lexington Books, 1978.

Sundquist, J. L. *Dispersing Population: What America Can Learn from Europe*. Washington,
D.C.: Brookings Institution, 1975.

————. "A Comparison of Policy-Making Capacity in the United States and Five European Countries: The Case of Population Distribution." In *Population Policy Analysis*.
Edited by M. E. Kraft and M. Schneider. Lexington, Mass.: Lexington Books, 1978.

U.S. Bureau of the Census. *Projections of the Population of the United States: 1982–2050* (advanced report). Current Population Reports, Series P-25, No. 922. Washington, D.C.: U.S. Government Printing Office, 1982.

U.S. Congress. *Declaration of U.S. Policy of Population Stabilization by Voluntary Means.* Hearings before the Special Subcommittee on Human Resources of the Committee on Labor and Public Welfare, U.S. Senate, 92nd Congress, 1st Session, 1971.

—————. *Final Report of the Select Committee on Population.* U.S. House of Representatives, 95th Congress, 2nd Session, 1978a.

—————. *Consequences of Changing U.S. Population.* 3 vols. (*Demographics of Aging, Baby Boom and Bust, and Population Movement and Planning*). Hearings before the Select Committee on Population, U.S. House of Representatives, 95th Congress, 2nd Session, 1978b.

—————. *U.S. Immigration Policy and the National Interest.* Committee on the Judiciary, U.S. House of Representatives and Committee on the Judiciary, U.S. Senate, 97th Congress, 1st Session, 1981.

—————. *National Population Policy.* Hearings before the Subcommittee on Census and Population of the Committee on Post Office and Civil Service, U.S. House of Representatives, 97th Congress, 2nd Session, 1982.

van de Walle, E., and Knodel, J. "Europe's Fertility Transition: New Evidence and Lessons for Today's Developing World." *Population Bulletin* 34, no. 6 (1980): 1–43.

Weber, J. A. *Grow or die!* New Rochelle, N.Y.: Arlington House, 1977.

Westoff, C. F. "Marriage and Fertility in the Developed Countries." *Scientific American* 239 (1978): 51–57.

Whisler, M. "Population Policy Implementation: Local Growth Management Strategies. In *Population policy analysis.* Edited by M. E. Kraft and M. Schneider. Lexington, Mass.: Lexington Books, 1978.

Part IV

AGENDA SETTING: THE ROLE OF INFORMATION

PUBLIC OPINION, PUBLIC POLICY AND MEXICAN IMMIGRATION

Brian Loveman and C. Richard Hofstetter

> The fundamental basis of all legislation upon this subject, state and federal, has been, and is, race undesirability. . . . The simple and single question is, is the race desirable? . . .
>
> Attorney General of California, 1913

I. INTRODUCTION

Immigration policy is an issue that generates intense emotions in the United States. It is also an issue that confronts policymakers with a series of harsh economic, social and political questions for which there are no ready answers. Indeed, our lack of reliable basic information in this area is immense.

There is no accurate estimate of the number of undocumented immigrants in the United States (4–12 million?).[1] There is no reliable estimate of taxes paid by undocumented immigrants to local, state and federal governments. There is no reliable survey of the increased demands on public services by undocumented immigrants that might alter

259

the quality, character or extent of such programs as public education, public transportation, public housing, social welfare, and health programs or even public recreation.[2] There are no reliable data on job displacements related to undocumented immigrants nor to the economic benefits to the economy of the United States attributable to the contributions made by undocumented workers.[3] Indeed, there is no critical survey at all of the qualitative cultural, social or political contributions by undocumented immigrants to the United States during the last five decades of this century.[4]

Notwithstanding this lack of the most basic information on the immigration issue, most Americans oppose large scale immigration—legal or illegal—into the United States. Recent national surveys confirm that a growing number of Americans favor decreasing the level of immigration to this country regardless of the source of that immigration. In short, it appears the world's "huddled masses" are no longer welcome in this country, if indeed they *were* ever welcomed—outside the pages of high school civics texts and conventional mythology of an earlier time.

Despite seemingly overwhelming public opposition to increased immigration, the most recent legislation on the issue debated in Congress (Simpson-Mazzoli Immigration Reform and Control Act, 1982,S 2222) provides, among other things, amnesty for an undetermined number of undocumented immigrants (estimated in the millions). The statute also attempts to better regulate the immigrant flow by applying sanctions against employers who "knowingly" employ undocumented workers. The contradictory policy messages conveyed by such legislation (increasing the future risk of would-be undocumented immigrants, while increasing the stakes of immigration at the same time; the hope of an additional amnesty at some point in the future) is consistent with the domestic political and economic contradictions in U.S. immigration policy as well as with the complexity inherent in immigration policy for U.S. officials who formulate foreign policy. It is also consistent with the mixed message contained in the recommendations of the bipartisan Select Commission on Immigration and Refugee Policy which worked from August 1978–April 1981. The Commission's recommendations included (1981):

- Improved border enforcement and increased funding of the Border Patrol;
- A fully automated system so that the INS can keep track of alien arrivals and departures;
- Endorsement of the Refugee Act of 1980;
- Legislation making it illegal to hire undocumented workers;
- A reliable method of identification for employees, proving legal status;

Table 1.   Should Legal Immigration be Kept at Its Present Level, Increased, or Decreased?

| | % of Respondents Favoring* | | |
Survey and Date of Interviewing	Present Level	Increase	Decrease
American Institute of Public Opinion (Gallup Poll), December 1945 (asked about persons from Europe)	32	5	37
American Institute of Public Opinion, June 1965	39	8	33
American Institute of Public Opinion, March 1977	37	7	42
**San Diego Survey, 1979	30	15	45
Associated Press-NBC News Poll, August 1981	27	5	65
**Houston Survey	27	6	54

Notes:

*Missing data ("don't know" or unascertained responses" are not reported here. However, it is significant that the proportion of respondents not expressing any opinion declined from 20 percent in the Gallup, 1965, survey to only 3 percent in the most recent, Associated Press–NBC Poll. Thus, rising levels of public information (or misinformation) about immigration have been translated into a more "restrictionist" climate of public opinion.

**San Diego Survey from C. Richard Hofstetter and Brian Loveman "Communications Media and Perceptions of Undocumented Immigrants: The Case of San Diego". Paper prepared for presentation at the Annual Meetings of the International Communication Association, Acapulco, Mexico, May 1980. Houston Data from Loveman and Hofstetter, Study in progress, 1982–1983.

Sources of data: Gallup, 1945: "The Gallup Poll: Public Opinion", 1935–1971, Vol. 1 (1935–1948) (New York: Random House, 1972), p. 555. Gallup, 1965: "Gallup Political Index", August 1963, P. 15. Gallup, 1977: "The Gallup Poll: Public Opinion 1972–1977" (Wilmington Del.: Scholarly Resources, Inc. 1978), Vol 2 (1976–1977), p. 1050. AP-NBC Poll, 1981: "The San Diego Union", August 17, 1981, p. A–9.

After Wayne A. Cornelius "America in the Era of Limits: Nativist Reactions to the 'new' Immigration". Working Papers in U.S.—Mexican Studies 13 Program in United States—Mexican Studies UCSD, 1982: 11.

- A program to legalize illegal aliens now in the U.S. (amnesty);
- An increase in numerically limited immigration from the present 170,000 to 350,000 per year, increased by 100,000 extra per year for the first five years to wipe out backlogs.

Within American society, the basis for a dilemma of public conscience surrounds immigration issues. The dilemma is based on a series of factual values and mythical beliefs which are woven into the texture of society. Most Americans trace their own ancestry to some other country, and many of their ancestors came to the United States when few if any practical restrictions against immigration existed. Most Americans express belief in the propriety of the so-called work ethic that people should benefit by the fruits of their honest labor, and most believe that undocumented immigrants work tremendously hard, do labor others will not do, and have come to the U.S. in order to make economic gains. Finally, it appears that most Americans benefit materially, whether directly or indirectly, from the presence of undocumented immigrants (see below). At the same time, people express considerable anxiety about being overwhelmed by a vast tide of non-whites who neither speak the "American" language nor behave in ways similar to native born Americans. As with other instances of racism and nativism, undocumented immigrants are held in awe for their prodigious feats of labor and despised for job competition at the same time. So acts of brutality are committed against undocumented immigrants on a daily basis. Although civilized people decry such wanton acts of brutality, a strange, convenient ignorance of the victimization exists, and this, too, is a concommitant of the "new American Dilemma."

II.   OBJECTIVES OF THE PRESENT STUDY

This study, part of a larger ongoing concern with the policy implications of undocumented immigration into the United States, explores the political and policy implications of significant contradictions between "public opinion" and public policy on the immigration issue. The study also discusses the complexity of immigration policy issues, especially in light of public perceptions of what is involved. Finally, the study discusses the various policy implications. In particular, this paper reports findings from a public opinion survey conducted in San Diego, California, regarding immigration into the United States and then examines (1) the possibility of enforcing current and proposed U.S. immigration policy, (2) the political implications of the constraints on law enforcement in the immigration field, (3) the domestic policy implications of contradictions between public opinion and political realities related to undocumented immigration, and (4) the foreign policy implications of American public opinion and public policy regarding undocumented immigration.

III.   PUBLIC OPINION ABOUT UNDOCUMENTED IMMIGRATION

The San Diego Survey

According to published estimates, the border areas between Mexico and San Diego County, California—and especially the San Diego-Tijuana city interface—account for as much as 40 percent of all undocumented immigration from Mexico to the United States. While it is well known that a large percentage of undocumented immigrants do not remain in San Diego County, there is a considerable presence of undocumented immigrants in the barrios of southern San Diego County, in coastal and inland towns, and in the agricultural districts in northern San Diego County. Tiny barrios and "drop points" dot coastal and inland northern San Diego County. And while the modal immigration is to the Los Angeles basin and northward, communication, social and economic exchanges between this area and the San Diego area are nearly sufficient to consider both areas as one. Only the interposition of Camp Pendleton has prevented the formation of a single gigantic, contiguous urban area.

Undocumented workers perform an important role in the San Diego County economy. Recent research suggests that undocumented workers account for 35–59 percent of hired labor in San Diego County agriculture; undocumented workers also occupy a significant percentage of retail and service jobs (including jobs in the large tourist industry) in the regional economy and, to a lesser extent, are employed in construction and manufacturing.

The visible participation of undocumented immigrants is reinforced by local media coverage. San Diego County residents receive considerable exposure to media content concerning undocumented immigration. In a related study conducted by the authors, San Diegans report having seen considerable coverage of undocumented immigrants in the various mass media. Indeed, mass media reports during the period of the study tended to emphasize the numbers of people entering the U.S. illegally, employment situations of undocumented immigrants (including both aspects related to job competition and non-competitive forms of work), and, to a lesser extent, the victimization and other problems undocumented workers faced.

San Diegans also reported considerable exposure to media about ". . . what happens to illegal immigrants from Mexico once they get into the United States." About 29 percent reported more than ten newspaper stories about what happens, while 21 percent reported having seen more than ten television programs about what happens to undocumented aliens once they are in the United States. About 29 percent said they had had more than ten conversations about undocumented immigrants in this country. Over 48 percent, moreover, said they had read more than ten news stories about undocumented immigrants from Mexico during the six months prior to the interview. Over 30 percent reported exposure to more than ten television programs, and 43 percent said they had had more than ten conversations during the time period about undocumented immigrants. In this sense, the study discussed in the following text focuses on issues of relatively high salience in the everyday lives of the public. *Public Opinion,* in the classical sense, on this issue is not simply an artifact of survey methodology but rather a part of the every-day reality of the San Diego region.

Method and Findings

Extensive telephone interviews were conducted with 500 adults during late summer and early fall, 1979. Although a number of broader public policy items were used in the survey, most interviewing focused on attitudes and beliefs about undocumented immigration.

The sample was designed to represent all adults in the larger San Diego, California area who could be contacted by residential telephone, approximately 95 percent of the adult population. Sampling was based on standard random digit-dial procedures due to the very large number of residences with either unlisted numbers, about 30 percent, or new listings not yet published in a telephone directory, five to ten percent.

Interviewing was conducted by a staff of trained interviewers employed by the survey unit in the Social Science Research Laboratory at San Diego State University. The refusal rate among eligible respondents was approximately 30 percent, a proportion doubtlessly inflated to some extent by a heat spell during the most intensive phase of interviewing. All interviews were conducted in English; only two interviewers reported not having been able to complete an interview because of language problems between an English language interviewer and a non-English language respondent.

The sample appears to represent the larger San Diego population fairly well. In comparison to data from the 1975 and 1980 censuses, the most appropriate population parameters available, sample estimates are somewhat higher on education and income than parameters for 1975 and within sampling error of parameters for 1980. The results, of course, are in accord with social trends during the years between the sample and the censuses. Minorities, especially Mexican-Americans, are underrepresented in the sample, probably due to greater difficulty in contacting them by residential telephone. As noted, the deficiency is not due to language problems in the interview.

Key Variables

A general attitude about legal immigration was measured by asking respondents: "In general, do you think that the number of people allowed to immigrate to the United States should be increased, decreased, kept about the same as it is now, or haven't you given the matter much thought?" More specific attitudes about immigration from certain nations or areas were measured by asking: "Some people say immigration has positive effects on San Diego. Others say it has negative effects. How about you? Do you think that immigration from Western Europe has had a positive effect, a slightly positive effect, a slightly negative effect, a negative effect, or no effect at all on San Diego?" Variations of the item were repeated for Asia, Africa, Latin American, the Middle East, Mexico, and Canada.

Perceptions of "problems" caused by "illegal immigration" to the United States in general and from Mexico in particular were measured by asking respondents to rate the "importance" of each as a problem. Open-ended items were asked to tap imagery and beliefs about undocumented immigrants from Mexico. These included: "What negative effects do illegal immigrants have on the way you live?" (asked of the 28 percent of the sample who asserted that the immigrants had some kind of negative effects ". . . on the way you live."), "Now, thinking more generally about San Diego, what would you say are the most important problems that illegal immigrants cause to San Diego?" (asked of all respondents), and "What are the most important benefits that San Diego gains from illegal immigrants?" (asked of all respondents).

Respondents who said immigrants used services were also asked the following about services: "Which services do you believe illegal immigrants use most in San Diego?", "Have you personally heard of cases where illegal immigrants used public services in San Diego?", and among those who claimed to know personally of cases where illegal immigrants used services, "Which services were those?".

Standard media exposure items were used to measure general exposure to television, television news, newspapers, and to interpersonal discussion. More specific exposure items were also used to tap recall of exposure about "illegal immigration." These were: "During the last six months, about how many (newspaper stories/television programs/conversations) have you (read/seen/heard) about illegal immigration from Mexico?" Respondents were also asked items in the same format concerning media content ". . . about what happens to illegal immigrants from Mexico once they get into the United States?"

Information was measured in several ways. Aided recall items were employed to measure information about Mexico, Baja California, Tijuana, Mexican nationals' expenditures in the United States, and estimates of the number of Mexicans and Latin Americans ". . . caught on the average day trying to enter the United States illegally in San Diego?" Information was also measured by tabulating the number of responses to open-ended items concerning the good and bad effects of undocumented immigration to the United States noted above.

Finally, a series of standard socio-economic, demographic, and quality control items were asked during interviewing.

General Perceptions

In the data collected for this study of citizen attitudes in San Diego, a marked tendency existed for the public to evaluate the effects of immigration *according to the source* of immigration. National or regional location of origin made considerable difference in the perceived effects of immigration.

When asked the question, "In general, do you think that the number of people allowed to immigrate to the United States should be increased, decreased, kept about the same as it is now, or haven't you given the matter much thought?", almost half the public believed immigration should be decreased. Over 70 percent believed it should be decreased or kept the same. Only 15 percent of the public believed more immigration to the United States should be permitted.

However, when asked specifically about the effects on San Diego of immigration from particular world regions, some dramatic differences in perceptions emerged. Data are reported in Table 2, below.

Perceptions of negative effects on San Diego were lowest for Canadian and Western European immigrants, and slightly higher for Africans. Immigrants from Latin America, the Middle East and Asia were perceived to have negative effects by over 30 percent of the public. While Mexico is obviously a part of Latin America, perceptions of the negative impact of Mexican immigration were substantially higher than for Latin American immigration more generally. To be noted, however, almost as many people believed that Mexican immigration has positive effects (46

Table 2. Evaluations of the Effects of Immigration from Selected Areas on San Diego by Source of Origin[a]

	Negative or Slightly Negative	None	Positive or Slightly Positive	DK/NA
Canada	11.8%	24.4	47.8	16.0
Western Europe	16.6%	19.6	48.8	15.0
Africa	21.6%	26.0	29.2	23.2
Asia	35.8%	9.0	40.0	15.2
Middle East	32.2%	14.0	35.8	19.0
Latin America	30.6%	12.0	36.8	20.6
Mexico	40.0%	5.0	46.4	8.6

[a]N = 500.

percent) as believed that Canadian or Western European immigration has positive effects. This was also true for immigrants from Africa, Asia and the Middle East. However, those respondents who believed that Mexican immigrants had some positive effects overwhelmingly limited their answers to narrow labor market-oriented responses.

When asked what benefits San Diego gains from illegal immigrants, respondents mentioned very few. Over 50 percent of those queried mentioned "cheap labor," "doing work Americans won't do," or "necessary for agriculture." There is a clear recognition that undocumented immigrants are a valuable source of labor: most (over 90 percent) of the respondents *could think of no other benefit San Diego gained* from undocumented immigrants. This was true despite the appearance of feature stories in Los Angeles and San Diego newspapers predating the survey which documented the large contributions of Mexican shoppers to the San Diego economy and the importance of Tijuana for the local tourist industry. In this sense the public seemed to perceive Mexican workers as little more than "cheap labor" who, while serving valuable economic functions, also generate unfortunate economic and social costs.

To a certain extent, of course, these perceptions were influenced by the salience of the issue of *illegal* immigration to the United States and the degree to which such illegal immigration is perceived as largely consisting of Mexican immigration. When asked to indicate the importance of the problem of illegal immigration to the United States, over 85 percent of the public categorized illegal immigration as a "very important" or "important" problem. When asked where they believed most illegal immigrants came from, over 90 percent responded Mexico. And over 86 percent of the public believed that illegal immigration from Mexico is a "very important" or "important" problem in the United States. Thus, for people in San Diego, illegal immigration has been a highly salient policy issue and that issue has been associated to a large extent with undocumented workers from Mexico.

These general perceptions are related to specific beliefs about the "most important problems" that illegal immigrants cause for San Diego. Most frequently mentioned were the impact of undocumented workers on employment (over 40 percent of the public), the cost of providing public services such as welfare, medical care or schooling (30 percent) and law enforcement problems (25 percent of the public). Notwithstanding these general perceptions, when asked whether illegal immigrants from Mexico "have any negative effects on the way you live," only 28 percent replied in the affirmative. Almost 70 percent of the public in San Diego believed that illegal immigrants did not create any negative impact on the way that *they* lived. Those persons who believe that undocumented immigrants have a negative effect on the way they live, listed job competition, criminal activity, especially burglary, and increased costs of government to provide services to undocumented immigrants. In general, however, despite an overwhelming belief that illegal immigration is an important problem, the vast majority of the public could think of no way in which such immigration affected *their own lives* negatively. Those who did identify effects in their own lives were concerned primarily with economic issues (jobs, cost of government) or security of property (burglary).

One important component of these costs perceived by respondents was the utilization of public facilities by undocumented immigrants. Over 70 percent of the public believed that undocumented workers use many or some public services. Most frequently mentioned as services used by illegal immigrants were welfare (44 percent), health and medical services (47 percent), schools (22 percent), and transportation (18 percent). When asked whether they had personally *heard of cases* in which illegal immigrants had used public services in San Diego, less than half responded affirmatively (47 percent). Welfare, health and school facilities were most frequently cited by those with hearsay knowledge of service utilization by undocumented immigrants.

Interestingly, only 26 percent of the public claimed to *know personally* of a case in which illegal immigrants utilized public services. Welfare, health and medical facilities, schools and transportation were mentioned most frequently as services used by illegal immigrants by members of the public who claimed to have personal knowledge on this subject.

Finally, although relatively few respondents claimed to know personally of cases in which illegal immigrants lived in their neighborhoods or used public services, a majority of the public *believed* that illegal immigration decreased job opportunities in San Diego (59 percent), decreased job opportunities for teenagers (58 percent), increased the level of crime in San Diego (57 percent), and increased the amount of taxes people paid (54 percent). Significant minorities of the public, moreover, believed that illegal immigrants decreased the availability of housing (34 percent, even though 82 percent believed that there was *no effect* in *their* neighborhood), decreased the availability of welfare benefits for citizens (35 percent), negatively affected the quality of health care available (29 percent), and negatively affected the quality of public education (34 percent), parks (29 percent), and transportation (18 percent) in San Diego. Some 28 percent of the public also believed illegal immigrants helped to increase inflation.

More generally, respondents in the sample tended to view illegal immigrants from Mexico as a valuable labor commodity which otherwise made very little, if any, positive contribution to San Diego or to the United States. Indeed, the Mexican immigrant was generally perceived as a burden on the taxpayers and as a source of criminal activity. A significant minority of respondents even believed that undocumented Mexican immigrants contributed to inflation in San Diego and the United States.

It is clear from the survey that San Diego residents have little appreciation for undocumented immigrants, except as agricultural laborers, gardeners, domestic servants, waiters, and other low paying, low status and difficult labor. Of course, they do recognize the contributions of Mexican workers in these areas. People in San Diego resent paying tax dollars for public services for undocumented immigrants. They resent "good jobs" being taken from Americans by undocumented workers and they blame undocumented immigrants, among other things, for increases in crime, crowding of recreational facilities and non-availability of low income housing.

San Diego residents do not appear to be pleased that enforcement of current immigration law fails to achieve its primary purpose, strictly limiting the *number and type* of immigrants entering the United States. The survey data also suggest that people in San Diego would support "guest worker" or "temporary worker" or other such "bracero-type" programs which might allow Mexican workers temporary opportunities to work at "jobs Americans won't do" while minimizing the tax burden (in terms of public services used) occasioned by such workers.

Thus, translation of public opinion in San Diego and, by implication from the other surveys reported above, of American public opinion into immigration policy would entail a number of specific components: first, effective restrictionist policies combined with, second, "guest-worker" type programs which, third, produce little or no job displacement for U.S. workers, and, fourth, place limited demands on public services, facilities and income transfer programs. Whatever the special character of such policies, in order to "fit" public opinion they must be perceived very broadly to possess these basic components.

IV. THE COMPLEX WORLD OF IMMIGRATION ISSUES AND POPULAR PREFERENCES

The United States is a sovereign nation with recognized national boundaries. As with most contemporary nations, these national boundaries resulted in part from conquests and wars. In the case of the United States' boundary with Mexico, a mid-nineteenth century war incorporated almost one-half of Mexico's national territory into the United States. The United States has the right, recognized under international law, to control immigration into its territory and to prohibit non-resident aliens without proper authorization from taking employment or utilizing "free" public services. Sovereign nations universally attempt to exercise these rights, whether within the confines of Western Europe, among socialist nations of Eastern Europe, or among the numerous nations located in Africa, Asia, or Latin America.

The sovereign right to control immigration into a nation does not guarantee its political or economic feasibility. Relatively low levels of government control over the daily lives and geographical mobility of American citizens and residents makes enforcement of immigration laws more difficult in the United States than in most other nations of the world. The blessings of liberty also impede vigorous enforcement of existing immigration legislation. The ethnic, racial, and religious pluralism of the society also makes recognition of aliens by such overt characteristics as color, language, or behaviors impossible. Substantial public opposition to national identity cards or to work permits, moreover, makes it difficult to institute such federal programs to assist employers— even if they were anxious to cooperate—in screening out ineligible workers.

In a similar vein, it is unreasonable to expect that any proposed sanctions against employers for "knowingly" hiring undocumented immigrants could be rigorously enforced while protecting employer rights against the common risk of fraudulent documents. For this and a number of other reasons, most reform legislation along these lines has been opposed in Congress by employer groups since the early 1950's.[5] Even if some sort of employer sanctions were eventually legislated, such legislation will inevitably face serious court challenges by employer groups. Similarly, civil rights groups and other groups representing minorities will challenge the law's validity since they accurately anticipate the discriminatory labor recruitment consequences that would almost certainly result from laws requiring employers to refuse employment to "undocumented aliens."[6]

At the present time approximately one million undocumented immigrants/visa violators are apprehended by the Immigration and Naturalization Service each year. The majority of apprehended persons are Mexican nationals.[7] Most Mexican nationals enter the United States seeking economic opportunities unavailable in their native land. For the most part, they do not reject Mexico or Mexican nationality, nor do they intend to reside permanently in the United States.[8] Many, in fact, travel illegally between the United States and Mexico from time to time to fulfill a variety of family, business or social obligations. Often, undocumented immigrants return permanently or semi-permanently to Mexico with a stake earned in the United States.

As with most historical migrant streams, however, a certain (apparently growing) number of Mexican immigrants establish "permanent" residence in the United States.[9] In addition, the demographic composition of the migrants appears to have changed in the last decade, with increasing numbers of immigrants coming from urban (in contrast to the predominantly rural origin of much earlier undocumented immigration) places in Mexico and with family members accompanying many more of the immigrants than in the past (Bustamante, 1978). In addition, females make up a larger share of the recent migrant population (Grennes, 1980; Herrand and Falasco, 1982).

Current enforcement of U.S. immigration law makes apprehension for illegal entry into the United States by Mexican nationals relatively painless. Most undocumented immigrants, regardless of the number of previous apprehensions, are allowed "voluntary departure." The voluntary departure procedures spare undocumented immigrants from a formal record of illegal entry, which would act as an obstacle to future legal immigration, and saves American taxpayers the cost of formal deportation proceedings (Piore, 1977).[10]

For present purposes, however, the most important characteristic of the voluntary departure procedure is that many Mexican undocumented immigrants, after being returned across the border, simply turn around and re-enter the United States. According to the presumed effect of immigration law, a third detention for illegal entry could lead to a formal deportation hearing and risk of a prison sentence for future detentions. In practice, this rarely occurs inasmuch as it is much more expedient to allow successive voluntary departures, thereby avoiding the costs of administrative and judicial proceedings.[11] This practice also corresponds to the reality of a lack of suitable facilities to "warehouse" hundreds of thousands of undocumented immigrants. Thus, even if unsuccessful until the fourth or fifth attempt, the consequences of apprehension by the INS or Border Patrol are typically so insignificant that economic necessity "pushes" Mexican nationals back across the border.

As noted earlier, pending immigration legislation, the Simpson-Mazzoli Immigration Reform and Control Act, proposes "amnesty" for selected undocumented immigrants, and sanctions against employers who "knowingly" hire "illegal aliens." The proposed legislation also suggests increased authority/resources for the INS and the Border Patrol.

Under present enforcement practices, these "reforms" will inevitably fail to achieve the intended results. Amnesty is an inducement to other undocumented immigrants to enjoy the same good fortune some years from now. Employer sanctions are inherently unenforceable in the unorganized service sector and difficult to enforce in agriculture. In urban industrial and manufacturing units, periodic raids can temporarily "rescue" jobs filled by undocumented immigrants, but employer sanctions will be resisted in the courts, unsystematically enforced, and ultimately rejected with the political leverage of employer groups, minority groups and civil rights activists. The Simpson-Mazzoli legislation as currently proposed (spring, 1983), moreover, raises numerous constitutional issues in regard to Fourth Ammendment protections of citizens, residents and undocumented immigrants alike. Constitutional issues will inevitably lead to significant litigation concerning "seizure" of the work force, "probable cause," "reasonable suspicion," and other similar challenges to INS enforcement practices.

The only guaranteed "success" of such reforms will be increased expenditures for INS. This increase in resources may also increase the number of undocumented immigrant detainees, since INS will, presumably, increase enforcement of laws which are currently less rigorously enforced due to shortages in personnel and equipment. The detainees will, in turn, accelerate the revolving door process of illegal entry/voluntary departure/re-entry. If the INS uses "increased detentions" as justification for future funding—to do an even better job—this dynamic may well lead to even higher funding levels as the voluntary departure/illegal entry merry-go-round is accelerated.

So long as would be immigrants *perceive* lack of social and economic opportunities or view political repression in their local areas as worse than the most miserable conditions of migrant farm laborers, or garment district sweat shop workers, no moderate "reforms"in immigration law will control illegal entry into the United States, at least not in a way that most Americans would regard as minimally effective. Rigorous enforcement of existing labor laws, including minimum wage requirements and health and safety standards as well as greater encouragement for union organization, might decrease employer incentives for employing undocumented immigrants. Such measures would do little, however, to deter effectively the employment of undocumented workers in agriculture, service industries, and non-unionized construction industries.

Present conditions in Mexico are too grim to expect most undocumented immigrants to press for payment of minimum wages or enforcement of health and safety laws if "fortunate" enough to earn dollars for themselves and their families in the United States. Wage differentials on the two sides of the border have increased with recent devaluations of the Mexican peso. This makes even U.S. minimum wages (or less) still more attractive to Mexican nationals. In a similar vein, the American historical record on enforcement of such legislation in the multifaceted, fragmented and relatively complex service sector or in agriculture is not very impressive even without considering the case of undocumented immigrants. Particularly under the current (Reagan) Administration, it is unrealistic to expect massive commitments of resources for the increased regulation of business entailed by such proposals. One would expect even less support for unionization drives among agricultural workers or systematic increases in minimum wage rates.

It is generally believed that INS has a budget so small in relation to the existing flow of immigrants that it cannot possibly enforce current immigration law. Given the strengthening of both "push" and "pull" factors which contribute to increasingly large flows of immigrants from Mexico, the lack of enforcement can only worsen. And, as INS becomes responsible for increasing levels of activity under immigration reform laws, politically unrealistic amounts of resources would appear necessary to maintain even existing levels of performance in enforcement. It may be, of course, that strict enforcement of U.S. immigration law would require more resources than presently are expended on "providing services" to undocumented immigrants *and* intensify hostility along the border.

In reality, of course, *enforcement practices* may be more important than levels of funding or the number of personnel. Mandatory prison sentences for first-time offenders instead of "voluntary departure," for example, would most certainly discourage undocumented immigrants. But enforcement of increasingly rigorous laws (and laws which might just be more effective in stemming the flow of undocumented immigrants) would require substantial expenditures for administrative and judicial proceedings as well as for construction of detention facilities. Such expenditures would probably produce some reduction in undocumented immigration. Of course, to the extent that such enforcement practices serve as a deterent to undocumented immigration, administrative and judicial costs would likely decline after several years. But it is likely that costs would far exceed current expenditures for a very long time under existing conditions. A much more extreme measure, advocated only by those with the most extreme exclusionist views, involves the deployment of military patrols and creation of "no man's lands." The harsher measure might be even more effective but at a cost in ethical if not monetary terms that most regard as too high to pay.

Such policies, of course, would represent outrageous, inhuman and un-American methods for enforcing immigration legislation. Unfortunately, as long as the alternative to illegal entry into the United States for millions of Mexican nationals is unemployment, underemployment, hunger and misery for themselves and their families, only such drastic, radical and morally outrageous enforcement of immigration law is likely to limit substantially illegal entry into the United States. This is a part, albeit a small part, of the ethical dilemma policymakers face concerning the problem of undocumented immigration. This conclusion is not a happy one for U.S. policymakers nor does it portend an amicable future for U.S.-Mexican relations.

V. POLICY ALTERNATIVES AND POLITICAL IMPLICATIONS

Political Implications

The current policy debate ignores or rejects the obvious *benefits* to diverse American and Mexican interests in the present circumstances of undocumented immigration. Colorado Governor Richard D. Lamm, for example, recently noted that:

> Our immigration system today serves no one's interest, except a few fortunate souls able to come into the United States while millions wait. Certainly the source countries are not helped. They lose their most productive and skilled workers. Certainly the American people are not helped. More people means more pressure on our own resources, more energy use, more traffic, more fertile farmland used for housing, more unemployment.[12]

Governor Lamm is simply wrong. Dollars sent from undocumented immigrant workers to families in Mexico constitute a valuable, indeed indispensable, source of foreign exchange for Mexico and source of subsistence for millions of Mexicans *in Mexico*. The dollar flow from the United States to Mexico also constitutes a political and economic prop to the Mexican political system, thereby reducing the threat of widespread protests and violence. American urban consumers are subsidized by undocumented immigrants in many guises: the most significant of such subsidies include relatively low prices for food and domestic services (for example, gardners, maids, and construction repairs). Tourist and restaurant industries throughout the Southwestern United States depend on undocumented immigrant labor, as does agriculture. And many who purchase houses or housing have been, however unknowingly, subsidized in their possessions by the labor of undocumented immigrants.

As suggested above, the most recent study of the impact of undocumented immigrants in San Diego County estimated that 34–59 percent of hired labor in agriculture consists of undocumented workers. It was estimated, moreover, that 50–62 percent of these jobs would go unfilled (at present wage rates and working conditions) if undocumented workers were unavailable.[13] Although such counterfactual arguments remain problematic because one can never literally test the consequences of the counterfactual assumption, the projections do represent the best available evidence on employment impact. Even if the projections considerably overestimate the role of undocumented immigrants in this sector because of error to fluctuations in economic, social, and local employment conditions at some time in the future, the remaining figures are still substantial in their significance.

Just as consumers benefit from the presence of undocumented immigrants, so do employers whose firms' profitability and competitiveness depend on relatively low wage structures, non-unionized labor, and "flexibility" in personnel management. Such employers in Southern California County range from flower growers and small construction firms to manufacturers of simulated panelling for recreational vehicles or the host of companies which provide services directly to consumers.

Certainly there are costs associated with these benefits. Job displacement, marginal declines in labor wage rates, declines in quality of working conditions associated with availability of migrant labor, pressure on public services, and income transfer programs all result to some extent as a consequence of the undocumented immigrant or undocumented worker.[14] These issues become increasingly salient in times of economic recession, as they have historically.

Calls for political resolution of the "immigration issue" typically coincide with unemployment of American workers. Economic crises tap the reservoir of underlying beliefs and attitudes about immigrants and immigration. The complex array of benefits to employers, consumers and workers are much less apparent than the list of costs provided by Governor Lamm: ". . . more pressure on economic resources, more energy use, more traffic, more fertile farmland used for housing, more unemployment."

While Governor Lamm's words are moderate and his message sincere, if economic conditions continue to deteriorate in the United States, the political language of immigration restriction will certainly grow more recognizably nativistic and racist in tone. As undocumented workers move out of the agricultural fields and into urban manufacturing and service employment in ever increasing numbers, their visibility increases and resentment by threatened sectors of the American public intensifies. As economic conditions worsen, previously "undesirable" jobs are viewed more favorably by unemployed Americans. Reductions in coverage or eligibility for social security programs, adoption of "workfare" type programs requiring people to work for "food stamps" or other essentially welfare benefits, or reductions in minimum wage coverage (for instance, eliminating certain age groups or job categories from coverage) put more Americans into direct competition with undocumented immigrants for domestic service, gardening, restaurant, tourist services and lower-paying construction work. Efforts by housewives, retirees, or students to supplement family income or partially to replace income lost by the principal wage earner still further intensifies competition for relatively low-paying work.

The belief held by large numbers of Americans that undocumented immigrants negatively affect job opportunities and living conditions in the United States provides ammunition for a frontal assault by some politicians on the "wetback problem." If such an assault gains widespread support, it will intensify racial polarization in border communities from San Diego to Brownsville. Increased demands for control of undocumented immigration or increased public clamor for such control *necessarily* threatens the life style and security of Latino and "Latin-looking" citizens and residents of the United States, if only by imposing the inconvenience-harassment of occasional checks for documents, searches, and erroneous detentions. In one sense such policies and procedures create a second-class citizen, a citizen subject to document checks based on the possibility of being in the United States illegally. Since most United States citizens do not carry birth certificates or other universal identity cards on their persons, the fear of mistaken apprehensions or even mistaken deportation could erode the everyday quality of life for Latinos in the United States. Unfortunately, one has only to look to the Great Depression years or to the INS "Operation Wetback" (1954) to find precedent for the mistaken deportation of Americans of Mexican ancestry.

In summary then, unsophisticated and literal translation of public opinion regarding undocumented immigration into effective restrictionist policy would necessitate harsh enforcement practices, disruption of important sectors of the U.S. economy (especially, but not limited to, agriculture, tourism and urban service sectors in the Southwestern United States) and sharply increased racial and ethnic conflict. Yet hard economic times and the increased political saliency of the immigration issue which accompanies periods of recession and depression provide ample opportunities for some politicians to exploit the latent nativistic and racist sentiment which waxes and wanes among Americans.

Domestic Policy Implications

As indicated, policies which purport to restrict immigration cannot succeed without substantial resource commitments and intensification of repressive enforcement measures. Ironically, such measures, if successful, would contribute to price inflation for basic foodstuffs and specialty crops, damage the tourist and restaurant industry in the Southwestern United States, deprive middle and upper class Americans of low-wage domestic servants and gardeners, and even adversely effect numerous small businesses and marginal construction firms unable to pay union wages or to comply with social security, labor and safety legislation. In short, removal of large numbers of undocumented immigrants would cause substantial short-term disruptions in Southern California and throughout the Southwestern United States.

Thus, public policy cannot literally enforce public opinion in regard to substantially reducing the flow of immigration from Mexico without seriously damaging American businesses and inconveniencing millions of American households. It would be possible, however, to satisfy public opinion and most economic needs by combining harsh enforcement measures against undocumented immigrants (if these were politically and economically feasible) with "guest worker" type programs for selective (favored) sectors of the American economy (those sectors which can demonstrate low levels of "substitutability" of local labor at market wage levels in the absence of immigrant labor).

Such a policy would require (1) enforcement of severe penalties against detained undocumented immigrants and employers who hire undocumented workers; (2) workable procedures for documenting and admitting "guest workers" for selected U.S. employers, and (3) adequate provision for the health and welfare needs of contracted labor.[15] Each of these requirements would generate considerable and intense political debate. Both moral and practical objectives would necessarily be raised against mandatory prison sentences for detained undocumented immigrants. This is also true in the case of guest worker proposals, with certain elements of organized labor in the U.S. an obvious political adversary.[16] The final requirement, adequate provision for health and welfare needs of guest workers, raises the additional question of which levels of government or of the private sector should share in paying the costs of such programs.

The political implications of decisions undergirding these three measures are sweeping. It is difficult to imagine Congress successfully legislating policies which would speak to each of these concerns in a public forum. Can we really threaten Mexican citizens with long prison terms for illegal entry into the United States? Can we afford (economically) to carry out the threat? What retaliatory steps might Mexico take? What would the costs be in increased racial and social polarization in the United States? What industries would effectively be subsidized, at what cost to which competing domestic labor pools and under what kinds of conditions?

It should be clear that even if such policies were approved, they would not address the issues raised by the unorganized service sector (domestics, gardeners, barbers, waitresses, and so on), nor would they entirely eliminate undocumented immigration. The policies would, however, allow the basic thrust of American public opinion on the immigration issue to be translated into public policy without disrupting those sectors of the American economy most dependent on undocumented immigrant labor. Moreover, to the extent that (1) the threat of prison serves as a deterrent and that (2) the current response to undocumented immigration consists primarily of voluntary departure for repeat offenders, then the immediate incarceration of detainees and mandatory prison sentences would ultimately reduce the workload of INS/Border Patrol personnel. It would also raise the morale of such personnel who, under present conditions, view their mission as both thankless and impossible to achieve.

The conclusion that incarceration of undocumented immigrants would reduce INS/Border Patrol workload may be more problematic than the conclusion that incarceration would boost morale and increase work efficiency. The assumption is premised on the notion that the same proportion of violators would be apprehended as now and that this proportion would decline due to the harsher policy. Indeed, more efficient work performance might actually increase the workload of INS/Border Patrol personnel if larger proportions of undocumented immigrants were apprehended, for it appears that only a very small fraction of the total flow of undocumented immigrants are apprehended under existing circumstances. Unfortunately, this must remain conjecture, since no precise estimates of the numbers of persons engaged in illegal immigration are available, nor are reliable data available indicating the precise extent of recidivism.

The Cost?

The cost of such "reforms" would entail a higher repressive alteration in immigration law enforcement procedures that would inevitably threaten the civil rights of numerous American citizens and legal residents as INS seeks to ferret out undocumented immigrants in neighborhood and workplace raids, individual seizure operations, and generally intensified enforcement activities. In addition, these policies would require major investment in new and expanded prison facilities, shortrun disruptions in some economic activities, and provisions for governmental/private sector institutions to administer contract labor programs. Each of these requirements implies significant obstacles, to say the least. In fact, it is quite likely that proposals for harsher immigration policies are based on assumptions that are politically unrealistic in light of recent historical experiences in states along the border.

Foreign Policy Implications

Undocumented immigration to the U.S. from Mexico is primarily the result of the inability of the Mexican political and economic systems to provide opportunities for a decent quality of life for millions of Mexican citizens. In a sense, then, the flow of undocumented immigrants to the United States is a political and economic safety valve for Mexico. In addition to removing literally millions of people from the Mexican labor market, undocumented immigration to the United States may provide Mexico with several billion dollars a year in remittances back to family members. Indeed, in the late 1970's Fagen suggested such remittances exceeded Mexican income from all tourist-related activities and were ". . . a crucial if not always acknowledged component of Mexico's balance of payments" (1977, p. 689). A more recent estimate by Robert Bond, the risk analyst for First National Bank of Chicago, suggests the Mexican workers in the U.S. remit approximately $3 billion per year to Mexico.[17] Thus, the contribution of the U.S. safety valve to political stability in Mexico should not be underestimated.[18] Massive deportations of undocumented immigrants back to Mexico would most certainly disrupt Mexico's precarious economic and social situation as well as severely strain U.S.-Mexican relations.[19]

Political stability in Mexico contributes to U.S. national security in a variety of ways, including insuring the availability of energy products (especially petroleum), guaranteeing a mutually beneficial exchange of goods and services, and allowing the 2000 mile long border between Mexico and the United States to be lightly monitored by U.S. military forces. Effective insurgency and/or social upheaval in Mexico would necessarily create a national security threat to the United States, particularly under present political circumstances in Central America and the Caribbean.

Leftist-oriented political movements, often supported or encouraged by Cuban and by non-Western hemisphere powers, pose a genuine threat to U.S. hegemony in its traditional sphere of influence. Upheaval in Mexico could provide great opportunities for expansion of Cuban, Soviet or other influences even if insurrectionary forces were ultimately defeated by the Mexican military and conservative political allies.

The U.S. has a significant stake in the ability of the Mexican political and economic systems to maintain relative stability and internal peace. Literal implementation of U.S. public opinion on questions of immigration would no doubt seriously threaten the Mexican regime's political and economic resources, especially given the heavy cash flow requirements of the existing internal and international debt of Mexico's public and private sectors. It would also intensify the traditional antagonism of Mexican nationalists toward the U.S. while eroding the underpinnings of Mexican-United States relations within the Inter-American system (Garner, 1981, pp. 184–185). It is also useful to point out that American financial interests are among the most important lenders to Mexico so that defaults on interest or principal could cost Americans billions and possibly undermine confidence in the banking system.

The serious foreign policy and national security implications of U.S. immigration policy also offer valuable opportunities for American policymakers to contribute to resolution of the immigration dilemma. Any policy that U.S. policymakers adopt which assists Mexican economic development and job creation (preferential tariff treatment for Mexican products, low-interest, long-term credit for agricultural development, or guaranteed prices for petroleum products, possibly similar to the way that the Soviet Union subsidizes Cuban sugar) will reduce the pressures for immigration to the United States. Obviously, the United States cannot, nor should it, solve Mexico's basic imbalances in income distribution nor reform Mexico's political system nor force changes in birth rates and population growth. The U.S. can, however, improve conditions in Mexico somewhat and thereby respond indirectly to political demands in the United States for immigration restriction.

Such policies require explicit formulation of a new "special relationship" policy toward Mexico (and, most likely, Canada as well) with respect to trade and related economic issues. From a national security standpoint this is an entirely justifiable approach which other American allies and trading partners must come to understand. U.S. interests require that Mexico be treated preferentially, that the Mexican economy, both public and private, receive special treatment from U.S. policymakers, and that U.S. policies favor particularly the development of Mexican agriculture and the creation and expansion of export-oriented industries.

Mexico is presently the third largest U.S. trading partner, after Canada and Japan. However, while trade with Mexico accounts for approximately five percent of total U.S. exports and less than five percent of all U.S. imports, from 1970 to 1980, the United States received from 54 to 71 percent of all Mexican exports while providing from 60 to 64 percent of all Mexican imports. In absolute terms, the value of U.S. imports from Mexico increased from $1.2 billion to $12.5 billion per year during the decade. Exports to Mexico exceeded $15 billion per year by the end of the decade.[20]

Thus, Mexican-United States trade produced a deficit trade balance for Mexico and intensified Mexican dependency on the United States for a broad variety of fabricated products as well as for *basic foodstuffs*.

For a variety of reasons, Mexico now depends on the United States for substantial quantities of corn, beans, sorghum, wheat, soybeans, sunflower seeds and rice. U.S. farm sector exports to Mexico exceeded $2 billion in 1980, and produced the first agricultural trade deficit for Mexico with the U.S. since the end of World War II. The trend continued through the end of 1982.

There are no technical or economic reasons why Mexico could not be self-sufficient in corn, beans, rice or even soybeans and soybean products (meal and oil). These items alone accounted for approximately $1 billion per year in imports in the early 1980's. U.S. foreign policy, particularly technical and economic assistance directed toward the Mexican small farm sector on concessionary terms, could improve Mexican food production, create employment in rural Mexico and, thereby, reduce to some extent migration pressures directed at urban centers in Mexico and at the U.S.

In order to further improve Mexico's economic position, the United States could devise policies acceptable to domestic interests that skirt the difficulties inherent in requests for applications of the "countervailing duty" provisions of U.S. trade law and allow Mexico to take full advantage of Mexican domestic fiscal incentives for exports (CEDI), tax credits for industrial decentralization and regional development (CEPROM) and subsidized export financing (FOMEX).[21]

In the long run, a stable and economically sound Mexico serves the national interest and national security of the United States. Mexican economic development, particularly agricultural development and growth of export-oriented jobs and of manufacturing and service sectors, contributes to reduced immigration pressures. With this in mind, it may better serve long-term U.S. interests to compensate U.S. firms against Mexican "dumping" (whether this be southern Florida citrus and vegetable growers or manufacturers of bathing apparel and leather products) rather than penalizing Mexican products with "countervailing duties." Similarly, it would be possible to expand the items Mexico is eligible to export to the United States under the terms of the Generalized System of Preferences by waiving the "competitive need" criteria and emphasizing *bilateral* treaties rather than insisting on Mexican acquiesence to the GATT.[22]

Although such policies might be resented by other trade partners, once the U.S. officially asserts a policy of "special relationship" with Mexico, exclusions for Mexico (or for both Mexico and Canada) on the basis of geographical contiguity or "national interest" or "good neighbor," do not necessarily imply similar exclusions for any other nation. Indeed, there is a notable lack of *bilateral* treaties in force between the U.S. and Mexico regarding trade, which could be remedied with a new policy initiative on the part of the United States. Likewise, the border industries program could be further encouraged, providing increased employment, technology transfer, technical education, and secondary economic benefits to Mexico and to U.S. consumers.[23]

Foreign policy toward Mexico *is* a special case for the United States. Responding to this reality pragmatically would not only contribute to ameliorating the immigration issue for the United States, but also corresponds to a moral, humane and laudable intent to improve living conditions south of the Rio Grande.

Such a policy initiative also implies some confrontation with U.S. interests, both employers and labor, which might be forced to compete with Mexican interests accorded favorable treatment by new U.S. trade and economic policies. Mexican policymakers might soften opposition to these policies in the United States by implementation of reciprocal concessions toward selected U.S. exporters, investors or workers. Naturally, like their U.S. counterparts, Mexican policymakers must consider carefully the domestic political and economic reactions to such policies.

Despite the inevitable difficulties, however, creative foreign policy initiatives provide important opportunities for the U.S. and Mexico greatly to improve conditions on both sides of the border. Indeed, it may be that a creative foreign policy initiative toward Mexico is also the best policy instrument available for U.S. policymakers to deal with domestic political pressures for restraint of immigration.

ACKNOWLEDGMENT

Special acknowledgement is owed to Professor William Simon, Department of Sociology, University of Houston, for his many criticial and helpful comments. This paper would have been better had we been able to follow even more of his sage advice.

NOTES

1. Thus Siegel *et al*'s (1980, p. 20) preliminary review of existing studies of the number of illegal residents in the United States concludes:

> We have unfortunately been unable to arrive at definite estimates of the number of illegal residents in the United States or the magnitude of the illegal migration flow. The phenomenon we have sought to measure, but its nature is not an easy one to deal with. Researchers and policymakers will have to live with the fact that the number of illegal residents in the United States cannot be closely quantified.

See also Population Reference Bureau, Inc., (1982).

2. Early studies of the impact of undocumented immigrants on public services suggested low rates of utilization of income transfer programs (AFDC, unemployment insurance, food stamps, health care, and so on). Some more recent studies provide contradictory evidence. While substantial controversy continues to exist on this issue, the Federation of American Immigration Reform, a restrictionist lobby, utilizes the recent data to conclude:

> There are several reasons to oppose illegal immigration: the impact of illegal immigration on the poor in America, its impact on our population growth and environment, its erosionof our national sovereignty, or the fact that it is a socially evil system which encourages exploitation. .

> The mounting costs of social services should be added to these reasons. I am not suggesting that costs are the major reason to work against illegal immigration. I am saying something far less sweeping but, I believe, far more compelling: if illegal immigrants could be exploited to subsidize benefit programs, it would be unworthy of us to toerate illegal immigration for these subsidies. But it is mistaken to believe that illegal immigrants are being efficiently and effectively exploited for the economic benefit of our government. Those who use that supposed benefit to apologize for the other social ills of illegal immigration are simply misled. Illegal immigrants aren't a bargain.

For a variety of approaches to these problems and for a survey of the literature, see North (1981), Simon (1981), Community Research Associates (1980), Cross and Sandos (1979), Cornelius et al (1982, chapter 4), Cross and Sandos (1981, chapter 6), Conner (1982), Comptroller General of the U.S. (1977), and Mines and Martin (forthcoming). The last paper examines a number of theories concerning labor market impacts of immigrants or potential "guest workers."

3. Efforts to estimate "job displacement" effects of undocumented immigrants necessarily involve relatively arbitrary assumptions about "substitutability" and availability of domestic labor by economic sector and specialized work functions. See, for example, Community Research Associates (1980, Chapter 2 and pp. 289–290).

4. There is, of course, a voluminous literature on immigration to the U.S. and varieties of immigrant experiences. See, for example, Jones (1960) and Dinnerstein (1979).

5. There is also, however, substantial support for such a program as evidenced by the public opinion research reported by the American Institute of Public Opinion, (November, 1980), and the San Diego *Union*, (November 30, 1980, p. A-22).

6. For description of previous unsuccessful efforts of this sort in California (the Arnett Law, 1971), see Calavita (1982). In November, 1982, Professor Carl E. Schwarz reported on a panel entitled "The Federal Courts and Undocumented Immigration: Recent Decisions and their Implications," that in eight states with "employer sanction" type legislation, enforcement was minimal. According to Schwarz, the harshest enforcement occurred in Virginia (1979–1982) where seven prosecutions resulted in two convictions and employers were fined $80.00 and $55.00, respectively, along with suspended sentences. Wayne Cornelius added that ". . . this approach to immigration control has already been tried in a dozen U.S. states that have passed such legislation since 1971, and in at least twenty other countries around the world. The results have been virtually identical in each case: employer penalties have *not* reduced the hiring of illegal immigrants, and often have created additional problems" (Cornelius, 1982, p. 6).

7. These 1 million apprehensions do not imply 1 million *different* people. Repeat offenders significantly reduce the number of *persons* apprehended. Cross and Sandos (1979, p. 83) suggest a deflation factor of 1.89 based on recent research in Mexico.

8. In addition, a number of Mexican citizens with "green cards" commute daily across the border to work. Although they technically violate U.S. law, no systematic effort exists to end the practice. It may be that *legalizing* this common practice would fill the needs of U.S. employers and the life style preferences of many Mexican nationals.

9. For a classical statement of the pattern, see Piore (1979).

10. In the U.S. in 1982, less than 30 immigration judges were available for formal deportation hearings. If only ten percent of detainees requested such hearings, the American judicial immigration apparatus would be overwhelmed, at least in its present circumstances.

11. There are, however, exceptions. In a recent case an undocumented immigrant was "punished" for requesting a jury trial, thereby imposing costs on American taxpayers. The U.S. District Judge in the case imposed a two year prison sentence and $2,000 fine *for each offense*. because "All I can see is he was just thumbing his nose at our judicial system (by requesting a jury trial)." A Federal Appeals Court vacated this decision, as reported in the Los Angeles *Times* (October 20, 1982).

12. As reported in the San Diego *Union* (March 28, 1982, pp. 4, 6).

13. See, for instance, Community Research Associates (1980, p. 59).

14. Recent federal case law, as well as some state and local decisions, have supported undocumented immigrant eligibility for education programs, emergency and non-emergency health care, participation in unions and protection of labor legislation, and even as victims of violent crime. On the other hand, some federal agencies have recently (1982) adopted administrative barriers to undocumented immigrant access to federal programs, including to the food stamp program, subsidized housing and school lunch programs.

15. Mines and Martin (forthcoming) suggest that guest worker programs must deal with at least the following four issues: (1) U.S. labor market tests to certify employers' labor needs, (2) details of the labor migration arrangements, (3) employment and non-employment rights of guest workers, and (4) circumstances under which guest workers can adjust status to become permanent residents. There is no doubt that a number of practical problems must be resolved if temporary worker programs are to be successful in the United States. These include efforts to avoid the difficult test of exploitation that often characterized the old *bracero* programs.

16. There is no doubt that reservations toward such a policy would be expressed by some economic interests and by labor groups in the United States which might be potentially affected adversely by Mexican competition. In the long run, however, the benefits to the U.S. of a strong Mexican economy and stable Mexican political system would outweigh the domestic costs of preferential trade treatment and economic assistance to Mexico.

17. Cited in *Business Week* (February 28, 1983, p. 44).

18. The Cuban press clearly recognizes the policy and propaganda implications of U.S. immigration policy in relation to hemispheric relations. A story which is prototypic in *Granma* (February 6, 1983, p. 11) suggests that American authorities are "hunting" undocumented immigrants in a sporting fashion.

19. In December, 1982, the Mexican Senate passed a resolution expressing its "alarm and concern" about the implications of the proposed Simpson-Mazzoli legislation. Such "intrusion" into U.S. "domestic" policy-making by the Mexican legislature is *very* uncharacteristic of the Mexican political process.

20. Basically, when a country's competitiveness for a product has been established, "competitive need" is lost, thereby removing that product from duty-free eligibility under the terms of the General System of Preferences (Title V of U.S. Trade Act of 1974).

21. Again, the Cuban press recognizes the importance of U.S.-Mexican trade policy and exploits the injury to Mexico caused by U.S. insistence on Mexican adherence to GATT. See, for instance, *Granma,* (February 6, 1983, p. 11).

22. John M. Garner, Economic Officer, U.S. Embassy in Mexico, noted that ". . . except for a bilateral textile agreement, there are no bilateral treaties in force, not even a Friendship, Commerce and Navigation (FCN) Treaty, defining the legal bases of the bilateral trade relationship." (1981, p. 170). See also, Purcell (1982).

23. Notwithstanding leftist critiques of the border industries (maquiladoras) and complaints by U.S. business, recent studies indicate a positive balance for this program. See Seligson and Williams (1982).

REFERENCES

Barrientos, Guido A., et al. "What Drives Mexican Illegal Border-Crossers into the U.S.? A Psychological Approach." *New Scholar,* forthcoming.

Bustamante, Jorge. *La Imigracion Indocumentado en Los Debates del Congreso de Los Estados Unidos.* Mexico, D.F.: Ceniet, 1978.

Calavita, Kitty. "California's 'Employer Sanctions': The Case of the Disappearing Law." San Diego: Center for U.S.-Mexican Studies, University of California, 1982.

Community Research Associates. *Undocumented Immigrants: Their Impact on the County of San Diego.* San Diego, Ca.: n.p., 1980.

Comptroller General of the U.S. December. *Impact of Illegal Aliens on Public Assistance Programs: Too Little is Known.* Washington, D.C.: Government Printing Office, 1977.

Conner, Roger. "Breaking Down the Barriers: The Changing Relationship between Illegal Immigration and Welfare." Washington, D.C.: FAIR Immigration Paper IV, 1982.

Cornelius, Wayne. "Simpson-Mazzoli vs. the Realities of Mexican Immigration." Paper presented at the Fourth Annual Earl Warren Memorial Symposium, University of California at San Diego, 1982.

Cornelius, Wayne, et al. "Mexican Immigrants and Southern California: A Summary of Current Knowledge." Working Papers in U.S.-Mexican Studies, No. 36. San Diego: Center for U.S. Mexican Studies, 1982 (Mimeo).

Cross, Harry E., and Sandos, James A. "The Impact of Undocumented Workers on the United States." Columbus: Batelle PDP Working Paper No. 15, 1979 (Mimeo).

Cross, Harry E., and Sandos, James A. *Across the Border: Rural Development in Mexico and Recent Migration to the United States.* Berkeley, Calif.: Institute of Governmental Studies, 1981.

Dinnerstein, L., et al. *Natives and Strangers: Ethnic Groups and the Building of America.* New York: Oxford University Press, 1979.

Fagen, Richard. "The Realities of U.S.-Mexican Relations." *Foreign Affairs.* XX(1977): 689.

Grennes, Ronald A. June 6, 1980. "Impact of the Urban Mexican Workers on the United States." Congressional *Record.* S Doc. 6424. Washington, D.C.: Government Printing Office, June 6, 1980.

Herrand, David M., and Falasco, Dee. "The Socio-Economic Status of Recent Mothers of Mexican Origin in Los Angeles County: A Comparison of Undocumented Migrants, Legal Migrants, and Native Citizens." Paper presented at the Annual Meetings of the Population Association of America, San Diego, 1982.

Jones, Maldwyn Allen. *American Immigration.* Chicago: University of Chicago Press, 1960.

Mines, Richard, and Martin, Philip L. "The U.S. Guest Worker Debate." *New Scholar,* forthcoming.

North, David S. *Government Records: What they Tell Us about the Role of Illegal Immigrants in the Labor Market and in Income Transfer Programs.* Washington, D.C.: New Transcentury Foundation, 1981.

Piore, Michael J. "Undocumented Workers and U.S. Immigration Policy." Paper presented at the Annual Meeting of the Latin American Studies Association, Houston, Texas,
1977.

Piore, Michael J. *Birds of Passage: Migrant Labor and Industrial Societies.* New York:
Cambridge University Press, 1977.

Population Reference Bureau, Inc. *Immigration: Questions and Answers.* (1982).

Purcell, John F. H. "Trade Conflicts and U.S.-Mexican Relations." San Diego: Program in
U.S.-Mexican Studies, 1982. (Mimeo).

Select Commission on Immigration and Refugee Policy. *U.S. Immigration Policy and the
National Interest.* Washington, D.C.: Government Printing Office, March 1981.

Seligson, Mitchell A., and Williams, Edward J. *Maquiladoras and Migration.* Austin, Texas:
University of Texas Press, 1982.

Siegel, Jacob, et al. *Preliminary Review of Existing Studies of the Number of Illegal Residents in the
United States.* Washington, D.C.: United States Bureau of the Census, 1980.

Simon, Julian L. "What Immigrants Take from and Give to the Public Coffers." *Appendix
D.* Staff Report of the Select Commission on Immigration and Refugee Policy Papers.
Legal Immigration to the United States. Washington, D.C.: Government Printing Office,
April 20, 1981.

EVALUATING THE CHANGING DEFINITION OF A POLICY ISSUE IN CONGRESS:
CRIME AGAINST THE ELDERLY

Fay Lomax Cook and Wesley G. Skogan

I. INTRODUCTION

There is a growing body of research in political science and in mass communications on agenda-setting—that is, on the question of how social conditions come to be defined as social problems and political issues (e.g., Cobb and Elder, 1971, 1972; Cobb, Ross, and Ross, 1976; Eyestone, 1978; McCombs and Shaw, 1972, 1977; Roberts and Bachen, 1981). Much political science research examines how particular problems, in the form of specific legislative proposals, are placed on the formal political agenda and then are processed further in the legislative arena. Much mass communication research examines how the mass media influence the salience of issues on the public and the governmental policy agendas. Less attention has been paid to how social conditions are perceived and framed as social problems in the first place. In addition to understanding how a bill becomes a law and how the media keep a policy problem high in salience on the agenda, we need to know how conditions become defined as specific problems for which redress is then sought.

This chapter suggests that the framing of political issues is not a cut-and-dried process. Events in the world do not clearly fall into slots with a problem label, and problems do not always have clear policy implications. Rather, complex and ill-understood conditions can be defined as a problem in various ways and emerge as a political issue taking on any of a variety of formulations. As it then competes for a place on the policy agenda, this issue can form and re-form itself yet further, reflecting the fact that it was not solely molded by a clear mandate concerning the nature of the problem.

The research reported here examines the changing definitions of one social problem in the criminal justice field—crime against the elderly. Concern about this problem emerged as an issue on the Congressional policy agenda in the early 1970s and achieved relatively high public salience. But during the decade in which it has remained an active concern of many Americans, the problem has been defined in several different ways. The first half of this chapter describes these problem metamorphoses—what we call the "life course" of the crime-and-the-elderly problem. The second half examines how each of the problem formulations stands up to tests of how well it fits the social conditions it presumably represented. Often it does not. This does not mean the elderly do *not* have a crime problem—our data clearly indicate otherwise. Rather, it means that the claims in this area were not often on the mark with regard to identifying the problem. This analysis indicates that the crime problems facing the elderly mostly resemble those plaguing all Americans. Victimization and fear of crime are high for city dwellers, the poor, racial minorities, and a number of other identifiable categories of people. However, it does not appear that an age-based definition of the problem—however politically attractive it may be—serves as well to identify a key group for tackling crime. Americans are clearly committed to serving the needs of the elderly (Cook, 1979), but the needs-identification process has not served them well in this case.

II. THE LIFE COURSE OF A POLICY ISSUE, 1970–81

In order to examine the life course of an issue on the policy agenda, we must first ask *which* policy agenda? Cobb, Ross, and Ross (1976) have distinguished between two—public agendas and formal agendas. By formal agendas they mean the set of issues discussed by government bodies, such as the U.S. Congress, that can decide on courses of action to be followed. By public agendas, they mean the set of issues which capture some degree of public attention at a particular time. The mass media are variously assumed to reflect or form this set, as well as to reflect or form the saliency of a particular issue on the agenda at a particular time. Such public agendas can then feed into formal agendas by influencing what is on them, how salient specific issues are, and how the issues are defined.

Since the number of potential policy issues far exceeds the capabilities of decision makers and members of the public to process them, issues must compete for a place on the policy agenda. In the competition, some issues achieve visibility and others do not. The issue of crime against the elderly is one that made it onto both the public agenda and the formal agenda. The issue received attention from the mass media and the U.S. Congress as well as from agencies within the federal bureaucracy and elderly interest groups. This attention grew from the early 1970s to 1978 when issue concern seemed to peak. Since 1978, much—though not all—of this attention has sharply decreased.

To operationalize the life course of the crime-and-the-elderly issue on the public agenda, we conducted a content analysis of articles on the subject that appeared in the *New York Times* between 1970 and 1981. Since research has shown that the mass media affect the policy priorities of the general public (e.g., Cook et al., 1983; see review of literature in Roberts and Bachen, 1981), it seems valid to use a widely read national newspaper such as the *New York Times* as a proxy for the public agenda. Figure 1 shows the life course of the crime and the elderly issue there. The number of articles in the *New York Times* increased from nine in the period from 1970–72 to 160 from 1973–75. The number remained high from 1976 to 1978 but dropped steadily after 1978.

Figure 2 shows the life course of the crime and the elderly issue in the U.S. Congress over this same time period. Before 1970 there had never been a Congressional hearing on the topic. Between 1970–72 there were six; between 1976–78 there were 15. After 1978, there were only five. The dash line in Figure 2 shows the number of times in Congress that there was mention made—through a speech or the introduction of legislation—on the topic of criminal victimization of the elderly. These increased from seven between 1970–72 to 17 between 1973–75 to a high of 49 between 1976–78. After 1978, Congressmen introduced legislation and discussed the issue on the floor of Congress much less frequently.

Clearly, it appears that in the space of one decade, we have seen the salience of the crime and the elderly issue rise and fall on both the public and the formal policy agendas. The life course of this issue prompts us to ask: Is it "right" that it should be decreasing in salience on the policy agenda?

Figure 1. The Life Course of the Crime and the Elderly Issue on the Mass Media Agenda, 1970–81

Source: Compiled by the authors from a content analysis of the *New York Times*. The authors relied on the *New York Times Index* as a locator of the articles and then read each article to verify that it should be included.

The first step toward answering this question is to dissect the issue and understand exactly what it was about the problem of criminal victimization of the elderly that concerned the public and policymakers. We conducted a content analysis of every mention that was made about crime and the elderly in Congress. The analysis included reading every speech, proposed bill, etc. that was on the topic and recording how each defined the problem. That analysis revealed the problem was defined in at least four ways, having to do with rates of criminal victimization, economic and physical consequences of victimization, fear of crime, and consequences of fear:

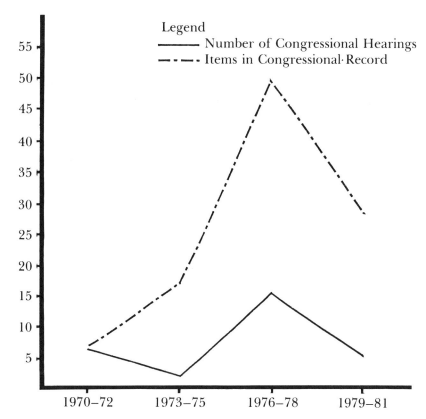

Figure 2. The Life Course of the Crime and the Elderly Issue on the Congressional Agenda, 1970–81

Source: Compiled by the authors from content analyses of the *Congressional Record* and from Congressional Hearings found through the *Congressional Information Service Index* (CIS). The *Congressional Record Index* and the *CIS Index* were used as locators of items, but all items were then read to verify that they should be included.

1. The elderly are more likely than other age groups to be criminally victimized.
2. When victimized, they are more likely than other age groups to suffer severe economic and physical consequences.
3. They are more likely than others to be fearful of crime.
4. The consequences of fear are more severe for them; i.e., fear causes them to be "prisoners in their own homes."

In addition, the content analysis of the *Congressional Record* revealed that the way in which the problem of crime and the elderly was formulated shifted over the 1970–1981 period. Figure 3 shows the pattern of these shifts in formulations. In the early years, 1970–72, the preponderance of the definitions of the problem were about rates of victimization (the elderly are more likely to be victimized than other age groups) and fear of crime (these high rates make the elderly more fearful of crime than other age groups). In the period 1973–75, the definition of the problem as one of higher crime rates for the elderly diminished somewhat, while the claim that the elderly were more likely than younger adults to be physically and economically injured by criminal attacks increased.

By the period 1976–78, the problem definition that was most often heard was that the elderly were more fearful of crime than others. The

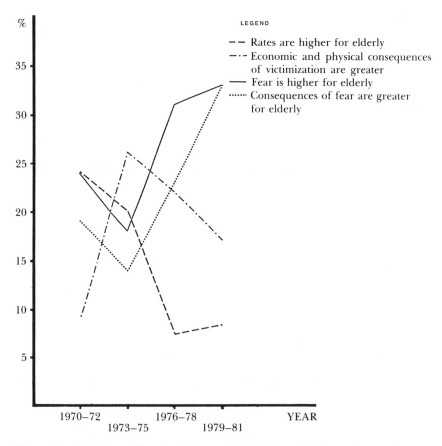

Figure 3. Problem Formulation and Reformulation about Crimes Against the Elderly

definition of fear as a problem was linked with its presumed consequences of being a "prisoner in one's own home." That definition of the
problem remained salient in the 1979–81 period as well. Clearly, between 1970–81, the formal agenda in Congress concerning crime and
the elderly was reformulated.

III. EMERGENCE ONTO THE POLICY AGENDA: A PROBLEM OF HIGH CRIME RATES

Issues emerge on the formal policy agenda in different ways. Cobb,
Ross, and Ross (1976) have proposed three models for understanding
different conditions under which this occurs. Their models are based on
whether critical actors are inside or outside government and on the
extent to which these actors attempt to engage the support of the general public as well as government bureaucrats: the outside initiative model,
the mobilization model, and the inside initiative model. A model of
agenda-setting developed recently by Cook (1981)—the convergent
voice model—more accurately portrays the emergence of the issue of
crimes against the elderly onto the policy agenda.

The convergent voice model describes issues that are independently
and similarly articulated by several different groups at the same time. In
the case of criminal victimization of the elderly, the 1971 White House
Conference on Aging, Hearings of the House Select Committee on
Aging, and the mass media all focused attention on the victimization
problems of the elderly in 1971. All seemed to have operated independently, and all converged on the same definition of the problem. The
issue was then legitimized through social science data, media attention,
discussion by high officials, and endorsement by appropriate interest
groups. In addition, what we call the issue climate was ripe for such a
problem to achieve public visibility; that is, the issue of criminals vic-
timizing senior citizens brought together in one package three themes
that were already very visible: crime, victims, and the elderly (Cook,
1981).

In this early process of the issue coming onto the policy agenda, the
"converging voices" initially identified the problem as one of higher
rates of victimization for older people. The news media, some academic
experts, and political spokesmen suggested or implied that the elderly
were more victimized than other groups in the population. For a variety
of reasons, some of which we speculate about below, many believed that
rates of victimization of the elderly were distinctively high, certainly
above those for other adults. This was seen as a particular problem in big
cities where, as most people know, violent crime is heavily overconcen-

trated. It was assumed that criminals there were particularly prone to victimize the vulnerable elderly. It also was widely asserted that this high rate of criminal victimization of the elderly was a special problem requiring a unique policy response, not simply a reflection of a general crime problem calling for a general solution. For example, according to Senator Harrison Williams:

> Elderly tenants in private and public housing in many of our big cities are the most vulnerable victims of theft, violence, rowdyism, and outright terrorism. . . . Many older persons lock themselves within their apartments night and day and dread every knock on the door. Do we need any more reason to act on an emergency basis? (U.S. Congress, 1972, p. 481)

How accurate were such claims about the elderly's crime problem? In this section, we shall see that most claims about rates were in fact misleading. Perceptions or assumptions about the nature of the crime problem facing the elderly were at variance with what we now know about their actual condition. How could this have happened? Issues get onto policy agendas based upon some type of definition of the problem or the public need. The specification can come from various sources—observations of reputed experts, investigative reports by the news media, testimonials by people who have been afflicted by the problem, compilations of case studies, and social science research.

In the case of criminal victimization of the elderly, the early definition of the problem was on the basis of newspaper accounts, testimonials of elderly victims, and social science research based upon samples consisting exclusively of elderly persons. The problem with using newspaper accounts as the basis for understanding social problems is one of selection bias. Newspaper journalists and their editors feature dramatic, eye-catching events with a prominence which depends upon whatever other events which may have occurred and are considered "bigger news."

The problem with using testimonials of elderly victims was that they were carefully chosen to testify because they were articulate and because they were terribly brutalized. They were not representative of all elderly victims. Since only elderly victims were chosen, one got no sense of whether the elderly were so differently victimized from other age groups that different policies should be developed to aid them.

The problem with social science research using samples just of elderly persons was that the data could only be used to generalize to them. When properly conducted such research *can* describe the rate at which elderly persons are victimized, the kinds of crimes they experience, and the manner in which they are victimized. However, most of these studies were haphazard or used very limited samples of older people, or they were limited to only a few neighborhoods, and even the higher-quality studies generally did not result in data which could be used to compare elderly victims to those of other ages. Thus, from such research, it was impossible to document that the elderly were the age group most vulnerable to crime, that the crimes that were committed against them were different from those committed against other groups, or that the process of their being victimized was different from that by which other groups were victimized.

In short, research using only elderly respondents, testimonials of elderly victims, and newspaper accounts cannot validly be used to discern the problem of crimes against the elderly for policy making purposes. Nonetheless it was, for no other data were available in the early 1970s. This condition changed in the mid-1970s. The Omnibus Crime Control and Safe Streets Act of 1968 established the Law Enforcement Assistance Administration (LEAA) within the United States Department of Justice. LEAA was charged with the responsibility of developing statistical information regarding crime and criminal justice in the United States. To develop statistical information about crime, LEAA established the National Criminal Justice Information and Statistical Service, now the Bureau of Justice Statistics (BJS). BJS began methodological planning in 1969 and field tests in 1970, to conduct a nationwide survey of households that would provide data on personal and household victimizations (Skogan, 1981).

Beginning in 1973, large-scale national victimization surveys have been conducted continuously for the Bureau of Justice Statistics by the U.S. Bureau of the Census, in person-to-person interviews in respondents' homes. In the survey about 136,000 persons are interviewed twice in a year. They are the residents who are 12 years and older of about 60,000 sample housing units. Each month, residents of a separate probability sample of 10,000 households (about 22,000 individuals) are interviewed. The survey has a panel design: these respondents are reinterviewed every six months for up to three years. After six interviews the monthly sample is "rotated out" and a new independent probability sample of 10,000 households replaces them.

For each crime incident that occurred, the respondent is asked questions about the events surrounding the victimization—when, where, and how it occurred; the characteristics of the offender, and threats and/or weapons used in the incident. Victims are asked about the physical consequences of each crime incident—what injuries were suffered, whether medical attention was needed, whether medical insurance covered the treatment. Finally, victims are asked about the economic impact of victimization—the amount of cash taken; the value of the property taken; how much, if anything, was recovered by the police or through insurance. In addition to examining the absolute amount lost, the data allow

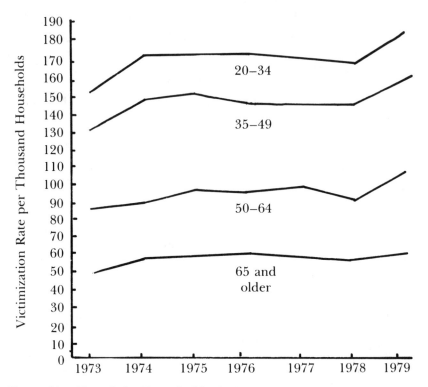

Figure 4A.   Trends in Household Theft By Age of Head of Household

one to compare that figure to family income. Information is collected from both victims and non-victims on such subjects as education, migration, labor force status, occupation, and marital status. In this section and the sections to follow, we will report on our analyses of these data to assess the accuracy of the various formulations in which the problem of the elderly with crime was cast.

Crimes may be categorized as household crimes (burglary, simple theft without illegal entry into a house—also known as household theft, and motor vehicle theft) and personal crimes (rape, robbery, assault, and personal theft—i.e., usually purse-snatching and pocket picking). These incidents vary greatly in frequency. The non-violent property crimes of burglary and household theft occur much more often than the violent crimes of rape, robbery, and assault. For example, together, burglary and household theft constituted 89 percent of all the incidents covered in the victim survey in 1976 and 1977.

Looking at this point another way, 15.7 percent of those interviewed in 1976 and 1977 reported something in their household was stolen in

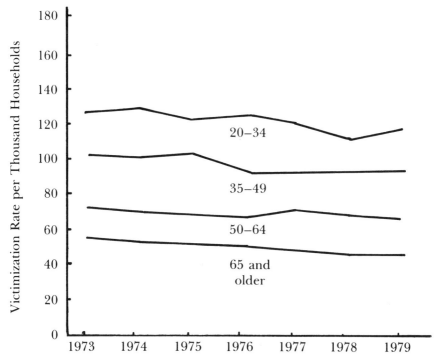

Figure 4B. Trends in Burglary By Age of Head of Household

Source: Criminal Victimization in the United States, yearly

the last 6 months and 3.95 percent of respondents reported that their household was burglarized, while far fewer reported a personal victimization. Only 1.25 percent reported an assault, .30 percent reported a robbery, .07 percent reported a rape, and .10 percent reported a personal theft such as pocket picking or purse snatching. Thus, it should be clear that while crime may be a frequent topic of conversation, it is a relatively low frequency event. The fact that it is such a low frequency event explains why we need extremely large numbers of respondents to locate a large enough sample of persons who have been criminally victimized, especially if we want to categorize victims by age groups.

Since it could be argued that any one year might represent an aberration, we present in the figures to follow breakdowns in crime rates by crime and by age categories for each year between 1973 and 1979. Figures 4A and 4B show trends in household theft and burglary for households headed by persons in different age brackets, from 1973 until 1979. Losses most frequently hit households headed by younger adults. In each year, victimization declined with age. With regard to burglary, people of various age cohorts also retained the same relative position over time. There were few changes in rates of victimization between 1973 and 1979 for burglary, and households headed by those over 65 were the least likely to be involved.

In regard to theft, in 1974 and again in 1979, household rates generally rose, but least of all for persons 65 and over. Victimization rates for motor vehicle theft, the other household crime discussed in the National Crime survey, are not shown in the figures due to space limitations, but they displayed the same relationship to age as well as the same stability over time.

Figures 5A and B and Figure 6 show the relationship between age and crimes against persons for every year between 1973 and 1979. Figure 5A shows teenagers and young adults to be most likely to be victims of assault. The likelihood of assault then declines with age. Victimization by

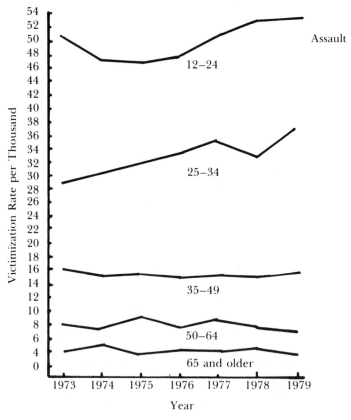

Figure 5A. Trends in Assault by Age, 1973–79

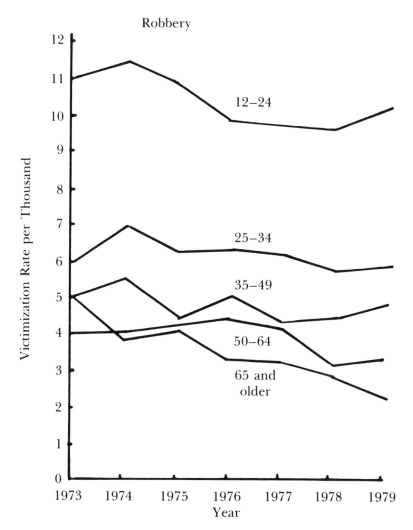

Figure 5B.   Trends in Robbery by Age, 1973–79

assault drops off very sharply in middle age. For those in their teens, twenties, and early thirties, the frequency of assault has been on the upswing. However rates of assault against the 35 and older set have been low and stable since 1973.

Robbery is theft or an attempted theft during which the victim is confronted by an offender who uses or threatens to use violence. Because force or threat of force is involved and because robbery is usually committed by persons who are strangers to the victim, it is a particularly

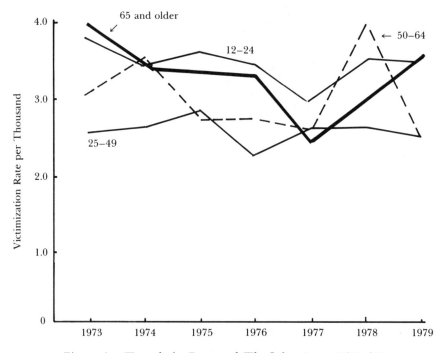

Figure 6.   Trends in Personal Theft by Age, 1973–79

Source: Criminal Victimization in the United States, yearly

fear-provoking crime (Skogan and Maxfield, 1981). Figure 5B documents that the proportion of persons indicating they have been robbed
in the NCS declines with age. Respondents in the youngest age categories were most likely to experience a robbery, while those in the oldest
category were least likely to be robbed in all years except 1973. There
appeared to be a small upturn in national robbery rates in 1979, but
rates for adults 65 and older continued to decline.

Purse snatching and pocket-picking together make up a crime category we have dubbed "personal theft." Both involve limited victim-offender contact, and are defined in part by the absence of the use of
force. Since in the United States few men carry purses or pocketbooks,
the pool of persons who are at risk for purse snatching is composed
almost exclusively of women. On the other hand, a significant number of
women report having their pocketbooks "picked," so in that case they
are numbered along with males as potential victims.

Women are most likely to report doing things which would minimize
their chances of victimization by these crimes, by exercising a great deal
of caution in their everyday activities (Skogan and Maxfield, 1981).

However, since many of those criminals engaged in purse snatching in particular prey opportunistically on passers-by, it is a crime which cannot be avoided completely through the exercise of common sense by potential victims. Elderly women, because of both their age and sex, are thought to be among those least capable of offering resistance to purse snatchers and nimble-fingered "pickers," and thus may be especially vulnerable to those crimes.

Figure 6 reports for each year between 1973 and 1979 the rate at which people in several age categories experienced a purse snatching or pocket picking. For the first time, the story about what happens to the elderly is not simple. In 1973, the oldest along with the youngest respondents experienced the highest rates of victimization, while by 1977 those 65 and older had dropped *below* everyone else. Then, in 1979 rates for the elderly jumped again to the highest position, a place shared again with the youngest respondents. Of course, low overall rates for such thefts result in instability in the data. This makes it difficult to draw any clear conclusions about the trends in personal theft from older people. The best summary of the data is that, overall, the elderly are essentially the same as other adults in regard to their experiences with purse snatching and pocket picking.

In summary, the prevalence of victimization turned out to be much lower among the elderly than for others in almost every category of crime. This finding was the same for each year between 1973 and 1979. Although it is not reported here, we also broke the data down into five-year age intervals. The story continued to be the same: the frequency of experiences with crime decreased with the passing years, and those under 25 were by far the most likely to report being victimized. Only in one category—personal theft—was this general decline tempered in any significant way. For purse snatchings and pickpocketing, older adults report levels of victimization which—although still usually below that threatening high-risk younger persons—put them on a par with other mature adults.

Thus, social science data alone would not confirm the validity of positioning the criminal victimization of the elderly issue on the formal governmental policy agenda as a problem of rates of crime being higher for them than for other groups. However, it must be remembered that it was during the years 1970–72 when these claims were most frequently made and it was not until 1973 that the Department of Justice implemented the National Crime Survey (NCS) which could be used to test such claims. Although news of the NCS results began to slip out in 1974, the first published report of the 1973 results did not appear until 1975 and the final report did not appear until 1976. These data showed the elderly to be the group least likely to experience crime. The decline in the number of claims in the *Congressional Record* that the problem was one of rates parallels the years in which the NCS data were made available. As can be seen in Figure 3, the number of claims about rates being the primary problem dropped in 1973–75 and dropped even more dramatically in 1976–78. The drop in these claims was clearly justified by the data.

IV. DEFINING THE PROBLEM AS SEVERE ECONOMIC AND PHYSICAL CONSEQUENCES

As the definition of the problem as one of rates decreased in frequency, the claim emerged that the elderly's problem was that they suffered more severe physical and economic consequences than younger age groups. According to Clarence Kelly, the director of the FBI, in testimony before the U.S. House of Representatives Select Committee on Aging, "Physically, no group of citizens suffers more than our nation's elderly do at the hands of America's criminal predators" (April 12, 1976, p. 24). Later, he went further and stated, "Psychologically, financially, and physically, no group of citizens suffers more painful losses than our nation's elderly do at the hands of America's criminal predators."

Such claims were also made by journalists and political actors. Very rarely were systematic data reported to validate the claims. Individual case histories of victims provided the primary source of evidence, all of which featured the most heinous crimes and the most serious consequences. The frequency of such extreme consequences was not probed in the reports, and graphic detail prevailed over any sense of what was typical.

A second argument about crime and the elderly was theoretical, based on untested assumptions. If the elderly are poorer, frailer and less resilient than others—as demographic statistics and popular stereotypes suggest—then it seems to follow that, when victimized, the elderly suffer more than younger victims. This chain of reasoning depends on several assumptions whose validity has not been demonstrated. One assumption is that criminals use force to the same extent with elderly as younger victims. However, criminals could just as easily use less force with elderly victims, and it is not difficult to imagine why. They may think that less force is needed since less resistance will be offered; alternatively, criminals may fear stiffer legal penalties if they use force against senior citizens. Of course, if they *do* use less force, it may mean less severe consequences for them.

A second assumption was that criminals who rob the elderly are as systematic in "cleaning them out" as they are with younger victims.

Should this assumption be wrong, then it is also possible that the financial consequences of crime may be less for the elderly than others. In fact we have shown elsewhere that the modal perpetrator of predatory crimes against the elderly is an inexperienced juvenile acting alone who snatches a purse (Antunes et al., 1977). It is not an adult professional who knows how "to clean out the mark" or a gang whose members can physically detain victims and systematically rob them of all their possessions, who typically prey on the elderly.

A third assumption was the elderly are frailer, poorer, and more psychologically brittle in ways that affect the consequences of crime. But frailty, poverty, and psychic withdrawal increase with age even among the elderly, so those with these conditions in their most chronic form are likely to be the "old-old," the least numerous subpopulation within the elderly. Since such persons are likely to be home-bound because of their condition, they are least likely to be exposed to crime on the street and most likely to be at home to deter burglars. Those among the elderly whose condition might make them most vulnerable to severe consequences may be the persons least likely to encounter crime and to show up in crime statistics. The enhanced frailty, poverty, and psychic withdrawal and depression of the elderly need not inevitably lead to more severe consequences for them.

In the analyses to follow, we examine data from the National Crime Surveys for 1973 to 1977. We combine the data for all these years to aggregate enough crime incidents to break them down by age, type of crime, type of consequences, etc. There is a great deal of stability in crime rates by year for each age group (seen in Figures 4–6), and these data should present no problems of bias in interpretations.

Financial Consequences

Monetary loss can be incurred from the household crimes of burglary or simple theft (i.e., household larceny). It can also result from the personal crimes of robbery and purse-snatching and pocketpicking.

Figure 7 shows the median amount taken by burglars from homes with household heads of different ages. The data are based on the amount of cash reported stolen and the estimated value of goods removed. They are for "successful" crimes only—those in which something of value actually was stolen. Because there were a few very large losses, medians are presented here.

Figure 7 suggests the relationship between age and the value of goods burglarized is curvilinear. Loss increases from age 25 to 49, but decreases thereafter. There is no sign of greater absolute loss by the elderly. Age is related in much the same way to the median amount taken

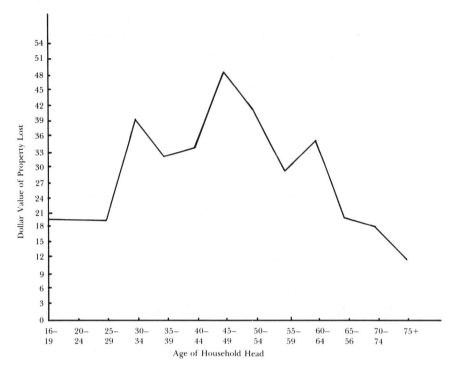

Figure 7. Median Value of Property Loss for Burglary for Households with a Head of 16 and over, 1973–77

in household thefts (not shown), which constitute about two-thirds of the property crimes against senior citizens. The major difference between burglary and household theft occurs for households with heads under 20 years of age, a very small group. They have among the lowest losses from burglary but the highest from simple theft. After age 30 the burglary and theft data are similar, showing that dollar losses are lower for households with elderly heads than for households with heads between 30 and 60.

However, it is important to note that households with elderly heads also tend to have lower family incomes. Thus, in 1976 and 1977 the reported median income of burglarized families with a head between 20 and 24 was $6,272; while for families with a head between 45 and 49 it was $13,611; and for families with a head between 65 and 69 it was $6,593. Since the ultimate impact of dollar losses depends in part on one's income, it is useful to express the amount lost in crime relative to total family income.

One simple way to do this is by expressing net dollar losses as a percentage of estimated monthly income. Net dollar loss is defined as the sum of the dollar value of goods taken and the property damage incurred during a crime minus the value of the goods recovered and insurance reimbursements for property loss and physical damage to the premises. NCS income measures cover the previous year. We divided these estimates by 12 to yield an average monthly income estimate. This form of measurement does not deal with the value of non-market goods and services received by families, and for our purposes we assume here that any age biases in income reporting are constant.

Figure 8 illustrates how age is related to net loss from burglaries expressed as a percentage of household income. The relationship is almost identical for household thefts (not shown). In each case, the highest relative losses are found in households with younger heads, and the level of loss falls preciptiously until about age 25. After age 25, income-adjusted losses rise with age but only to a small degree. This rise is strongest with household theft, where the increase is from a net loss of about 1% of monthly income at age 30 (the lowest point) to just over 2% by age 75 and above (the highest point).

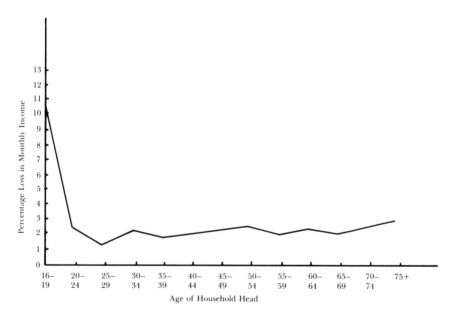

Figure 8. Net Loss from Burglary as a Percentage of Household Monthly Income, 1973–77

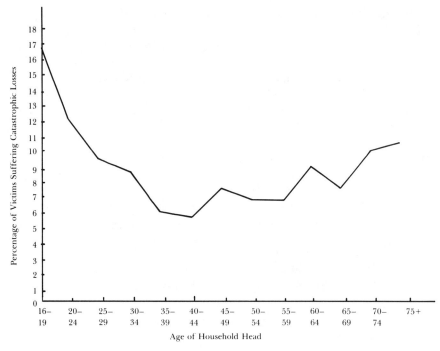

Figure 9. Percentage of Burglary Victims Who Suffered Catastrophic Losses in 1973–77

Another way of relating dollar losses to household income is to consider only "catastrophic" losses, defined here as losses totaling at least one month's income. We ask: Are net losses of this magnitude more common among elderly victims than others? Figure 9 provides the answer for burglary. The victims most prone to catastrophic losses are in households with younger heads (and lower incomes). However, victimized households with elderly heads are somewhat more likely to suffer catastrophic losses than households headed by other mature adults. Thus, about 9% of victims 60 and older suffer catastrophic losses compared to between 6.5% and 7% for households with heads between 35 and 59. The pattern is comparable for larceny where about 0.75% of the victims aged 30–59 suffer catastrophic losses and about 1.5% of the victims 60 and over do. It seems, then, that the net losses suffered by elderly victims are somewhat more likely to be catastrophic when compared to the losses of adults 30–59. But they are noticeably less likely to be catastrophic when compared to the losses incurred in households with heads younger than 30, and especially those with teenage heads.

Personal Crimes

Unlike household crimes, in which about 80% result in something being stolen, the majority of personal crimes do not involve the loss of objects of financial value. Indeed, most of the predatory crimes that survey respondents mentioned were attempted but not completed. The ratio of successful to attempted personal thefts is systematically related to age, with crimes against older people being more successful. When victims are under 40, less than 20% of the personal crimes involve loss, but by age 60 it is just under 40% and by 75 and above it is just over 50%. The criminal's success in gaining money or valuables from older victims reflects a lower level of resistance to criminals by senior citizens (Block, 1983). It seems unlikely, given the profile of typical offenders against older adults, that the higher ratio of success is due to more professional criminals. The typical offender against the elderly is a young black teen-ager acting alone who does not have a weapon.

Because not all attempts at personal theft are successful, we shall restrict the analysis of the median number of dollars lost to those incidents where a loss occurred. The unbroken line in Figure 10 shows that the median amount lost increases with age until about 40–49, and decreases thereafter. This is similar to the case with burglary (see Figure 7) where losses were also lower for persons 60 and over when compared to other mature adults.

The relationship changes once we compute net loss as a percentage of monthly income. Figure 10 shows that the relative loss is approximately constant from age 20 to 69, implying that persons between 60 and 69 are much like younger victims of mature age. But after age 70 loss relative to income increases. This is due to a sharp decrease in income of the 70+ age group.

Summarizing the financial consequences, households with elderly heads lose less from burglaries and simple thefts than do households with younger heads when we consider only absolute dollar losses. When we compute losses as a percent of monthly income, households with an elderly head tend to lose about the same or slightly more than other adults over age 20. With respect to personal crimes, again the elderly lose less absolutely. Relatively, however, the loss is higher for older persons over 70.

Physical Consequences

The physical consequences of victimization can be described in terms of a sequence of contingencies: Is the victim attacked? Does the attack

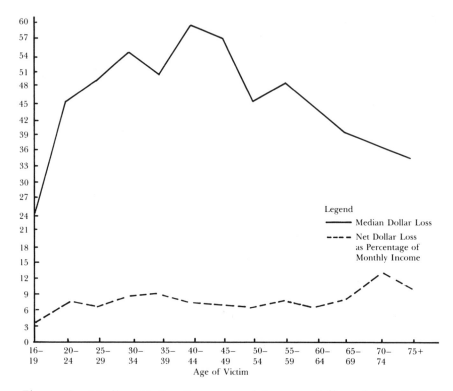

Figure 10. Median Dollar Losses, and Income Adjusted Net Dollar Losses, from All Incidents of Personal Crime with Loss, 1973–77

lead to injuries? Is the injury serious enough to warrant medical attention? Is the attention protracted and costly? We shall deal with each of these issues in the same sequence, progressively narrowing the sample base as we go along. That is, any analysis of injuries is restricted to victims who have been attacked; an analysis of whether medical attention is called for is restricted to victims who have been attacked and injured, etc. Since the number of persons who are injured by criminals and require hospitalization is quite small, the data we present are merged from 1973 through 1977.

The unbroken line in Figure 11 shows the percentage of victims 12 years and over in the nation who were physically attacked while a crime of physical contact was committed (note that we are *only* focusing on victims here). The trend declines rapidly for victims age 12 to 34, then stays fairly constant until age 60–64. Victims age 60–64 are less likely to be attacked than younger victims—in fact, they are the least likely age group to be attacked. Those aged 65–69 and 70–74 are about as likely to

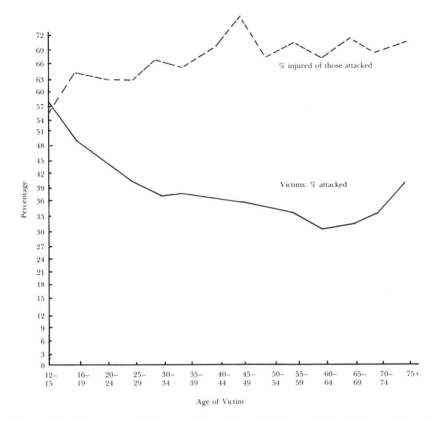

Figure 11. Patterns of Personal Attack and Injury, 1973–77 Age 12 and Over

be attacked as victims 30–59, whereas those aged 75 and over are attacked more frequently—at the rate at which 25–29 year olds are attacked.

Are these attacks more likely to result in injuries to the elderly then to others? The broken line in Figure 11 indicates the percentage of those attacked who reported injuries. It does not appear that older adults are more likely to be injured when they are attacked. This raises the issue of how much force criminals use against the elderly.

Are the injuries to senior citizens more likely to result in a need for medical care? The answer is clearly no. The results show that the likelihood of medical care increases from age 12 to about age 30, stabilizes at 45% by age 30, but drops again at age 60. The implication is that the crimes committed against the elderly typically involve less force when contact occurs.

This interpretation would be neatly corroborated if age were also related to the percentage of injuries serious enough to require medical care for which financial charges were made. But while the percentage of such injuries is approximately constant at 54% for victims between ages 20 and 59, it is somewhat lower for both the 60–64 and 75+ groups (50% and 42% respectively) but is higher for victims aged between 65 and 74 (about 60%). Similar instability is apparent in examining the medical dollar costs per injury. This instability probably arises because the base sample of reports is low. Indeed, when we collapse the age categories beyond 60 to create a single group of persons over 60 and consider the percentage needing medical care at some expense, we find that the data for seniors are like those for other adults. But the medical dollar costs tend to be highest in the group of persons over 60, both before and after they are expressed as a percentage of reported monthly income. Injuries to the elderly cost more, but we cannot be sure to what extent these expenses were out-of-pocket or met by insurance, Medicare, or Medicaid.

In summary, the overall physical consequences of victimizations are no more severe for elderly adults than for younger adults. The elderly are not the most likely to be attacked, and when attacked they are not more likely to suffer injuries. Moreover, their injuries are no more likely to require medical care than those of younger adults. However, their injuries are slightly more likely to result in medical care for which charges are made and the median dollar costs of medical care are slightly higher than for younger adults. Nonetheless, we cannot be sure to what extent these latter differences are due to the fact that they are more likely to be covered by some form of government supported insurance (Medicare and Medicaid) than younger adults.

Based on the evidence presented above, it is clear that the re-definition of the crime problem facing the elderly as one of *more severe physical and economic consequences* also does not correspond with our best data on their actual problems. Claims about this definition of the problem were most frequent from 1973–75. During the 1976–78 period they declined. This was the period when NCS findings were gaining widespread attention. As with rates, the drop in volume in these claims was justified by the data.

V. DEFINING THE PROBLEM AS FEAR AND CONSEQUENCES OF FEAR

From the time when the crime and the elderly issue first emerged onto the policy agenda, claims about the problem of fear of crime were numerous. During the 1976–78 and 1979–81 periods when other claims about the elderly's special crime problems diminished, these increased. If one re-examines Figure 3, it is clear that within the U.S. Congress fear of crime and consequences of fear for the elderly were the major concerns within this issue area. How accurate were these concerns?

Researchers who have examined both victimization rates and the concerns expressed by older persons agree that high levels of fear are more frequently reported and seem to have a great effect upon senior citizens (Clemente and Kleinman, 1976; Sundeen and Mathieu, 1976). A national survey conducted in 1974 asked people to rate the seriousness of a number of specific problems in their own lives. More elderly persons (23%) ranked "fear of crime" as a very serious problem than ranked poor health (21%), "not having enough money to live on" (15%), loneliness (12%), and "not enough medical care" (10%) as very serious problems (National Council on the Aging, 1975, p. 31). Interestingly, for those *under* 65 fear of crime was also among the two most highly-ranked personal problems, standing just below "not enough money." Overall, 23 per cent of the elderly and 15 per cent of those under 65 indicated that fear of crime was a "very serious" problem for them personally. Between 1974 and 1981 these percentages rose very slightly for the elderly (to 25 per cent), and somewhat more for those under 65 (to 20 per cent) (National Council on Aging, 1981).

These data are frequently cited to support the contention that the fear of crime is a problem which disproportionately affects the elderly (for example, Curtis, 1978), although the differences—while statistically significant—are not overwhelming. These observations led Cook and Cook (1976, p. 643) in an early article to conclude that "the major policy problem associated with the elderly and crime is probably not crime *per se*. Rather, the problem is related to the elderly person's fear of crime and the restrictions to daily mobility that this fear may impose." They concluded that "the policy response to victimization of the elderly should be targeted to alleviating fear" (p. 644). The National Council on Aging (1975) survey also indicated this was the popular perception of the issue. In that survey respondents *under* 65 were asked what they *thought* were the serious problems facing the elderly; 50 per cent indicated "fear of crime" was a very serious problem in old age. By 1981 this figure had risen to 74 per cent (National Council on Aging, 1981).

Previous research has not been specific about the content of the elderly's fear of crime. Are the elderly fearful of every sort of crime or only of selected offenses? Are they fearful under all conditions and in every aspect of their daily lives or are they fearful only under selected circumstances and at specific times? Does fear mean that the elderly see a great deal of crime around them or do they believe that whatever crime there is is likely to involve them—that they are special targets? Do the elderly think that the things they do to protect themselves from crime actually work or do they believe that they are completely vulnerable? These and other questions remained unanswered.

There have been a number of efforts by researchers to clarify the meaning of the concept of "fear of crime" (DuBow, 1979). While there is no clear consensus on what "fear of crime" means or how it is best measured, there are three dimensions along which many specific fear-related perceptions can be described: concern, personal risk, and threat of crime. By societal *concern* about crime we mean the assessment that crime is a serious problem for a community. This distinction follows that made by Furstenberg (1971). Concern is a judgment about the seriousness of events and conditions in one's environment. The second common meaning of fear (Furstenberg's other meaning) is the perception that one is likely to fall victim. Since the first surveys sponsored by the Crime Commission (Biderman, et al., 1967), researchers have been asking people to rate their chances of being victimized. For example, respondents may be asked to rate "how likely" they are to be attacked or burglarized, on a scale ranging from "not very likely" to "very likely." Those ratings of *risk* have been used as measures of fear. The concept of *threat* of crime lies at the nexus between concern and personal risk. People feel threatened when they believe that something *could* happen to them, even though for a variety of reasons—including that they may have done a great deal to protect themselves—they may not necessarily feel that it is likely to happen to them. Threat is measured by questions that ask "How safe *would* you feel *if* you were out alone?" or "How would you feel if you were approached by a stranger on the street or heard footsteps in the night?"

The concepts of concern, personal risk, and threat cover most of the assertions which have been made about the distinctive fear problems facing the elderly. It also is often claimed the urban elderly are overconcentrated in bad neighborhoods and are concerned about conditions and crime in their neighborhood. And it is claimed that the elderly feel hopelessly vulnerable to crime, which can be evaluated using measures of self-diagnosed risk. Finally, it is claimed the elderly are "prisoners of fear," traumatized by the thought of venturing out because of the risks they would face. This assertion can be tested using data on perceived threat of crime.

For each claim there are two research questions: are the elderly fearful, and are they distinctively more fearful? In this section, we define the elderly population as persons sixty years of age and older. A close examination of age-specific levels of fear indicates this is an optimal cutting point, and it is one which defines a pool of elderly respondents large enough to examine accurately in some of the smaller surveys we use. To examine fear of crime and its behavioral implications we turn to a number of surveys of large American cities which have employed identical or similar questions about those topics. Being big cities, they are all places where problems of fear and victimization are significant. By examining surveys which have been conducted in a number of cities, we hope for some generality in our conclusions. No single national survey duplicates the data we needed; rather, we rely upon multiple replications across time, cities, and surveys to gain the same end.

Concern About Crime

A number of claims have been advanced that the elderly are more concerned than other age groups about the level of crime and disorder around them. The best data for evaluating these claims may be the reports of elderly persons themselves. We have examined four sample surveys in which residents were asked to rate a variety of crime conditions in their own neighborhoods, conducted in Chicago, San Francisco, Philadelphia, and Hartford, Connecticut. By examining responses by age groups we can assess the possibility that, while the elderly may report adverse local conditions, other city dwellers also face the same problems.

Our first comparison is the assessments of crime-related neighborhood deterioration and deviant behavior. These include ratings of the extent to which respondents in these four surveys were concerned about youthful harrassment, unseemly public behavior, and building abandonment. In each case they were asked "how much of a problem" each of these conditions was in their neighborhood. Respondents could indicate each was a "big problem," "some problem," or "almost no problem." The ratings of these conditions are presented in Table 1.

Few of the petty "incivilities" which plague many urban residents seemed to be problems significantly related to age. In Table 1 the incidence of concern about teenagers, vandalism, "people using illegal drugs," "drunken men on the street," and "prostitutes on the street" is summarized. The only significant differences fall to the disadvantage of *younger*, not older, residents. These forms of deviant public behavior are violations of what James Q. Wilson (1975) called "standards of right and seemly conduct." He argued that they are read by "proper" citizens as signs that the social order is in disarray. While over one-fifth of those interviewed in these cities seemed bothered by these activities, neither youths, drugs, prostitution, nor public intoxication seemed to particularly plague the neighborhoods of elderly residents. If anything, those *under* sixty are more likely to report that they represent major neighborhood problems. This negative relation between old age and perceptions of neighborhood deterioration obtains even when we control for race.

Table 1. Perceptions of Neighborhood Deterioration as a
Neighborhood Problem, by Age

Problem Area	Age Group	Percent Think a "Big Problem" in Their Neighborhood			
		Hartford (1975)	Philadelphia (1977)	Chicago (1977)	San Francisco (1977)
Teenagers Hang-	under 60	32*	22	22	12
ing Around	over 60	21	20	30	12
Vandalism	under 60		20	20	10
	over 60		21	21	11
Drug Use	under 60	29*	24	25	15
	over 60	16	14	27	6
Drunks on Street	under 60	22*			
	over 60	10			
Prostitution	under 60	17*			
	over 60	9			
Abandoned	under 60		14	12	3
Buildings	over 60		8	10	1
(Number of cases)		(537)	(479)	(417)	(447)

Note: Asterisks indicate differences significant at the P < .05 level. Blank entry indicates no comparable
question. The number of cases varies slightly from question to question; averages are given here.

These are neither white elderly nor black elderly problems in these
cities. Blacks (and another population subgroup, women) were more
likely than their counterparts to sense neighborhood decline, but within
racial groups and sexes the elderly still were less likely to report that
these conditions constituted a "big problem."

When we turn to concern about serious crimes, some distinctive concerns of the elderly begin to emerge. In these four cities survey respondents were asked to rate "how much of a problem" three types of
crimes presented in their neighborhood. The crimes were burglary, robbery, and assault. Each of these crimes involves the threat of serious
injury or financial loss. Each is relatively frequent and potentially could
strike any urban dweller. Neighborhoods in which they are rated big
problems are fearsome places indeed. The data on these ratings are
summarized in Table 2.

Overall, burglary was the crime most frequently rated a "big problem." For that crime the only significant age difference in ratings was in
Hartford, where those under sixty were more likely to be concerned.
However, in all three cities surveyed in 1977, "people being robbed or
having their purses or wallets taken on the street" was more frequently
cited as a big problem by the elderly. Those differences were quite
substantial, and point to concern about neighborhood "mugging" as a
special problem for the elderly. The only remaining significant age dif-

Table 2.   Perceptions of Major Crimes as Neighborhood Problems, by Age

		Percent Think a "Big Problem" in Their Neighborhood			
Major Crime Problem	Age Group	Hartford (1975)	Philadelphia (1977)	Chicago (1977)	San Francisco (1977)
Burglary	under 60	32*	16	19	20
	over 60	16	18	23	20
Robbery	under 60	20	12	23	15
	over 60	20	24*	39*	27*
Assault	under 60	16	6	9	7
	over 60	14	8	13	19*
(Number of cases)		(537)	(433)	(401)	(452)

Note: Asterisks indicate differences significant at the $P < .05$ level. The number of cases varies slightly from question-to-question; averages are given here.

ference reported in Table 2 was for assault, but that difference appeared for only one city.

Perceived Risk of Victimization

The concerns about crime analyzed above were ratings of neighborhood problems. Those ratings reflected assessments about "what's going on" there. Assessments of risk, on the other hand, are perceptions of the likelihood of things "happening to me." Perceptions of risk often are recommended as measures of "fear" (Yin, 1980; Biderman, et al., 1967), for they reflect the perceived probability of personal involvement in victimization situations. If they are realistic reflections of patterns of victimization, they generally should be lower than risks perceived by younger persons; on the other hand, if they are a source of distinctive concern among the elderly and an indicator that senior citizens are plagued by fear, they should be higher.

In this analysis we report upon five city surveys which gathered people's assessments to their risk of victimization, the four utilized above and a survey conducted in Kansas City, Missouri. In each study respondents were asked to estimate how likely it was selected crimes would involve them. In Kansas City, respondents were asked to rate their chances of victimization on a six-point scale ranging from "very improbable" to "very probable." In the other cities they were asked to choose a position on a zero-to-ten scale which was not labeled at each point; respondents were told to "let the zero stand for no possibility at all of something happening," and the ten for it being "extremely likely that something could happen" and to choose a value in that range.

Table 3. Estimates of Risk of Victimization For Major Crimes, by Age

		Average "Risk Estimate" for Major Crime Types				
Type of Crime	Age Group	Hartford (1973)	Philadelphia (1977)	Chicago (1977)	San Francisco (1977)	Kansas City (1973)
Burglary	under 60	4.9*	3.6	4.1	3.9	4.8
	over 60	3.7	3.8	4.2	3.4	4.6
Robbery	under 60	3.7	3.2	4.2	3.2	4.4
	over 60	4.0	3.0	4.4	3.8	4.5
Assault	under 60	3.2	2.5	3.2	2.6	4.1
	over 60	3.7	3.0	3.6	3.7*	4.4*
Purse or Wallet	under 60	4.2				
Snatched	over 60	4.9*				
(Number of cases)		(537)	(453)	(428)	(430)	(1160)

Note: Asterisks indicate differences significant at the P < .05 level. In Kansas City, respondents were asked to rate their risks on a one ("very improbable") to six ("very probable") scale. All others employed a one–to–ten scale *without* labels for each scale position. The number of cases varies from question to question; averages are given here.

Source: Computed by the authors from original data.

Table 3 presents the distribution of these estimates of risk of victimization, by age, for each of the five cities. On the whole, residents of these cities gave the highest ratings of risk to burglary. This is congruent with the frequency of burglary in contrast to personal crimes. However, burglary is numerically almost four times as frequent as any of these personal crimes, and this great difference in rates of victimization is not accurately reflected in these assessments of risk. In each of these cities, residents of all ages overestimate the relative risk of violent crime.

There are few significant differences between those under sixty and those sixty and older apparent in Table 3. Only one of those differences is replicated in more than one city. Those under sixty in Hartford were more likely to perceive high risks of burglary, and the elderly in the same city were more fearful (by this measure) of purse snatching. The most consistent relationship between age and estimates of risk of victimization involved the crime of assault. In the three cities surveyed in 1977 the wording of this crime question referred to attacks by a stranger in a public place in the respondent's neighborhood, while in the other cities it was somewhat less explicit. In all five communities older persons reported higher-than-average risk estimates for assault. However, only two of those differences were significant.

While these risk estimates point to the conclusion that the elderly perceive somewhat higher levels of risk for street crimes, the differences reported in Table 3 are not large and not often significant. Note also the elderly do not see themselves as particularly likely to fall victim to the one major crime which they consistently rated a "big neighborhood problem." Perhaps the most interesting point to be made of Table 3 is that these estimates of risk all are relatively low, in absolute terms. For assault and robbery they average near the lower third on the "zero-to-ten" scale that was proffered. Despite widespread discussion of rising crime rates during the decade that preceded these surveys, on the "no probability" to "extremely likely" response dimension that was employed in the questions, both of these groups of adults appeared to be quite similar and to consider themselves relatively safe.

Threat of Crime

In addition to concern and perceptions of risk, there is a third aspect of fear of crime which may distinguish the elderly from other adults—the threat of crime. By threat we meant the *potential* for harm which people feel crime holds for them. The concept of threat is distinct from those of risk and concern. Because people may adopt tactics to reduce their vulnerability to victimization, the threat of crime may not be reflected in assessments of the actual probability that something will happen. Because many people may believe that they are capable of dealing with crime in their neighborhood or that it will not strike them personally, the threat of crime also is distinct from concern about the issue as a community problem. Threat, on the other hand, is a perception that something untoward could happen when (and if) one is exposed to risk of victimization. Data from numerous surveys indicate that the threat of crime is felt most strongly by the elderly, and in comparison to measures of risk or concern, questions measuring threat clearly differentiate senior citizens from the remainder of the adult population.

There are, of course, a number of potential risks that people face. Available survey data dwell upon one threat, personal violence. Numerous surveys have inquired about how afraid or unsafe people would feel *if* they were exposed to personal attacks. Virtually all of them employ one of two questions to measure that threat. They are:

How safe do you feel or would you feel out alone in your neighborhood at night?

and

Is there any area right around here—that is, within one mile—where you would be afraid to walk alone at night?

The respondents in these surveys are asked to choose among four answers in reply to the first question, alternatives that range from "very safe" to "very unsafe." The latter question usually demands a "yes-or-no" response. The first item has been included in all of the city victimization surveys conducted by the Census Bureau and in various surveys by other organizations. The latter question is employed by the National Opinion Research Center (NORC) in their yearly national survey, and by the Gallup Poll organization.

This chapter employs city and national surveys which have used these items in order to assess the extent to which the threat of personal violence differentiates the elderly from the remainder of the adult population. The national survey data was collected by NORC over the period 1973–1978, which bridges the time-span of all of the surveys analyzed in this volume. Here we will also report the results of five Census Bureau surveys conducted in 1973 in the nation's largest cities. Another was fielded in 1974 in Portland, Oregon. Finally, we combine the results of parallel surveys conducted in Chicago, San Francisco, and Philadelphia in 1977, which were reported upon earlier in this chapter. Because of the large size of these surveys we will refine the age categories used to examine the distribution of the threat to five-year age intervals. The relationship between age and the threat of crime in all of these surveys is summarized in Figure 12.

These surveys all point to the same general conclusion: the perceived threat of personal attack in a public place is relatively low among younger respondents, then climbs in frequency. In each survey there is a tendency for those under fifty or so to report similar perceptions of threat and for threat to then grow more rapidly with age.

This expression of fear is very much confined to *nighttime* risks. When contrasted with the daylight hours, it is clear that for most people the threat of crime rises as the sun goes down. For example, in the Census Bureau's surveys in five cities about 48 percent of all residents indicated some degree of concern about going out alone after dark, but only 11 percent had any hesitation about their daytime safety. The elderly were more likely than others to express uneasiness about their safety during the day (17 percent as opposed to 9 percent under sixty years of age.) In the survey in Hartford, 28 percent of those over sixty expressed at least some worry about "street crime" during the day, but that figure stood at more than 60 percent after dark. A Texas survey using similar measures also indicates that this fear is confined to on-street as opposed to at-home risks. In that study (a statewide mail questionnaire with a reasonable rate of return) older people were more likely than others to indicate fear of walking alone, but were *less* likely to express fear about being home alone at night (Jeffords, 1980).

The relationships between age and perceptions of threat documented in Figure 12 are all extremely strong, especially in contrast to the sometimes significant but rarely impressive differences between the elderly

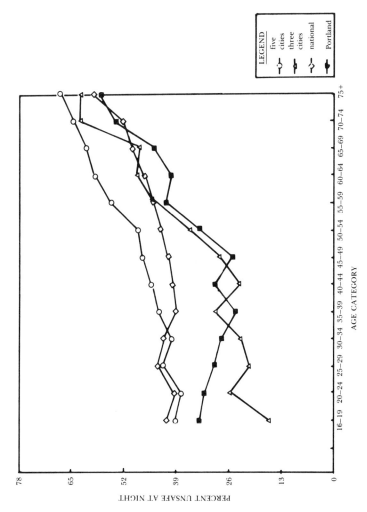

Figure 12. Age and Threat of Crime

319

and others on measures of concern and risk. The age-threat linkage has been replicated across cities, across most of the 1970s, and across nations as well (Sparks, et al., 1977). It is an extremely robust correspondence, suggesting that it reflects powerful social and psychological forces which are not idiosyncratic to individual jurisdictions or particular events.

Are the Elderly More Fearful?

There have been numerous claims advanced concerning the fears of the elderly with regard to crime. We find that a quarter of the urban population is concerned about crime and their general level of assessed risk is only moderate, but their perceived threat of after-dark violence in public places is quite high. Many of the concerns and risks we investigated proved to be general ones, however. On those dimensions the elderly were distinctive only in two regards: they were significantly more likely to report higher levels of risk of assault, and they were substantially (as well as significantly in a statistical sense) more likely to report street robbery was a big problem in their community. In most ways the elderly closely resembled other urban dwellers. In particular, it did not seem they were disproportionately concentrated in "bad neighborhoods" or more threatened by minor crimes and incivilities not otherwise reflected in victimization studies.

The concern of the elderly with street predation was mirrored in our data on potential, rather than realized, threats of crime. We found extremely strong and distinctive relationships between age and the threat of personal violence after dark. Even during the daylight hours many elderly reported that they were fearful, and they were distinctive in this regard as well. However, the level of threat that was registered in these surveys was far more substantial for "after dark" risks. We interpret those as expressions of concern about potential victimization because they do not strongly parallel age differences in victimization or assessments of risk. Rather, the elderly seem distinctively to fear what *could* happen to them *if* they were exposed at places and times that would put them at risk. Using this quite restricted definition of fear, the elderly are indeed distinctively threatened by crime, both in big cities and for the nation as a whole.

VI.   THE CONSEQUENCES OF FEAR

Here we turn to another important aspect of the "fear of crime" problem, what people *do* about it. It is widely claimed the elderly are the prisoners of their own fear, with adverse consequences for the quality of their lives. The high level of perceived threat of victimization among the elderly documented above makes it tempting to identify those actions as reactions to crime. However, it is likely that at least some portion of this reduced risk is derivative rather than conscious in origin. It may simply be attributable to problems attendant to old age. One should not only look to crime to account for the limited exposure to risk of personal crime of many elderly persons. The "prisoners of fear" concept implies that the daily activities of older persons are significantly shaped by their perceived threat of victimization, a conscious strategy.

This analysis deals with two general classes of responses to crime: those which serve to limit people's risk of personal attack and those which reduce the vulnerability of households to property crime, burglary, and home invasion. The former involve either taking positive "risk management" measures when exposed to risk, or more passively limiting one's exposure to risk in the first place. Household protection measures include "target hardening" tactics designed to make a dwelling more difficult or risky to enter and routine measures intended to increase the actual or apparent level of surveillance protecting a residence.

Table 4 presents findings concerning the age distribution of such activities in a number of cities. It indicates the percentage of respondents above and below the age of sixty who reported taking various household surveillance and target hardening measures. The statistically significant comparisons reported there indicate no particular tendency for older respondents to live in better-protected places. There were no age-related differences in the frequency of leaving lights on, and younger respondents more often reported living in households with dogs ("because of crime" in Kansas City, as a "watch dog" in Portland). The elderly were more likely than others to report having outside lights in Kansas City, but less likely in Portland: the same sort of reversal characterizes the data on light timers in Kansas City and Cincinnati. In two cities, seniors were more likely to report installing special door locks (but in Portland it went the other way by the same margin), and in Kansas City they more often mentioned installing window bars or special locks—but there were no differences across age in other places. Other indicators revealed no significant differences among age groups.

Personal Precautions

Rather than taking measures to reduce their risk of property crime, it may be that older people are more likely to try to reduce their likelihood of victimization on the street. For example, they may go out less frequently during the day and at night than do younger adults. If it is true that they feel they cannot go out, crime exacts a heavy toll on the quality

Table 4. Frequency of Efforts to Reduce Household Victimization, by Age

		Community				
Activity	Cincinnati	Kansas City	Portland	Three–City	Hartford	Chicago–Metro
Surveillance						
Outside Lights						
Under 60		35	52*			29
Over 60		45*	41			26
Light timer						
Under 60	17	16				
Over 60	11	26*				
Have a dog/watch dog						
Under 60		31*	41*			
Over 60		23	21			
Leave lights on when gone						
Under 60			79	82		
Over 60			81	80		
Target Hardening						
Special door locks						
Under 60	39	40	36*		51	
Over 60	39	49*	27		59	
Special window locks or bars						
Under 60		23		44	45	38*
Over 60		30*		46	46	27
Peephole at door						
Under 60		12		62		
Over 60		12		63		
Burglar Alarm						
Under 60	3	7	6			
Over 60	1	7	7			
Fence						
Under 60		28				
Over 60		30				

*Difference significant at P < .05 level.

Note: Wording of questions varies somewhat in different surveys. The items are quite comparable, however. "Over 60" category includes sixty-year-olds.

Source: Computed by the authors from original data.

of their life. Survey data probing the fear behavior nexus is presented in Figure 13. It examines the relationship between fear and two different forms of social activity for those in various age brackets. Figure 13a employs responses to a question in surveys conducted in the nation's five largest cities, about "going out" for entertainment. Average responses

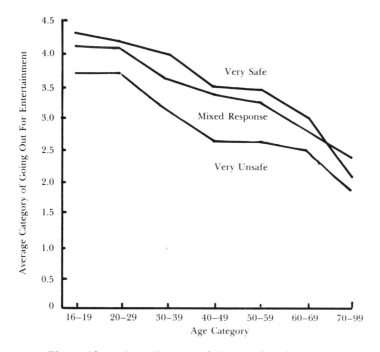

Figure 13a. Age, Fear, and Recreational Activity

Source: Computed from Census Bureau Surveys in Five Largest Cities

concerning how frequently respondents went out for entertainment are presented for those reporting varying levels of perceived threat of crime, in ten-year age categories. In general, this form of mobility decreased with age *and* fear. Those indicating they were "very unsafe" were particularly likely to report going out less frequently. Differences across age appear to be greater than differences between those reporting different levels of fear, a conclusion supported by a multivariate analysis (not shown) examining the comparative impact of both measures on behavior.

A similar pattern, but one suggesting even greater fear-related differences in behavior, is found in Figure 13b. It links age, fear, and another form of activity—"going out after dark"—among respondents to surveys in Chicago, Philadelphia and San Francisco. Again, average exposure levels (measured as reports of the number of times people went out after dark during the week before the survey) declined with age and fear. What is more apparent in this figure than in the last is there also is less *variation* among the elderly—and particularly among those 70 and older—with regard to their behavior. In comparison to

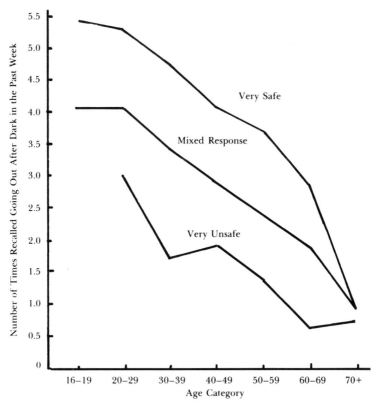

Figure 13b.   Age, Fear, and Routine Neighborhood Activity

Note: Too few cases in the "very unsafe" 16–19 age category
Source: Computed by the authors from three-city data

others, senior's activities seem to be dominated by their age and less affected by differences in their level of fear.

Both of these analyses suggest the same conclusions. Age and this measure of threat of crime seem to be independently related to reduced mobility among persons of all age groups. Within each fear category mobility continued to decline with age. This decline in mobility with age *independent* of levels of threat remains substantial. In eight other cities surveyed by the Census Bureau using the same questionnaire the correlation between age and this measure of going out for entertainment was −.41, and controlling for perceived threat of crime reduced the partial age-mobility correlation only to −.38 (Garofalo, 1980). The figures for the five city surveys used here are the same to two decimal places. A great deal of reduced mobility among the elderly (and others) may be attributable to constraints or conditions other than crime or fear. Age differences appear greater than differences across levels of fear in both cases. Relative to other age groups, fear seems to make less of a difference for the elderly.

Risk Management

While many older Americans report greatly limited mobility, those who do venture forth seem to do so with considerable boldness. When we examine the ways in which they act to manage their risks when they *are* in what are often thought to be more risky situations, the elderly do not seem to be especially cautious.

Table 5 documents the frequency with which those over and under sixty in these city surveys indicated taking each course of action. The most common strategy turns out to be resorting to the automobile. Across the four cities where residents were quizzed about this strategy, the elderly were more likely to report this action in two of them. While this places the elderly squarely among other adults, it should be noted that they take to the road with some frequency despite generally low levels of automobile ownership. Over 20 percent of those over 60 who were interviewed in the NCS lived in households without a car.

Table 5. Frequency of Efforts to Reduce Personal Victimization, by Age

Protective Measure	Community				
	Philadelphia	Chicago	San Francisco	Hartford	Kansas City
Take escort					
Under 60	38	38	31	30	
Over 60	35	53*	52*	24	
Drive rather than walk					
Under 60	62	62	51	66	
Over 60	55	58	82*	69	
Take protection when walk					
Under 60	30	31	20	8	17
Over 60	25	24	27	10	18
Avoid areas of neighbor- hood					
Under 60	36*	44	32		
Over 60	20	44	28		

Note: Asterisks indicate differences significant at the <.05 level. "Over 60" category includes sixty-year olds.

Source: Computed by the authors from original data.

The next most common defensive strategy employed by residents of these cities was to walk with others when out after dark. In two of the four cities in which people were quizzed about this strategy the elderly more often indicated they had adopted it at least "sometimes." But in the remaining cities nonsignificant differences favored younger respondents instead. "Avoiding dangerous areas" also is a strategy commonly adopted by residents of these cities to avoid crime. In Philadelphia and San Francisco younger persons were more likely to report trying this, but there were no age-linked differences in describing this kind of maneuver in Chicago. Finally, in four cities respondents were asked about carrying "things" for protection on the streets at night. Taking protection was (on a hopeful note) the least commonly employed defensive strategy in each of the cities surveyed. There were no clear age-related differences in the frequency with which people questioned in these surveys did so.

These data suggest that when they do go out after dark the elderly are not distinctively more likely than other adults to employ defensive strategies which greatly limit their freedom of action. They do so too often, to be sure: when a fifth of the urban population is "taking protection," and two-thirds are no longer walking the streets of their own neighborhoods, it is clear that crime is having a tremendous impact on their lives. The elderly simply are not unique in their response to neighborhood crime. It also must be remembered that for older Americans these "normal" levels of caution serve to further reduce the exposure to risk of a population which already does not venture forth very often. The two factors taken in combination result in a "net exposure level" for the elderly which is very low.

Fear and Behavior

In many ways the attitudes and behaviors explored in the last two sections of this chapter have been consistent. In large areas of concern they have pointed to a surprisingly *undistinctive* salience of crime among senior citizens. There is considerable evidence that the distinctive concerns of the elderly are few and clearly focused upon personal attack, primarily after dark. They did not report disproportionate concern about household burglary or property crime, nor did they perceive their neighborhoods as excessively plagued by the minor "incivilities" of urban life. This is congruent with the generally typical behavior of elders toward those problems. There is a correspondence between at least one crime which does hit the urban elderly with average frequency—predatory street crimes—and their concerns and behaviors. Predatory street crime, which seems to have the strongest effect upon its victims, is among the most important threats facing the elderly. This seems quite consistent with their perceptions of those threats. As we saw above, street robbery and purse snatching were the major crimes which the urban elderly were significantly more likely to identify as "big problems" in their neighborhood. And this is also consistent with their higher levels of perceived threat of personal attack after dark.

In this light it is surprising how limited the behavioral component of that concern seems to be. In this chapter we have seen that among the elderly only behavioral restrictions seem to be distinctively frequent. They report not going out very often, relative to their younger counter-parts. However, much of this restricted behavior appears to be deriva-tive rather than conscious in origin. Much of the limited mobility which protects them stems from health, age, and other concerns. Even in the larger cities which have been surveyed many elderly report doing rela-tively little about crime. It is unsurprising that more of the elderly report not going out after dark because of crime, but that only 9 percent of them fell in this category was unexpected.

Others have come to the same conclusion. M. Powell Lawton (in press, p. 21) notes:

> Repeatedly, in looking at the research in this area one is struck by the contrast between the extreme anxiety over crime as expressed by older people, and on the other hand, the smaller-than-expected effects of crime on their behavior or psycho-logical wellbeing . . .

In his study of elderly in public housing Lawton could find no significant impact of crime or fear on their behavior. Fear was not related to the frequency of either on-site or off-site activity, nor to the frequency with which the elderly visited with friends or relatives, walked their area, or other self-reported measures of personal mobility. He concluded that the findings:

> [G]ive no support to the idea that elderly tenants respond to victimization, high crime risk, or even fear of crime, by becoming housebound (Lawton and Yaffe, 1980, p. 778).

In its national survey, the National Council on Aging (1975) found that in a number of major areas of life the general public seemed to have an exaggerated view of the importance of the problems facing the el-derly. In several issue areas—including crime—those under 65 gave "aging problems" a higher significance rating than did the elderly them-selves. The "prisoners of fear" issue may be another example of this phenomenon. While their perceived threat of crime is high, in many ways the elderly take no more precautions than the rest of us, even in big cities where that threat is presumably more realistic. Perhaps the aged ". . . are not as easily daunted as our stereotypes of the 'vulnerable elderly' might have thought them to be" (Lawton and Yaffe, 1980, p. 778).

VII. SPECIFICATION AND RE-SPECIFICATION OF A POLICY ISSUE

We have seen that over the span of one decade the crime and the elderly problem has been re-specified in the U.S. Congress at least three times—from a problem of especially high rates of crime to a problem of especially severe physical and economic consequences from criminal victimization, and then to problems of especially high levels of fear of crime and severe consequences resulting from that fear. Based on our analyses of the data, we concluded that most of these definitions of the problem were inappropriate. Those who serve the elderly face a surprisingly heterogenous constituency. Their constituents voice a variety of concerns, and in addition the media, other practitioners, and the views of the general public on what the "real" problems facing the elderly are become mixed into the brew. Most of the resulting formulations of those crime problems which were cast into the congressional hopper were off the mark.

Rather than older persons being the most likely age group to be victimized, they are the least likely group to be the victims of most household and personal crimes. For the crimes of purse snatching and pocket picking, they are no different from other age groups in the rate of victimizations they suffer.

When the definition of the problem switched from one of high rates to one of severe consequences, it seemed a logical re-specification. But when researchers began to probe the National Crime Survey for an understanding of crime's consequences, it soon became clear that the consequences it measures were no greater for older persons than for others.

The final specification of the crime and the elderly problem was one of especially high levels of fear and consequences of that fear. In this chapter, we examined three different conceptualizations of fear of crime—concern about neighborhood crime, personal feelings of being at risk, and perceptions of threats of crime lurking in wait. Our data for this analysis were not national, but were drawn from studies replicated in a number (up to eight) of major U.S. cities. Of these conceptions of fear of crime, the elderly's special fear seems to be most concentrated in the third. Older city dwellers are more likely to report feeling threatened by potential personal violence after dark. Even during daylight hours many older persons reported they felt threatened. Thus, older people seem especially to fear what could happen if they were at risk. However, in terms of consequences of fear, the elderly do not seem unique. Although there is a decline in mobility for older persons in cities, this decline does not seem to be due to fear of crime.

According to Wildavsky (1979, p. 36), the art of policy analysis consists in finding problems worth solving. But the translation of social conditions into clearly defined social problems for which policy solutions are available is often difficult. In the case reported here, a variety of definitions of "the problem" emerged, and none of them appears on the basis of our analysis to represent those social conditions adequately. The best-fitting specification of the issue is one of fear of crime among the urban elderly. However, claims that the elderly are widely held prisoner by their fear are misleading. Rather, the crime problems of the elderly are the same as the crime problems of the rest of us, albeit with some special expression of concern about street robbery and purse snatching. Measured by their behavior and most of their expressed concerns, the impact of crime upon the quality of their lives is about the same as that of other city dwellers.

There are ample reasons for placing crime near the top of the policy agenda, if only because opinion polls throughout the 1970s and early 1980s indicate that Americans of all ages would have it there. However, it appears that *need-based* rather than *age-based* criteria should decide at whom crime policies and programs are targeted. In a number of policy areas there is growing recognition that "needs" criteria which cross-cut age-based qualifications for benefits may more efficiently address particular problems. Often more of the elderly than others may qualify on the basis of those criteria, but that does not make them "elderly problems."

In the case of crime, even this "age-based" view of the problem does not seem to be particularly appropriate. The elderly have many real and serious problems that are in fact more severe for them than for younger adults. Scarce resources can probably best be targeted at alleviating those problems. Defining every problem that elderly persons face as a distinctive problem for the elderly may seem to be a useful political strategy. As Cook (1979) has documented, there is deep public support for serving the elderly. Linking them to neighborhood or urban problems or to broad and widespread social problems like crime might seem a useful strategy for tackling those issues. However, if every problem that Congress considers is claimed to be more severe for the elderly, then the possibility exists that an opinion backlash against the elderly could occur and that we could reinforce the misperception of "the old" as a problem group and run the risk "of stigmatizing rather than liberating older people from the negative effects of the label 'old'" (Neugarten, 1982, p.

27). Our analyses and those by others indicate crime and fear of crime are indeed problems, for city dwellers, declining urban regions, the poor, racial minorities, teenagers attending bad schools, women living alone, public housing residents, and a variety of others. But that list is so broad that the crime problem is a generic one and should be understood—and dealt with—as such.

In *Speaking Truth to Power,* Wildavsky says "Always, we must be prepared to learn that we are wrong" (p. 59). For if the problem as perceived does not really exist, then time and money are likely to be wasted in action. And as Popper (1972) tells us, "It is through the falsification of our suppositions that we actually get in touch with 'reality.' It is the discovery and elimination of our errors which alone constitute that 'positive' experience we gain from reality" (p. 361). Such falsification of suppositions in the policy arena is more difficult than it sounds, for the "facts of the case" are not the only basis for political action. Values, beliefs, and multiple problem definitions compete in the cauldron from which political decisions emerge. However, in this chapter we have seen a case in which a social problem underwent multiple redefinitions in the U.S. Congress and then declined in salience on the policy agenda . . . . and the evidence presented here would suggest rightly so.

REFERENCES

Antunes, George E., Cook, Fay Lomax, Cook, Thomas D., Skogan, Wesley G. "Patterns of Personal Crime Against the Elderly: Findings from a National Survey." *The Gerontologist* 17 (1977): 321–327.

Biderman, Albert D., Johnson, Louise, McIntyre, Jeannie, and Weir, Adrianne. *Report on a Pilot Survey in the District of Columbia on Victimization and Attitudes Toward Law Enforcement.* Washington, DC: President's Commission on Law Enforcement and Administration of Justice, 1967.

Block, Richard. "Victim-offender Dynamics in Stranger to Stranger Violence." Unpublished paper presented at the Thirty-third International Course on Criminology, Vancouver, BC, March, 1983.

Clemente, Frank, and Kleinman, Michael B. "Fear of Crime Among the Aged." *The Gerontologist* 16 (June 1976): 207–210.

Cobb, Roger W., and Elder, Charles D. "The Politics of Agenda-Building: An Alternative Perspective for Modern Democratic Theory." *The Journal of Politics* 33, no. 4 (1971): 892–915.

Cobb, Roger W., and Elder, Charles D. *Participation in American Politics: The Dynamics of Agenda-Building.* Boston: Allyn and Bacon, 1972.

Cobb, Roger W., Ross, Jennie-Keith, and Ross, Marc H. "Agenda-building as a Comparative Political Process." *American Political Science Review* 70 (1976): 126–137.

Cook, Fay Lomax. "Crime and the Elderly: The Emergence of a Policy Issue." In *Reactions to Crime.* Edited by Dan A. Lewis. Beverly Hills, CA: Sage Publications, 1981.

Cook, Fay Lomax. *Who Should Be Helped? Public Support for Social Services.* Beverly Hills, CA: Sage Publications, 1979.

Cook, Fay Lomax, and Cook, Thomas D. "Evaluating the Rhetoric of Crisis: A Case Study of Criminal Victimization of the Elderly." *Social Service Review* 50 (December 1976): 632–646.

Cook, Fay Lomax, Tyler, Tom R., Goetz, Edward G., Gordon, Margaret T., Protess, David T., Leff, Donna R., and Molotch, Harvey L. "Media and Agenda-Setting: Effects on the Public, Interest Group Leaders, Policy Makers, and Policy." *Public Opinion Quarterly, month/quarter season?* 1983.

Curtis, Lynn. "Statement on Violent Crimes Against the Elderly." Testimony before the House Select Committee on the Aging, Washington, DC U.S. House of Representatives, Ninety-Fifth Congress, 2nd Session (June 1978), Committee on Publication No. 95–146.

Downs, Anthony. "Up and Down with Ecology." *Public Interest* 28 (1972): 38–50.

DuBow, Fred. *Reactions to Crime: A Critical Review of the Literature.* Washington, DC: U.S. Government Printing Office, 1979.

Eyestone, Robert. *From Social Issues to Public Policy.* New York: John Wiley, 1978.

Furstenberg, Frank F. "Public Reactions to Crime in the Streets." *American Scholar* 40 (Autumn 1971): 601–610.

Jeffords, Charles R. "The Impact of Age upon the Fear of Crime." Unpublished paper presented at the Annual Meeting of the Academy of Criminal Justice Sciences, Oklahoma City, Oklahoma, March 12–14, 1980.

Lawton, M. Powell, Nahemow, Lucile, Yaffe, Silvia, and Feldman, Steven. "Psychological Aspects of the Fear of Crime." In *Crime and the Elderly.* Edited by Jack Goldsmith and Sharon Goldsmith. Lexington, MA: Lexington Books, 1977.

Lawton, M. Powell, and Yaffe, Silvia "Victimization and Fear of Crime in Elderly Public Housing Tenants." *Journal of Gerontology* 35 (1980): 768–779.

Lawton, M. Powell. "Crime Victimization and the Fortitude of the Aged." *Aged Care and Services Review,* forthcoming.

Lindbloom, Charles E., and Cohen, David K. *Usable Knowledge.* New Haven: Yale University Press, 1979.

McCombs, Maxwell; and Shaw, D. L. "The Agenda-Setting Functions of the Mass Media." *Public Opinion Quarterly* 36 (1972): 176–87.

McCombs, Maxwell, and Shaw, D. L. "Agenda-setting—the Political Process. In "The Emergence of American Political Issues: The Agenda-setting Function of the Press." Edited by D. L. Shaw and Maxwell McCombs. *Communication Research* 1 (1977): 131–166.

Mitchell, Douglas E. "Social Science Impact on Legislative Decision Making." *Educational Researcher* 9 (1980): 9–19.

Morgenthau, Hans J. *Scientific Man vs. Power Politics.* Chicago: University of Chicago Press, 1946.

National Council on the Aging. *The Myth and Reality of Aging in America.* Washington, DC: National Council on the Aging, 1975.

National Council on the Aging. *Aging in the Eighties: America in Transition.* Washington, DC: National Council on the Aging, 1981.

Neugarten, Bernice. *Age or Need? Public Policies for Older People.* Beverly Hills, California: Sage Publications, 1982.

Popper, Karl R. *Objective Knowledge: An Evolutionary Approach.* New York: Oxford University Press, 1972.

Roberts, Donald F., and Bachen, C. M. "Mass Communication Effects: *Annual Review of Psychology* 32 (1981): 307–56.

Skogan, Wesley G. *Issues in the Measurement of Victimization.* Washington, DC: Bureau of Justice Statistics, U.S. Department of Justice, 1981.

Skogan, Wesley G., and Maxfield, Michael. *Coping with Crime: Individual and Neighborhood Reactions.* Beverly Hills, CA: Sage Publications, 1981.

Sparks, Richard F., Genn, Hazel, and Dodd, David J. *Surveying Victims: A Study of the*

Measurement of Criminal Victimization, Perceptions of Crime, and Attitudes to Criminal Justice. New York, John Wiley, 1977.

Sundeen, Richard A., and Mathieu, James T. "The Fear of Crime and Its Consequences Among the Elderly in Three Urban Communities." *The Gerontologist* 16 (June 1976): 211–219.

U.S. Congress, House of Representatives. *Crime Against the Elderly: Hearings Before Select Committee on Aging.* Nineth-Fourth Congress, 2nd Session, 1976.

U.S. Congress, Senate Special Committee on Aging. *Hearings before the Subcommittee on Housing for the Elderly.* Ninety-Second Congress, 2nd session, August, 1972.

Weis, Carol H. *Social Science Research and Decision-Making.* New York: Columbia University Press, 1980.

Wildavsky, Aaron. *Speaking Truth to Power: The Art and Craft of Policy Analysis.* Boston: Little, Brown, and Company, 1979.

Wilson, James Q. *Thinking About Crime.* New York: Basic Books, 1975.

Wilson, Janes Q. *Social Science and Public Policy.* In *Knowledge and Policy.* Edited by Lawrence E. Lynn. Washington: National Academy of Sciences, 1978.

Yin, Peter P. "Fear of Crime Among the Elderly: Some Issues and Suggestions." *Social Problems* 27 (April 1980) 492–504.

VETERANS PREFERENCE:
A POLICY IN CONFLICT WITH EQUAL
EMPLOYMENT OPPORTUNITY[1]

Laura L. Vertz

I. INTRODUCTION

Many analysts of public personnel policy view veterans preference as a personnel policy which constrains the implementation of equal employment opportunity. In general, equal employment opportunity refers to efforts made to recruit and promote minority candidates to positions *for which they are qualified*. Because equal employment opportunity policy requires that minority applicants fulfill job qualification standards before they are hired or promoted, it is consistent with the underlying and most basic operating principle of the civil service: the merit principle (Stone, 1982; Vertz and Wells, 1982).

In contrast, veterans preference policy consists of nonmerit-oriented advantages given to veterans by virtue of their status as veterans. Thus, the conflict between veterans preference and equal employment opportunity occurs to the extent that the preferences given to veterans constrict the ability of qualified minority candidates to receive appointments. In addition, particular aspects of veterans preference, such as preference in reductions-in-force, may limit employment opportunities of minorities in other ways. The conflict between veterans preference and equal employment opportunity may be said to affect employment opportunity for all nonveterans. However, as a protected class, women tend to be viewed as the most adversely affected by veterans preference.

In analyzing the conflict between equal employment opportunity and veterans preference, the effects of veterans preference policy are compared against a standard supplied by the merit principle. Because equal employment opportunity is consistent with the merit principle, deviations from merit caused by the use of veterans preference policy can be viewed as potentially limiting equal employment opportunity.

This evaluative standard will be employed in this paper. An empirical analysis of veterans preference policy will be conducted in order to isolate the ways in which it conflicts with the merit principle. The purpose of using such a standard is to make inferences concerning the impact of veterans preference policy upon equal employment opportunity, particularly as it applies to women.

What are the conditions which need to be identified in order to conclude that veterans preference conflicts with merit, thereby constraining equal employment opportunity? At a minimum, the methodological standard applied to assess conflicts with equal employment opportunity should be that veterans preference is associated with decisions to hire, the GS level at which individuals are hired, or their current GS level. However, an even stricter standard will be imposed. In order for veterans preference policy to be concluded to be in conflict with equal employment opportunity policy, it must be shown that it has an *independent* impact in these areas which is not shared with merit-oriented criteria (such as job qualifications) or gender (which may be the result of other forms of discrimination). The independent impact of a preference for veterans upon initial and current GS level will be measured with statistical techniques which will provide controls for gender and job qualifications.

Thus the purpose of this paper is to build upon previous analyses of the conflict between veterans preference policy and the implementation of equal employment opportunity in public sector employment. In pursuit of this objective, the paper will contain five parts:

1. The history of veterans preference policy will be reviewed. This section will provide an information base on the development of veterans preference policy in the United States and will end with an overview of the current details of the policy.
2. Previous research on veterans preference has emphasized its effects upon the decision to hire. The purpose of the section is to

point out how previous analyses view the conflict between merit and veterans preference.

3. Data obtained from the Office of Personnel Management will be used to describe the current effects of veterans preference within the major departments of the federal government. This section will add to previous analyses by giving a comprehensive overview of the status of veterans compared with women in federal employment. Gammas and partial gammas will be used to assess the independent impacts of veterans preference and gender upon current GS level.

4. Using multiple regression analysis, a more detailed individual level analysis will compare the relative effects of veterans preference, job qualification factors, and gender upon GS level. The analysis will measure the independent impact of veterans preference for the current position held by individuals and also for their first position held within the organization. Survey data obtained from the Milwaukee District Office of the Internal Revenue Service will be used in this part of the analysis.

5. The paper will conclude with a discussion of the justifications for veterans preference policy. An argument will be made concerning which justification appears to be most consistent with the effects of the policy. Derived from this discussion will be suggestions for policy reform.

II. THE HISTORY OF VETERANS PREFERENCE IN THE UNITED STATES: A BRIEF OVERVIEW

Prior to World War II, veterans preference largely consisted of informal norms giving preference to veterans in hiring and promotion within the civil service. As Stahl (1976, p. 154) has observed, ". . . statutory provisions on the subject were confined to rather general statements of policy enjoining appointing officials to give disabled or other veterans (and eventually their wives) preference over others of equal qualifications." Stahl has also noted that norms in favor of hiring veterans during this period were quite strong, often exceeding the statutory requirements.

Historically, veterans preference in the United States began with the desire of several early presidents to appoint veterans to government posts.[2] President Jackson vigorously applied the norm of appointing veterans in his personal and political appointments. Likewise, following the Civil War a norm in favor of hiring Union army soldiers was observed in governmental appointments.

This norm became formalized in the act of 1865, which later became section 1754 of the Revised Statutes. This first formal statement of the norm of preference applied only to disabled veterans and it was later incorporated in the Civil Service Act of 1883. The result of the incorporation was to establish a priority of preference over merit. Hence, at the same time that the merit principle received formal statement (in the Act of 1883), it was also stated that merit hiring was not to detract from the preference awarded disabled veterans in the federal government.

During the same period in which the 1883 Act was passed, several states also initiated preference statutes. At the state level, preference often applied to both disabled and nondisabled veterans. Following World War I, a new preference statute extended coverage at the federal level to apply to all veterans, their widows, and the wives of disabled veterans. The new preference statute, enacted on July 11, 1919, was interpreted by the attorney general to extend preference over all other persons eligible to appointment. In other words, at this stage in preference policy, it was interpreted as absolute.

Statutes enacted following World War II specified veterans preference policy in much greater detail. The Veterans Preference Act of 1944 formalized the point system for preference for disabled and nondisabled veterans along with the "rule of three" (Davis, 1980; Stahl, 1976). The resultant hiring procedures specified the addition of ten points to the scores received by disabled veterans and five points for nondisabled veterans in civil service examinations. The "rule of three" provision entailed compiling a register of applicants ranked according to job qualifications (in which the examination score is usually the most overriding consideration). The top three names are given to the appointing official who then selects one of the three candidates. In addition, the Veterans Preference Act specified that disabled veterans are to be placed at the top of the register regardless of qualifications, except for a few professional positions (Stahl, 1976). Nondisabled veterans, as described above, receive five bonus points which raises their ranking on the register compared with nonveterans with equal test scores.

Currently, veterans preference applies to:

1. appointment to positions. Hiring of veterans is accomplished by points added to test scores coupled with the rule of three.
2. employee appeals processes.
3. reduction-in-force (RIF's). Veterans are the last to be cut from positions during employee lay-offs. However, at the state and local levels, the RIF preference is often not a part of their preference systems.
4. promotions in some states and localities. This provision does not

apply in the federal civil service (Campbell, 1978; Davis, 1980; Nigro and Nigro, 1982).

III. THE EFFECT OF VETERANS PREFERENCE UPON HIRING: SOME RESULTS FROM PREVIOUS RESEARCH

There are two ways in which veterans preference policy may have an impact upon the administration of public personnel. One is in the process of appointing individuals to governmental positions. The second is in the experiences that individuals have during their tenure within public sector organizations. Both of these are important insofar as the effects of veterans preference conflict with merit considerations. In this section, the focus will be upon the first possible effect of veterans preference policy; that is, the analysis will deal with the impact that veterans preference has upon hiring. As such, the purpose of the section is to identify whether or not veterans preference constrains merit hiring and to isolate where some of the conflicts with the merit principle occur.

Previous analyses of veterans preference policy can be categorized as belonging to two distinct periods. The early period of research largely compared veterans with nonveterans in order to ascertain possible conflicts with merit. More recent analyses compare women and veterans. Again, the purpose of these studies is to determine whether conflicts with the merit principle exist. Each of these strands of research will be discussed in turn.

In an early analysis of the civil service, Miller (1935) compared the rating of veterans and nonveterans applying for specific positions in order to demonstrate the conflict with merit. Several instances of conflict were observed. For example, Miller found that the highest rating achieved by a veteran for the position of accountant was 81.5. The highest score for a nonveteran was 90.8. In this case, 16 non-veterans with higher scores than the veteran hired were passed over in order to hire veterans for accounting positions (Miller, 1935, p. 281). A more extreme example cited by Miller was for the position of scientific assistant in public health. Here the highest veteran scored 68 compared with 95 for the highest nonveteran. Seventy nonveterans with higher qualifications were passed over in hiring for the position. Miller also demonstrated that in the civil service system as it existed prior to World War II, 447 of the 1996 disabled veterans earned ratings of less than 70 percent in the examinations which resulted in their appointments (Miller, 1935, p. 282). Finally, he also found that veterans were hired primarily in the highest salary grade ($3,000 and over). For this grade, veterans comprised over 51.5 percent of the total appointments made in 1930–31 and 62.5 percent in 1932–33.

Miller's findings apply to an earlier era of veterans preference policy, and some would no longer apply to its current implementation. For example, veterans are currently required to achieve passing grades on civil service examinations before they are eligible for bonus points. In addition, in hiring procedures the preference is usually restricted to five or ten points, depending upon a veteran's classification. Nevertheless, these safeguards do not prevent the civil service from being plagued by problems similar to those noted by Miller.

The current emphasis upon the implementation of equal employment opportunity policy has resulted in the research focusing on the possible constraint that veterans preference places upon the merit hiring of women. Campbell (1978) compares the position of veterans and women in order to ascertain the effects that veterans preference has on merit hiring. He finds that veterans comprise 25 percent of the labor force; yet, they hold over 50 percent of the jobs in the federal government. Moreover, he finds that 65 percent of the upper level management positions are filled by veterans. In citing a Professional Administrative Career Examination (PACE) summary, Campbell shows that in 1976, 19 percent of those eligible for entry level positions (GS 5 and GS 7) were veterans and 41 percent were women. Yet, in hiring, veterans comprised 29 percent of the total hired, while women constituted only 31 percent of the selected group.

Fleming and Shanor (1977, p. 46) also cite PACE data in describing the effects of veterans preference upon hiring. Again, the data describe application to entry level positions (GS 5 and GS 7) which can potentially develop into professional management positions. For fiscal year 1975, males filed 128,362 applications, females filed 88,839 applications, and veterans (comprised of both men and women)[3] filed 50,428 applications. The percentages in each category which passed the civil service examination include 49.9 percent for males, 51.2 percent for females, and 42.9 percent for veterans. The percentages hired in each category were 12.7 percent of the males, 6.6 percent of the females, and 17.5 percent of the veterans. Thus, while the female pass rate was somewhat higher, a larger percentage of veterans were appointed to positions. The authors also cite very similar results for hiring in fiscal year 1976.

The effects of absolute preference systems upon hiring also deserve some consideration. Absolute preference refers to a system where eligible veterans are hired before any nonveteran is considered. Absolute preference differs from the more common point-bonus system in that bonus points do not preclude the hiring of nonveterans (although it is likely to inhibit it). With absolute preference, nonveterans are seldom hired.

Fleming and Shanor (1977, p. 22) discuss the impact that absolute preference systems have on the merit hiring of women. They cite an example from the preference system in Massachusetts, which was the basis for the case *Anthony v. Massachusetts.*[4] The plaintiffs challenged the absolute preference system on the grounds that it prevented women from being hired in civil service employment. The plaintiffs had tied for the highest grade on a civil service examination but were ranked 57th and 58th on a register behind 56 veterans, all of whom were male and 54 of whom received scores lower than they did. In this case, the court ruled that veterans preference had a discriminatory impact upon a constitutionally protected group, i.e., women.[5] The result of such an impact was to directly contradict merit.

Several additional details are also worthy of mention. The Veterans Readjustment Benefits Act of 1966 provided for peacetime veterans with at least six months of service to also qualify for veterans preference (Stahl, 1976). In 1976 Congress made veterans preference unavailable to future enlistees. This was probably done at the behest of the Civil Service Commission and with the recognition that both the draft and the Vietnam era had ended (Fleming and Shanor, 1977). Since April 1970, federal agencies have been able to offer absolute preference to veterans for certain positions in grades one to five. These appointments are convertible to career positions provided the veteran completes a self-development program. Appointment to jobs at GS level three or lower can be made solely on the basis of the veteran's military experience provided that the agency feels that the veteran can perform the duties of the job (Levitan and Cleary, 1973).

In summary, the veterans preference policy which is currently implemented in the United States is one of the strongest preference systems in the Western World. As Stahl notes (1976: 154): ". . . it is clear that in its enthusiasm to guarantee preference for veterans the Congress went well beyond basic preference policy and legislated personnel employment procedures to a degree of detail unparalleled anywhere else in the world." Thus, the legal requirements of veterans preference policy appear to be very strong. In the next section, some of the empirical effects of the policy will be analyzed.

These findings illustrate the adverse impact that veterans preference policy can have on the ability of nonveterans to be hired in public sector employment organizations.[6] More specifically, the results indicate that veterans preference constrains employment opportunities of women. The effects of the policy were found to apply to the point-bonus system in hiring. In addition, the effects were even more extreme for absolute preference systems.

IV. THE EFFECT OF VETERANS PREFERENCE WITHIN THE FEDERAL GOVERNMENT: A COMPREHENSIVE OVERVIEW

In the previous section, the effects of veterans preference policy upon government hiring decisions were considered. Previous analyses, however, do not indicate in a systematic fashion how the decisions are aggregated into a comprehensive pattern of government employment. Current patterns of employment reflect not only the initial decision to hire, but also at what level individuals are hired as well as other experiences that they may have within government organizations. This section will deal with the second way in which a preference for veterans may have an impact on the administration of public personnel. Here we will investigate whether veterans preference policy affects the experiences that individuals have once the decision is made to hire them for government positions.

In considering these effects, the central question is: What is the relationship between veterans preference and current governmental position? The research goal is to ascertain whether or not individuals with veterans preference appear to be advantaged once they are hired within the public sector. In a manner consistent with hiring decision results, the hypothesis which is tested is that having veterans preference will be positively associated with occupying a higher GS level.

This hypothesis will be tested with data for all major federal departments obtained from the Office of Personnel Management. The data describe federal personnel as of March 13, 1982 in the following agencies: Air Force, Department of Agriculture, Army, Department of Commerce, other Defense activities, Department of Justice, Department of Labor, Department of Energy, Education Department, Environmental Protection Agency, General Services Administration, Department of Health and Human Services, Department of Housing and Urban Development, Department of Interior, National Aeronautics and Space Administration, Navy, State Department, Transportation Department, Treasury Department, and Veterans' Administration. These data represent 1,321,806 federal civil service employees.

In order to test the hypothesis with these data, a crosstabulation of veterans preference and GS level is provided in Table 1. The veterans preference variable is divided into three categories: persons not entitled to veterans preference; nondisabled veterans (entitled to a 5 point preference): and disabled veterans, spouses of deceased or disabled veterans, or mothers of disabled veterans (entitled to a 10 point preference). GS level is also collapsed into three categories: GS 1–6; GS 7–11; and GS 12 and higher.

Part A of Table 1 contains the results for all federal civil service employees found in the agencies listed above. There exists a rather moderate relationship between veterans preference and GS level, the gamma coefficient being slightly over .3. The table shows that a majority of those without preference (52.8 percent) are located in GS levels 1 through 6. Those with a five point preference are mainly found in GS 7 through 11, but also comprise the largest number located in GS 12 and higher. Disabled veterans are located at higher GS levels than nonveterans, but are not as heavily concentrated in the GS 12 and higher category as are nondisabled veterans.

Table 1 also contains the same table constructed for those departments which display the strongest and weakest relationships between veterans preference and GS level. The purpose of including these tables is to indicate the range of the strength of the relationship over all of the major federal departments. (Here, and below, selected single agency results are presented to abbreviate the presentation; however, tables for all agencies listed above are available from the author upon request.) As can be seen in part B of Table 1, the Labor Department has a strong relationship between veterans preference and GS level. The gamma for this relationship is .593. Over 70 percent of nondisabled veterans are found in the GS 12 and higher category. For those without veterans preference, the largest number are found in GS 1 through 6 (41.1 percent of those with preference are located here).

The weakest relationship is found in the Department of Health and Human Services. The relationship in this case continues to hold, although the gamma statistic is only .304 (part C). Nondisabled veterans are found in equal proportion in GS levels 7 through 11 and 12 and higher. In contrast, both disabled veterans and those without preference are found in equal proportions in GS 1 through 6 and 7 through 11. In general, the differences in percentages are less extreme than for the other examples contained in Table 1. Nevertheless, the overall pattern is found, although in a more modest form.

Given the relationship between veterans preference and GS level, the next question that warrants investigation concerns the extent to which veterans preference adversely affects the experiences that women have in public employment. In analyzing this question, it is necessary to first establish the strength of the relationship between gender and veterans preference. It would be of little surprise to find that most veterans are men. However, the purpose of this analysis is to find out what the rela-

Table 1.   Relationship Between Veterans Preference and GS Level

A. For All Agencies:

	Veterans Preference			
	No pref.	5 points	10 points	Total
GS Level 1–6	432,936 52.8%	112,828 28.3%	39,867 39.7%	585,631 44.4%
7–11	279,483 34.0%	165,898 41.6%	40,758 40.6%	486,193 36.8%
12 and higher	108,346 13.2%	120,346 30.2%	19,759 19.7%	248,451 18.8%
Total	820,765 100.0%	399,072 100.0%	100,384 100.0%	1,320,221 * 100.0%

Gamma = .341   *Deviations from the total of 1,321,806 are due
                                to missing values.

B. For the Labor Department—The Strongest Relationship:

	Veterans Preference			
	No pref.	5 points	10 points	Total
GS Level 1–6	4,624 41.4%	332 7.7%	181 17.2%	5,137 30.9%
7–11	3,239 28.8%	906 21.0%	278 26.4%	4,423 26.6%
12 and higher	3,388 30.1%	3,075 71.3%	596 56.5%	7,059 42.5%
Total	11,251 100.0%	4,313 100.0%	1,055 100.0%	16,619 100.0%

Gama = .593

Table 1. (*Continued*)

C. For the Department of Health and Human Services—The Weakest Relationship:
Veterans Preference

	No pref.	5 points	10 points	Total
GS Level 1–6	41,708 41.9%	5,732 23.8%	2,596 43.1%	50,036 38.6%
7–11	42,614 42.8%	9,619 39.9%	2,195 36.5%	54,428 42.0%
12 and higher	15,155 15.2%	8,712 36.2%	1,228 20.4%	25,095 19.4%
Total	99,477 100.0%	24,063 100.0%	6,019 100.0%	129,559 100.0%

Gamma = .304

Source: Compiled by the author from data supplied by the Office of Personnel Management.

tionship is between gender and veterans preference *among those individuals currently employed in the federal government.*

The results are found in Table 2. There is a very strong relationship between gender and veterans preference for all of the examples contained in the table. Part A contains the results for all personnel; a gamma of .792 is seen. The Department of Transportation displays the strongest relationship among the agencies. The gamma statistic for the relationship between gender and veterans preference in this case is over .9 (see part B of Table 2). Even for the Interior Department, the department with the weakest relationship, the correlation is over .7 (part C). These results stem primarily from the fact that for every agency, approximately 90 percent of the women do not have veterans preference. The strong correlation between these variables is found consistently across the various departments.

The investigation of whether veterans preference adversely affects women within the federal government entails an additional consideration. It has been established that veterans preference is moderately associated with GS level and that gender is strongly associated with veterans preference. From these findings, a third question is derived: What is the relationship between gender and GS level? The hypothesis to be tested is that women will tend to be located at lower GS levels, while men will be located at higher levels.

Table 3 contains these results. The overall level of association between

Table 2. Relationship Between Gender and Veterans Preference

A. For All Agencies:

	Gender		
	Women	Men	Total
Veterans Preferance No. pref.	572,827 88.0%	247,938 37.0%	820,765 62.2%
5 points	51,750 7.9%	347,322 51.9%	399,072 30.2%
10 points	26,338 4.1%	74,046 11.1%	100,384 7.6%
Total	650,915 100.0%	669,306 100.0%	1,320,221 * 100.0%

Gamma = .792

*Deviations from the total of 1,321,806 are due to missing values.

B. For the Trasportation Department—The Strongest Relationship:

	Gender		
	Women	Men	Total
Veterans Preference No. pref.	11,043 91.3%	8,435 21.5%	19,478 37.9%
5 points	777 6.4%	26,328 66.9%	27,105 52.8%
10 points	280 2.3%	4,439 11.3%	4,719 9.2%
Total	12,100 100.0%	39,202 100.0%	51,302 100.0%

Gamma = .909

Table 2. *(Continued)*

C. For the Interior Department—The Weakest Relationship:

	Gender		
	Women	*Men*	*Total*
Veterans Preference	19,821	19,741	39,562
No. pref.	90.7%	60.6%	72.7%
5 points	1,702	11,654	13,356
	7.8%	35.8%	24.6%
10 points	302	1,158	1,460
	1.5%	3.6%	2.7%
Total	21,825	32,553	54,378
	100.0%	100.0%	100.0%

Gamma = .712

Source: Compiled by the author from data supplied by the Office of Personnel Management.

Table 3. Relationship Between Gender and GS Level

A. For All Agencies:

	Gender		
	Women	*Men*	*Total*
GS Level	433,934	151,697	585,631
1–6	66.7%	22.7%	44.4%
7–11	184,725	301,414	486,139
	28.4%	45.0%	36.8%
12 and higher	32,256	216,195	248,451
	4.9%	32.3%	18.8%
Total	650,915	669,306	1,320,221 *
	100.0%	100.0%	100.0%

Gamma = .722

*Deviations from the total of 1,321,806 are due to missing values.

(continued)

Table 3. *(Continued)*

B. For NASA—The Strongest Relationship:

	Gender		
	Women	Men	Total
GS Level 1–6	2,878 56.4%	687 4.6%	3,465 19.5%
7–11	1,594 31.2%	3,284 25.9%	4,878 27.4%
12 and higher	634 12.4%	8,803 69.5%	9,437 53.1%
Total	5,106 100.0%	12,674 100.0%	17,780 100.0%

Gamma = .870

C. For the Department of Education—The Weakest Relationship:

	Gender		
	Women	Men	Total
GS Level 1–6	1,171 39.4%	284 15.6%	1,455 30.4%
7–11	1,094 36.9%	515 28.3%	1,609 33.6%
12 and higher	704 23.7%	1,020 56.1%	1,724 36.0%
Total	2,969 100.0%	1,819 100.0%	4,788 100.0%

Gamma = .539

Source: Compiled by the author with data supplied by the Office of Personnel Management.

gender and GS level found in part A is .722. Part B of the table again presents data for the department displaying the strongest relationship between the two variables. The gamma coefficient for NASA is nearly .9. Even the Department of Education, the weakest case (part C), reveals a strong relationship. Here gender is associated with GS level with a .539 gamma statistic.

These three findings—moderate to strong relationships between veterans preference and GS level, gender and veterans preference, and gender and GS level—leave us with an interesting problem. Since both gender and veterans preference are related to GS level, the possibility of spurious correlation arises. Is the relationship between gender and GS level spurious, that is, dependent upon veterans preference policy? Or, is the relationship between veterans preference and GS level spurious, dependent upon gender? The possibility also exists that both gender and veterans preference have an independent impact on GS level. In order to address this problem, we will look at the relationship between gender and GS level controlling for veterans preference and the relationship between veterans preference and GS level controlling for gender. Table 4 contains these results.

Part A of Table 4 contains the results for the relationship between gender and GS level when controlling for veterans preference. As can be seen, there is no change in the relationship when controls for veterans preference are applied. The zero-order gamma for the relationship is .722; the first-order partial gamma is .716. Thus, the relationship between gender and GS level remains strong even after controlling for veterans preference.

The relationship between veterans preference and GS level when controlling for gender is contained in part B of Table 4. The zero-order gamma for the relationship is .341. However, when controls are applied for gender, no relationship between veterans preference and GS level is found to exist. The partial-gamma in this case is −.054. Hence, when controlling for gender, there is no relationship between veterans preference and GS level.

These results indicate that the relationship between veterans preference and current GS level is completely dependent upon the covariation between gender and veterans preference. It appears that it is not veterans preference, but rather gender, that is associated with current GS level in federal employment. The implication of this finding is two-fold. First, while veterans preference policy was found in previous studies to affect the initial decision to hire it does not appear to affect current GS level.[7] Second, throughout the federal employment, gender appears to be strongly related to current GS level. Identifying the content of the gender bias is outside the scope of the current research. However, it is clear that veterans preference policy does not account for it.

There are, however, some limitations to the analysis presented above. First, in analyzing the relationship between veterans preference and current GS level, it is impossible to isolate the relative effects of initial position versus an individual's other experiences within the organization. Because veterans preference was found to be only spuriously relat-

Table 4. The Effects of Gender and Veterans Preference Upon GS Level with Relevant Controls

A. The Relationship Between Gender and GS Level Controlling for Veterans Preference:

	No Preference		5 Points		10 Points	
	Women	*Men*	*Women*	*Men*	*Women*	*Men*
GS 1–6	374,820 65.4%	58,116 23.4%	39,533 76.4%	73,295 21.1%	19,581 74.3%	20,286 27.4%
GS 7–11	167,721 29.3%	111,762 45.1%	10,892 21.0%	155,006 44.6%	6,112 23.2%	34,646 46.8%
GS 12 and higher	30,286 5.3%	78,060 31.5%	1,325 2.6%	119,021 34.3%	645 2.4%	19,114 25.8%
Total	572,827 100.0%	247,938 100.0%	51,750 100.0%	347,322 100.0%	26,338 100.0%	74,046 100.0%

Zero-Order Gamma = .722   First-Order Partial Gamma = .716

B. The Relationship Between Veterans Preference and GS Level Controlling for Gender:

| | Women | | | Men | | |
	No Preference	5 Points	10 Points	No Preference	5 Points	10 Points
GS 1–6	374,820 65.4%	39,533 76.4%	19,581 74.3%	58,116 23.4%	73,295 21.1%	20,286 27.4%
GS 7–11	167,721 29.3%	10,892 21.0%	6,112 23.2%	111,762 45.1%	155,006 44.6%	34,646 46.8%
GS 12 and higher	30,286 5.3%	1,325 2.6%	645 2.4%	78,060 31.5%	119,021 34.3%	19,114 25.8%
Total	572,827 100.0%	51,750 100.0%	26,338 100.0%	247,938 100.0%	347,322 100.0%	74,046 100.0%

Zero-Order Gamma = .341   First-Order Partial Gamma = −.054

Source: Compiled by the author with data supplied by the Office of Personnel Management.

ed to GS level, this does not leave us with a problem of interpretation. However, if veterans preference had been found to have an independent impact, the precise reasons for this impact would have been unclear. This potential problem could have been averted and some potentially interesting results obtained if the effects of veterans preference and gender could have been assessed for both the first GS level held within the organization and current GS level. Unfortunately, the nature of the data provided by the Office of Personnel Management permitted only the analysis of current GS level.

Another problem with this analysis is that the variables allow for only a very gross picture of the relative effects of veterans preference and gender. An analysis based on only three variables does not allow for an in-depth analysis of either the factors associated with attainment of a high GS level or how veterans preference is related to them. Additional variables not provided in the data analyzed here such as education, experience, and other merit related variables are necessary.

From both the earlier studies and the results in this section, it can be concluded that at least two non-merit factors are related to GS level: gender and veterans preference. However, despite its apparent role in initial hiring decisions, veterans preference policy appears to have no independent association with current GS level. These results point to the needs of analyzing initial GS level in addition to current GS level and of adding other individual level merit-oriented variables in order to ascertain relative effects. An analysis addressing these needs is presented in the next section.

V.   THE EFFECTS OF VETERANS PREFERENCE WITHIN THE FEDERAL GOVERNMENT: AN INDEPTH ANALYSIS

Both of the missing factors cited above, merit-related variables and initial GS level, are crucial in an analysis of veterans preference policy. Merit considerations are important for they will allow more precise statements as to the possible conflicts between veterans preference and the merit principle. Results from an analysis which incorporates initial GS level will help to isolate which factors are associated with the initial level at which an individual is hired compared with the factors related to an individual's other experiences while located within a government organization.

The incorporation of these additional variables in this research is achieved through the use of data obtained from a survey of employees at the Milwaukee District Office of the Internal Revenue Service. The organization contains approximately 400 employees. A simple random sample of 201 were surveyed and 167 returned completed questionnaires, resulting in a response rate of 83 percent. From the information obtained in the survey, the following variables are used:

1. *Veterans Preference:* A dichotomous variable measuring whether or not the respondent indicated having veterans preference.
2. *Gender:* A dichotomous measure for the respondent's gender, with the higher value for males.
3. *Current GS level:* The respondents' self report of their current GS level. For those located in the Senior Executive Service, GS level was estimated at 16.
4. *Initial GS level:* The respondents' self report of the initial GS level which they held within the Milwaukee District Office.
5. Merit related variables: The four merit related variables used may also be referred to as job qualification variables. They are:
   a. Education: An ordinal scale, ranging from 1 to 5, for the respondents' highest educational level achieved. Possible responses are grade school, high school, some college, undergraduate degree, graduate degree.
   b. Experience: Respondents' total years of experience in the federal government.[8]
   c. Non-federal Experience: A dichotomous variable measuring whether or not the respondent indicated that previous jobs held outside the federal government helped to prepare the individual for their current job.
   d. Merit Award: A dichotomous variable indicating whether or not the respondent reported having received a merit award.

The analysis is performed in two parts. First, the relative effects of gender, veterans preference, and job qualification factors upon current GS level are assessed. Second, an analysis of the impact of these same factors on initial GS level is conducted. Multiple regression analysis is used to estimate several equations for each dependent variable. Table 5 contains the first set of equations.

Equation 1 in Table 5 compares the relative effects of merit related variables and veterans preference. Overall, these variables explain 53 percent of the variance in current GS level. The most important variable in the explanation is education; a one unit increase in education is estimated to increase current GS level by 2.72 levels. In terms of the magnitude of the relationship, veterans preference is the second most important variable. Respondents with preference are estimated to be 1.38 GS levels above similar individuals who do not have preference. The esti-

Table 5. The Relative Effects of Gender, Veterans Preference, and Job Qualifications on Current GS Level

Equation 1: The Effects of Job Qualifications and Veterans Preference
Current GS Level = 1.02 + 2.72*Education + .10* Experience + 1.38* Veterans Preference + .43 Merit Award
(.64)   (.24)   (.16)   (.05)
+ .10 Non-federal Experience
(.10)

$R^2 = .53$

Equation 2: The Effects of Job Qualifications and Gender
Current GS Level = −2.69 + 2.14*Education + 2.67*Gender + .08*Experience + .36 Merit Award
(.51)   (.36)   (.20)   (.05)
+ .34 Non-federal Experience
(.05)

$R^2 = .60$

Equation 3: The Effects of Job Qualifications and Veterans Preference Controlling for Gender
3A: Effects for Women
Current GS Level = 2.58 + 1.97*Education + .03 Experience + 1.04 Veterans Preference + .46 Non-federal Experience
(.55)   (.09)   (.08)   (.08)

$R^2 = .29$

3B: Effects for Men
Current GS Level = 1.84 + 2.29*Education + .13*Experience + .85 Merit Award + .37 Non-federal Experience
(.63)   (.39)   (.14)   (.06)
− .20 Veterans Preference
(−.03)

$R^2 = .47$

Note: Figures in parentheses are standardized regression coefficients. Asterisked figures are unstandardized regression coefficients statistically significant at the .05 level.

352

mate for the experience variable is also statistically significant, although the magnitude of the relationship is quite low. The unstandardized regression coefficient is only equal to .10. The relative effects of these three variables may be assessed with the standardized regression coefficients. The beta for education is a very strong .64. This is followed by betas of .24 for experience and .16 for veterans preference.

Consistent with the analysis presented earlier for all major federal agencies, the impact of gender on current GS level is also assessed. Once again, the job qualification variables are also incorporated into the equations. These results are contained in Equation 2 of Table 5. The total variation in current GS level explained with this set of variables is .60. Education is again found to be the best explanatory variable. The strength of the relationship with GS level is, however, somewhat reduced when compared with the first equation. Another strong relationship is found between gender and GS level. Being a man is estimated to increase an individual's current GS level by 2.67 levels. As before, the estimate for the experience variable is statistically significant, but the magnitude of the impact is very slight. The standardized coefficients for the three significant variables are .54 for education, .36 for gender, and .20 for experience.

These results are quite similar to those found in the overview of federal agencies. Both gender and veterans preference are found to be significantly related to current GS level. The strength of each of the relationships approximates that found earlier. In addition, two merit related variables, education and experience, are also important. Education turns out to be the single most important factor, while experience has only a slight relationship with current GS level. Thus it appears that merit related considerations are predominant in explaining current GS level. Nevertheless, both gender and veterans preference appear to have an independent impact.

At this juncture we are once again faced with the question of whether the relationship between veterans preference and current GS level is spurious. Equation 3 in Table 5 presents results which are intended to disentangle the independent effects of gender and veterans preference on current GS level. The model is estimated separately for women and men, thereby holding the effects of gender constant. Equation 3A contains the equation estimated for women in the sample. The only variable which is statistically significant in this equation is education. This relationship is weaker than similar ones seen in the earlier equations. An increase in one unit of education is estimated to increase GS level by only 1.97 levels. While the magnitude of the relationship for veterans preference is quite high (1.04), the estimate is not statistically significant, and the standardized coefficient suggests that it has very little independent effect in the equation (.08). The amount of variation in current GS level explained by this equation is .29, a figure also smaller than those obtained in earlier equations.

In contrast, the results for men are somewhat stronger: 47 percent of the variance is explained. Merit related variables appear to be more important for men. Both education and experience are statistically significant (and the merit award variable is quite close to being significant at the .05 level). The relationship between education and GS level is such that a unit increase in education increases GS level by 2.29 units. The standardized coefficient in this case is .63. The estimate for experience is also quite strong. The standardized coefficient equals .39, while the unstandardized estimate is .13. The veterans preference variable has the smallest independent impact of all the variables in the equation. The standardized regression coefficient is −.03. In addition to not being statistically significant, this coefficient is also not in the hypothesized direction.

These results indicate that when controls are applied for gender, the relationship between veterans preference and GS level once again disappears. The strong results seen for education seem to indicate that merit considerations are very important in contributing to an individual's current GS level. However, gender is also found to have a strong and independent impact on GS level. Thus, merit related factors do not exclusively explain GS attainment. They appear to be predominant,[9] but gender is important as well.

The findings for current GS level largely replicate the results obtained for the federal departments concerning the relative effects of gender and veterans preference. To move the analysis one step further, it is necessary to also assess their impact on initial GS level. Table 6 presents these results.

Equation 1 again presents the results for the impact of job qualification factors and veterans preference. For initial GS level, the only variable with explanatory power is education. Compared with the results for current GS level, the magnitude of the relationship is substantially reduced. An increase in one unit of education is estimated to increase initial GS level by 1.67 levels. The estimate for the education variable is the only statistically significant one in the equation. The independent impact is .54; all other variables have standardized coefficients less than .06. Veterans preference is the least explanatory of all the variables for initial position, the standardized coefficient equalling only .03. The total variation in initial GS level explained in the equation is .30.

Adding gender to the equation, the explanatory power is increased slightly (Equation 2). The total percentage of variance explained is 33 percent. Note that both education and gender have statistically signifi-

Table 6. The Relative Effects of Gender, Veterans Preference, and Job Qualifications on Initial Gs Level

Equation 1: The Effects of Job Qualifications and Veterans Preference

Initial GS Level = −1.36 + 1.67*Education + .26 Non-federal Experience + .20 Merit Award + .01 Experience

$\quad$ (.54) $\qquad$ (.05) $\qquad$ (.04) $\qquad$ (.04)

R² = .30 $\qquad$ − .19 Veterans Preference

$\qquad$ (−.03)

Equation 2: The Effects of Job Qualifications and Gender

Initial GS Level = −1.44 + 1.36*Education + 1.15*Gender + .18 Non-federal Experience + .12 Merit Award

$\quad$ (.44) $\qquad$ (.21) $\qquad$ (.04) $\qquad$ (.02)

R² = .33 $\qquad$ − .01 Experience

$\qquad$ (−.02)

Equation 3: The Effects of Job Qualifications and Veterans Preference Controlling for Gender

$\quad$ 3A: Effects for Women

Initial GS Level = 1.62 + .92*Education + .37 Merit Award − .02 Experience + .43 Veterans Preference

R₂ = .22 $\qquad$ (.41) $\qquad$ (.10) $\qquad$ (−.11) $\qquad$ (.06)

$\quad$ 3B: Effects for Men

Initial GS Level = −1.87 + 1.63*Education − 1.40*Veterans Preference + .71 Merit Award − .03 Experience

$\quad$ (.41) $\qquad$ (−.23) $\qquad$ (.11) $\qquad$ (−.08)

R² = .28 $\qquad$ + .18 Non-federal Experience

$\qquad$ (.03)

Equation 4: The Effects of Job Qualifications and Veterans Preference For Men within Subsets of Initial GS Level

$\quad$ 4A: Initial GS Level Less Than GS 5

Initial GS Level = 2.28 + .04 Education + .88 Non-federal Experience − 1.64 Veterans Preference

R² = .31 $\qquad$ (.04) $\qquad$ (.40) $\qquad$ (−.51)

$\quad$ 4B: Initial GS Level Between GS 5 and GS 8 (inclusive)

Initial GS Level = 6.72 − .21 Education + .04 Non-federal Experience − .21 Veterans Preference

R² = .02 $\qquad$ (−.09) $\qquad$ (.02) $\qquad$ (−.11)

$\quad$ 4C: Initial GS Level Greater Than GS 8

Initial GS Level = 8.00 + 2.00 Education + 1.50 Non-federal Experience + 1.00 Veterans Preference

R² = .27 $\qquad$ (.46) $\qquad$ (.28) $\qquad$ (.23)

Note: Figures in parentheses are standardized regression coefficients. Asterisked figures are unstandardized regression coefficients statistically significant at the .05 level.

cant relationships with initial GS level. With gender in the equation, the magnitude of the relationship for education is substantially reduced. Education increases GS level by 1.36 levels: male gender increases it by 1.15 levels. The standardized estimates are .44 and .21 for education and gender, respectively.

The results found for the veterans preference variable are counter intuitive. Why is there no relationship between veterans preference and initial GS level, when there is for veterans preference and current GS level? The possibility exists that gender masks the relationship with initial GS level. Therefore, the equations again are estimated separately for women and men. These results are found in Equation 3.

The results for women in large measure parallel those found in Equation 1 of this table,[10] and need not therefore be discussed here. However, the results for men are very interesting. Education is again primary. The standardized coefficient equals .41, while the unstandardized estimate suggests that a unit increase in education increases GS level by 1.63 levels. Surprisingly, veterans preference also has a statistically significant relationship with initial GS level. By holding gender constant, it can be seen that gender, indeed, is masking the relationship in Equation 1. Even more interesting is the fact that the relationship is the opposite of that hypothesized. Individuals with veterans preference are estimated to be located 1.40 GS levels below those without preference. The total variation explained with this equation is 28 percent.

This relationship between initial GS level and veterans preference is contrary to our expectations. The relationship between veterans preference and GS level hypothesized throughout this research is that having veterans preference is positively associated with occupying a higher GS level. The hypothesis is consistent with an incentive model for the utilization of veterans preference. The incentive model suggests that veterans preference gives veterans an incentive to apply for higher level positions than they are truly qualified for (e.g., see Miller, 1935). The preference, from this perspective, gives veterans a competitive edge which results in their being hired at higher GS levels than comparable nonveterans.

However, another possibility also exists. This alternative may be referred to as the safety net model. The safety net model suggests that veterans will not apply for jobs that tax their level of qualifications for to do so might result in their failing to be hired. With preference, if veterans channel their efforts at GS levels slightly below their qualifications, they will be nearly assured of receiving appointments. Given the way the civil service system operates, once a position is obtained, tenure will result in advancement.

From the results seen in Equation 3 of Table 6, it appears that the latter possibility holds. Yet, because this result is inconsistent with previous work, it deserves further investigation. In Equation 4 of Table 6 the analysis for men is divided into subsets of initial GS level in order to test for the conditional validity of the safety net and incentive models. The two models suggest that veterans direct their job searches to positions either above or below the points at which they are normally qualified. If both models are partially correct, that is, each holds for some veterans, and the propensity to search above or below is independent of veterans' qualifications, then evidence consistent with each model will be seen at different points in the job structure. If the safety net model holds, the strongest negative relationship between veterans preference and initial GS level should be seen within the lowest GS subset. If the incentive model has any applicability, it should be found in the highest GS subset.

Equation 4A contains the results for the lowest subset, initial GS level being less than GS 5. The results are consistent with the safety net model. Merit variables[11] do not explain initial GS level when it is less than GS 5. However, the relationship with veterans preference is very strong and in the negative direction. Having veterans preference is estimated to reduce an individual's GS level by 1.64 levels. The standardized regression coefficient equals $-.51$, and the total variance explained is 31 percent.[12]

For the middle subset (GS levels 5 through 8), none of the variables are associated with initial GS level. Equation 4B shows that neither merit nor veterans preference explains the variation in initial levels 5 through 8.

However, in Equation 4C, the variables once again explain a substantial amount of the variation. Both merit and veterans preference explain initial GS level when it is greater than GS 8. One unit of education increases initial GS by 2.0 levels; one unit of non-federal experience increases initial GS by 1.5 levels, and veterans preference increases initial GS by 1.0 level. These results are consistent with the incentive model. Job qualifications are important, but veterans preference gives an incentive (and means) to obtain an initial position which is one GS level higher than that which might normally be obtained.

From all of these indepth results, several conclusions can be drawn. First, it appears that, as with the findings for all the major federal agencies, veterans preference is only spuriously associated with current GS level. Gender appears to be the most important non-merit explanatory factor, while education is the most important merit factor. Second, gender and education both make significant contributions toward the explanation of initial GS level. Veterans preference is found to be a less important factor; however, it has an important effect when controls for gender are applied.

The results found for veterans preference appear to be primarily consistent with the safety net model as outlined above. However, it is found that the incentive model is also partially operative. Both models are interpreted as conflicting with the merit principle. Consistent with this, both models can be seen as adversely affecting employment opportunities for women. The incentive model provides for veterans being hired in upper level positions at GS levels which exceed their qualifications. This makes it difficult for nonveterans to be hired in upper levels of the bureaucracy. The safety net model makes it even easier for veterans to be hired over nonveterans. This, again, can adversely affect the ability of women to be hired.

One caution in interpreting these results needs to be expressed. The findings in this section are based upon one sample drawn from a single district office. While the results for current GS level are consistent with those found for all federal agencies, no such check of the generalizability of results exists for initial GS level. Therefore, these findings must be replicated in order for general statements to be made concerning their applicability to all federal civil service employment. Until then, these results must be viewed as tentative.

VI.   CONCLUSION: SOME POLICY SUGGESTIONS

The Veterans preference policy may be at odds with the merit principle in three ways: the decision to hire, the level at which individuals are hired, and other experiences that they have while located in public employment. Each of these possibilities was explored in this paper with the following results:

1. Veterans preference was seen to have a large impact on hiring decisions.
2. Veterans preference was also seen to have an effect on the initial GS level held by individuals. The evidence suggests that the incentive model holds for some veterans while the safety net model applies to others.
3. Veterans preference was found to be only spuriously related to current GS level. It was found to have no independent effect when controls for gender were applied.

These results help to identify where the most severe conflicts with the merit principle occur. Veterans preference policy causes deviations from the merit principle in public sector employment primarily in the area of hiring. This result can be interpreted as suggesting the contradiction between equal employment opportunity policy and veterans preference occurs in the decision to hire and the GS level at which individuals are initially hired.

Currently, the conflict between veterans preference and equal employment opportunity has been resolved by placing a priority on veterans preference over equal employment opportunity of women and other minorities. This prioritizing receives formal recognition in the law. As Fleming and Shanor (1977, p. 60) point out, challenges to veterans preference under Title VII of the Civil Rights Act of 1964 are prohibited within the Act itself in section 712.

From a normative perspective, the question which arises from the analysis is: Should veterans preference take priority over equal employment opportunity? Since government has stated as its responsibility the implementation of equal employment opportunity policy, should veterans preference automatically take precedence over equal employment opportunity in government employment? The answer that appears to be most reasonable and most consistent with the nature of the political system in the United States is no. No single policy should be designed to take priority over all others, particularly insofar as it advantages a single group (i.e., veterans) to the detriment of all others. If a pluralist society is assumed, the conflict between the merit principle and veterans preference should be resolved through compromise.

In order to initiate a compromise situation, several reforms in veterans preference policy are necessary. These reforms can be derived from a change in the justification of the policy. Currently, the policy is most consistent with a benefits justification. This means that veterans perference is conceptualized as a part of the overall veterans' benefits package. The goal of veterans preference policy is to reward veterans for their service to the country and to recognize society's gratitude for their efforts (Stahl, 1976; Fleming and Shanor, 1977). Given this justification, veterans have a right to apply for preference whenever they desire. This leaves very little room for possible compromise with the goals of equal employment opportunity policy.

The change suggested for veterans preference policy is to make the various details of the policy more consistent with a readjustment (rather than benefits) justification.[13] The readjustment justification has as its goal the rehabilitation and relocation of those suffering economic and social dislocation as a result of wartime service (Stahl, 1976; Fleming and Shanor, 1977). The readjustment justification allows for compromise with equal employment opportunity because certain limitations on veterans preference follow from this justification. First, limitations may be placed on the length of time that an individual is eligible for preference, namely, only as long as it reasonably takes for readjustment. Second, since the policy under this justification is not viewed as a benefit, it would no longer be justifiable to have preference provisions which result in the hiring of veterans to the exclusion of all others. Finally, a readjustment justification implies that conflicts with the merit principle would be tolerated only for those veterans truly suffering from economic and social dislocation.

The specific policy reforms derived from a readjustment justification include the following:

1. The length of time following an armed conflict that veterans are eligible for bonus points in hiring needs to be severly reduced. Veterans preference should be applied for no more than a limited period beyond the completion of the conflict.
2. Veterans preference should only apply to wartime veterans.
3. Absolute preference in hiring should be eliminated. Only the point-bonus preference system in hiring should be used.
4. Veterans preference should not result in any individuals being given top priority on the hiring register. This means that disabled veterans should no longer be automatically placed at the top of the register. However, if it is established that disabled veterans suffer severly from economic and social dislocation, their bonus points might be increased.
5. Other forms of preference which are unrelated to readjustment, but rather have long term effects, should be eliminated. These include preference in promotion, RIF's, and employee appeals processes.
5. Some mechanism for the determination of those suffering from economic and social dislocation needs to be developed. Preference in hiring should apply only to those individuals who qualify based on these criteria.

All of these reforms, with the exception of the fifth, refer to hiring. If implemented, the anticipated impact of the reforms is to reduce the effects that veterans preference policy has in the area of hiring. The reforms suggested concerning promotions, RIF's, and employee appeals processes are suggested primarily because these facets of the current policy are *logically* inconsistent with a readjustment justification. However, the empirical impacts of these parts of the policy have not been clearly identified in this paper. Their gross effects were touched upon in the analysis of current GS level, and here, effects of the policy were found to be spurious. However, more research into the impact of each of these policy details needs to be conducted for this reform to be made with confidence.

A readjustment focus, then, allows for compromise between the implementation of veterans preference policy and equal employment opportunity policy by reducing the adverse impact of veteran preference upon the hiring of women in public sector employment. The suggestions for policy reform are very modest and completely consistent with the norms of the political system in the United States. They provide for policy modifications which will incrementally advance employment opportunity for women and other nonveterans. While more radical policy analyses are also consistent with the empirical findings contained in this research, policy suggestions derived from such analyses are less likely to be implemented within the existing political structures.

NOTES

1. The author wishes to thank John P. Frendreis for his helpful comments on earlier drafts of this manuscript.

2. Most of the information pertaining to pre-World War II veterans preference is obtained from Miller (1935).

3. Even though women are contained in the veterans category, they comprise only a very small proportion of the total. The largest percentage of women in the armed services prior to 1976 was 5 percent. See Fleming and Shanor (1977, 13) for data on the proportion of women in the military.

4. 415 F. Supp. 485 (D. Mass., 1976).

5. In a subsequent decision, *Washington v. Davis* (426 U.S. 229, 1976), determinations resting solely upon discriminatory impact were disapproved.

6. It is unfortunate that most of the data presented in this section are from individual cases. The exception to this is the PACE data which are systematically collected. The reason for the lack of data in this area is that recruitment data are seldom made available in order to protect the privacy of employee records.

7. This may, in part, be due to the fact that the federal preference system does not allow for promotion preference. It does, however, give preference in RIF's and employee appeals processes which potentially could affect current GS level.

8. Two other experience questions were asked, one for years of experience in the IRS and one for years of experience in current position. All three questions correlated very highly, exceeding .8. Therefore, the decision was made to include the variable for total federal experience in the analysis.

9. In interpreting the explanatory importance of education, it should be noted that veterans receive educational benefits in addition to veterans preference in public employment. Therefore, if this paper had intended to explore the effects of all of the benefits that veterans receive upon current GS level, the effects might be even more substantial. Estimating the impact of the total veterans' benefits package on women in employment is beyond the scope of this paper. Yet, the potential for the overestimation of merit effects and the underestimation of gender effects is noteworthy. In addition, the results in Equation 3 of Table 5 indicate that merit-related variables are less explanatory for women than men, although education is still quite important for women. This is further evidence that some kind of gender bias is operating within the federal civil service.

10. Non-federal experience is not included in this equation because it did not meet the tolerance level assumptions in SPSS. While the assumptions can be manipulated to provide for its inclusion, the effects of such a variable are so small that it can be assumed that it has no impact.

11.   Only education and non-federal experience are included in these equations to abbreviate the presentation. Other variables were not seen to have an impact and were therefore excluded.

12.   Note that none of these results are statistically significant. This is largely due to the number of cases for each of the equations. The total number of men in the data set is 74. When this is divided into three subsets, the N is such that statistical significance is difficult to obtain. Yet, the variation explained by the equations and the strength of the relationships are consistent with the findings based on all men. Thus, the findings are interpreted as representative of the sample. Since the results for the sample achieved significance, they are, in turn, viewed as representative of the Milwaukee IRS population.

13.   This analysis is not intended to imply that veterans are not deserving of some benefits. Rather, it is an attack on the use of public employment as a benefit because of the impact that such a policy has on women and nonveterans. If employment is to be viewed as a benefit for veterans, then incentives for such employment must be directed to both public and private sector employment. If such policies are not undertaken, then the ramifications of the current policy warrant the reforms suggested.

REFERENCES

Campbell, Alan K. "Civil Service Reform: A New Commitment." *Public Administration Review* March/April (1978): 99–103.

Civil Service Commission. *Thirty-Sixth Annual Report.* Washington D.C.: Civil Service Commission, 1919.

Davis, Charles E. "A Survey of Veterans Preference Legislation in the States." *State Government* 53 (1980): 188–191.

Fleming, John H., and Shanor, Charles A. "Veterans Preference in Public Employment: Unconstitutional Gender Discimination? *Emory Law Review* 26 (1977): 13–64.

Levitan Sar A., and Cleary, Karen A. *Old Wars Remain Unfinished: The Veteran Benefits System.* Baltimore: The Johns Hopkins University Press, 1973.

Miller, John F. "Veteran Preference in the Public Service." In The Commission of Inquiry on Public Service Personnel, ed. *Problems of the American Public Service.* New York: McGraw-Hill Book Company, Inc., 1935.

Nigro, Felix A., and Nigro, Lloyd G. *The New Public Personnel Administration.* Itasca, Ill.: Peacock, 1982.

Stahl, O. Glenn. *Public Personnel Administration*, 7th Edition. New York: Harper & Row, 1976.

Stone, Alan. *Regulation and Its Alternatives.* Washington D.C.: Congressional Quarterly, 1982.

Vertz, Laura L., and Wells, Joan A. "Recent Trends in EEO Policy: Affirmative Action versus the Merit Principle in an Era of Deregulation." Presented at the Annual Meeting of the Southwest Social Science Association, San Antonio, Texas, March 17–20, 1982.

Biographical Sketch of the Contributors

Ellen Boneparth is Associate Dean, School of Social Sciences and Associate Professor of Political Science, San Jose State University. She is the founder and Director of the Aegean Women's Studies Institute. Her most recent work is *Women, Power and Policy,* an edited volume published in 1982.

James W. Button is Associate Professor of Political Science at the University of Florida. He is the author of *Black Violence: Political Impact of the 1960s Riots,* and has published a number of articles on black politics in the South.

Fay Lomax Cook received her Ph.D. from the University of Chicago in 1977. She is currently an Assistant Professor at Northwestern University with a joint appointment between the School of Education and the Center for Urban Affairs and Policy Research. She is the author of *Who Should Be Helped? Public Support for Social Services* and the co-author of *Setting and Reformulating Policy Agendas: The Case of Criminal Victimization of the Elderly.*

Norman Furniss is Professor of Political Science and Director of the West European Center at Indiana University. His major research interests are in contemporary West European politics, comparative public policy analysis and issues of property rights. He is co-author of *The Case For The Welfare State.*

Malcolm L. Goggins is an Assistant Professor of Political Science at the University of Houston—University Park. He received his Ph.D. from Stanford University, where he also taught in the Department of Political Science, the Human Biology Program, and the School of Medicine. His specialty is health policy and politics. Dr. Goggin has contributed to several books on public policy and is currently writing two books— one on the governance of science and technology and one on a theory of public policy implementation.

C. Richard Hofstetter has been a professor at San Diego State University and the University of Houston. He has written numerous articles in the areas of public opinion, mass media, research methods, and political behavior.

Michael E. Kraft is Professor of Political Science and Public Administration at the University of Wisconsin, Green Bay. He received his Ph.D. from Yale University (1973) and has held positions at the University of Wisconsin, Madison and Vassar College. He has written extensively on environmental policy and politics and on population policy, and is co-editor of *Population Policy Analysis: Issues in American Politics* (1978) and *Environmental Policy In the 1980s* (1984). Current research focuses on the use of risk analysis in environmental regulation, institutional capabilities for population planning in the United States, and environmental policy change in the Reagan presidency.

Howard Leichter is Professor of Political Science at Linfield College in Oregon. He received his Ph.D. at the University of Wisconsin—Madison. Professor Leichter is the author of three books—*Political Regime and Public Policy; A Comparative Approach To Policy Analysis; American Public Policy In A Comparative Perspective* (co-authored with Harrell Rodgers) and numerous scholarly articles. His primary area of research is comparative public policy.

Brian Loveman is Professor of Political Science at San Diego State University. He has authored numerous books and articles concerning Latin American politics, agrarian reform in Latin America, the role of the military in Latin American regimes, and immigration problems.

Neil Mitchell is a doctoral student in Political Science at Indiana University. His dissertation concerns the causes, content, and consequences of changes in U.S. business ideology. His research interests are in comparative politics, policy, and political theory.

Harrell R. Rodgers, Jr. is Professor of Political Science at the University of Houston—University Park. He is a policy analyst who specializes in social welfare programs and issues of poverty, the impact of civil rights laws, and political economics. His latest books include *The Cost of Human Neglect: America's Welfare Failure; American Public Policy In A Comparative Context* (with Howard Leichter); and the second edition of *Unfinished Democracy: The American Political System* (with Michael Harrington).

Richard K. Scher is Associate Professor of Political Science at the University of Florida. He is co-author of *Florida's Gubernatorial Politics in the Twentieth Century,* and has published other works on political leadership and civil rights in the South. He is currently engaged in an interpretive study of politics in the contemporary South.

Wesley G. Skogan is Professor of Political Science and Urban Affairs at Northwestern University. He is author of *Coping With Crime,* and edited *Sample Surveys of the Victims of Crime.* He is the general editor of a series of volumes on victimization and fear of crime being published by the Bureau of Justice Statistics, and wrote the lead monograph in that series, *Issues in the Measurement of Victimization.* With Fay L. Cook he is the co-author of a forthcoming book, *Setting and Reformulating Policy Agendas.*

Laura L. Vertz is an Assistant Professor of Political Science and Public Administration at North Texas State University. Her research interests include the areas of public personnel policy, political behavior, and intergovernmental relations. She has contributed to several journals and edited volumes including *Social Science Quarterly* and *Comparative Politics.*

Author Index

Subject Index